fP

Also by Howard Kurtz

Media Circus: The Trouble with America's Newspapers

Hot Air: All Talk All the Time

Spin Cycle: Inside the Clinton Propaganda Machine

The Fortune Tellers: Inside Wall Street's Game of Money, Media, and Manipulation

Reality Show

INSIDE THE LAST GREAT
TELEVISION NEWS WAR

HOWARD KURTZ

FREE PRESS
New York   London   Toronto   Sydney

Free Press
A Division of Simon & Schuster, Inc.
1230 Avenue of the Americas
New York, NY 10020

First Free Press hardcover edition October 2007

FREE PRESS and colophon are trademarks of Simon & Schuster, Inc.

For information about special discounts for bulk purchases,
please contact Simon & Schuster Special Sales at 1-800-456-6798 or
business@simonandschuster.com

Manufactured in the United States of America

10   9   8   7   6   5   4   3   2   1

Library of Congress Cataloging-in-Publication Data

Kurtz, Howard
    Reality show : inside the last great television news war / Howard
Kurtz.—1st Free Press hardcover ed.
        p. cm.
    ISBN-13: 978-0-7432-9982-4
    ISBN-10:   0-7432-9982-5
    1. Television broadcasting of news—United States—History.   2. Television news
anchors—United States—Biography.   I. Title.
    PN4888.T4K87 2007
    070.1'95—dc22   2007027144

For Sheri,
who tolerated my channel-surfing
through endless newscasts,
and Abby,
who demanded the Food Network instead.

CONTENTS

INTRODUCTION

I grew up with a black and white television set on a rusty metal stand in my bedroom, and when you wanted to change programs you had to get up and turn this round metal protrusion–it was, I believe, called a dial—from Channel 2 to Channel 4 or Channel 7 or the handful of local stations.

This did not seem like a terribly heavy burden at the time. I had, and this may be hard to grasp, no computer. No VCR. No fax machine. No e-mail. No voice mail. No FM radio, no tape cassettes, no DVDs, no music player capable of holding thousands of songs. There were no blogs to read, no Web sites to surf, no video-on-demand to download.

If you wanted news, you bought a newspaper in the morning, and if you wanted more up-to-date news, you bought an afternoon paper, one of which I delivered for a time, stuffing the copies into a canvas bag that hung from my bike's handlebars. And if, during or after supper, which was generally eaten together by families, you wanted the latest available information from the rest of the world, you turned on the network news at 6:30.

No wonder it loomed so large in our lives. The news at that hour was fresh, there was film from around the country, and tuning in was a shared experience, not unlike watching the comedians, singers, and jugglers on Ed Sullivan. With little in the way of competition, Walter Cronkite, along with Chet Huntley and David Brinkley, enjoyed an enormous market share, to use a modern sales term. Never mind that their broadcasts were primitive by today's standards, with public officials droning on at length, reporters holding microphones while interview subjects fumbled for answers, and little sense of drama or storytelling. The newscasts fit the times, and the anchors fulfilled our needs.

Fast-forward a few decades. I am totally wired, from the hundreds of cable choices on my TV set, complete with digital recording device, to the 170 channels on my car's satellite radio, to the blessing and curse of my constantly buzzing BlackBerry. As a reporter for *The Washington Post,* I am surrounded by news, practically choking on news, all day long. As the host of CNN's media program, *Reliable Sources,* I am immersed in the making of television. As a journalist who has patrolled the media beat for seventeen years, I am intensely interested in the gathering and shaping and communicating of information.

A few short years ago I realized that I was increasingly missing the network newscasts, for reasons that were all too familiar. I got home too late, or was busy making dinner, or was distracted by a dozen other things. When I had the set on, I realized that I already knew the details of the top stories and often clicked it off. Sometimes I was on the computer, where any story, it seemed, was at my fingertips within seconds.

I was losing the habit.

When there was a big, breaking scandal or a hot political campaign, I usually found time to watch. The rest of the time, not so much. Without really thinking about it, I was concluding that the newscasts had little to offer me that I couldn't get, in timelier and more compelling fashion, elsewhere. The world had changed since the days of my little black and white set with the gnarled antenna, and so had I.

The tectonic plates of network news were about to shift. The men who had dominated the television landscape for more than two decades—Dan Rather, Tom Brokaw, and Peter Jennings—were nearing the end of their long run. I had gotten to know them reasonably well over the years, understood their strengths and weaknesses, and had a hard time imagining the evening news without them. In times of crisis and celebration, of triumph and tragedy, they were there, as entrenched a trio as had ever peered out from the small screen. What would television news be like without them? Would their successors be able to fill their sizable shoes? Or had we, as a country, simply moved on? Without Dan, Tom, and Peter, would the whole shaky edifice just collapse?

The question, I realized, was this: What did it mean to be an anchor—a big-time, globe-trotting, perfectly lit, multimillion-dollar anchor—in the first decade of the twenty-first century? It was fashionable in some circles to deride anchors as absurdly overpaid news readers, but they also had to be able to ad lib for hours on end, flying blind as it were, when dramatic events erupted. Rather, Brokaw, and Jennings had formed an emotional connection with the audience precisely because they served as national hand-holders when the *Challenger* blew up, when a president was impeached, when the World Trade Center towers came crashing down, when American troops were marching through the desert toward Baghdad.

But the job description was changing. When big stories broke, the country increasingly turned to cable, to channels that trafficked in news and opinion around the clock, not just in carefully circumscribed half-hours amid a panoply of sitcoms and dramas and reality shows. And the big, lumbering broadcast networks were all too happy to cede that turf, the breaking-news turf, to their younger cousins. News was expensive, messy, unpredictable, labor-intensive, and far less lucrative than *Survivor* or *E.R.* or *Ugly Betty* or *Desperate Housewives.* The desperate networks had found a way out. They would show up on ceremonial occasions, such as presidential inaugurations and conventions, and wave the corporate flag, but for them news was essentially a time slot, a niche market in their sprawling business.

The final proof, as if any were needed, came when the greatest natural disaster ever to strike the United States hit the coast of Louisiana and Mississippi in the summer of 2005. The networks did a fine job covering Hurricane Katrina, but their employers did not go wall to wall, did not blow out the schedule, did not forgo commercials as they had in the days after 9/11. If you wanted to know what was happening with the drowning of the city of New Orleans in mid-morning, or mid-afternoon, or mid-evening, you had to turn to CNN, or Fox News, or MSNBC, or the Internet. The morning shows and the evening newscasts packaged the disaster, chronicled it with skill and grace and emotion, but disappeared after their allotted minutes. The same thing happened in the summer of 2007 when the anchors raced off to Minneapolis after a major bridge collapsed during rush hour.

Yet the three network newscasts, for all their flaws and shortcomings, remained the biggest game in town, reaching a combined nightly viewership of 25 million Americans. But the shrinkage was impossible to miss. Two and a half decades earlier the audience had been twice as large, 56 million viewers, and far younger than the graying crowd that still gathered for the old ritual that had once been indispensable and was now merely a lifestyle choice.

Where once there were just three alternatives for the day's national headlines, hundreds of thousands now beckoned, shiny and seductive. We were hurtling into an era of personalized news, of custom-tailored news, of opinionated news, of satiric news, of fact-free news, of skip-the-vegetables-and-have-the-ice-cream news, if indeed anything resembling news was on the menu. Younger people, especially, wanted what they wanted when they wanted it, whether it was radioed, video-streamed, satellited, blogged, or podcasted their way. They might get their fill from *Howard 100 News,* on Howard Stern's new Sirius radio channel, or Google News, a constantly updating compendium powered by computer algorithms, or dig the stories at *Digg.com,* where the most popular pieces were voted by users onto the Web site's home page. They might prefer fake news from Jon Stewart and Stephen Colbert on Comedy Central, or exchanging tidbits with buddies on *MySpace.com,* an Internet portal site snatched up by Rupert Murdoch that boasted an astonishing 60 million members. The notion of waiting around for some authority figure in New York to deliver the headlines from behind an anchor desk was almost quaint.

The larger reality was that all of organized journalism was in deep trouble, as I was painfully aware after a professional lifetime in the trenches. I had worked for one afternoon paper, *The Washington Star,* that abruptly shut down; then *The Washington Post,* which had been growing by leaps and bounds when I joined, eventually started losing readers and trimming its staff like most big-city dailies. Newspapers, in fact, had been declining for a generation. Their combined circulation, a robust 62 million in 1970, had dropped to 55 million in a much larger country, with such blue-chip names as *The New York Times* and *Los Angeles Times* cutting staff, curtailing news space, and killing sections, while entire chains, such as Knight Ridder and the Tribune Company, sold themselves off. Network magazine shows, which once filled every night of the schedule, had dwindled to a precious few. Cable news channels were drawing a relatively tiny audience compared to the big networks, rarely averaging more than 1 million viewers and sometimes drawing just a few hundred thousand. Newsmagazines were struggling as well, with *Time* and *U.S. News & World Report* enduring several rounds of painful layoffs. The most successful political magazines, from *National Review* and *The Weekly Standard* to *The Nation,* were all losing money, and the venerable *New Republic* cut its weekly publication schedule in half.

Deep down, media executives wondered whether the younger generation cared about news at all, or whether its members were content to play Xbox games, instant-message each other, download songs from iTunes, and find apartments and dates on *Craigslist.*

News organizations were reluctant to accept their share of the blame, although they had turned much of the news into a commodity that seemed ial, stilted, and remote from most people's lives. But the media universe had also splintered into a thousand fragments as people got their news not just instantaneously but tailored to their outlook and preferred delivery method—Fox News or PBS, Rush Limbaugh or Air America, iPod or cell phone. At the same time, public trust in big news outlets was plunging to record lows. As the country grew dramatically more polarized in the era of George W. Bush and the Iraq war, liberal bloggers and radio hosts denounced the MSM, or mainstream media, as hopelessly biased toward the White House, perhaps with greater ferocity than conservative commentators ripped the same targets as unfair to their side.

In the midst of this free-fire zone, high atop a hill, behind glittering gates that once seemed impregnable, the network anchors were trying to hold together a tattered coalition of the middle. At a time when families no longer gathered around an electronic hearth, the networks had to deliver news that was neither too sophisticated nor too dumbed-down, too left or too right, too elite or too obvious. They still sought a mass audience when the very concept sounded like a twentieth-century relic, now that people could download their own music and movies rather than having a handful of corporate suits choose it for them. The *YouTube* generation, which enjoyed making and circulating its own videos, was reclaiming control of a process that had once been beyond the reach of ordinary folks.

The upheaval at the broadcast networks, after so many years of relative stability, was for these proud organizations a time of both immense opportunity and extraordinary vulnerability. Their task was far greater than simply replacing the anchor-monsters, as industry insiders called them, with younger journalists who would have to labor mightily to earn the respect that the veterans had commanded. Their challenge was nothing less than to rescue a creaky franchise that was threatened by faster technology, edgier alternatives, and the disintegration of a unified audience.

The moment seemed ripe, then, for a book-length examination of network news at a critical juncture. I wanted to get inside the culture, to understand the process and the pressures, to document how the anchors and correspondents and producers decide what is news, how they package that news, and how their personal predilections and biases influence these choices. What impact did their reporting have on politics, on war, on the country itself? Were they merely summarizing and synthesizing what was out there or bringing new facts to light? Were they putting a spin on the news? How did the anchors see themselves, assert themselves, and market themselves in an age of celebrity?

They operated, after all, under a constant barrage of criticism, their work and their words picked apart by thousands of bloggers and ideological watchdogs. Where Cronkite was once dubbed the most trusted man in America, the new anchors bobbed along in a sea of distrust that enveloped the media institutions of which they were the most visible symbols. The same technological tools that enabled the networks to put their broadcasts online also allowed anyone with a modem to post their denunciations on a daily basis, or to fire them off to the anchors themselves. What was it like, I wondered, to be in the eye of the electronic storm?

In this endeavor, I enjoyed an extraordinary degree of access to journalists and executives at all levels of these communications companies. Those involved shared their thinking and writing in ways that greatly illuminated what transpires behind the cameras. When I describe their conversations, interactions, and beliefs in these pages, it is based either on direct observation or hundreds of interviews with one or more of the participants involved at any given moment. All this material unfolds against the backdrop of their broadcasts, the product by which they are ultimately judged, in an effort to explain how those programs are pieced together under tight deadlines and why they play up some subjects and largely ignore others.

As I quickly learned, the anchors, their staffs, and their bosses are acutely aware of the obstacles looming in their path. Watching a half-hour newscast at 6:30, after all, is a practice that began nearly sixty years ago, and no one in the modern age has managed to slow the erosion of the audience.

I knew, as I set out on this project, that all the networks were confronting a daunting transition, one that would require new anchors to establish themselves and gradually win the trust of their viewers. I had no idea of the twists of fate that would, with startling swiftness, plunge the process into turmoil.

CHAPTER 1

Changing of the Guard

The courting of Brian Williams unfolded amid the stately splendor of the second floor of the Harvard Club.

Seated around an alcove in front of a window of the nineteenth-century building on Manhattan's West 44th Street, near a library packed floor to ceiling with twenty-five thousand books, the former volunteer fireman from New Jersey was listening to an offer that once would have seemed unimaginable.

It was a cold winter day in 2002, and Williams, perfectly coiffed and impeccably dressed as always, had been a correspondent and substitute anchor for NBC News for nine years. But his heart had always been with CBS. He had grown up watching Walter Cronkite, had so idolized the man that when he was hired by the local CBS station in New York, he had asked a colleague to show him what he considered a shrine: the newsroom wall that had formed the backdrop for Cronkite's spare, black and white broadcast. It was just a faded wall in a sad little back office now, but it symbolized the reverence with which Williams held the storied network.

He had been lured from WCBS to the massive art deco tower at 30 Rockefeller Plaza by Tom Brokaw himself, with enticing words about the possibility of one day inheriting his NBC anchor chair. Williams was perpetually described in the press as being groomed for the job. Enough with the grooming! He was beginning to feel like a prize poodle. Williams was just impatient enough, just ambitious enough, that he had agreed to this secret meeting with his competitors, to consider the tantalizing possibility of defection.

In one chair sat Les Moonves, president of the CBS television network, a former actor with leading-man looks and the silky-smooth manner of a Hollywood deal-maker. In the other was Andrew Heyward, the news division president, an erudite Harvard graduate with graying hair and a dark mustache.

The two men had a simple proposition for Williams.

They were offering him Dan Rather's job.

The pitch was based on emotion and carefully calibrated to appeal to Williams's sense of tradition and history. CBS was home, they said, it was where he had grown up and ultimately where he belonged. They would bill it as the prodigal son's return.

This was heady stuff for a guy who had never graduated college, who had announced the news as a grade-schooler through a paper towel roll, who had washed out in his first television job, a $174-a-week gig at a station in tiny Pittsburg, Kansas.

But Williams had serious concerns about joining the third-place *CBS Evening News* and the battered news operation, eroded by years of budget cuts, of what had once been called the Tiffany Network.

"I would need this to happen along with a totally revitalized news division and a huge investment on your part," he said.

The talk turned to whether Cronkite, who had remained a friend since Williams had left Channel 2, would appear at a celebratory news conference.

"I would only invite him if it meant a return to the great days of CBS," Williams said.

Moonves and Heyward assured him that this was precisely what they had in mind. Moonves felt that Rather had had an illustrious career, but he was seventy-one and the ratings weren't getting any better. It was time to line up a younger successor. And as Moonves knew all too well from his days in Hollywood, he needed someone who, if not yet a celebrity, had the potential to blossom into a bankable star, someone who could deliver at the box office.

Moonves cautioned that Williams could not immediately ascend to the anchor chair, which at the moment was occupied by the proud Texan who had held it for more than two decades. Williams would serve as a featured correspondent for a time, to allow the CBS audience to become acquainted with him, and then would take his place in the coveted seat. Moonves and Heyward even offered to set a date, in a year or so, for the incumbent's departure. Dan Rather would be out, and Brian Williams would be in.

He promised to think it over. The whole idea struck him as rather romantic.

They left the library one at a time, so as not to be spotted in public.

This was a serious approach, Williams thought. The discussion had been so specific, down to the level of whether Williams would also appear on CBS radio. At the same time he was miffed at the notion of having to serve an apprenticeship as a correspondent. That struck him as a tad condescending. He didn't have anything to prove. Still, Moonves was promising him the anchor chair. It was a bird in the hand. The future at NBC, despite his years as the leading understudy, was less clear.

When Tom Brokaw caught wind of the offer, he called Williams at home.

"You're not really going to do this?" Brokaw asked in his rich, deep baritone. "If loyalty means anything to you . . . These last few years have been about one thing: the passing of the baton to a new generation."

Williams was mush in his hands. As he hung up the phone, he wondered: *What were you thinking?* He felt . . . dirty. How could he have considered a life outside the family?

When Brokaw had mentioned loyalty, it struck a nerve. Williams's father had that quality in spades, had been married to the same woman for fifty years. Maybe he was turning into his dad. Brokaw had done an enormous amount for his career, and Williams owed it to him to stick with NBC.

There was already a clause in his contract requiring NBC to pay him a huge amount of money if he didn't succeed Brokaw. But Williams had been around the business long enough to understand that no deal was final until the ink was dry. His flirtation with CBS, however fleeting, persuaded his bosses that time was of the essence. Brokaw had already been in talks about eventually stepping down, but now the process took on a new urgency. The handoff clearly had to be speeded up. On May 28, 2002, network executives took the unusual step of announcing that Brian Williams would succeed Tom Brokaw as the anchor of *NBC Nightly News,* but not for another two and a half years. As the country's top-rated anchor, Brokaw would get one last victory lap that would carry him through the end of the 2004 presidential campaign, and Williams would get the official designation of anchor-in-waiting, poised to become the first man since the early 1980s to break into the triumvirate that had dominated the television landscape for so long.

This was a valuable prize indeed, but in truth it was losing some of its glitter. The job lacked the sheer stature it had held when Brokaw first took over, the number of viewers were dwindling each year, and the broadcasts had faded in importance amid the explosion of alternative news sources.

Williams understood all this as he prepared to steer the ship, and he was determined to stem the tide. These network news operations, he felt, were too important to be allowed to wither and die. He knew what Brokaw and his brethren had meant to the country, and the enormity of the shoes he was trying to fill, but he had some ideas about modernizing the franchise and extending its reach.

All those years he had filled in on *Nightly News,* Williams had felt constrained. It was Tom's program, and he was like a visitor in a friend's home who had to be careful not to disturb the furniture. But when he took over, Williams wanted to make it his broadcast. He would cast about for new ways to connect with the audience. He carried a BlackBerry and an iPod, was a regular reader of blogs, and was fully plugged into the wired world. Williams felt that it was time to pull back the curtain, to let viewers in on the way that newsroom decisions were made and give them a chance to talk back. Imagine how fascinating it would have been, when he was growing up, to know what Cronkite was thinking, to know what Huntley and Brinkley were doing behind the scenes. Maybe, he thought, he would start his own blog.

Williams realized how lucky he was to have climbed to the top rung of NBC News. He had never expected it to happen, not to a college dropout who had spent years knocking around local television, not to someone who had endured too many jokes about being a good-looking lightweight. Now that he had finally made it, he wanted to keep the anchor job for the next twenty years. And this, he knew, this was the real challenge—he wanted to make it a job worth keeping.

*   *   *

When viewed through the hazy lens of memory, Rather, Brokaw, and Jennings loom like journalistic giants, stomping through history as they interviewed world leaders and raced off to war zones and disasters.

In the grittier reality, each man faced substantial difficulties and internal backbiting as they presided over the transformation of television news from dignified public trust to budget-squeezed business unit.

The tug of war between news and commerce can be traced to television's earliest days, when NBC's first news show, anchored by John Cameron Swayze, was called the *Camel News Caravan,* and even Edward R. Murrow had to balance his controversial *See It Now* documentaries with a celebrity chat show called *Person to Person*. The mythical golden age probably never existed.

But in a time of few choices, everyone watched. In 1980 *U.S. News* was asking: "Is TV News Growing Too Powerful?" The magazine, noting the launch of a tiny Atlanta start-up called CNN, observed that "the audience for TV network news has exploded in the past year." The most popular show on the tube—drawing an impressive 36 million viewers—was *60 Minutes*. But within a few short years all three networks were sold to corporate conglomerates, touching off a series of cost-cutting battles that left considerable blood on the floor.

The laments often sounded by media graybeards about the deterioration of these once-proud franchises seems rooted in nostalgia for the era when there were three television alternatives for national news, along with PBS. Who, really, would want to go back to those days? We take for granted the instantaneous availability of information, yet wonder why a form of news delivery invented in the late 1940s isn't as important as it used to be. In some ways, of course, it is far better—those early, plodding, black and white newscasts would seem as primitive as telegraph machines today—with a depth and texture, on longer pieces, that was well beyond the reach of the pioneers.

Today's evening newscasts, with their glitz and technological prowess, would be barely recognizable to the viewers of even a quarter-century ago. In an age of MTV attention spans, everything moves faster. The stories (a minute forty-five is considered a substantial piece). The sound bites (eight seconds if the speaker is lucky). The tantalizing teases (*"Coming up, a story you won't want to miss . . ."*). The back half of the broadcasts is so heavily tilted toward health and medicine that they might be confused with an episode of *E.R.*

Network news executives can hardly be blamed for the fact that the ground has shifted beneath their feet, turning what once reigned as the fastest medium into a lumbering giant. But they do bear some responsibility for their shrinking audiences. They cut back drastically on coverage of the rest of the world, deeming such news expendable until 9/11 rendered this approach embarrassingly myopic. They succumbed to the sensational, from an immersion in local crime to a fixation on celebrity trials, in search of a quick ratings fix. They stuck with rigid, traditional formats—their idea of a major innovation was having the anchor stand for part of the show—that tightly packaged the news but made it seem more artificial. They grew comfortable with their aging audience, offering little to younger viewers who were already skeptical of passively receiving predigested facts from an authority figure behind a desk.

Perhaps most important, they hitched their collective wagons to three men who had over the years formed a unique connection with the country, even as they approached senior citizen status, their very longevity making them a comfortable presence in our lives. Their careers, and the forces that shaped them, are crucial to understanding the rise and eventual decline of network news. Through wars and riots, conventions and campaigns, terror attacks and natural disasters, they ministered to their flock, some of which had fallen away but returned to the fold in time of crisis. At the beginning, though, these men were seen as callow, untested, and ambitious, perhaps unworthy to carry the mantle of their illustrious predecessors.

CHAPTER 2

No Pretty Boy

From the moment he ascended to the anchor chair, Tom Brokaw had trouble being taken seriously.

It wasn't a lack of journalistic experience. Brokaw had been a local newsman and a White House correspondent who had held his own against Dan Rather during Watergate and the years that followed.

The problem, for some people at least, was that he was too cute.

"He looks so good that people instinctively take him less seriously," said *The New York Times.*

He was "younger, richer, prettier," said *The Washington Post.*

One critic talked about his button nose.

"I'm not looking to be the Farrah Fawcett of TV news," Brokaw was forced to declare.

Others saw him as somehow more frivolous because he had served as cohost of the *Today* show, engaging in some of the unavoidable fluff required by morning television, chatting up actresses from *Dallas* and other light fare.

Brokaw quickly grew tired of this sort of patter, which seemed to encapsulate the mixed expectations of a network anchor. It was, on the one hand, a showbiz job, graded as theater, and on the other the pinnacle of the news business, a post of grave responsibility and enormous impact. Brokaw understood, too, that he looked younger than he was. But the pretty-boy coverage was, in his view, just journalistic laziness, by writers who hadn't bothered to learn that he had been a convention floor reporter or had covered the pope or had flown all night to report on the assassination of Egyptian leader Anwar Sadat.

This was the precursor of a debate that would surround a generation of anchors to come, whether they were hard-core reporters or entertainers, and whether the ability to have fun on the air detracted from the seriousness of their mission.

The son of a hard-hat worker who grew up in Yankton, South Dakota, Brokaw started out doing the weather in 1960 for a Sioux City, Iowa, station. In 1973, when he was a reporter and anchor at KNBC in Los Angeles, NBC News tapped Brokaw as its White House reporter. When Barbara Walters left the *Today* show in 1976 to become the first female network anchor, on ABC's evening news—in what would become a disastrous and short-lived partnership with Harry Reasoner—Brokaw got the nod. He worked so hard as Jane Pauley's cohost, and was so versatile, that the executive producer, Steve Friedman, dubbed him "Duncan the Wonder Horse."

Brokaw eventually grew weary of the showbiz side of the program, and in 1980 the other two networks made a run at him. Brokaw was particularly charmed by Roone Arledge, the charismatic president of ABC News. Arledge wasn't sure that the boyish-looking Brokaw had the heft to be the solo anchor of *World News Tonight*—a judgment he later came to regret—but thought that he would make a terrific correspondent and anchor. Arledge dangled before him an astonishing sum of money.

"This is irresponsible, what you're offering," Brokaw told him. "This is wacky. You cannot be serious about this."

Brokaw wasn't sure where he fit in at NBC, which had recently hired the far more experienced Roger Mudd after he lost out in the anchor sweepstakes at CBS. Brokaw finally concluded that he should accept the Arledge offer. He told his wife, Meredith, of his decision.

"I think that's the right call," she said.

Brokaw poured himself a large scotch, stared out the window, and realized that he had been with NBC his whole adult life and just couldn't leave. He promptly informed Arledge of his change of heart.

Days later Brokaw was staying at a friend's house in the Hamptons when Arledge somehow tracked him down and called at 7 A.M. "It doesn't make sense," Arledge insisted. Roone just never let go.

At NBC, however, there was a catch. In luring Mudd from CBS, the network had made him a contractual promise that he would succeed John Chancellor in the coveted chair.

But Mudd, knowing full well that NBC was anxious to keep Brokaw, urged him to stay during a lunch at the Four Seasons. Mudd waived his right to be the sole anchor, and on July 1, 1981, NBC announced its new team:

Brokaw in New York, Mudd in Washington. Brokaw's salary more than doubled, from $400,000 to a reported $1 million a year.

But they were no Huntley and Brinkley. It was difficult for two men to share twenty-two minutes of airtime, and the ratings were lousy. "I think we've got to look at this thing," Brokaw told Mudd after less than a year, but his partner insisted that they were doing just fine. Brokaw, though, sensed that NBC was going to drop one of them, and he was convinced it would be him. Roger just seemed smoother and more established, and he had been a network reporter when Brokaw was still in Omaha.

Brokaw was wrong. After two years NBC benched Mudd and handed him the ball. Mudd complained about "a built-in anti-Washington bias among senior management. They think most Washington news is 'inside' and boring." Brokaw understood that Mudd was bitter, having lost two network anchor jobs, and he was saddened that their friendship did not survive the rupture.

Brokaw settled more comfortably into the *NBC Nightly News* chair over the next three years. But he faced a different kind of challenge in 1986 when General Electric acquired NBC, and the rest of its parent company, RCA, for $6.2 billion. The new corporate owners, headed by Jack Welch, began cutting jobs, but more important, a culture clash emerged between GE and what had been a free-spending news division in which limousines and first-class flights were a way of life. GE's insistence that each company unit, including news, show how it could shrink its budget by 5 percent was seen as blasphemy. Brokaw was unsettled. For the first time he felt like a cog in a machine.

And it was, in fact, a very different kind of corporate machine. Welch wanted to know how much each story covered by NBC cost, how many of those stories got on the air, and how often each correspondent appeared on each newscast. He insisted that the money-losing division break even. Brokaw felt that there could be greater efficiencies, but how did you value the services of an investigative reporter like Brian Ross, who was on the air less often because difficult digging could take weeks?

During the same period Brokaw tried to broaden his approach, to move away from the old "newscast of record" model by doing fewer stories at greater length. He also began to establish himself journalistically, especially on the world stage. He landed the first American television interview with Soviet leader Mikhail Gorbachev in 1987. On the night Bob Dole lost the 1988 New Hampshire primary, Brokaw, who was with George H.W. Bush, asked Dole if he had any message for the vice president. "Stop lying about my record," Dole growled. That all but ended his candidacy, and it was years before Dole, who felt set up, spoke to Brokaw again.

Brokaw also covered the turmoil in Eastern Europe and was at the Berlin Wall when it came down in 1989. He stumbled two years later, when his broadcast carried the name and picture of Patricia Bowman, who had accused William Kennedy Smith of rape and had wanted her identity protected.

The next few years were a difficult time for Brokaw. Some people on the fifty-second floor, in the executive suites at 30 Rock, did not think he was the future of NBC News, deeming him incapable of lifting the newscast into first place. *Nightly News* was stalled, and it wasn't clear how to restart the engines.

It was then that CBS News made a play to steal Brokaw from NBC. Howard Stringer, the president of CBS's news division and a longtime friend, made a very serious offer for Brokaw to jump ship. The pitch was for Brokaw to become a correspondent for *60 Minutes*. Don Hewitt, the executive producer who had launched the program in 1968, tried to persuade Brokaw as well.

It was a fairly audacious move. Brokaw thought about it long and hard. Being a network anchor was terrific, but how long was he prepared to keep banging his head against the wall? The people upstairs didn't seem to have much confidence in him. GE executives couldn't decide if they loved NBC or not. For all his fame, he was an expendable commodity. He had no illusions about that. But Brokaw decided to make one more push at NBC. He felt the tug of loyalty to his colleagues. For him to bail out would be traumatic for everyone in the news division.

The network kept tinkering with the nightly news. Jeff Zucker, a twenty-seven-year-old wunderkind, was named the program's new executive producer. This would have been unremarkable, except for the fact that Zucker was holding on to his job as *Today*'s executive producer as well. Zucker was young and arrogant and filled with boundless energy and had not the slightest doubt that he could do both jobs well. After six weeks he realized the arrangement was impossible and abandoned the evening job.

Months later Zucker gave up his *Today* post to launch a prime-time newsmagazine with Brokaw and Katie Couric, his new morning star. Brokaw agreed to assume the extra workload because he felt that NBC News needed a hit evening show after a series of failures and the rupture of *Dateline*'s credibility after the program staged the fiery crash of a General Motors truck. The new program, called *Now,* leaned heavily on crime and sensationalism, as was evident from the teasing headlines:

"Was sex with children part of this group's teachings?"

"Coming up: One family's desperate search for their daughter."

"Herman and Druie Dutton, ages fifteen and twelve, shot and killed their father."

"How would you feel about sharing your spouse?"

"They're armed and dangerous, and they could come into your home and take you away."

Couric tried to land the first interview with Tonya Harding, the bad-girl ice skater who had orchestrated an attack on rival Nancy Kerrigan, but lost out to CBS's Connie Chung, who had her own magazine show, *Eye to Eye.*

Brokaw, for his part, wanted to do more serious issues. He was conflicted by his role on *Now.* It wasn't true that they pursued stories only for the ratings, but they couldn't very well go out of business, either. Couric, too, acknowledged that ratings were the driving force behind many of their prime-time pursuits. *Now* lasted one year.

When O.J. Simpson was accused of murdering his wife, Nicole, and her friend Ron Goldman in 1994, Brokaw and *Nightly* jumped on the story with more force than their rivals, sometimes airing two segments a night. After a jury acquitted the former football star, he agreed to an exclusive interview with Brokaw and Couric on *Dateline* but backed out seven hours before airtime. In a cringe-inducing choice of words, Simpson told *The New York Times* he had heard that "Tom Brokaw was sharpening knives for the interview."

Brokaw felt that the newscast had gotten a nice lift by broadcasting from Atlanta during the network's coverage of the 1996 Summer Olympics. And when Simpson was embroiled in a civil suit over the killings that stretched into 1997, Brokaw's broadcast led with the O.J. saga night after night, sometimes with as many as three reports. While cutting back on political coverage, Washington scandals, and foreign news, Brokaw was also adding a mix of softer stories on genealogy, baldness remedies, daydreams, a dog on death row, bad sportsmanship, no-fault divorce, Dennis Rodman, and Rosie O'Donnell. And the combination seemed to be working. During a ten-week stretch, Brokaw's newscast pulled ahead of ABC's *World News Tonight,* which had led the field for eight years, in every week but one.

The tabloid fare, always a tantalizing option, had given the broadcast a boost. Brokaw made no apology for the heavy diet of O.J. and harmless features. These were not the traditional stories that everyone had grown up with, but those reports—on subcommittee hearings and political developments—were part of the reason that people felt more distanced from television news. He was breaking the mold, getting away from Washington and politicians on soapboxes. The new approach might not fall within the traditional parameters of important journalism, he felt, but it also had value.

Once Brokaw grabbed hold of the ratings lead, he never relinquished it. *Nightly* remained firmly ensconced in first place. In 1998, when he published his book *The Greatest Generation,* about World War II veterans, Brokaw seemed to acquire more gravitas along with his graying hair. He felt that veterans, and many of their families, were seeing him in a new light. Those around him believed that Brokaw was acquiring a new confidence on the air, that he truly had become America's anchorman. No longer was he the too-cute kid from the Midwest. He was at once more established and more relaxed, taking off summers to spend at his Montana ranch.

On Election Night 2000, after all the networks had awarded Florida to Al Gore and then withdrawn the prediction, George W. Bush was one state away from being able to proclaim victory. In the early-morning hours all the network anchors suffered the humiliation of prematurely projecting Bush as the winner in Florida and the next occupant of the White House. But it was Brokaw who came up with the best line. "We don't just have egg on our face," he said the morning after the biggest fiasco in the history of television news. "We have a whole omelette."

The following summer, as he took an unprecedented ten-week vacation, Brokaw was thinking hard about hanging it up. The truth was, he was bored out of his gourd. He was spending more time in Montana with Meredith. He wanted to go steelhead fishing in the fall. He didn't need to be an anchor anymore. He had done it all. The challenge was gone. He felt he had played out the string and was ready to move on.

But life changed on September 11, 2001. It fell to Brokaw, Rather, and Jennings to guide a shaken nation through the trauma of the worst terrorist strikes on American soil. There was no way that Brokaw could leave, not now. He was fully immersed in perhaps the biggest story of his career.

Life in television news began returning to normal. But the definition of normal had changed, and Brokaw routinely devoted a substantial portion of his broadcast to war and terrorism and homeland security, leaving less time for the fluffier features of years past.

Brokaw's thoughts turned again to retirement the following spring. He had finally fought his way to the top. There wasn't much left for him to accomplish. Very few men walked away from these jobs, but Brokaw believed there could be more to life than sitting behind an anchor desk.

CHAPTER 3

Hurricane Dan

Dan Rather, who had first made his name covering hurricanes, was not a natural anchor, not with his stormy intensity and slightly eccentric style. But in the early months of 1980, everyone wanted him.

After nearly two decades at CBS News, he was in the thick of a race to succeed Walter Cronkite, who was so revered that his shadow all but eclipsed those who were eyeing his chair. Rather, who had clawed his way up the network ladder from Sam Houston State Teachers College, was by no means assured of the job and was competing with the more urbane Roger Mudd, the more literary Charles Kuralt, and, as a long shot, his scrappy fellow Texan Bob Schieffer.

Roone Arledge, the ABC sports impresario who had taken over the network's news division three years earlier, was determined to hire Rather and make him a star anchor; Brokaw was not yet available.

"I think you'd be fabulous on *World News Tonight*," Arledge told Rather. Arledge already had an anchor in Frank Reynolds, but he nonetheless dangled the prospect of a $2 million salary and a regular role on *20/20, Nightline,* and the network's Sunday morning show. Arledge even hosted a dinner party at his apartment for Rather and his wife, Jean. Rather was so excited by their conversations that he began referring to ABC News as "we."

At NBC Bill Small, the news division president, also made Rather a lucrative offer, promising the anchor job either with John Chancellor or on his own after Chancellor moved on to become a commentator. CBS responded by promising the top spot to Rather and offering him more than double the compensation of the legendary Cronkite, who was paid just under seven figures.

Rather's friends urged him to leave CBS, saying that he would never match Cronkite's legacy. Cronkite, for his part, encouraged Rather to stay. "You're a CBS man," he said.

Rather, who even in private could talk like a medieval knight, called Arledge to say that he was staying at CBS. "Roone Arledge, know this now and know it always: Dan Rather will walk through fire in a gasoline suit for you."

In the end Rather took less money to stay at CBS, though his new package, at more than $2 million a year, was a tremendous boost from the $225,000 he had previously been earning. Once the deal was announced, Rather made the cover of *Time* as "The $8,000,000 Man." He always kept in mind that his father, who had been a ditch digger, never made more than $11,200 a year. But with the money and the publicity came immense pressure. "Some people have told me, 'You're crazy to stay at CBS. The first guy after Walter Cronkite is going to get his head blown off,' " Rather said.

Rather would transform the job in unexpected ways, sparking questions about his personality, his temper, his ideology, and ultimately his ethics—a new model, a post-Cronkite model, of the anchor as controversial celebrity.

It was not an easy transition. Rather was a hot personality in a cool medium. He had been, by accident, the first television journalist to report that John Kennedy had died on that awful day in Dallas in 1963. He had been, not at all by accident, the reporter who mouthed off at a 1973 news conference when Richard Nixon asked whether he was running for something and Rather shot back, "No, Mr. President, are you?" He was, quite in character, the *60 Minutes* correspondent who dressed up in peasant garb to slip into Afghanistan, earning the indelible nickname Gunga Dan.

But from March 9, 1981, when he took over for Cronkite, Rather often seemed stiff, tense, or uncomfortable in the chair. He tried wearing a sweater. He tried signing off, strangely, with "Courage." As a reporter in the field, he was in his element; during live events he was indefatigable; but on the set he soon ceded the first-place status he had inherited.

It wasn't long before Cronkite turned against Rather and the broadcast. When he agreed to relinquish the anchor chair, he felt emphatically that he was not retiring from broadcasting or from CBS. He was shocked to learn that he would almost never be asked to appear on the network again. Cronkite came to believe that this was solely Rather's doing, that the new man had made a policy of freezing out his predecessor. The way he had been shafted was just unbelievable, Cronkite felt. For the rest of his life he would regret stepping down when he did.

Rather saw things very differently, believing that Cronkite had just gotten bored sailing his boat and wished he had not abandoned the chair and missed the era of big multimillion-dollar salaries.

As the *CBS Evening News* slipped to second place, and briefly to third, there were even whispers that Cronkite might come back. Rather was stung when a producer stood outside his door and declared loudly, "Rather's through, he's doomed. He won't be here when spring comes."

The broadcast bounced back into first place after Van Gordon Sauter became the news division president and ordered up softer, more emotional stories—he liked to speak of television "moments"—that were ridiculed in media circles but embraced by Rather, despite his predilection for hard news. But Rather, who was becoming known for his down-home prairie metaphors—saying that someone was "mad as a rained-on rooster" or "if a frog had side pockets, he'd carry a gun"—brushed off the detractors.

Rather soon felt battered by unrelenting criticism from the Reagan administration that his broadcast, far more than NBC and ABC, was airing slanted or unfair stories. It was not the first time that he had found himself at odds with a Republican administration, and it would not be the last.

Rather, who had grown up in segregated Houston, believed that his liberal reputation stemmed from his coverage of the civil rights battles of the early 1960s, when in some parts of the South his network was known as the Colored Broadcasting System. To him, the label was laughable. After all, he was a Texan who had served in the Marines and gone to a state teachers' college, hardly the profile of a northeastern liberal. But he underestimated the impact of his battles against Nixon, and by the early 1980s Jesse Helms, the conservative Republican senator from North Carolina, was fronting a business group angling to take over CBS with the appeal that Helms would become "Dan Rather's boss"—and fire him.

That effort fell short. But when billionaire businessman Laurence Tisch bought a controlling interest in CBS in 1986, the network's journalists were stunned by the slashing reductions in their news budget. Worse, they were taken aback by the bottom-line mentality that viewed news not as a sacred trust but as just another product that had to eke out a profit. What ensued was a very public war against the chief executive of the Loews Corporation over the issue of layoffs; Rather rallied the news troops, publishing a remarkable op-ed piece in *The New York Times* headlined "From Murrow to Mediocrity?"

Rather's behavior appeared increasingly erratic, particularly his 1987 decision to walk off the set rather than truncate the *CBS Evening News* after a U.S. Open tennis match ran long. The network went to black for seven excruciating minutes. By then Rather's dominance was fading as well. Tisch wondered aloud why the number-three anchor was being paid the number-one salary.

An even more bizarre tableau unfolded at the start of the 1988 presidential campaign, when what was supposed to be a routine interview with the vice president, George Herbert Walker Bush, turned into a ten-minute shouting match on the *CBS Evening News*. Rather pressed Bush about the intricacies of the Iran-contra affair, the vice president accused him of distorting the facts, and the country was divided over the confrontation. The overwhelming majority of Republicans concluded that the anchor had been unfair, while most Democrats sided with Rather. The episode left a residue of overheated partisanship that Rather would never be able to shake.

By 1993 Rather's star had fallen sufficiently that CBS executives began pressuring him to accept a female coanchor as a way of lifting him out of the ratings cellar. Rather, whose permission was required under his contract, reluctantly agreed to share the anchor desk.

It was a disaster from the start. Connie Chung believed that she would be a full coanchor, including on big breaking stories, while Rather had thought he was taking on a junior partner. Chung's fate was probably sealed in 1995 when she persuaded House Speaker Newt Gingrich's mother—assuring her it was "just between you and me"—to reveal that her son had called the first lady, Hillary Rodham Clinton, a "bitch."

CBS pulled the plug on the dual-anchor format soon afterward. Rather's side accused Chung of using a scorched-earth strategy to cover her journalistic shortcomings, while Chung's partisans blamed a sexist power play that never gave her a fair chance.

Even the city's tabloids chose up sides.

"CUNNING BACK STABBER," the *Daily News* said of her.

"DAN'S DOUBLE CROSS," the *New York Post* said of him.

Just as Rather had survived the Chung experiment, he outlasted Larry Tisch as well. In 1995 the corporate titan sold the network for $5.4 billion to the Westinghouse Electric Corporation, which in turn sold CBS to the communications giant Viacom for $37.3 billion four years later.

In the late 1990s Rather was disgusted by the Monica Lewinsky scandal, saying that he didn't get into journalism to chase sex stories. His detractors saw Rather as simply applying a different standard to a Democratic president who had clearly lied.

In the summer of 2001 the media went utterly wild over the disappearance of Chandra Levy, a former House intern who police sources said had had an affair with California congressman Gary Condit. While Connie Chung, by then with ABC, snagged an exclusive interview with Condit, and while Tom Brokaw's *NBC Nightly News* ran ten stories on the case in the space of a week, Rather's *CBS Evening News* refused to cover it.

Rather's producer, Jim Murphy, a goateed man with a sharp eye and sharper tongue, announced that he was "sick to my stomach" over the media's behavior and said that the story was "nauseating" and "beyond tasteless" and not worth Rather's time. The message was that CBS was making a lonely stand for quality news. Murphy was also mindful about not saddling Rather with stories the anchor would regard as frivolous. In such cases, the staff had observed more than once, Rather appeared to deliberately mispronounce words as a way of signaling his displeasure.

Nearly two weeks later CBS correspondent Jim Stewart learned that FBI officials were unhappy with the way the District of Columbia police were handling the Levy probe and had transferred it to the bureau's elite "cold case" unit. That, Murphy felt, was news, and they had it exclusively. But Rather strongly disagreed that it was a story.

"We've taken a stand," Rather told his producer. "Without any serious evidence, why should we be out there?" Murphy felt that they were letting the desire for favorable publicity about their principled position get in the way of their news judgment. But Rather would not budge, and they were at an impasse.

Andrew Heyward, the CBS News president, called in from a vacation in Belgium. Heyward wondered why CBS wasn't running the Stewart scoop.

"Andrew, this could be easily solved," Murphy said. "You know what the rules are." The long-standing agreement was that no story would air on the *CBS Evening News* if either Rather or Murphy strenuously objected.

"Do you want me to tell Dan to go home and get someone else to do it?" Murphy asked.

Heyward said that he did not.

"This is easily solved if you just order us to do it."

"I don't do that," Heyward said. He had never issued such an order during his tenure running the news division.

In the end Rather agreed to air Stewart's report, which some critics promptly derided as an excuse for CBS to get in the missing-woman game.

Less than two months later terrorists armed with box cutters hijacked airplanes and flew them into the World Trade Center and the Pentagon. The overheated coverage of the murder of Chandra Levy came to be viewed as an irresponsible interlude before journalists were rudely reminded that there were groups around the world plotting to kill large numbers of innocent Americans.

The new, sober-minded era played to Rather's strengths. His flag-waving patriotism was on display when he cried at David Letterman's side during a rendition of "God Bless America." Rather praised George W. Bush's performance as commander in chief and said that he was an American first and a journalist second.

As the United States geared up to invade Iraq, he landed what turned out to be the last interview by a Western journalist with Saddam Hussein, just as he had managed to interview the Iraqi leader on the eve of the Persian Gulf War. Some criticized Rather for not asking more confrontational questions, but few denied that he had pulled off a major coup.

Rather made headlines again in the spring of 2004 when he and his *60 Minutes* producer, Mary Mapes, obtained photos documenting some of the appalling abuses by American guards at Abu Ghraib prison.

Despite his journalistic accomplishments, Rather remained the most polarizing of the three network anchors. And in the heat of the 2004 general election campaign, he handed his critics a loaded revolver.

It was, in retrospect, a remarkably reckless act. Five days after Mapes obtained what purported to be thirty-year-old memos about Bush's National Guard service, Rather was on *60 Minutes Wednesday* making explosive charges that he could not possibly back up. He did not know where the documents, said to have been written by Bush's long-dead squadron commander in the Texas Air National Guard, had come from. Mapes's source, Bill Burkett, an anti-Bush zealot with a history of self-described mental problems, never adequately explained the provenance of the papers. Two handwriting experts retained by CBS had warned of problems with the documents, and a third said that he could not authenticate them. Rather felt that a retired colonel had vouched for the documents, when they had only been read to him over the phone.

The night before the story was tentatively scheduled to air, Rather was sitting at the anchor desk, with less than half an hour before the start of the *Evening News*. He called Josh Howard, who had recently been named executive producer of *60 Minutes Wednesday,* and asked what they were doing to promote his story.

"We're not," Howard said. "We haven't gotten the lawyers to sign off. The script isn't finished. We haven't even talked to the White House. I'm not going to start promoting a story when we don't know what we have."

That was not the answer Rather wanted to hear.

"Other people are chasing this story," he said. "We're going to lose our exclusive. We have to get our hooks into the story."

When Howard again refused, Rather raised the stakes.

"I'm going to give one of the documents to *The New York Times* to run in Wednesday's paper," he said. "They'll have to credit CBS News. That way we can put our stamp on it."

"You can't do that either," Howard said. "We haven't finished vetting this." Rather grumbled and hung up. To raise the specter of giving away a scoop to a competing news outlet was practically unheard of.

Howard, who had once been an *Evening News* producer, had never been subjected to this kind of pressure. He did, however, have a backup plan. They were still in rerun season, so if the Guard story failed to get the green light, he had a previously aired program ready to go.

That evening Dan Bartlett, the White House communications chief, called CBS to ask about the widely rumored Guard story and whether he could present the president's side. Bartlett said that he would agree to be interviewed by Rather only if he could first examine the ancient memos.

At 7:45 the next morning CBS faxed the documents to Bartlett's office. When torrential rains kept Rather in New York, John Roberts, the White House correspondent, showed up instead at 11:15. The situation, as Bartlett saw it, was absurd: How was he supposed to verify in just three hours a bunch of papers that ostensibly came from a dead man?

Bush told Bartlett that he had no recollection of having seen the memos, but then, he wouldn't necessarily have been shown documents from a commander's personal file. When Roberts conveyed this information to CBS, Josh Howard and his staff stopped trying to authenticate the memos, inexplicably treating Bartlett's lack of a denial as confirmation that the story was true.

One hour before airtime Andrew Heyward gave final approval for the story. At 8 P.M. on September 8, 2004, eight million people saw Rather accuse the president of having received favorable treatment in the National Guard.

An initial wave of bloggers at Web sites such as *Power Line* and *L*

Green Footballs, followed by several major news organizations, reported that the memos were almost certainly not typed on an early 1970s government typewriter and were more likely computer-generated forgeries.

At this point Rather proceeded to dig himself into a deeper hole. He dismissed much of the criticism as coming from "partisan political operatives" and told one colleague, "I have never been more confident of a story in my life." As the questions mounted, Andrew Heyward also dug in his heels, saying he saw "no percentage of possibility" that CBS had been duped. Rather stuck to his guns, even after Marian Carr Knox, the eighty-six-year-old secretary to the late squadron commander, said she had never typed the memos and that they were fakes.

Jim Murphy felt that Rather and the news division needed to come clean in a day or two and put the sordid mess behind them. Murphy was stunned to learn that Mary Mapes was continuing to work on pieces for the evening news that defended her work. Bill Burkett, whom CBS had repeatedly described as an "unimpeachable source," had told Mapes that someone handed him the documents behind some hog barn at an agricultural fair. A high school student would not have believed that. Murphy called *60 Minutes* and said that independent journalists with no connection to the fiasco needed to take over.

The next night Rather, Heyward, Howard, Mapes, Senior Vice President Betsy West, and others gathered in West's office for a damage control meeting that dragged on almost until midnight. Despite the mounting questions, Rather was unyielding: We are right, we are confident, and we stand by our story. If outside experts are criticizing the documents, we will find our own experts to defend them.

Josh Howard could not sleep. At 4:53 A.M. he sent an e-mail to West, suggesting that CBS say the following: "We're continuing to investigate, and if we were the victims of an elaborate hoax, no one would be more anxious to get to the bottom of it than CBS News." West responded that the network should "not even concede that we think it could be a hoax."

Jeff Fager, the executive producer of *60 Minutes,* had lunch with Rather and urged him to begin backing away from the story. "These documents are suspect," Fager said. Rather would not give an inch.

But he no longer had the final word. On Sunday, September 19, Heyward showed Rather a statement that he planned to issue, saying that CBS could not authenticate the documents and had been wrong to rush the story to air. The next night, after twelve days of dogged defensiveness, Rather apologized on the air. Burkett, Mapes's source, had admitted lying, but Rather also knew that he himself had fallen short, that he had not been as careful on the explosive story as he should have been.

Yet even as Les Moonves, the CBS president, said that he would appoint an independent panel to examine the Guard story, Rather insisted that it was true.

The consensus view among CBS's most experienced journalists, even those who liked Rather and admired his long and tenacious career, was that he had mainly himself to blame. Rather, they felt, had long been overexposed, and worse than that, he was stretched far too thin. He was brought into too many stories at the tail end, handed three questions on a blue card for the final interview with some big shot. He was flying around the country doing stand-ups. Instead of being a reporter, and he had once been a great one, he was increasingly playing a reporter.

There was a famous tale in the news division that during a special event in Washington several years earlier, Rather had looked up and asked his staff, "Where are my final thoughts?"

Bob Schieffer, who had known him for more than three decades, felt that CBS expected too much of Rather. It had begun in the early 1980s, when the networks decided to make their anchors virtual logos for the company, rather than just the lead correspondents. In the long run, Schieffer felt, that was a mistake. Each of the ventures in which Rather was involved— evening news anchor, *48 Hours* anchor, *60 Minutes* correspondent, radio commentator—was a full-time job. Sometimes, Schieffer believed, Dan was running so fast from one assignment to the next that he must have been worn out.

There was one more thing that no one at CBS could figure out: Given Rather's contentious history with the Bush family, given the history of attacks on him as a liberal ideologue, how could he not have been more careful? How could he have risked his career and credibility on such a shaky story? And the bottom-line question: Could Rather survive?

Murphy felt it was obvious to anyone that Rather would have to leave the broadcast. But Dan, he saw, had a hard time believing that. After all, the man had given his entire working life to the network, had performed extraordinarily well under incredibly dire circumstances, had risked his life dozens of times. And now the company seemed to be turning on him.

CHAPTER 4

The Comeback Kid

Peter Jennings was a complete flop as an anchor.

He wasn't ready, and he wasn't very good.

He was twenty-six years old.

Less than three years later, in the fall of 1967, ABC pulled the plug on *Peter Jennings with the News*. Jennings had been the youngest person ever to anchor a network newscast, which made it all the more difficult for him to compete against Walter Cronkite and the team of Chet Huntley and David Brinkley. His low ratings, his Canadian accent, and his lack of experience with American subjects—Jennings was sometimes derided as an "anchorboy"—contributed to his demotion. He was replaced by Bob Young, a little-known London correspondent.

Jennings claimed, not very persuasively, that it was his decision, that he wanted to return to field reporting. But there was another reason as well: Jennings, who had just turned thirty, knew that he wasn't qualified to sit in that chair. Network executives made no attempt to change his mind.

Jennings was acutely sensitive about the fact that he had dropped out of high school in Ontario after the tenth grade. Much of his career was dedicated to acquiring, through travel, books, and conversations with academics and experts, the knowledge he had never obtained in school. Ironically, the man who came to be viewed as the most cosmopolitan and erudite of the anchors had never gone to college.

As the son of Charles Jennings, the first news anchor and eventually the news chief at the Canadian Broadcasting Corporation, the young man seemed destined for a career in broadcasting. At nine he was hosting a weekly CBC radio show for kids called *Peter's People*. As a young man he landed a spot at an Ontario radio station, and the private network CTV soon tapped Jennings as coanchor of its new late-night newscast. His work in the States, including his coverage of the Kennedy assassination, caught the attention of ABC, which hired him as a reporter in 1964. A year later he was the network's anchor, although ABC's stature was so slight that *The New York Times* devoted only four sentences to his selection, as the second item of a roundup column.

Losing that job forced him to acquire what many in today's generation would regard as a mere accoutrement for fronting a newscast: nuts-and-bolts reporting experience around the globe.

Jennings moved to Beirut, as the first U.S. television correspondent based in the Arab world, and remained there for seven years. He covered the Yom Kippur War and the Lebanese civil war, and he developed a lifelong fascination with the Middle East and world affairs that would later be a hallmark of his broadcast. Critics would pummel Jennings for being overly sympathetic to the Arab cause, but he always insisted that his approach was balanced rather than reflecting unblinking favoritism toward Israel and the West.

With his good looks, dashing manner, and ever-present trench coat, Jennings was the personification of the suave foreign correspondent and, as his friend Ted Koppel liked to put it, catnip to women. It was no accident that he would be married four times.

Jennings eventually landed in London, and in 1978 Roone Arledge had the idea of using a three-anchor, multicity format for the last-place *ABC Evening News*. Frank Reynolds became the chief anchor, in Washington, with Max Robinson in Chicago and Jennings in London. The three-headed beast proved unwieldy, and detractors likened it to a journalistic version of Arledge's *Wide World of Sports*.

When Reynolds died in 1983, Arledge quickly decided to junk the three-anchor approach. He approached Ted Koppel, the *Nightline* host, about the job, but Koppel, who had always been bored by the prospect of anchoring the evening news, said that Jennings would be the best choice. Jennings, too, was reluctant. He loved England, loved his globetrotting lifestyle, and viewed anchors as high-priced slaves. In the days before Reynolds's death, Arledge had been forced to fly to London just to persuade him to substitute in Washington.

Jennings had other drawbacks as a solo anchor, in Arledge's view. He disdained certain stories that had mass appeal, detested the spotlight, and pronounced certain words in the British manner. But Arledge regarded him as handsome, authoritative, hardworking, and the best ad-libber in the business.

When Arledge asked Jennings, over a long dinner at Alfredo's restaurant in Manhattan, to return to New York as the anchor of *World News Tonight,* Jennings proffered a long list of reasons why he didn't want the job. He and his third wife, Kati Marton, wanted to stay in Europe, and he didn't think he knew enough about American politics and issues to succeed in New York.

Finally Arledge invited the couple to his Long Island retreat, in Sagaponack, and Kati, a former ABC foreign correspondent, urged her husband to take the plunge. "You *have* to take it, Peter," she said. "You'd never forgive yourself otherwise."

It was a very big job, Jennings thought. He had to ask himself: Was he qualified? Was he emotionally ready? He concluded that fourteen years after leaving New York as an anchor failure, this time he was fully prepared.

But Jennings told Arledge that he didn't want to give up reporting entirely, and he didn't want the boss to name a new chief foreign correspondent for a year in case he decided to reclaim his old job. Arledge reluctantly agreed.

First Jennings faced the little matter of cultural readjustment after seven years out of the country. He was somewhat unplugged from American politics. He mispronounced the name of Bowie Kuhn, the baseball commissioner, on the air. He clearly had some catching up to do.

Jennings soon settled into the job but eventually found himself reporting to a new set of bosses. In 1985 Capital Cities, a little-known newspaper company that owned seven television stations, bought ABC for $3.5 billion. As with Laurence Tisch and General Electric, Cap Cities brought to the network a frugal, budget-trimming culture that collided with the free-spending ways that ABC had adopted, especially in a news division that was playing catch-up with its long-established rivals.

The summer of 1987 was a difficult time for Jennings. He enjoyed the social whirl with Kati, whether at their Central Park West apartment or at home in the Hamptons, but amid reports that she was having an affair with another journalist, they separated. Liz Smith, who had called them the perfect couple, disclosed the split in her *Daily News* gossip column. *USA Today* ran a story. Jennings was humiliated, both by the breakup of his family—they had two young children—and by all the press coverage. It was the worst thing that had ever happened to him. The couple reconciled for a time but later divorced.

Jennings was struggling with a strained relationship at work as well. He kept clashing with Bill Lord, his executive producer, over the content of *World News Tonight.* After one such squabble Lord ordered him to run a closing piece on the marital problems of Princess Diana and Prince Charles. Jennings wrote a condescending lead-in about "gossip at the highest level. We're never quite certain whether it's because the British press is having a quiet week or because they know it sells newspapers." Lord defended the story—it was *news*—but Jennings had more clout than any producer. A few weeks later, Lord was replaced.

Things settled down at the newscast, but another corporate shake-up lay ahead. In 1995 the Walt Disney Company bought the network for the stunning sum of $19 billion. ABC was now part of a conglomerate whose best known symbol was a mouse.

Later that day, in a closed-circuit news conference beamed to ABC employees around the country, Jennings asked Disney chief Michael Eisner and Thomas Murphy, the Cap Cities chairman, about "the sheer size of the company and the sheer concentration of power, too much being held by too few hands. Is that good for the public?" Eisner said the combined company did not have too much power, but that to maintain a serious news operation, "you have to have sufficient size to be able to compete."

Despite the shifting ownership, Jennings had in recent years led *World News Tonight* into first place, a remarkable accomplishment given his failure the first time around. But when the O.J. Simpson frenzy got under way, Jennings did as little as he could get away with on the broadcast. All the buzz was about NBC, which was blanketing the trial, feeding the public appetite aroused by the live coverage on CNN. Jennings knew that some people thought he was being pompous in refusing to pander to the passions inflamed by a single, racially charged murder trial, but he felt that he was right. Other ABC executives pushed for Jennings to emulate what he called the "populist" newscast at NBC by including more stories on health care and pieces that pushed emotional buttons.

ABC began inching in that direction, but this was not a good fit for Jennings, and more people were sampling *NBC Nightly News* during the Simpson mania. Jennings lost the ratings lead to Tom Brokaw in 1997. He concluded that he had made a mistake with the move toward populism and had blurred the newscast's identity. He was determined to return to his journalistic roots.

Whatever Jennings's personal preferences, the truth was that all the network newscasts were gravitating in the same direction. ABC, like its rivals, had drastically cut back its web of overseas bureaus in the years since Jennings had gone to Beirut, and he was acutely aware that no reporter could be dispatched to a foreign country without the accounting department demanding to know in advance how much it would cost. While Jennings was interested in Washington news, *World News Tonight* did far fewer of what he called "process pieces" about battles within the administration and Congress. Each of the anchors had to modify his beliefs to accommodate the realities of the marketplace.

Jennings was not the easiest man to work for. He could be demanding, moody, and remarkably thin-skinned, despite his outwardly unruffled air. He sometimes demanded top-to-bottom script rewrites from his correspondents and would argue with them, sometimes vigorously, about what was, or was not, the essence of the story.

Although Jennings slipped into second place, he continued to draw plaudits for his versatility as an anchor, whether he was covering foreign news, making prime-time documentaries, or producing shows aimed at children. His personal life settled down, too, with his fourth marriage, in 1997, to Kayce Freed, a former *20/20* producer two decades younger than he was.

After the September 11 attacks, Jennings played the same calming role as the other anchors, perhaps even more so, given his relaxed and unhurried demeanor even in the face of gut-wrenching crisis. He almost lost it when his children called in from different parts of the country, but he felt that the anchor's job was to hold it together at a time of tragedy. Still, his air of assurance masked an inner tension that prompted him to begin smoking again, a habit that he had kicked many years earlier, when he sometimes sneaked off-camera cigarettes during live events.

For all his accomplishments, Jennings remained the least publicized of the anchors, and the reason was clear: He didn't much like talking about himself. He felt he was a lousy interview subject, hemming and hawing and declining to take a clear position on anything. Unlike Rather and Brokaw, he appeared on few television chat shows and did not regularly call in to Don Imus's freewheeling radio show. Jennings loved to gossip about the business away from the cameras, but he generally declined to play the publicity game. He was even low-key about his 2003 decision to finally become an American citizen.

Four weeks before the 2004 election Jennings took the stage at the ornate New York Public Library, seated next to his longtime rivals, Rather and Brokaw, their strange friendship forged by shared membership in a very exclusive club. Rather had considered pulling out of the panel discussion, for he had been pummeled over the previous four weeks about his disastrous

National Guard story. Rather looked pained on the stage as he declined to answer questions about the Guard fiasco, a difficult stance for a proud man whose natural instinct was to punch back.

Jennings credited bloggers with first questioning whether the Guard documents were fake and did not accept Rather's defense that the online attackers were politically motivated. "I don't think you can just say this is a universal 'let's get CBS,' " Jennings said. But he also took a diplomatic approach to Rather's crisis, declaring, "I don't think you ever judge a man by one event in his career."

Brokaw was far more willing to take Rather's side and seemed almost angry at what his former competitor on the White House beat was going through. He accused the Internet critics of mounting "a kind of political jihad against Dan Rather and CBS News that is quite outrageous." Brokaw said the *60 Minutes* report was "a big mistake" but that it had produced an attempt to "demonize" Rather through "demagoguery."

It was the last time the three anchors would be in the same room.

When the Indian Ocean tsunami devastated several countries on Christmas Day, Jennings drew fire from some commentators for failing to travel to the region. He just didn't feel well. It seemed like he had a bad cold that he was unable to shake.

Three months later Jennings got the real diagnosis: lung cancer. He was determined to beat it, but the disease had already progressed considerably. Surgery was no longer an option. It seemed unthinkable: The man who had always seemed the picture of health and vigor was suddenly fighting for his life.

Jennings tried to restrain himself when he told his executive producer, Jon Banner, about the diagnosis. "I promise not to make you cry if you won't make me cry," Jennings said.

The country got the news on April 5, 2005, at the end of *World News Tonight.* Jennings taped the announcement so he wouldn't get too emotional on a live broadcast. It was classic Jennings, betraying not an ounce of self-pity. He took part of the blame: "Yes, I was a smoker until about twenty years ago, and I was weak and smoked over 9/11." He joked about his upcoming chemotherapy: "I wonder if other men and women ask their doctors right away, 'Okay, Doc, when does the hair go?' " He vowed to continue to do the broadcast. But his words were undermined by his voice. The strained, rasping voice, so smooth and resonant in normal times, now made clear how sick he really was. No one outside his circle of family and friends would ever hear his voice again.

In a note to his staff, the sixty-six-year-old anchor said: "There will be good days and bad, which means that some days I may be cranky and some days really cranky!"

In the space of four months and four days, all the network anchors had relinquished their posts, but none under circumstances as sad as these.

Charlie Gibson, the cohost of *Good Morning America,* and Elizabeth Vargas, an anchor for the magazine show *20/20,* were named as temporary substitutes. But Jennings remained involved with *World News Tonight* almost to the end, constantly calling or e-mailing Banner with suggestions.

He cared deeply about the broadcast, even if he was too sick to speak on camera. Everyone at ABC hoped and prayed for his recovery.

The end came all too swiftly. On August 7, 2005, surrounded by his family, Jennings passed away.

Several weeks later the titans of the media world, and two thousand ordinary fans, gathered at Carnegie Hall to bid Jennings farewell. Dan Rather and Tom Brokaw were there, and Brian Williams and Bob Schieffer, and Elizabeth Vargas and Bob Woodruff, and Diane Sawyer and Charlie Gibson, and Katie Couric and Matt Lauer, as well as Cokie Roberts, Sam Donaldson, Barbara Walters, Larry King, Bill O'Reilly, and Jon Stewart. The Royal Canadian Mounties marched, and Yo-Yo Ma played the cello. Some of those on ABC's staff wore blue bracelets emblazoned with the words, "What Would Peter Do?"

There was much chatter, outside the theater and in the aisles, about the passing of an era. The assembled generally agreed that things would not be the same for the next generation, that they would never command the audience share that Jennings and his contemporaries had in their heyday, that their stature, although no one said so out loud, would never reach the same heights. And yet the younger anchors and anchors-in-waiting were just starting to devise ways to connect with an audience weaned on instant online information and a thousand media alternatives. None of them would ever be Peter Jennings, a journalist struck down in his prime. They would have to find their own way.

CHAPTER 5

Heir Apparent

Brian Williams felt stranded in Secaucus.

Here he was, the loyal soldier, the designated successor to Tom Brokaw, the future face of NBC News, and he was stuck in a former Hartz Mountain warehouse in the swamps of New Jersey, doing a cable show that almost no one watched.

It had made sense once, back in the summer of 1996. When the network launched its cable channel, MSNBC, in a joint venture with Microsoft, Williams was quite gratified to have an hour-long news program in prime time. The new channel might be available in only 25 million homes, but *The News with Brian Williams* was conceived as a sophisticated look at the day's events, a chance to give an up-and-coming star some valuable flight time in the news cockpit.

But now, in 2003, Williams could not have felt more out of the network loop. It wasn't that he was worried about the future. He had a virtual lock on Brokaw's job. It was right there in his contract: If for some reason NBC decided at the last minute not to elevate him to anchor, the network had to pay him the astonishing sum of $10 million. That, even by GE standards, was more than a rounding error.

Still, given his status as the prince-in-waiting, wasn't it in NBC's interest to be showcasing him in as prominent a way as possible? Instead, he spent most of his time in the Secaucus offices of the country's third-place cable news channel, putting on a program that was seen by perhaps 300,000 people. In the immediate aftermath of the Iraq war, Williams was relegated to the cable ghetto. Nor did things improve when *The News* was moved to CNBC, a business network whose ratings had been sinking since the dot-com bubble burst on Wall Street, and which seemed unsure what kind of programming to air at night.

It was a Jekyll and Hyde existence. On some days, when Brokaw was off, Williams would bask in the splendor of 30 Rock, using a borrowed office to prepare for a 6:30 newscast that would be seen by 10 million people. But on those days he would also be on the phone with his New Jersey producer, pressing Ctrl-Alt on his keyboard to toggle between his scripts for *NBC Nightly News* and for the cable program that would be seen by a minuscule audience at eight o'clock. Williams seemed to thrive on the juggling act. But then Brokaw would return to work and Williams would retreat into the shadows, banished to the relative obscurity of a channel where he reached fewer people than the *Newark Star-Ledger.*

His sense of isolation was exacerbated by Neal Shapiro, a quiet, unpretentious man who had succeeded the hard-charging Andrew Lack as the president of NBC News. Shapiro was, in Williams's view, painfully introverted and did not seem to regard the care and feeding of the network's next anchor as an important aspect of his job.

Shapiro, for his part, viewed himself as a big cheerleader for Williams who had drafted a plan to raise his profile by sending him out on major stories and to meetings with affiliate stations. But as Williams saw it, Shapiro had no idea of the qualities required to be a network anchor or the skills that Williams brought to the studio. In fact, it was downright insulting. The two men rarely spoke. They once went five and a half months without a conversation. Intentionally or not, Shapiro made Williams feel like a basketball sub consigned to the end of the bench, not a franchise player.

Finally Williams decided to go over Shapiro's head. He complained to Jeff Zucker, who had become the network's entertainment czar, and to Robert Wright, the NBC president, about his cable exile.

"This is killing me, guys," Williams said. "You're warehousing me."

It was a rare period of frustration for a perpetually tanned man who radiated optimism and who rarely, even in private, seemed less than eventempered. Williams never forgot where he came from—a store manager's son who grew up in Elmira, New York, and Middletown, New Jersey—or how he had bombed in his first television job.

He had caught the bug early. As an elementary school student, Williams fantasized about becoming a television anchor. His father worked first for Corning Glass Works, then as a manager at the W. T. Grant department store. When his tightfisted dad finally bought a color television for their three-bedroom ranch in Elmira, it was a major event for his son, who watched Cronkite, Huntley, and Brinkley and harbored a secret, outlandish dream to someday join their ranks.

As a teenager, Brian was at home in the white, blue-collar community of Middletown, spending time with the police dispatcher, the Amoco gas-pumper, the bartender at the local bowling alley. As a young man he worked at Sears, went to church on Sunday, and spent weekends in bars along the Jersey Shore. He graduated from Mater Dei, a Roman Catholic high school. Williams also worked as a volunteer fireman, building an unshakable cama-raderie with the gang at Firehouse 11.

He didn't venture beyond the county line at first, enrolling at Brookdale Community College, then moving to Catholic University in Washington, where he helped pay the tuition by writing press releases. Williams later transferred to George Washington University but never graduated. He was ashamed of being a dropout, and, like Peter Jennings, later overcompensated by immersing himself in the world of books.

His one foray into politics came when Williams landed an internship in Jimmy Carter's White House that later turned into a sometimes-paying job. Williams would deny any Democratic pedigree, joking that if he had been any lower in the pecking order, his job would have included shrubbery maintenance.

In 1981 Williams got a job at a tiny station called KOAM in the Kansas town of Pittsburg, near the Missouri border, where he anchored the news and shot and edited his own stories. He worked seven days a week. The station's general manager, Bill Bengston, found him eager to learn and des-perate to get into the business. So desperate, in fact, that when Bengston told him that his name was "too East Coast Catholic" and he would have to change it, Williams, feeling crushed, prepared a speech for his parents. He was too anxious about succeeding to get the joke.

The unpaid bills and college loan debt piled up as Williams labored for meager wages, and when his Dodge Dart died one day in a cornfield, Bengston helped arrange a loan for a Ford Escort. But not even a new set of wheels could get Williams to a bigger market. He sent his audition tape to stations in Tulsa and other midsize cities without a nibble. He had no health insurance and sometimes was forced to skip meals. Clearly, he had failed.

Williams packed his dog, Charlie, into a Ryder truck, drove to Washing-ton, moved into a basement apartment, and took a courier's job at the National Association of Broadcasters, delivering documents in a red station wagon. It was a huge comedown.

But he kept trying to get his foot in the door, answering a want ad for a weekend job running the Chyron machine—which superimposed head-lines and people's names on the screen—at Washington's WTTG. The pay was sixty bucks a weekend. But his smartass personality caught the eye of the news director, who gave him a tryout as a reporter and then assigned him to cover such issues as airport noise in northern Virginia.

Williams called himself a "young fogy," and his colleagues noticed. He once brought six button-down shirts and a blazer on a sailing trip to the British Virgin Islands, where everyone else was wearing T-shirts, and bus-ied himself reading books and magazines on airplane design.

One day he filled in for Maury Povich as the host of Channel 5's talk show *Panorama,* working with the program's producer, Jane Stoddard. He told a colleague that afternoon he had met the woman he wanted to marry. She found him funny yet studious enough to keep the *Almanac of American Politics* near his bed. They started dating soon afterward.

Finally things began falling into place. Williams got a job at WCAU, the CBS station in Philadelphia, where he worked closely with a new writer and producer named Steve Capus, an easygoing Frank Zappa fan with glasses and a neatly trimmed black beard. Williams would ride around in a van, cov-ering the suburbs of South Jersey, filing two stories a day, one for the 5 o'clock newscast and another for the 6 o'clock edition. He didn't always like what he was doing, but he was determined to punch the proper tickets.

In 1986 Brian Douglas Williams and Jane Stoddard were married in Con-necticut. The following year the network moved Williams to its flagship, WCBS in New York, the station that he had grown up watching. When Williams, who wanted to develop as a correspondent, told the station man-ager he was not looking for an anchoring job, his agent kicked him under the table.

His new job had him constantly in motion. Williams became the chief correspondent for the eleven o'clock news, covering murders, fires, acci-dents, and other nighttime mayhem. Within two years he was anchoring the noon news. Williams's goal, his dream, was to succeed Jim Jensen, the craggy veteran who anchored the 6 o'clock news. He began filling in regu-larly when Jensen took a leave to treat his addiction to Valium and alcohol. Williams was the reliable understudy, hoping for a shot at the main role.

One afternoon in 1993 Williams was in his fire boots, covering a power-ful nor'easter on the FDR Drive, when his cell phone rang. It was an exec-utive at NBC News, asking if he would be willing to meet with Don Browne, the acting president of the news division.

"I'm up to my ass in water," Williams shouted into the phone. "What's this about?"

The woman said that Browne wanted to talk to him about opportunities at NBC. They met at a Sixth Avenue restaurant called Corrado's. It turned out that they had grown up within a few miles of each other. Browne said that the network was interested in having him anchor the Saturday edition of *NBC Nightly News,* be the primary substitute anchor on the weekend edition of *Today,* and fill in for the *Today* newsreader during the week. Williams was dumbfounded. He had had very little anchoring experience, didn't really think of himself as an anchor, was only the noon guy at Channel 2. He was thirty-four years old, and this was clearly a terrific opportunity.

Browne sent in Tom Brokaw to close the deal. Brokaw strongly hinted at the possibility of succession if Williams could earn his spurs. NBC's news division, he noted, had been decimated by the recent *Dateline* scandal. The newsmagazine had tried to show that a General Motors truck was unsafe by orchestrating a crash, and the rigging led to a spate of firings and the settling of a lawsuit brought by GM.

"Look around," Brokaw said. "This is a good place to come at this time. If you survey the field, there aren't a lot of folks lined up behind me."

CBS executives, knowing that Williams's wife spoke Russian and had lived in Vladivostok and St. Petersburg, offered to make him Moscow bureau chief. But Williams concluded that the posting would be too arduous for a young couple starting a family.

On the local front, Bud Carey, the general manager of WCBS, wasn't playing. "I just don't see Brian as an anchor," he said.

On his last day at WCBS Howard Stringer, president of the CBS Broadcast Group, invited Williams to his office for a gathering over bagels. Williams explained that he hadn't been shopping himself, that the NBC approach had come out of the blue.

"How is it that you're leaving?" said Peter Lund, a CBS executive vice president.

"Ask Bud Carey," Williams replied. "He didn't match the offer."

Andrew Lack, one of the gruff veteran producers at CBS, wished Williams well. "Good luck over in that shithole," he said.

Williams had barely settled in at 30 Rock when, a few months later, NBC News named Lack as its new president. Williams sent him a note. "Welcome to the shithole," it said.

In 1994 Lack decided that his weekend anchor needed some seasoning and named Williams the network's chief White House correspondent. It was, in some ways, the perfect job for Williams, whose obsession with presidential history bordered on the fanatic.

But once the Republicans won control of both houses of Congress that fall, covering Bill Clinton proved to be less than glamorous. The correspondents often found themselves sitting in their tiny booths in the basement of the dingy pressroom, killing time, while Newt Gingrich was making news at the other end of Pennsylvania Avenue. Williams wasn't happy unless he was on the air, and increasingly, he wasn't. He lobbied for his stories every day and sometimes wrote scripts just for the exercise.

The dry spell ended with the Oklahoma City bombing and the run-up to the 1996 presidential campaign, and Williams became more visible to the television audience. He even appeared on *The Tonight Show,* where Jay Leno introduced him as "the handsomest White House correspondent."

The joke captured something of a whispering campaign against Williams. With his perfectly coiffed brown hair, chiseled features, winsome smile, Brooks Brothers suits, presidential cufflinks, and Ralph Lauren ties, Williams looked as though he had just stepped out of the pages of *GQ.* That made it easy for his detractors to dismiss him as a pretty boy, a glib local TV guy who hadn't earned his reporting spurs. Williams began to win converts with his hard work at the White House, but the lightweight image lingered.

Williams also learned that he could antagonize critics in high places. One night, with his glasses fogged as he was draining pasta at his Washington home, his daughter handed him the phone. It was Bill Clinton, yelling as loudly as he had ever heard a human being yell. "Goddammit, I don't know what you people think you're doing," the president bellowed. "You just think you can put any old piece of shit on the air!" Williams had reported that a senior administration official had made fun of Lamar Alexander's Republican presidential campaign, and Clinton thought he had made it up. Williams was mightily offended. The senior official was George Stephanopoulos, who had blamed a dropped cell phone connection for the misunderstanding. "You know you said this," Williams told him. Such was the nature of life on the White House beat.

Williams was excited when he was first dispatched to the fledgling venture known as MSNBC. Tom Brokaw wasn't wild about the idea of losing Williams as a *Nightly* correspondent. But he understood that the network was trying to give MSNBC a strong launch by populating the channel with familiar names.

The News with Brian Williams began life as a tony and substantive report. Jack Welch, the General Electric chairman, called the new program a "contemporary *MacNeil/Lehrer.*" When the broadcast debuted on July 15, 1996, the lead story was about President Clinton and the Whitewater scandal, followed by reports on the presidential campaign; the resignation of Arkansas governor Jim Guy Tucker; Russian leader Boris Yeltsin rescheduling a meeting with Vice President Al Gore; and strife in Northern Ireland. Not until the seventh story did Williams turn to the guilty plea of Dallas Cowboys star Michael Irvin in a cocaine case. On his third night he threw away the scripts to cover the crash of TWA Flight 800, a baptism of fire from which he emerged unscathed.

But within a year, as MSNBC stumbled into the first of a series of identity crises and began canceling shows, the high-minded mission of the Williams broadcast seemed to evaporate. Brokaw might have paved the way with his orgy of O.J. coverage, but Williams took things to a different level. In a word, his newscast went tabloid.

Not all the time, of course. But for weeks after the car-crash death of Princess Diana, Williams was leading with Di stories night after night. If it wasn't the princess, it was the assault charges against sportscaster Marv Albert, a saga that included tales of biting women, three-way sex, and Albert's acquaintance with a transvestite.

On one evening during the fall of 1997 Williams led off with two reports on Diana. The next night the lead story was the death of an eighteen-year-old MIT student from a drinking binge, followed by a piece on whether Diana's limo driver was an alcoholic. Williams then introduced "the murder-suicide that shook the Ivy League"—which, as it turned out, had occurred at Harvard back in 1995 but was the subject of a new book. The night after that the top story on *The News* was "Teenage Rage," about a string of murders by teenagers. Even Williams felt compelled to ask a guest: "Is this just the kind of theme stories that the news media latch onto?" But he had little time to ponder the question before Williams was on to the next crime story, about the release from prison of a woman convicted in the manslaughter death of a man who had molested her son. Then it was back to the dead MIT freshman.

Williams was conflicted about his detour into the gutter. He was not entirely comfortable with what now passed for news. The truth was, he hated the Marv Albert story. He understood that news organizations had ways of sneaking sleazy stories into the lineup under a thin veneer of sociology.

Behind the scenes, Williams expressed concern about the broadcast's direction, and one night he argued against making Albert the lead story yet again. Publicly, however, he defended the program, saying that viewers had always found crime stories to be news. He said that people of his generation were fascinated by Princess Diana, that she was their girl, and that naturally there would be huge public interest in her death. He denied trying to pump up his ratings. It was almost a badge of honor, in fact, that when his show was replayed on CNBC, he lost two-thirds of the audience that had been watching Geraldo Rivera's talk show. The debate, as Williams saw it, was between "back fence" stories—the kind that the neighbors would gossip about—and "civics lesson" stories, which tended to involve government and diplomacy. Sometimes civics just lost out.

In the spring of 2002, after the secret meeting in which Les Moonves offered him the CBS anchor job, another network came calling. David Westin, the ABC News president, arranged a rendezvous in a Manhattan hotel. Westin was not about to negotiate over Peter Jennings's job. He had a different idea. Westin asked Williams if he wanted to anchor *Nightline.*

This was a stunner. The prestigious program, considered by many to be the gold standard of nightly television news, already had an anchor in Ted Koppel, the man who had launched the show twenty-two years earlier. But Koppel had cut back his workload to three nights a week, and it was not clear how much longer he planned to stay. Westin was casting about for a younger successor.

Williams promised to think about it. The idea was just plain intriguing. *Nightline,* he felt, really fit his personality. He could put his stamp on the late-night program, present himself as a cross between Charlie Rose and Jack Paar. But in the end it wasn't on the same level as being a network anchor, and he had already realized how difficult it would be to walk away from NBC.

Brokaw was determined to step down on his own timetable, and the renewed sense of purpose he had felt after the 9/11 attacks was starting to fade. For him, the events of February 2, 2002, had been a turning point. Brokaw and his wife were on a friend's yacht in the Caribbean, and at 10 in the morning he had just plunged into the water when he saw a friend frantically waving at him from the dive boat. The space shuttle *Columbia* had blown up. They made it back to the mother ship, and when Brokaw called the office, he was told that he could get a charter flight from St. John's to Florida. He left Meredith a note and threw some things together for the trip. At 4:30 that afternoon, Brokaw was on the air from Cape Canaveral. He didn't want to live like that anymore, taking satellite phones out into the ocean, never truly being on vacation.

Brokaw concluded that he had one last presidential campaign in him, but he knew that the NBC brass were worried about losing Brian if the situation dragged on much longer. So he came up with the idea of announcing his retirement way in advance—far earlier, in fact, than any network anchor had ever done.

In the final negotiations Williams signed a seven-year contract that was worth more than $20 million, although the press reported a figure about half that amount. The length of the deal was important to him because he had grown up listening to his father talk about job security.

On May 28, 2002, Robert Wright, Andy Lack, Neal Shapiro, Tom Brokaw, and Brian Williams faced a group of reporters at 30 Rock and made the announcement. Brokaw would work for another two and a half years, and then Williams would take his chair.

Williams heaped praise upon his friend, saying theirs had been "the most extraordinary relationship, most generous relationship to date in television news at the network level." He recalled the terror attacks of nine months earlier. "On those days when the Big Three earn those salaries for the year, that's the gut check. That's when Americans make the crucial decision: *Do I want him holding my hand?*"

It would be some time, however, before Williams got to hold the audience's hand from 30 Rock, except as a substitute anchor. His frustration mounted as he largely remained in cable exile for the next eighteen months. Finally, at the beginning of 2004, NBC recalled him for network duty, and the cable news show that he anchored would soon be abolished. At last he was getting high-profile assignments: trips to the Middle East and forays to Florida hurricanes and a prime spot at the political conventions.

Brokaw, meanwhile, was savoring his final months on the job, content that he had made the right choice and was ready to move on. In the run-up to the Democratic convention in Boston, Brokaw was quoted as saying that these gatherings produced little news but were a good opportunity to see old friends.

At a panel discussion at Harvard with the other anchors, Peter Jennings took a jab at him. "Perhaps for Tom it's as much a social occasion as it is for some of the delegates," Jennings said. "I think of it more as a target of opportunity."

Brokaw was steamed at how his meaning had been twisted and was noticeably cool to Jennings at the conclave. Later in the week the ABC anchor called.

"Lad, I'm told I may have ruffled your feathers somewhat," Jennings said.

"Peter, we'll be friends forever, but sometimes you don't think about what you're saying."

It was strange, Brokaw thought, the way he and Jennings and Rather had competed against one another for so long that there was now an unshakable bond among them. He also thought back to his rocky transition into the anchoring business. He sat down and wrote a letter to Roger Mudd, from whom he had been estranged since their partnership broke up. I am very much aware, Brokaw wrote, that I could not have had this career were it not for your generosity many years ago.

Brokaw also knew that Brian was impatient for his long-awaited opportunity. Being the backup quarterback was a tough job.

His last hurrah was the night of the 2004 election, which dragged on for hours with Bush one state short of victory. Dan Bartlett, Bush's communications director, sent Brokaw an e-mail in the early morning hours, saying, Why don't you call Nevada and New Mexico, you know we've got this won. Bartlett was trying to start a network stampede that would prompt John Kerry to concede. Brokaw e-mailed back: "If you know that you have won the presidency, you don't need me to say it."

In the final days before the handoff, Brokaw gave Williams the sleeping bag he kept in his office closet and offered some words of advice: Take the broadcast on the road when you can. Pick three or four issues and make them your own. And don't read the television critics.

"Everyone's going to write about you," Brokaw said. "Everyone's going to have something to say, and you must force yourself to ignore it all. You can't be defined by outside forces."

There was one critic, though, that Williams could not ignore. Jane, his wife, told him that he had to lose his chief sartorial affectation: the pocket handkerchief.

"I've never liked it," she said.

"You're kidding," Williams replied. He promptly ditched the pocket square.

Williams brought a very different background and cultural sensibility to the job. He was forty-five years old with a wife, two teenage children, a dog, and a rabbit. He lived in the Connecticut farmhouse in New Canaan where Jane had grown up. He was a big NASCAR racing buff who took his son to the speedway on Saturday nights and drove on a dirt track during vacations in Montana, where he owned a half-interest in a local team. Williams had asked to meet Dale Earnhardt at one NASCAR event, and they started lunching together at 21 and traveling together to races across the South. Earnhardt left a voice-mail message for Williams in early 2001, shortly before he was killed in a car crash, and the anchor kept Earnhardt's number-three decal on his Lexus. On his office wall—along with autographed photos of Lyndon Johnson, Joe DiMaggio, Ted Williams, and Mickey Mantle—was a framed shot of Brian Williams and Dale Earnhardt, right after the racer had won the DieHard 500 in Alabama.

Williams was determined to infuse the broadcast with the values that reflected his life experience. As a guy who went shopping with the family at Target, he wanted more coverage of small-town America and the problems facing parents in everyday life.

Neal Shapiro was all but certain that the ratings would decline. After all, the audience was losing Brokaw, their trusted friend, and would likely flip around for a while. The hope was that they would eventually come back.

Steve Capus, the broadcast's executive producer, could not imagine the kind of pressure that Williams must have felt. By anointing him two and a half years early, Capus believed, NBC had avoided the messy gossip and maneuvering that usually surrounds a succession, but had also put Brian under a tremendous amount of scrutiny. If he couldn't hold Brokaw's audience, there would be no one else to blame.

As the big day finally drew near, it still felt to Williams like Tom's broadcast. He was a little apprehensive, but it wasn't like he hadn't anchored from Studio 3C hundreds of times over the past decade. The way he figured it, the audience would either come to him or it wouldn't. Why, after all, did people prefer one anchor over another? It was, Williams felt, the ultimate subjective business.

Rather was seen as aggressive, tightly wound, unpredictable, and with his down-home Texas metaphors, a bit corny. Jennings was the unhurried, urbane internationalist who perhaps carried a whiff of condescension. Brokaw was the earnest, down-to-earth midwesterner who had forged a connection with the World War II generation. And Williams, who seemed friendly and a bit bland, simply wasn't well known enough to have fixed an image in the public mind.

Brokaw signed off for the last time on December 1, 2004: "That's *Nightly News* for this Wednesday night. I'm Tom Brokaw. You'll see Brian Williams here tomorrow night, and I'll see you along the way."

The next night Williams began as if he had been sitting there all along. "America's new reality tops our news tonight," he said. "U.S. troops on the ground in Iraq, the violence there as the scheduled election approaches . . ." At the end of the show he thanked Brokaw, his family, his colleagues, and the viewers. "We'll continue to work each evening to earn and preserve your loyalty," Williams said.

At the end of the month Williams and the family left town for a Caribbean vacation. On New Year's Eve he was dancing with Jane when he felt his cell phone vibrate. It was the desk in New York. NBC had found a way to fly him to Indonesia to cover the tsunami that had devastated southern Asia. The timing was terrible, but this was what he had signed up for. After forty-four hours of traveling, Williams arrived in Banda Aceh and was almost overwhelmed by the scenes of death and destruction.

When Williams got back ten days later, Steve Capus noticed a change in his demeanor. Before, he had approached the broadcast as if he were still filling in for Brokaw. When Williams returned from Banda Aceh, Capus felt, he was carrying himself differently, more confidently, acting as if *Nightly* was now his newscast. It had taken a disaster, but Brian had found his voice.

CHAPTER 6

The Accidental Anchor

On the evening of October 13, 2004, Bob Schieffer took the stage in Tempe, Arizona, and handled the proceedings smartly and skillfully. But moments after the final showdown between George W. Bush and John Kerry, CBS viewers heard a different verdict.

"Many people may reach the conclusion this was the least interesting of the three debates," Dan Rather, Schieffer's colleague of three decades, declared on the network's postgame show. And again, minutes later: "I may be wrong, but I think some people will look at this third debate and say you needed a speed-yawning course to get through it."

Schieffer was stunned when he heard about the remarks the next day. The critics had all praised his performance. Les Moonves, the CBS president, had sent him a gracious note, and Andrew Heyward, the news division chief, had followed up with his own complimentary message.

What had gotten into Dan? It was childish, like a kid lashing out because he didn't get the ball. It made Rather look bad. Schieffer suspected that Rather was jealous that he had been chosen for the coveted assignment, rather than the anchor of the *CBS Evening News.*

The Bush campaign would have gone haywire had Rather gotten the nod from the debate commission. Among the Bushes, it was an article of faith that Rather was a liberal in anchor's clothing who bore a grudge against them. Just one month earlier Rather had done the badly botched *60 Minutes* report on the president's National Guard service, the fallout from which now threatened his career.

Although both men hailed from Texas, they could hardly have been more different. In television terms, Rather was hot, Schieffer was cool.

Rather was intense—even off camera he spoke with great fervor and urgency—while Schieffer always seemed relaxed and conversational. With his weathered face, narrow eyes, and big ears, Schieffer looked like your favorite uncle. Unlike Rather, he had allowed his hair to turn naturally white and had never shed his odd Fort Worth twang. Rather had lusted for Walter Cronkite's chair, while Schieffer, who had briefly harbored anchor dreams of his own, had settled comfortably into his niche of chief Washington correspondent and Sunday morning host.

They were friendly—Rather liked to refer to Schieffer as "Deputy Dog," as if he were some kind of funny sidekick—but not close. In the 1980s Rather had pushed for Schieffer to substitute for him when he was off. But there was never any question that Rather was the dominant force in the news division. Schieffer once twisted his ankle just before an Election Night rehearsal, and as the music began for the run-through, the pain became so excruciating that he interrupted the opening music to say that he could not continue. Eric Ober, the CBS News president, and other executives rushed onto the set—to make sure that Rather wasn't upset.

Rather was cool to Schieffer in the weeks following the debate. One problem was that Schieffer was on the road, promoting his book about the history of *Face the Nation,* which he had now hosted for thirteen years, and reporters were asking about the National Guard fiasco. At the time Heyward, Rather, and everyone else in CBS management were in a bunker, refusing to comment on the controversy. But Schieffer never felt constrained by the overly cautious CBS public relations apparatus. He had enough stature, and enough confidence in his judgment, that he refused to be muzzled.

"I cannot go out there and sell a book if I have to say no comment," he told Heyward. "If I say something you don't like, you can fire me."

The news division chief was clearly nervous. "Just be really careful," he said.

Schieffer was diplomatic, always praising Rather as a great reporter, but he would not defend the story. In the first days after the *60 Minutes Wednesday* segment blew up, Schieffer said the matter was "very, very serious" and that "somehow we've got to find a way to show people these documents are not forgeries." After Rather apologized on the air, Schieffer said: "Look, we made a terrible mistake. CBS has admitted it made a terrible mistake, and Dan has apologized. We take this very seriously, and some serious steps are going to have to be taken."

On Election Night, when the first wave of exit polls conducted for the networks showed Kerry with a comfortable lead, Karl Rove, the Bush White House strategist, called Schieffer to berate him.

"Those polls are wrong," Rove declared. "They can't be right."

"We're not reporting this, Karl. It's Drudge," Schieffer said. The networks never made their morning exit polls public, since the numbers were by definition incomplete, but the figures had leaked to the *Drudge Report* and other Web sites.

When Schieffer reported what Bush aides were saying about the vote projections, Rather dismissed it as White House spin. He kept asking Schieffer what remaining state Kerry needed to win the presidency. Schieffer said he wasn't sure that a Kerry victory was still possible.

Once Bush was reelected, the talk in media circles turned to whether Rather could survive. On November 24 Schieffer got the word only hours before the rest of the world: Dan Rather was stepping down as anchor after nearly a quarter century as the face of CBS News. Les Moonves had been talking to Rather about retiring after one more year, and now it became clear that the timetable would have to be speeded up. There was no question that he was getting out of town, figuratively speaking, one step ahead of the sheriff.

The outside panel, named by Moonves, was nearing the end of its investigation. Rather knew that he was likely to bear the brunt of harsh criticism, that the pressure for him to step down as anchor might well become unbearable, and that if he waited he would be seen as having been forced out over the debacle. Every professional obituary would be about his *60 Minutes* screwup, not the many accomplishments of his forty-year career. Rather also knew that if he delayed another week, he would be seen as upstaging Tom Brokaw's long-planned retirement. And so, just before Thanksgiving, Rather said that he would relinquish the anchor chair the following March, on the twenty-fifth anniversary of his debut as Cronkite's successor. Rather took great pains to say that this was his decision, and that it was not related to the investigation of the National Guard story. Very few people believed him. If he could have hung on for one more year, he would have wanted another year after that. Friends knew that he would never willingly give up that job.

Over the next few weeks Schieffer's name began popping up in articles as a potential replacement for Rather, at least on an interim basis. One such piece, by television writer Peter Johnson, appeared in *USA Today,* saying that Schieffer "could be tapped" as a temporary replacement. Schieffer called Johnson, whom he considered a friend.

"Let me ask you a question," Schieffer said. "When you put my name in there, were you just being nice to me, or did you actually base it on something?"

"Hell no, I had a really good source," Johnson replied. "I don't think he'd mind if I told you. It was Les Moonves. A couple of us cornered him at press tour," the semiannual gathering of television critics and industry executives in Los Angeles.

On January 10, 2005, the outside panel, chaired by former attorney general Dick Thornburgh and Lou Boccardi, who had been chief executive of the Associated Press, assailed CBS for having "failed miserably" to authenticate the purported thirty-year-old memos at the heart of the network's charge that Bush had received favorable treatment as a young lieutenant. Three top executives, including Josh Howard, who had run *60 Minutes Wednesday,* were forced out, and Rather's producer on the story, Mary Mapes, was fired. The investigators faulted Rather for being overenthusiastic in pursuing the story and overzealous in defending it for twelve long days after serious questions surfaced about whether the documents were fake, in part by mischaracterizing some of the evidence. Perhaps most damaging, the panel concluded that Rather had played a minimal role in producing the piece and never even saw the segment before it aired.

Walter Cronkite thought that the whole thing was a damn tragedy. The Guard story was a terrible mistake by Rather. Cronkite felt that Rather should have backed off the story right away when it began to crumble, but the real blunder, when others started getting fired, was that he didn't resign immediately.

On the morning the report was released, Janet Leissner, CBS's Washington bureau chief, told Schieffer that management wanted him in New York to anchor that night's evening news. Schieffer later learned that Rather had been pushing to anchor the broadcast himself. That was hard to fathom, since his conduct was a subject of the report that the program would have to address. In fact, the taped piece by correspondent Wyatt Andrews said that Rather had no comment. How would Dan have handled that from the anchor chair?

Five minutes before airtime Schieffer was told there was a technical glitch in loading Andrews's piece for broadcast. The conspiracy theorists, Schieffer knew, would never buy that explanation. Fortunately, the problem was resolved just before the program began.

The first week of February began auspiciously for Schieffer. He was at his alma mater, Texas Christian University, before a crowd of fifteen hundred, for a ceremony in which the journalism school was being named for him. The next day he flew back to Washington for President Bush's State of the Union address, which by tradition would include an off-the-record luncheon with the network anchors and Sunday talk show hosts.

That morning Peter Johnson reported in *USA Today* that CBS was about to name Schieffer as its interim anchor while searching for a permanent replacement. Nobody had bothered to tell Schieffer. Worse, the word had never gotten to Rather. Andrew Heyward had told Rather's agent, who failed to hook up with his client because of a misunderstanding about his schedule. Rather learned the news when he saw Johnson's article on the train ride from Manhattan to the nation's capital.

Rather threw a fit in the Amtrak car, cursing everyone in sight. He blamed Schieffer for plotting behind his back, although Schieffer had done nothing of the sort. The news forced Rather to confront the fact that he really had lost the anchorship and would soon be stepping down.

When Schieffer got to Washington, Heyward told him the plan was definite and that Schieffer would take over the evening news for six weeks, maybe two months, while the network looked for a permanent successor. Schieffer, who felt honored that CBS would turn to him in time of crisis, said that was fine with him.

A car and driver met Rather at Washington's Union Station, and the plan was for him to pick up Schieffer at the network bureau on M Street and ride together to the White House. But Rather was clearly in a foul mood. Schieffer got a call explaining that Rather was running late and wouldn't have time to pick him up. Schieffer took a taxi instead.

As a frequent visitor to the White House, Schieffer had a hard pass that allowed him swift entry at the Northwest Gate. Rather had no such pass, so he would have to present his identification at the guard's booth and wait to be cleared by the Secret Service. As Schieffer scanned his pass against an electronic eye, he saw Rather's limo behind him. He walked past a lone Marine sentry into the West Lobby, where Brian Williams, Tim Russert, Jim Lehrer, and Wolf Blitzer had already gathered. They all jumped to their feet and began singing "Anchors Aweigh!"

Schieffer looked alarmed. "Damn, be quiet!" he said. "Dan is right behind me." The other anchors were laughing and patting Schieffer on the back when Rather walked in a moment later.

"Congratulations," he said to Schieffer, and there were handshakes all around.

After the luncheon, as CBS staffers prepared to do the newscast from a law firm whose windows provided a money shot of the illuminated Capitol, Janet Leissner called Schieffer. "You really should talk to Dan," she said. "He's gone into his office and won't talk to anybody."

Schieffer felt awkward—he himself had had no advance warning of the news—but decided to approach his old friend. "Dan, I'm really sorry no one told you about this," he said. "This is just unconscionable that they treated you this way."

"I understand, Bob, that you didn't have anything to do with it," Rather said. The exchange was brisk and businesslike.

Les Moonves placed a congratulatory call to Schieffer. "Don't worry about ratings for a while," he said. "Just see if you can get people back in a better humor and focusing on work. We'll get past this."

*   *   *

Bob Schieffer had never expected to be anchoring a network newscast. His father had worked in a lumberyard and in construction, and his mother would have gone hungry during the Depression had her brother not quit elementary school for a drugstore job where the pay included a quart of milk and a box of saltine crackers. Schieffer, whose mother had instilled a sense of discipline—she once knocked him to the floor with a board for mouthing off—had begun his career at KXOL, a Fort Worth radio station. He later became a night-shift reporter for the *Fort Worth Star-Telegram,* making $115 a week and working until 2:30 A.M.

It was in that capacity that he answered a newsroom phone on November 22, 1963, and spoke to Marguerite Oswald, who told him that her son, Lee, was suspected of shooting President Kennedy. Schieffer gave her a lift to a Dallas police station and, with his Dick Tracy hat, was happy to let others assume that he was a detective. He got kicked out only after an FBI agent demanded to know who he was. Days later Dan Rather, a young CBS News reporter, called Schieffer to ask about getting in touch with Oswald's mother. Schieffer gave him the address, but *Life* magazine had already signed her to an exclusive contract.

After a stint covering Vietnam, Schieffer joined the NBC station in Fort Worth, WBAP, and tried to emulate Rather, who had drawn the attention of CBS News by covering a monster hurricane in Galveston. Schieffer drove through a major storm, but was so tired by the time the 10 P.M. news began that he dozed off after a commercial, waking only after a cameraman's shout.

He came to Washington in the first days of 1969, having signed with the independent station WTTG for a lesser salary than he was making in Texas.

Schieffer's job consisted mainly of doing stories that had appeared in that morning's *Washington Post*. Within months he grew bored and wanted to return to Fort Worth, but his wife Pat, who was nearly seven months pregnant, resisted.

Instead, Schieffer walked into CBS News without an appointment and got to see the Washington bureau chief, Bill Small, who, as it turned out, had been waiting for a local NBC reporter named Bob Hager and got the two confused. Small said that he wasn't interested in anyone with a regional accent. But it turned out that Small knew Schieffer's boss in Fort Worth and decided to hire him for $200 a week, plus a $50 fee every time he appeared on television or radio. Schieffer joined an all-star cast whose beat reporters, in the days when the networks commanded a huge audience, were famous in their own right: Rather, Roger Mudd, Marvin Kalb, and Daniel Schorr.

It was Walter Cronkite's broadcast, and Schieffer became accustomed to the torrent of WWs that emanated from the anchor desk, which was shorthand for "Walter Wants," usually some fact or detail shortly before airtime.

Rather had been anchoring CBS's fifteen-minute newscast on Sundays at 11 P.M., and when the Saturday evening job opened up, he and Schieffer were among those given tryouts. Rather got the job, and Schieffer was given the Sunday show as a consolation prize.

One week after Richard Nixon resigned, CBS made Schieffer the White House correspondent, replacing Rather, who believed that he had been forced out by pressure from some affiliate stations unhappy with his confrontational style. Rather was sent to New York to head the documentary unit.

In 1979 the network asked Schieffer to become cohost of the *CBS Morning News*. He was not particularly good at it, and after moving his family to New York, the grueling schedule—getting up at 4 A.M.—took a toll on his marriage to Pat. The problem was that Schieffer had never done much ad-libbing and did not know how to be a host. He was miserable, began drinking regularly, and felt himself in danger of becoming an alcoholic. The ratings kept dropping. But Schieffer stuck it out for nearly two years because he thought he still had an outside chance of succeeding Cronkite.

In 1980, when Rather was tapped for the anchor chair, the network granted Schieffer's request to send him back to Washington to replace Mudd, who had jumped to NBC after being passed over. Schieffer felt like a complete failure. The morning stint had been the worst experience of his life.

Over the next decade Schieffer became a fixture in the marble corridors of Capitol Hill. By the time he was offered the *Face the Nation* job in 1991, he had covered every major beat in Washington: the White House, the State Department, the Pentagon, and Congress. Now, instead of chasing down administration officials and committee chairmen, they came to him, often clamoring to be on the broadcast. It was frustrating for Schieffer that he could not convince CBS to expand the show to an hour, like NBC's *Meet the Press* and ABC's *This Week,* but his hard work and folksy style paid off and he eventually lifted *Face* into second place.

Life, however, soon threw him a curveball. In 2003, on his sixty-sixth birthday, he was diagnosed with the most aggressive grade-three form of bladder cancer. Schieffer was normally private about such things, but after talking things over with another cancer survivor, Hamilton Jordan, who had been Jimmy Carter's White House chief of staff, he decided to go public. On the Don Imus radio show, where Schieffer was a frequent guest, he talked about how his cancer was in remission after surgery and treatments that involved pumping tuberculosis bacteria into his bladder through a catheter. He felt that he had dodged a bullet.

The disease may have slowed him down, but it had also made Schieffer appreciate how fortunate he was. He took new pleasure in visiting his vacation home in Sea Island, Georgia, and ordered season's tickets for the new baseball team coming to town, the Washington Nationals. Schieffer was basically satisfied with his career. He had gone as far in the television news business as he expected to go.

Now, in the early months of 2005, on the verge of assuming the job he had once craved, all Schieffer had to do was put together a new evening newscast. Jim Murphy, who had produced the third-place *Evening News* for Dan Rather for the previous six years, had some ideas.

Murphy, a playful man with a high-pitched giggle, believed in building the program around the anchor, like custom-designing a car. Rather was serious, intense, and obsessed with hard news. Schieffer had an open, informal style, and after a decade and a half as the host of *Face the Nation,* he was good at asking questions.

A week before the debut, Murphy suggested to Schieffer over lunch that he should ask the correspondents some questions during the show. Schieffer was wary. In the tradition-encrusted structure of network newscasts, where every second was planned, that seemed like a radical departure.

Murphy had another proposal: Instead of having the anchor record all the headlines at the top of the show, what if Schieffer read the first one and tossed to several of the correspondents, each of whom would billboard his or her story? This, to Murphy, was TV 101. The grandfatherly Schieffer, at sixty-eight, wasn't exactly the sexiest guy on television. Murphy wanted to put pretty young faces at the top of the show. It was a no-brainer.

But Murphy couldn't make the sale. He asked for an audience with Andrew Heyward.

"This is ridiculous," Murphy told him. "Nobody is in fucking charge here." Heyward liked the idea of making changes, but Murphy found him to be overly cautious. They all wanted to do Cronkite's show.

The day before the relaunch Murphy again called Schieffer, who this time said that he would give the new approach a try. But the secret had to be spontaneity. During Schieffer's years as a correspondent, a producer would often call and ask: "What do you want for a question?" During the broadcast Rather would ask the suggested query, for which Schieffer would have an obviously prepared answer. It all seemed so prepackaged.

On March 10, 2005, the first broadcast of the *CBS Evening News with Bob Schieffer,* the anchor asked John Roberts about Bush's Social Security plan and Cynthia Bowers about a crime story. He seemed relaxed, as if he were interviewing guests on Sunday morning. Unlike Rather, who had left nothing to chance, Schieffer didn't tip off the correspondents in advance. This gave the exchanges an unscripted feel.

The difference was immediately apparent. The show seemed breezier. Rather than delivering the news from Mount Olympus, the anchor was just chatting with his reporters as if they were sitting at the local diner. Schieffer began asking questions every night.

"This really works," he told Murphy.

The initial reviews were good, but the ratings, which had been sinking under Rather, dipped even further the first month. Schieffer thought he knew why. Rather had become a supremely polarizing figure. The only people who were still watching the broadcast at the end, he felt, were diehard Dan fans, and they probably resented Schieffer for taking over. These were the people who truly hated George Bush and saw Rather as their hero.

Moonves called Schieffer to say that he liked the looser format, but in the press the focus was still on who would be Rather's permanent successor. For years John Roberts, the White House correspondent, had clearly been groomed for the post. He had been Rather's principal substitute. With his deep voice and thick shock of dark, slightly graying hair, the joke was that he even looked and sounded like Dan. Andrew Heyward had been pushing Roberts, as had his deputy, Marcy McGinnis.

There was only one problem: Les Moonves didn't want him. And

Moonves was the dominant personality at the network, whether he was in his Los Angeles office or, increasingly, at the New York headquarters. He thought Roberts was a nice enough guy, but he was unalterably opposed to giving him the top job. Roberts was the old guard, a continuation of the very thing that they were trying to get away from: the anchor as the outsize personality around whom everything else would revolve.

But if not John Roberts, then who? Moonves began saying that he might prefer to have multiple anchors, two or even three, and a more creative format. He did not want a single anchor delivering the news with the "voice of God."

Over lunch, another CBS executive told Moonves that when he said he didn't want a "voice of God" anchor, it sounded as though he was actually signaling that he didn't want another Dan Rather.

"That's what I was trying to tell them," Moonves said. "I just didn't want to say that in print. I didn't want a news organization that was all about one person." There was a tactical explanation as well: Since Moonves didn't have a hot young successor waiting in the wings, it made more sense to talk about multiple anchors.

The original plan to announce a new anchor in the summer of 2005 kept getting pushed back. Moonves wanted to see a pilot of what a revamped newscast might look like.

The first pilot featured John Roberts and an attractive reporter named Mika Brzezinski. But Moonves didn't see either one as anchor material and rejected the pilot. Why did the news division keep pushing Roberts?

"How many times do I have to tell them?" Moonves asked a colleague. "That's *not* what we're going to do. Don't they understand?"

Jim Murphy was asked to make a second pilot. He felt that it was a waste of time. Heyward wouldn't give him a budget for it or let him bring in any outside people. This was, to Murphy, an exercise in bullshit, an attempt to buy some time while CBS tried to lure Katie Couric from the *Today* show to the anchor chair.

Murphy churned out the pilot in a week. It opened with John Roberts walking around a futuristic set with two large video screens, but he was just one of several players. It was almost as if there were no anchor.

"What would you do if you had to either pull the plug on your dying spouse or lose $100,000 in retirement money?" Roberts began. "She had to make the choice, and we'll hear her story." A moment later Roberts said, "Let's get caught up with the Monday evening news," and Sharyl Attkisson appeared on the screen to tease the Supreme Court confirmation fight over the *other* John Roberts. Then, jarringly, there were pictures of a Florida hurricane, with Roberts providing the narration, and then he was back on camera for a few seconds to talk about how everyone was becoming "numb" to violence in Iraq, and then Sharyn Alfonsi appeared in Baghdad to talk about a bombing that had killed several children. There was no "Let's go to Sharyn Alfonsi" or "Thanks, John." Correspondents just kept popping up like special effects in an MTV video.

The pilot raced on: A couple of sentences from David Martin about military recruiting, from Mika Brzezinski about the drug Vioxx, from Sandra Hughes on how "California's action-hero governor may need more muscle than he had as Mr. Universe." Suddenly Roberts was back on the sprawling set: "You're getting your news tonight from CBS." It was so fast-paced, superficial, and disconnected that the effect was downright dizzying.

"I don't want to produce this kind of show," Heyward told Murphy, who wasn't crazy about the idea either.

Roberts couldn't figure out what was going on. The whole thing just looked like a futile exercise. Once the second pilot was rejected, Jim Murphy told Roberts that he had asked Heyward what they should do next and that the reply was simply, "Nothing." They both took that to mean that Heyward, who had run the news division for a decade, wouldn't be around much longer.

But Heyward was still making suggestions for the current incarnation of the *Evening News*. Murphy got into a heated argument with the boss.

"Why aren't you doing different stuff on the show?" Heyward asked.

"I'm doing the show that works for Bob," Murphy explained.

Heyward was adamant. "Nobody knows it's working," he said.

Murphy demanded a meeting with Moonves and was told that he would get one. But the sit-down never got scheduled.

Temptation reared its head when Murphy was offered a job producing a syndicated talk show for Jane Pauley, the onetime *Today* cohost, at nearly double his salary. But he felt committed to news and took a pass.

Schieffer, for his part, felt that the revamped newscast was starting to jell. You put on a story and ask the reporters to talk about it. You put on a sound bite from the president and ask the White House correspondent why he said it. With cable and all the other round-the-clock news outlets out there, Schieffer believed, why did you need a John Roberts to do a minute-and-a-half package on the same material with a stand-up on the White House lawn? Gloria Borger, Lara Logan, and Byron Pitts were especially good at fielding questions on the fly and providing insights. That, Schieffer felt, was the signature of the new program. Besides, no one knew who most of these kids were, and he needed to introduce them to the viewers. Familiarity, in Schieffer's view, was the first step toward credibility.

Some of the correspondents were nervous about the revised format and would ask for a hint about where their segment was going. Murphy enjoyed torturing them, and sometimes, for fun, he would even feed them the wrong intelligence. After all, Murphy felt, they were all smart enough to answer a fucking question without making a career-ending mistake.

Schieffer's two-month assignment stretched to three, then four and five. While he was having a great time, the commuting arrangement was hard on his wife, Pat, since he was spending the week in New York and then flying back to Washington on weekends to do *Face the Nation.* He joked that he might have to choose between the job and his marriage.

Moonves began meeting with Schieffer every couple of months in his New York office. The two men had never been close, but Moonves liked the changes that Schieffer had made, and the anchor came to respect the boss's judgment. Moonves said his thinking about news had evolved since he took over the network.

"I had such respect for CBS News," Moonves said. "I was in entertainment, and I just hesitated to interfere with the news department. But I should have."

Over lunch one day Moonves asked for advice on who should be the permanent anchor of the *CBS Evening News,* and they kicked around some names. "Look, I don't want the job," Schieffer said. "I may be the only person in America who doesn't."

During this period Moonves would ruminate aloud about what would jazz up the third-place program. *The New York Times Magazine* published a profile in which Moonves was depicted as supremely frustrated by the news division. "I want to bomb the whole building," he was quoted as telling friends.

Bob Schieffer was infuriated at the remark, and so were most of his colleagues. How could Moonves have possibly said that? One CBS correspondent e-mailed from Baghdad that here they were, getting their asses shot at, and Moonves was talking about blowing up the building. CBS reporters in New Orleans were sleeping on the sidewalks in the days following Hurricane Katrina. What was Les thinking?

When the two men later had lunch, in Washington, the explosive metaphor came up.

"Look, I just want you to know something," Moonves said. "Number one, I never said it to a reporter, and I said it two weeks after you started," meaning that the crack was no reflection on what Schieffer had done since then.

Schieffer acknowledged that he had criticized the remark. "I was kind of standing up for the troops and thought somebody ought to," he said.

Moonves didn't apologize, but he did make a small concession: "I probably shouldn't have said it."

Moonves also called John Roberts. He said that his comment had been taken out of context and that he hadn't meant to slight Roberts personally. It was the first time the two men had spoken in many months.

Rather called Schieffer one day to check on an agency that had offered him a speech. They had a cordial chat but made no plans to have dinner. Rather seemed very hurt by what had happened. Schieffer hadn't wanted to call him because that, in a strange way, would make it harder on Dan. There he was, sitting in the second-floor office that Rather had sat in for twenty-five years, occupying the job that was the be-all and end-all for him, personally and professionally.

Most CBS staffers, including Schieffer, felt that the network wanted Rather to leave. After relinquishing the anchor chair, Rather had been assigned to *60 Minutes Wednesday,* the program where the National Guard debacle had taken place, but when Moonves canceled the show, he moved Rather to the Sunday edition. The problem was, the program now had too many correspondents, from Mike Wallace at the octogenarian end to the younger Charlie Rose and Scott Pelley, all fighting for airtime. Rather went to China and North Korea, but those stories were delayed for months. The former anchor of the *CBS Evening News* was rarely on the air. Most insiders believed that CBS was trying to send a message to Rather, whose contract expired at the end of 2006. Fairly or unfairly, he was viewed as damaged goods. Why, his colleagues wondered, was Rather sitting in that office day after day, allowing himself to be humiliated?

In November and December the *Evening News* ratings finally started to climb. The broadcast gradually added about 700,000 viewers after Rather's departure and was gaining on second-place *World News Tonight.*

Schieffer had already renegotiated his contract once, when he got the anchor job, but it had been nearly ten months now of a backbreaking schedule and no end in sight. Schieffer joked that anyone would look good following a calamity, but he was proud of what he had accomplished.

"Dude, you should go to them and say you want to keep the job for a year," Murphy told Schieffer. He felt that CBS needed the goddamn credibility, and Schieffer had a boatload.

Schieffer soon asked for another renegotiation. The way he figured it, even if the network landed Katie Couric, he would be there at least through the first nine months of 2006. Her NBC contract didn't expire until May, and she probably had the standard clause barring her from appearing on a competing network for ninety days. If CBS wanted him to keep handling two jobs, the network would have to pony up. He was approaching his sixty-ninth birthday and wasn't doing this as a hobby. He had gotten over the thrill of being on television a long time ago.

In the middle of December Schieffer spoke to Couric. She had just completed ten years with the *Today* show in first place, a remarkable run.

"I just cannot make up my mind," Couric said.

"Well, I hope it works out," Schieffer told her.

Days later Schieffer told *The Philadelphia Inquirer* that Couric was "a big-time journalist" and that "I hope we can get her." Couric sent him a note. "You're very sweet to say those nice things," she wrote.

Schieffer wasn't sure that Katie Couric was the answer as CBS's next evening news anchor, but it would be good to get her in the tent. The network needed all the stars it could get.

CHAPTER 7

Dynamic Duo

Elizabeth Vargas looked like she was headed for a top anchor job at ABC News. She had that star quality, dark good looks and a winning smile married to a solid reporting background, and the network brass seemed to love her.

Then it all fell apart.

It was the summer of 1997, and Vargas had been expected to ascend to the coveted cohost job at *Good Morning America.* Instead, amid a round of nasty leaks and finger-pointing, she wound up leaving the show. What was particularly disheartening for Vargas was that she had been lured from NBC a year earlier and so became the focus of virulent gossip at two networks.

This was easily the most depressing episode of her career, but Vargas, publicly at least, refused to fight back. She knew how the game was played. Reporters who covered television just loved it when someone called and dished dirt, and the person being muddied, in this case, was her.

Friends begged her to let them defend her in the press, but Vargas refused. Her father had always told her, don't get down with the pigs. She was determined to take the high road. Perhaps, she would later conclude, that had been a mistake on her part. Maybe she should have played defense rather than ceding the field to her unnamed detractors. But she decided that it would be better to just take her lumps and move on. You couldn't control when bad things happened to you in the workplace, but one thing you could control was your reaction. There was no point in getting mad or trying to get even. Life was too short.

It was not the last time Elizabeth Vargas would draw the critics' ire. As a slender young woman with silky dark hair, flawless skin, Hispanic blood-lines, and a way of attracting prominent men, she often found herself becoming tabloid fodder. But she was also a determined journalist with a knack for overcoming setbacks.

The trouble began in the early weeks of 1996, when Vargas was negotiating a new contract with NBC. She was on her way up the network ladder as a correspondent, for *Dateline NBC* and for *Now with Tom Brokaw and Katie Couric,* and both ABC and CBS were courting her for their morning shows.

Suddenly an unnamed NBC executive told *The Washington Post* that the network was breaking off the talks because Vargas had insisted on assurances that she would be the eventual successor to Katie Couric at *Today.*

That, in Vargas's eyes, was hogwash. Couric was on maternity leave after giving birth to her second child, but there was never any question that she was coming back to what had recently become the top-rated morning show, and that she would be there for a good long while. Yes, Vargas had filled in for Couric periodically, and she had also been subbing as a coanchor for *Weekend Today,* but this talk that she was gunning for Katie's job was absurd. It was Jeff Zucker, the executive producer of *Today,* who had put Vargas on the show, but the truth was that she had no network anchoring experience. She felt like a fish out of water.

Three months after an NBC executive leaked to the press complaints that Vargas was being difficult, she signed with ABC to become the news anchor at *Good Morning America,* the number-three job. Vargas had found Roone Arledge, the ABC News boss who hired her, incredibly persuasive—it was impossible to say no to Roone—and she was drawn to an organization that included such glittering all-stars as Peter Jennings, Diane Sawyer, Barbara Walters, and Ted Koppel. At the same time she had to wonder: Will there be room for me?

The chatter in the press was that Vargas was fiercely ambitious, that she wanted to succeed Joan Lunden as Charlie Gibson's coanchor on *Good Morning America.* It proved to be a difficult transition. As Vargas saw it, Lunden was not happy about her being there. Vargas in no way felt that she had been hired to replace Joan and believed the veteran anchor was reading too much into her hiring. Of course, Arledge didn't help things with Lunden when he proclaimed that Vargas "could very well turn out to be her heir apparent" and "clearly will have a larger role."

Vargas was miserable. She told friends that Lunden barely spoke to her and that Gibson, who owed his job to Lunden, was also giving her the cold shoulder. It was hard to become the newest member of an anchor team that had been together for a long time, especially with the ratings slipping.

For public consumption, Vargas tried to knock down the notion that she and Lunden were engaged in a cold war. "We're both kind of bummed out that this is happening," Vargas said. Lunden took a matter-of-fact approach, saying: "ABC should be grooming someone else . . . They'd be idiots if they weren't, and Elizabeth would be an idiot if she didn't want my job." And no one had ever accused Vargas of being an idiot.

Vargas hunkered down in her new role. She interviewed Benjamin Netanyahu, the newly elected prime minister of Israel, handicapped the presidential debates between Bill Clinton and Bob Dole, profiled a Broadway choreographer, and during one segment was bitten on the arm by a toucan.

But the whispering campaign about the woman her enemies dubbed "Elizabitch" would not go away. In the spring of 1997 *TV Guide* got hold of an ABC News memo that made Vargas sound like a demanding diva. Her perks were said to include "two-camera shoots whenever it involves her interviewing somebody"; "hair and makeup at location"; what's more, "she doesn't want to be there if you're shooting B-roll," and producers should "always assume that she will be running a bit late (15–30 minutes)."

Vargas was hurt. It was hard to read things about yourself that you knew weren't true. Her peers were sympathetic. Diane Sawyer, Barbara Walters, and Matt Lauer called with messages of support. Even Joan Lunden offered a bit of sympathy.

But the well had been poisoned. Less than three weeks later ABC announced that Vargas was leaving *Good Morning America*. She was transferred to *20/20* and *Primetime Live* as a correspondent, would anchor *World News Saturday* and, the network said, occasionally fill in for Peter Jennings. Vargas was relieved, in a way, to return to reporting and to step out of the harsh morning spotlight. She had learned something about the snakepit of network news.

If Vargas had an innate resilience, she probably acquired it during her childhood as an army brat. She grew up constantly on the move, from Germany to Belgium to Japan, and without a television set. She learned to make her way in foreign cultures and to cope with constant anxiety while her father was serving a tour of duty in Vietnam. She was the product of a mixed culture herself, since her dad was Puerto Rican and her mother Irish-American.

Vargas got her first television job while still attending the University of

Missouri at Columbia, then made it to a Reno station in the mid-1980s. Her early efforts were painful. Vargas had never read fashion magazines as a girl, and producers had to teach her how to cut her hair and wear makeup.

She soon concluded that the only way to make any real money in local television was to become an anchor, so she applied for an anchoring job at KTVK, the ABC affiliate in Phoenix. The station manager, Phil Alvidrez, quickly realized that Vargas wasn't polished enough to anchor, so he hired her as a reporter. Alvidrez found her headstrong, ambitious, and passionate, but when he passed her over for a weekend anchoring job, Vargas quit to join WBBM, the CBS station in Chicago, as a reporter, and eventually she moved up to weekend anchor. After four years she made the jump to NBC News, about the same time that the network hired Brian Williams.

When Vargas returned to newsmagazine reporting at ABC after the *Good Morning America* debacle, she seemed to have an affinity for crime stories and tabloid topics. She covered murders in Yosemite National Park. She covered the murder of a suburban Oklahoma couple. She covered the murder of six-year-old JonBenet Ramsey. She interviewed the owners of two dogs that killed a San Francisco woman. She anchored a series of "Vanished" specials on, for example, the death of supermodel Gia Carangi. She hosted a special called "In the Shadow of Laci Peterson," questioning why similar cases involving a black woman and a Hispanic woman generated little publicity compared to the sustained media frenzy over Peterson, the pregnant California woman killed by her husband.

Vargas did other kinds of stories as well. She won an Emmy Award for anchoring live reports on the battle over sending six-year-old Elian González back to Cuba. She covered same-sex marriage and surrogate births and pediatric intensive care units. She interviewed the likes of Mick Jagger, Hugh Hefner, and Cat Stevens. Many of the stories she pursued seemed to have a strong emotional component, far removed from the world of politics, war, and diplomacy.

But none of these stories generated a smidgen of the publicity that surrounded her romance with Michael Douglas. Once they started dating, Vargas became a fixture in the gossip columns. She soon realized that it was impossible to date an actor that famous and not have the press swarm all over you. She had briefly drawn attention for going out with the singer Lyle Lovett, but Douglas was in a separate stratosphere.

"Hamptons buzz has it that **Michael Douglas** and 'Good Morning America' diva **Elizabeth Vargas** got better acquainted last weekend on the East

End," said the New York *Daily News,* which described her as "the fetching correspondent."

"Seems the budding romance . . . is still going strong—Douglas is said to be completely smitten," said the *Chicago Sun-Times.* " 'He's totally ga-ga for her,' says a close Douglas pal and business associate."

The *Globe* supermarket tabloid ran bathing-suit shots of Douglas and Vargas taken in Marbella, Spain.

By 1998 the *Daily News* was reporting: "**MICHAEL DOUGLAS** isn't giving ABC correspondent **Elizabeth Vargas** the exclusive anymore. He's also seeing Martine McCutcheon, who stars on Britain's 'EastEnders' series. Vargas is dating others as well."

And inevitably, the *Chicago Sun-Times* noted: "The New York press is churning over news that **Michael Douglas** has reportedly 'dumped' recent significant other and TV newsreader **Elizabeth Vargas** for *New York Times* columnist and avid Bill Clinton critic Maureen Dowd."

Actually, Vargas maintained that she broke up with Douglas. And after that the press lost interest in her social life, at least for a while.

In 1999 Shelley Ross, the executive producer of *Good Morning America,* asked Vargas to go to the U.S. Open in Queens and land an interview with tennis star Andre Agassi. The next Monday was a big day because the show was debuting its new Times Square studio. The problem was that Katie Couric already had Agassi lined up for *Today* on Monday. Vargas's assignment was to steal him away.

In the locker room Agassi introduced her to a longtime friend, a Grammy Award–winning singer and songwriter named Marc Cohn. They flirted during the men's singles finals the next day, and soon they were dating. It was an unlikely match in some ways, since Cohn was divorced, with two teenage children for whom he shared joint custody, and he preferred the arts section to the op-ed page. They fell in love at the dining room table of Vargas's Upper West Side apartment, which overlooked the Hudson River, and were married in 2002. The couple soon had a son named Zachary.

Her career was quietly progressing. On the day John F. Kennedy Jr. had been killed in a plane crash, Vargas had anchored for four hours before being relieved by Peter Jennings. He told Vargas that she had done well, and soon afterward she was tapped as an occasional substitute on *World News Tonight.* No other woman had ever backed up Jennings on a regular basis.

Vargas knew that if she made a mistake, if she somehow screwed up, she wouldn't be back. Sometimes Jennings would shoot her a quick e-mail when he returned from vacation, telling her what he thought of her broadcasts. If he said "nice job," Vargas was thrilled. Jennings was not an effusive man, so those two words constituted high praise.

In the fall of 2004 Vargas finally got the kind of high-profile job that had eluded her at *Good Morning America* when she was named a cohost of *20/20*. But all the press coverage was about the woman she was replacing, the woman who had been the first to coanchor a network evening newscast. Barbara Walters was the story. Vargas was an afterthought.

*   *   *

Bob Woodruff was sitting in his law office at Shearman & Sterling in San Francisco, watching the Persian Gulf War unfold on television, when the memories came flooding back.

He was making a rather comfortable $130,000 but kept reflecting on his experience in China two years earlier, when he wound up working as a translator and fixer for Dan Rather after the bloodbath at Tiananmen Square. Woodruff, who spoke Mandarin Chinese, had married his wife, Lee, shortly before heading to Beijing for a yearlong teaching assignment, and he got caught up in the excitement of working with a network news operation on a breaking story with international repercussions.

Now all Woodruff could think about was that he wanted to be covering the war. He was miserable practicing law, poring over tedious cases and getting home at midnight. He had tasted something that he was convinced would be far more fulfilling as a career. Lee Woodruff was pregnant with their first child but wanted her husband to be happy. There were friends who thought he was nuts, just absolutely out of his mind.

Woodruff was offered a job at KCPM, the NBC affiliate in Redding, California. The salary was $12,000 a year. He asked Lee what he should do. She did not want an unhappy husband and told him to take the job. At the beginning Woodruff was stiff and awkward. As he struggled to learn the craft, there were moments when he said to himself: *What have I done?*

Growing up in Bloomfield Township, Michigan, and later while at the University of Michigan Law School, he had never entertained thoughts of being a journalist. He had become a specialist in mergers and acquisitions and later in bankruptcy law. But now he began the long climb up the television ladder. After two years Woodruff jumped to the CBS affiliate in Richmond, Virginia, and two years after that joined the ABC affiliate in Phoenix. In 1996 ABC News hired Woodruff as a correspondent and stationed him in Chicago.

He was a dashing figure with thick, dark hair, a penetrating gaze, and what his wife called a "Ken-doll chin," and women often did double-takes when he passed. Beyond that, his affable manner and determined work ethic made him a popular figure at the network. Woodruff was soon moved to Washington to cover the Justice Department, but his real value to ABC was as a utility player overseas. In 1999 the network sent Woodruff to cover the war in Kosovo. He was transferred to the London bureau, and on September 11, 2001, he and Lee made plans to go out to dinner to celebrate their thirteenth wedding anniversary. When the terrorists struck, Woodruff called her to cancel. He had three hours to pack and fly to Pakistan, where he spent the next eighteen weeks.

Woodruff was brought to the New York headquarters the following year. During the 2003 invasion of Iraq he was embedded with a reconnaissance unit of the First Marine Division. Woodruff consciously modeled himself on Peter Jennings, whom he viewed as a mentor. Jennings was a demanding boss, insisting that no corners be cut, no issues oversimplified, no overreaching tolerated. That made some correspondents uncomfortable, but it only made Woodruff work harder. His goal, he often said, was "to be the best damn foreign correspondent I could be."

But while Woodruff was adept at parachuting into war zones, he was also tapped to anchor the Saturday edition of *World News Tonight*. "Be careful what you wish for," Jennings told him, "because you're going to end up in a chair and not out on the stories you love." Woodruff first filled in for Jennings in late 2004. "Don't screw it up," Jennings said with a brief smile.

Woodruff's greatest challenge, he felt, was balancing the enormous demands of his career with the need to help Lee raise their four young children. He and Vargas often talked about being pulled in two directions by work and family.

*   *   *

When Peter Jennings revealed that he had lung cancer in the spring of 2005, Elizabeth Vargas was shocked by the diagnosis. But she was not particularly surprised that she and Charlie Gibson were asked to fill in. They had been subbing on *World News Tonight* for several years, and besides, Jennings would surely be back in a matter of months. It was too devastating to contemplate any other possibility.

In the early summer Vargas began to suspect that Jennings's condition was worse than she had thought. "I think he might be out longer," she told

Gibson. "I think we need to take a week off to pace ourselves." The truth was, they were both exhausted.

ABC, she felt, was at a distinct disadvantage. It was Peter's show. They couldn't make any changes, and the network couldn't publicize her or Charlie, or anyone else, while they were just keeping the seat warm. She was acutely aware that she was filling in for someone else and didn't own the real estate.

On August 7, 2005, the day Peter Jennings died, Vargas got an urgent call from Denver. Her husband had been shot in the head in an attempted carjacking. Vargas was numb. This could not possibly be happening. The suspect, who surrendered to police after a five-hour standoff, had fired a shot into the van of Cohn's band after a concert. Police were stunned that Cohn had survived, but the bullet had been slowed by the windshield and by hitting the driver first, and the singer was not seriously injured. Vargas immediately flew to Colorado to be with her husband. The rest of the month was a blur.

When Cohn recovered and she returned to work, Gibson, who was working many evenings and then getting up early to do *Good Morning America,* had come down with pneumonia and dropped out of the rotation. In September ABC turned to Bob Woodruff to share the anchoring duties with Vargas. Some nights she was in the chair, other nights he took over.

But as the weeks dragged on with no announcement, Woodruff was growing anxious about whether he would get the job. He held a secret meeting with Sean McManus, the new president of CBS News, who thought that Woodruff was a terrific journalist and was very interested in hiring him, but not as an anchor. He figured that Woodruff's agent was engaging in a smart bit of positioning, allowing others to think that CBS might be dangling the anchor's job.

It had never occurred to Vargas to set her sights on the evening news job. She was extremely happy at *20/20.* She would have been just as pleased if Gibson was picked as Peter's successor. Charlie had toiled for the news division a long time and had earned his shot. While her bosses felt that *World News Tonight* suited her, Vargas believed that morning shows and newsmagazines were a better fit for her interests. She loved the mixture of hard news and cultural topics, enjoyed the more personality-driven stories.

The more that Vargas did *World News,* however, the more satisfaction she derived from her temporary role. When big news broke, you wanted to be in the chair. Everyone in the business felt that way.

David Westin faced one of the most difficult decisions of his tenure as the president of ABC News. A smooth-talking corporate lawyer with light brown hair, a relaxed manner, and an easy smile, Westin could have been cast in a movie about a senator. Nine years earlier he had succeeded the legendary Roone Arledge, facing considerable skepticism because he had no journalistic background. Westin had also survived some unfortunate publicity over an affair with an ABC staffer, Sherrie Rollins, the wife of Republican political consultant Ed Rollins, until both divorced their spouses and got married. What's more, Westin had won the job that Arledge's deputy, Paul Friedman, had hoped to get, and Jennings was extremely loyal to Friedman. "You've got to make Paul happy or you're going to have problems with me," Jennings had bluntly told him. Jennings was innately skeptical of the corporate suits, and that was how he initially viewed the latest news division president.

Westin had suffered his share of early embarrassments, most notably his decision to send Leonardo DiCaprio to interview Bill Clinton in the White House for an Earth Day special, prompting howls that he did not grasp the difference between news and entertainment. He had also been humiliated in 2002 when Disney tried to pull the plug on *Nightline* by giving its time slot to David Letterman, who ultimately decided to stay with CBS.

Earlier in the year Westin had all but prompted Ted Koppel to resign after twenty-six years as the *Nightline* anchor by setting conditions that he knew Koppel would reject, such as doing the program live every night at 11:35. Westin now faced a similar dilemma: He needed a new anchor for *World News Tonight,* and Charlie Gibson wanted the job.

By every conventional measure, Gibson was the logical choice. He was the most experienced and versatile newsman in the division, having patrolled a range of beats from Capitol Hill to London, and he was one of the most decent men in the business. He had cohosted *Good Morning America* once before and, when Westin was desperate to rescue the show, had agreed to a second tour. Gibson had again proved himself a trouper months earlier, filling in for the dying Jennings while also showing up for morning duty.

But Westin was acutely aware that Gibson was sixty-two years old, and he felt strongly that it was time to hand the reins to considerably younger journalists. He was also reluctant to take Gibson off the morning show, where he and Diane Sawyer worked so well and were finally making an impressive run at overtaking *Today* after a decade in which Katie Couric and Matt Lauer had ruled the morning news world. Westin spent part of the fall having long conversations with Gibson while saying nothing to Vargas or Woodruff, even though they were carrying the anchor load.

Gibson, for his part, viewed himself as a relic of the Cronkite era, and *World News Tonight* would be the capstone of his career. We all spent our lives trying to prove to our parents that we were worth a damn, he felt, and the evening news was the fulcrum on which the news division rotated. But Gibson also understood the new paradigm, that the morning shows, not the more prestigious evening newscasts, were the big revenue producers, generating hundreds of millions of dollars for the company. Gibson wanted the anchor post, but not at any price. If he were going to take Jennings's old job, he wanted to do it at least through the 2008 presidential election. The only leverage you had in negotiations, he felt, was if you could say no and still walk away happy. Gibson was perfectly prepared to do that.

Westin consulted with the charming, whispery-voiced Sawyer, who was not only the biggest star but the canniest politician at the network. She was known as a fierce infighter when it came to protecting her interests, and could be an unstoppable force when she set her mind to something.

Sawyer had toyed with the idea of making a run for the *World News* job. But she prided herself on never having taken a job away from someone else, first at CBS and later at ABC. If Charlie wanted that job, she could not wake up the next morning and say she wanted it, too, not if she wanted to live with herself. They were war buddies, and in her mind, Gibson had the right of first refusal.

"Charlie should be given an opportunity here," Sawyer told Westin. "He's earned it."

Westin agreed that Gibson deserved a fighting chance. He was willing to expose ABC to the risk that *GMA* would decline in the ratings. Westin consulted with his bosses at Disney, particularly Anne Sweeney, the network president, and they backed him up. But Westin did not want to give the job to Gibson and then have to manage another transition in a few short years. Besides, if he made Charlie the solo anchor, he didn't think Bob Woodruff would stay at ABC, and he might lose Elizabeth Vargas as well. Vargas was receiving strong feelers from the other networks and could bail if she was passed over. These were risks that Westin was not willing to take.

Westin sat down with Gibson and explained his thinking.

"I want to go to two people," he said. "I want to go to younger people. I want to have one of them on the road at all times. But I think Bob and Elizabeth need some more time to be introduced to the audience. I want you to be the principal anchor."

The cumbersome arrangement that Westin envisioned would cast Gibson as the lead anchor, Vargas as his coanchor, and Woodruff a sort of supercorrespondent who would be regularly featured on the program.

Gibson, said Westin, could have the chair for a year.

There was no way he could accept that, Gibson said, no way he would give up *Good Morning America* for such a short tenure. Three years, that was his minimum, take it or leave it.

"If it's just going to be for a year," Gibson said, "I've got a terrific job now and I'd just as soon stay there."

They would inevitably fight about budgets and priorities, Gibson said, and he didn't expect to win them all, but he wouldn't win any of the battles if he were just a transitory figure.

Westin said that he needed to give Bob and Elizabeth a starting date for when they would take over. He saw that the conversation was not going well. Westin said he was worried that Gibson had his heart set on the evening news.

"David, that's not true," Gibson said. "Either way this goes, I will be fine."

Gibson believed that if you took a job and people knew in advance the day you were going to leave, you never really had that job. He didn't like the idea of distorting the broadcast by featuring one correspondent night after night, regardless of what was in the news. And while Gibson thought that Westin's concept of a tag team in which young anchors took turns getting on airplanes was intriguing enough, he didn't agree with it. *World News* should have a single anchor.

But the two men continued to talk. Westin softened his position and offered Gibson the job for two years. He would leave the anchor chair in June of 2008.

"David, that's the *last* time you want to change anchors, in the middle of an election," Gibson shot back. The place needed a period of stability, especially after everyone had been rocked by Jennings's death.

It was, on one level, absurd. They were down to quibbling about four months, about whether Gibson would depart after the presidential primaries or the fall election. Westin could never adequately explain why two and a half years was an acceptable tenure and three was a dealbreaker.

The ball was in David Westin's court. In late November he called Gibson from Orlando and said they needed to meet.

When they got together, Westin returned to his concept of bringing Vargas and Woodruff along, of shifting the spotlight to a new generation. Three years, he said, was not going to work.

Gibson had heard enough. "This is about them," he said. "David, get on with it. Put them on now."

Diane Sawyer thought that what Charlie had done was insane, forfeiting the job by insisting on the precise length of his tenure.

"You should never, ever do that to yourself again," Sawyer told him. "This is the thing you've wanted your whole life. To lose it on this point of pride . . ." She could not understand his behavior.

Some ABC executives believed that Gibson had overplayed his hand. You got in that job, you took that chair, and if you did well, no one could take it away from you. But the deed was done. Gibson was out of the running.

The next day, Thursday, December 1, Westin met with Bob Woodruff in his office and had Elizabeth Vargas on the phone from New Orleans, where she was covering the aftermath of Hurricane Katrina. He offered them a coanchoring arrangement. "It is going to be hard to replace Peter Jennings, very hard," Westin said. But they would reinvent the show by keeping one or the other constantly on the road.

Woodruff was thrilled to accept. He told friends that the whole thing was just awesome. But his wife, Lee, had reservations about all the travel involved and the possible disruption of their family life. Her husband had just grabbed the brass ring, but could he still be a dependable father?

Vargas did not leap at the opportunity. She wasn't sure she wanted the job, this once-in-a-lifetime opportunity that almost anyone in network television would kill to secure. She hadn't been sure whether to hope that an offer came or not, and now that it had, she had to be convinced. She needed to have a very candid conversation with David Westin.

The problem was that she had a two-and-a-half-year-old son. She also had Marc, a touring singer who was hardly a stay-at-home husband. Marc Cohn was plainly reluctant to have his wife take on this demanding job. He was extremely proud of her career, but he also felt strongly that parents needed to be heavily involved in their children's lives.

Vargas knew how all-consuming the anchor job was. It was very daunting to take on that role under these circumstances. No working mother with a young child had ever coanchored a network newscast before. If Vargas was going to take the plunge, she could not do a half-assed job. It was only fair that she make an enthusiastic commitment to all that the job entailed. Could she find a way to do this and not completely check out as a mother?

Vargas and her husband agonized over the weekend as they played with young Zachary. On Monday morning she signed the contract. Hours later ABC News announced that the new anchors of *World News Tonight* were Elizabeth Vargas and Bob Woodruff. She was forty-three, he was forty-four. The Jennings torch had been passed to a new generation.

Westin's view was that he was not merely picking the kind of boy-girl team so common in local news. He liked to shock visitors by flatly declaring that network news was dead. What he meant was that the old-style anchor, as a presenter in the British style, was an anachronism. Jennings had often felt that being in the chair constrained him as a reporter, and Westin believed it was time to get the anchor out in the field as frequently as possible. The way to do that, he decided, was to have two of them.

He also concluded that network news had to get with the technological revolution, that they had to make news available as they reported it, rather than holding it for 6:30. Westin ordered up a daily Webcast, to be carried over the Internet at 3 P.M., that would be a kind of preview of that night's news show, a work in progress. He decided that *World News Tonight* should do a live broadcast for the West Coast, rather than pretending that a three-hour-old show was up to the minute. That meant an anchor had to stick around each night until 10 P.M. New York time. No single anchor could do all those things, which was why Westin felt he needed a duo.

Then he heard from Diane Sawyer again.

Sawyer was fascinated by the puzzle of television, by the challenge of moving the pieces around to make it smarter. She wanted a chance to replenish her hard-news chops. She asked Westin if she could substitute for a couple of months as the *World News Tonight* anchor. Her argument was that she could experiment with some new wrinkles before Westin relaunched the program with Bob and Elizabeth at the helm, and then they could make a big splash as the new kids in town.

"Don't worry, I'll do both shows," Sawyer said. "I will take my vitamins."

Westin didn't give her much reaction, and the proposal went nowhere. Sawyer concluded that he must have been concerned about hurting *Good Morning America* if she were stretched too thin.

A week after the announcement Vargas went to Baghdad for the Iraqi elections to choose a new government, and she spent time embedded with a U.S. military unit. She and her cameraman, Doug Vogt, visited a hospital emergency room, along with a ballet company that had been burned and bombed. She regarded it as one of the most fascinating assignments of her career, a glimmer of things to come.

The new team relaunched the show on January 5, 2006, with Woodruff in Iran and Vargas on the Manhattan set that had been designed for Jennings and that would have to be rebuilt for two anchors. They were crisp and competent, the stories substantive and solid, but the newscast lacked a certain warmth. Even when they were both in New York, they appeared on camera together only fleetingly at the beginning and end of each show, and barely acknowledged each other's presence. They saw themselves as reporters first and disdained what they called chitchat.

The critics were respectful, if lukewarm, but Vargas drew all sorts of gossipy appraisals, in part because she was that rarity, a female network anchor, as well as the first such journalist of Hispanic descent. "Vargas is hot, especially when artfully filmed from the side in her jeans on hurricane gigs," wrote Tina Brown, the former editor of *Vanity Fair* and *The New Yorker.* The *San Diego Union-Tribune* complained about Vargas's "histrionic" facial expressions and "dramatic vocal inflections."

Vargas tried to ignore all the blather about her style and what she was wearing. Women, she knew, were ripe targets for this sort of sniping. It was all a head game, and she refused to play. She was beyond the point of whining that Bob didn't get that kind of criticism. It was long past time for a woman to succeed in this job. Besides, between *World News Tonight* and her other job coanchoring *20/20,* she was too busy to dwell on her detractors.

Not that Woodruff got off scot-free. Maureen Dowd, the acerbic *New York Times* columnist, dubbed him a "pretty boy android." On Comedy Central, Stephen Colbert, the satirical commentator, branded him a "robot."

Woodruff cared about the criticism but tried not to let it bother him. He was surprised that so much of it focused on his appearance rather than his reporting. But he knew that people had to be comfortable with who was giving them the news, and he felt it would take time to build a bond with the audience. Until Jennings fell ill, Woodruff had never even been mentioned in a *New York Times* story.

Vargas suffered an unfortunate embarrassment during the first week, and it involved Jon Banner, the program's executive producer, a compact, balding man with an all-business demeanor. She had been dispatched to West Virginia in the wake of a fatal mine collapse, and ten minutes before the broadcast Banner called to discuss what would happen if Ariel Sharon, the Israeli prime minister who had just suffered a stroke, died while they were on the air. The producer said that Vargas should announce the death and then toss to Charlie Gibson and Barbara Walters, who were on the set in New York and could more easily handle the breaking elements from there. Vargas argued strenuously that she had been following the story on the wires and could handle any live interviews from her remote location in West Virginia. Banner went to Westin, who sided with Vargas, but the damage was done because a *New York Times* reporter happened to be there. The incident made her look as though she wasn't a decision-maker on the newscast that bore her name.

Vargas and Woodruff both took the criticism in stride. Their ratings had not been great in the first week, but they were trying to fill the considerable void left by Peter Jennings. They were just getting started.

CHAPTER 8

Pressing the President

Brian Williams was sitting in the cramped confines of the White House pressroom, waiting for his summons to the Oval Office.

He had already done a live shot for the *Today* show, touting his upcoming interview. And with a few spare moments he took out his BlackBerry and began blogging. He tapped out the first of several dispatches for NBC's Web site, giving online readers a sense of making the trip with him. It was 7:45 on the morning of December 12, 2005, and Williams was spending the day with George W. Bush.

For a network anchor, few assignments were more important, or more fraught with danger, than going toe-to-toe with the president of the United States. It was an unparalleled opportunity to make news, to match wits with the leader of the free world, to demonstrate your aggressiveness in holding the commander in chief accountable. But even at such a sensitive moment Williams felt that it was vital to remain connected to the wired world. Putting a taped interview on television was no longer enough, not in an age of instant information.

The day had a deeper resonance as well. Williams had been fascinated by the presidency since he was eight years old, when he wrote a letter telling Lyndon Johnson to hang in there and, miraculously, received a reply. During his internship in Jimmy Carter's White House he had roamed the corridors, somewhat starry-eyed, and had returned as an NBC correspondent during the Clinton presidency. He reveled in the grandeur of the place.

When the interview was scheduled, Williams quickly realized that he wouldn't have much time to chat with Bush en route to his appearance in Philadelphia. Tim Russert, NBC's Washington bureau chief, called Dan

Bartlett, the president's counselor, to argue for more time. Russert knew that Bush generally got in early and would probably give the anchor even more access than was on the schedule. Bartlett agreed to the additional time.

Williams wanted to make sure that he was fully prepared. The Friday before the Monday interview, he called Russert again. "Hate to do this to you, pal," Williams said, "but want to do a conference call after your show Sunday?" When Russert's *Meet the Press* ended, he chatted with Williams and Steve Capus, Williams's longtime producer, whose closeness to the anchor had clearly been a factor in his promotion to president of NBC News.

The most important issues by far, Russert said, were Hurricane Katrina and the Iraq war. "That's what's defining his presidency."

Russert offered Williams a parting bit of advice: "Get ready for the blogs, left and right, because no one's going to like it."

As it turned out, Williams had three cracks at the president: a few minutes in the Oval, a few minutes en route to Philadelphia, and again on the flight home. But the White House, he felt, was choreographing the sessions rather tightly. It was hard to concentrate on multiple topics and cogent follow-ups on the plane when Bartlett was twirling his finger and saying "wrap." With all the stopping and starting, Williams felt that he couldn't really get his mojo going. Spending some personal time with Bush, who liked to swear in private, was quite helpful in getting a sense of the man, but the on-camera portion—the only part the audience would see—was strictly limited.

Williams's style was unfailingly polite. When it came to conducting interviews, he was no Russert. "You are very kind to have us," he began.

Instead of simply asking about growing criticism that Bush was walled off from the real world, Williams showed him the cover of *Newsweek,* which pictured him inside a bubble, with the headline "Bush's World: The Isolated President—Can He Change?"

"Look what they've done to you," Williams said, as if some unseen enemy were rendering Bush a caricature. The president denied being in a bubble.

When Williams turned to Hurricane Katrina, a disaster that he had covered from New Orleans, he again used the semantic trick of attributing the criticism to others, although Williams himself had been saying the same thing. "After the tragedy," he said, "I heard someone ask rhetorically, 'What if this had been Nantucket, Massachusetts, or Inner Harbor, Baltimore, or Chicago, or Houston?' Are you convinced the response would have been the same? Was there any social or class or race aspect to the response?"

That got a rise out of Bush, who said the criticism was "absolutely wrong . . . You can call me anything you want, but do not call me a racist." Bush's tone of defensiveness was revealing.

Williams seemed almost giddy in his repeated blogging updates, one from the motorcade in Philadelphia and the final one an hour and six minutes before the start of *NBC Nightly News,* talking about the "thrill and great honor" of visiting the White House.

That sort of gushing brought Williams some mockery from the online pundits, one of whom compared him to Ron Burgundy, the buffoonish character depicted by Will Ferrell in the film *Anchorman.* But that was the nature of the blogging world, filled with ideologically charged insults, that Williams had chosen to join.

*　　*　　*

On the wall of Brian Williams's third-floor office at 30 Rockefeller Plaza hung a framed photo of the Warren Burger court, signed by each of the nine justices.

Williams was utterly immersed in the history of the Supreme Court. He followed the justices the way other men followed baseball players. When Bush nominated Samuel Alito to the court, Williams faced something of a dilemma. On the one hand, he considered a high court nomination the most important thing a president could do, short of declaring war. On the other hand, Senate confirmation hearings were not exactly scintillating television. He wasn't sure how much the audience really cared about this bookish lawyer facing off against a bunch of posturing lawmakers.

Williams spent some time surfing the Net, to get a sense of how the nomination was playing in cyberspace. He looked at a piece on *Slate* and checked out the conservative view on a blog called *Captain's Quarters.* Blogging, Williams believed, had changed the way people viewed these hearings by saturating the landscape with waves of instant punditry. Sometimes he wondered: If everyone out there was talking, was anyone listening?

The defining characteristic of cyberspace was that everyone's motives were questioned. Some on the left had concluded that Williams was a closet conservative. He carefully guarded his personal views, refusing to tell even his wife, Jane, how he voted, so she could preserve her deniability. But Williams was open to hearing conservative voices, and that, in the eyes of als, was unforgivable.

as, for example, the matter of Rush Limbaugh, the bombastic e who had revolutionized radio. "It's my duty to listen to Rush,"

Williams once said. "Rush has actually yet to get the credit he is due because his audience for so many years felt they were in the wilderness of this country. No one was talking to them."

Even praise for evenhandedness was held against Williams. Republican pollster Frank Luntz told congressional leaders in a confidential memo that Williams had emerged as the "go-to network anchor" because of his brains and "lack of detectable ideological bias." Some liberal groups viewed Luntz's endorsement as a GOP stamp of approval.

On the second day of the Alito hearings Williams and his producers had decided not to make it their lead story. After lunch he grabbed a cab for a quick errand and was listening to the hearings on the radio. Suddenly Ted Kennedy and Arlen Specter, the Judiciary Committee chairman, were getting into some kind of spat. The driver had arrived at Williams's destination on East 45th Street, but the passenger was transfixed. Kennedy was demanding a vote on some documents, and Specter was telling him that he would run the committee as he saw fit. Williams refused to get out. They sat there in traffic, cars honking all around them, as the anchor of *Nightly News* hung on every word.

Once he got back to 30 Rock, Williams huddled with his executive producer, John Reiss, a relaxed, pink-faced man with the air of a genial professor. They agreed that they would still lead the broadcast with the latest on stalled efforts to rebuild New Orleans. The Specter-Kennedy spat, after all, was about congressional procedures.

In the late afternoon there was another flare-up. Lindsey Graham, a Republican committee member, was making an impassioned speech. But it was hard to follow what was happening. MSNBC had broken away to talk with guests. Williams flipped to the other news channels. This was one of the things that made him angry about cable news. They went to great lengths to cover live events and then spent much of the time chattering away while actual news was unfolding. In the meantime Martha-Ann Alito, the nominee's wife, had fled the hearing room in tears.

Williams checked the Associated Press wire. He clicked on the gossipy *Drudge Report*. "ALITO WIFE LEAVES HEARING IN TEARS AFTER DEM ATTACK" was Matt Drudge's screamer. Everyone was depicting the Democrats as having made Mrs. Alito cry. The media had just botched it, Williams felt. It was Lindsey Graham who had elicited the tears with a dramatic recitation of what he described as the Democratic charges against her husband, including the question of whether he was a racist. With half an hour until airtime, Williams felt that Martha-Ann Alito had brought a badly needed touch of human drama to the dry legal proceedings. They would top the broadcast with a crying woman.

Sixteen blocks to the north, in the ABC newsroom on West 66th Street, a brownstone neighborhood near Lincoln Center, Elizabeth Vargas was watching the same scene. She had been frustrated by the difficulty of covering the Alito hearings, of getting at the larger issues during these abstract discussions of legal precedents. But the spectacle of this lovely woman dissolving into tears struck a nerve.

Vargas called George Stephanopoulos, the former Clinton White House operative who was now ABC's chief Washington correspondent.

"That just clinched it for Judge Alito," Vargas said. "We might as well start calling him Justice Alito."

At CBS headquarters on West 57th Street, tucked away near a car dealership between Tenth Avenue and the Hudson River, Bob Schieffer was also weighing the Alito story. He had been busy and had not seen the argument between Specter and Kennedy, or Alito's wife breaking into tears.

Schieffer kicked it around with his new executive producer, Rome Hartman, who had succeeded Jim Murphy when Murphy left the network after being passed over for a promotion. Hartman, a calm, graying *60 Minutes* veteran who still lived in Washington and commuted each Monday on the 6 A.M. shuttle, had joined Schieffer despite hesitations about leaving his cushy job. That day's hearing, Schieffer told him, didn't really move the ball forward. They decided to lead with an exclusive from correspondent Bob Orr, who had learned that when a group of miners had been trapped by an explosion in West Virginia—all but one had died, despite the embarrassing spectacle of the cable networks erroneously declaring them to be alive—a second team of rescuers had gone underground and was close to reaching the trapped men.

The next day Schieffer was kicking himself. At the very least he should have shown more of the footage of Specter squabbling with Kennedy. That pissing contest—*"You received my letter!" "No I didn't!"*—just showed the Senate at its absolute, petty worst.

Unlike the other anchors, who were cautious about leaning one way or the other, Schieffer didn't shy away from offering his opinions. This was an ingrained habit from all his years as a Capitol Hill reporter, when CBS was paying him to analyze what was likely to happen. The conversational format they had adopted for the broadcast was the perfect vehicle for the new anchor to slip in his views. Reflecting on how the Democrats had done in grilling Alito, he told viewers, "I don't think they really touched him up very badly." The next night Schieffer said flatly: "It appears that Judge Alito is going to be confirmed, if something doesn't go wrong here." Sure it was opinion, Schieffer thought, but it was an informed opinion.

Now that his words were being watched more carefully, Schieffer had become acutely aware of the online world. This blogosphere, my God, suddenly you had to respond to every complaint out there. But if he replied to every idiot who e-mailed him about something, he would just be giving that person legitimacy.

There were, in Schieffer's view, three kinds of blogs. Some were good and provocative. Others were simply partisan; they didn't want you to tell the truth or attempt to be objective. They wanted to own you. They wanted you to present their side and only their side. And then there were those written by people who just wanted to tear things up. They were like the kids back in Texas who used to chop off tomcats' tails with their hatchets. Just nuts on parade. He had to be careful not to get bitter about it.

*　　*　　*

The networks were voracious when it came to vacuuming up last-minute details on a breaking story. The competition was fierce, not just from rival broadcasts but from a thousand other outlets. And that left the evening newscasts vulnerable to being used.

On January 13, 2006, a Friday night, Williams led his newscast with the aftermath of a massive fire in New Orleans, and Bob Schieffer led with Bush warning Iran against developing nuclear weapons. But on *World News Tonight* Bob Woodruff started the broadcast this way:

"We begin tonight with breaking news out of Pakistan that could have major implications for the war on terror. Today, according to Pakistani military sources, U.S. aircraft attacked a compound believed to be frequented by high-level al-Qaeda operatives. And Pakistani officials tell ABC News that the number two man in al-Qaeda, Ayman al-Zawahiri, may have been among them." Brian Ross, ABC's chief investigative reporter, had the details.

Sean McManus, the new president of CBS News, was in a theater with his wife, watching the Steven Spielberg film *Munich,* about the Palestinian terrorists who murdered eleven Israeli athletes at the 1972 Olympics. McManus, a beanpole of a man with steel-gray hair and an easy laugh, had more than a passing historical interest in the subject. He had been in the ABC control room at the time. He was seventeen years old and hanging out with Roone Arledge, the ABC Sports president, while his sportscaster father, Jim McKay, found himself continuously on the air during an international tragedy.

The movie was more than half over when his cell phone vibrated. McManus stepped outside to take the call. A CBS producer told him of the missile strike in Pakistan. McManus had suddenly gone from a cinematic account of a terrorist incident to a real attack in the war on terror.

"How much confirmation do we have?" McManus asked.

Not much, he was told. McManus said that the network needed two sources for anything it wanted to report.

In the CBS control room, Rome Hartman was trying to see if they could match the ABC exclusive. Hartman thought that Brian Ross was a terrific reporter, although sometimes he found Ross's scoops to be overblown.

Hartman got word to David Martin, CBS's Pentagon correspondent, and got in the ear of John Roberts, who was stationed on the White House lawn. Schieffer was able to read only a few sentences late in the newscast, but when Martin told Hartman he had confirmed the essentials of the story, they hardened their language and moved it higher for the 7 P.M. feed.

NBC had been working on the missile story for hours. Jim Miklaszewski, the veteran Pentagon reporter, had the gist of it, but Brian Williams was skeptical about the administration's claim that Zawahiri might be dead, and he didn't want to lead *Nightly* with the story. This was, after all, a drone aircraft carrying four enormously lethal missiles, being flown by joystick from Langley, Virginia. Some civilians had obviously died, so Williams felt it was in the administration's interest to suggest that high-level terrorists had perished as well.

Williams, who always turned his eyes to the monitors on his right so he could check out the competition after introducing his first taped package, saw just after 6:30 that ABC was leading with the Pakistan strike. John Reiss, in the control room, asked Miklaszewski to see what else he could find out. They decided to bump up the story to the lead position when they revised the newscast at seven. Williams was always conscious that this was the feed that went to Washington, where *Nightly News* aired a half-hour behind the other two broadcasts.

Williams tossed to Miklaszewski, who said: "One official tells us that intelligence indicates it was a good possibility that Zawahiri was in the Pakistani village at the time of the air strike, but stresses there is no official confirmation that Zawahiri was indeed killed."

The situation remained murky. Two weeks later Zawahiri released a videotape in which he taunted President Bush about the failed attack:

"Bush, do you know where I am?" He might have chided the network newscasts as well.

The episode underscored how easy it was for the administration to spin news organizations, in a manner all too reminiscent of the media trumpeting the false claims that Saddam Hussein was harboring weapons of mass destruction. The newscasts could have reported the Pakistan missile strike without including the baseless speculation about Zawahiri, which they had no way of confirming. But in a hypercompetitive environment, no one wanted to lag behind the others if a top al-Qaeda terrorist had indeed been taken out.

*   *   *

Bob Schieffer had been stiffed, and he wasn't happy about it.

In the fall of 2004, the White House had promised him an interview with President Bush for the fiftieth anniversary of *Face the Nation.* The Friday before the long-planned Sunday program, Schieffer still hadn't gotten a definite answer. He called senior adviser Karl Rove at the White House.

"We're not going to do that," Rove said. "Hasn't anyone told you?"

No one had.

"It's your White House, but I can't believe this," Schieffer told him. He didn't believe in making threats, but didn't hide his feeling that he had been treated shabbily.

The situation was all the more frustrating because Schieffer had enjoyed a social relationship with Bush. In the early 1990s Schieffer's brother, Tom, became Bush's partner as an owner of the Texas Rangers. Bob, a baseball fanatic, had gone to games with the former president's son, and they spent time together at spring training. They also played some golf. Politics aside, Schieffer considered Bush a great guy.

The last time Schieffer had interviewed Bush was in early 2000, on the eve of the New Hampshire primary, when the Texas governor was widely viewed as trailing Senator John McCain. After the taping Bush said: "Bob, I don't want to say this publicly, but we're going to win here by a lot more than people think we are." McCain trounced Bush by 19 percentage points.

When Bush won the presidency, Schieffer felt that the situation was a bit awkward for him. But he had been around Washington so long that he was friendly with just about everyone. Now, despite their baseball socializing, he couldn't even land an interview with his fellow Texan.

The reason, Schieffer knew, was obvious: Dan. Bush and his top aides didn't want anything to do with CBS because of what they saw as Rather's ideological opposition to the 43rd president. Whatever Schieffer wanted from the White House, the answer seemed to be no.

After Schieffer succeeded Rather in the anchor chair, *The New York Times* wondered in a front-page story whether he had a conflict of interest in covering Bush, who had appointed Tom Schieffer first as ambassador to Australia and then as the U.S. envoy to Japan. The CBS press office didn't want Schieffer to comment for the story, but he thought that was ridiculous. He wasn't going to let some nervous spokesman dictate what he could say when his reputation was at stake.

When Andrew Heyward stepped down as CBS News president—the fallout from Memogate had overshadowed his final year—and Sean McManus succeeded him, Schieffer saw the opportunity for a fresh start. He took an immediate liking to McManus, who had been running CBS Sports for nearly a decade until Les Moonves had stunned him with an offer that only his father's pal Arledge had ever received: to run both a network news division and a sports unit at the same time. McManus had a fondness for sports clichés, referred to the *Evening News* as the "telecast," and faced a major-league learning curve when it came to national and world events.

Schieffer took McManus on a courtesy call to the White House, where they met with Dan Bartlett and tried to clear the air. Finally, in January 2006, the White House offered Schieffer an interview with the president.

Schieffer, who planned to run a longer version on *Face the Nation,* asked for a walking conversation on the White House grounds before the formal sit-down. Shortly before the appointed hour, a midlevel aide called to say that the president was behind schedule and would have to do the sit-down first—and any time used for the walking part would have to be subtracted from his allotted thirty minutes. Schieffer called Bartlett.

"The president always looks better when he's more relaxed," Schieffer said. "It's better for both of us if we just give him a few minutes to collect his thoughts." Bartlett agreed.

Schieffer knew that Bush would not be expecting softballs. Bush, he felt, wanted the anchor to throw the high, hard one and see if he could hit it. Schieffer was no grandstander, but had a disarming way of cloaking his tougher queries in neighborly, conversational tones.

"Last summer, it seems to me, Mr. President, public support for the war began to erode," he offered. "Why do you think that happened?"

Rather than demand that Bush defend his domestic eavesdropping program, carried out without court orders, Schieffer asked: "Do you believe that there is anything that a president cannot do if he considers it necessary in an emergency like this?" Bush, taken aback for a moment, said that a president could not order torture, or the assassination of a foreign leader, and then offered his standard defense of the spying program.

When they were finished, they began chatting off the record, just two Texans shooting the breeze. Schieffer turned the conversation to Bush's reticence about sitting down with journalists.

"It's none of my business, and I don't give advice to politicians, but the best way to communicate with people is still the one-on-one interview," Schieffer said.

"You may be right," Bush said. "I'm going to think about that."

The interview made headlines. Tim Russert called afterward to congratulate Schieffer. Russert was a burly, down-to-earth Irish-American from Buffalo, and although his program *Meet the Press* was far ahead of *Face the Nation* in the ratings, what most people didn't know was that the two men were good friends. Professionally, Schieffer felt, he would cut off Russert's nuts if he had the chance, and he was sure his pal would do the same.

The most important thing about the interview, Schieffer believed, was that it had taken place at all. This was a major breakthrough. It meant that CBS and the Bush White House were back on speaking terms.

CHAPTER 9

Wounded in Action

Bob Woodruff walked toward the news desk, dressed in an open-necked blue shirt and black pants. He was hitting the road again.

"I'm so jealous," Elizabeth Vargas said. "I love going to Israel."

It was shortly before noon on January 23, 2006, and Woodruff was about to leave for the airport en route to Jerusalem to cover the first democratic election in the Palestinian territories. They chatted about the difficulty of sleeping on the twelve-hour flight, for which she said she needed an Ambien.

Minutes later Woodruff slung his black computer bag over one shoulder, a duffel bag over the other, and pulled his roll-on suitcase past her corner office.

"Fly safe," Vargas said.

Woodruff found himself absorbed by the trip. After the Palestinian elections, he was at a checkpoint in Amman, heading into Jordan, when he called Jon Banner at 2:30 A.M. New York time to say that he was turning back and returning to Israel. Word had just arrived that the terrorist group Hamas had pulled off a stunning upset and won control of the Palestinian authority.

Two days later Woodruff was in Iraq, preparing to join the Army's Fourth Infantry Division and travel as an embedded correspondent. He sent an e-mail to his ABC colleague Martha Raddatz, who had been to Iraq several times. "Tell me everything you know, girlfriend," Woodruff wrote.

On Sunday, January 29, Woodruff and cameraman Doug Vogt left an Army Humvee to ride with an Iraqi convoy for a story on whether the embattled country's armed forces were capable of assuming part of the military load from the Americans.

As the convoy rolled, Woodruff stood up in the turret of the tank while Vogt videotaped him, a report that would show him on the move, very much in war mode. He was wearing a helmet and a rather short flak jacket but no protective goggles.

"We're on patrol with Iraq's Ninth Division," Woodruff said, shouting to be heard over the din. "There's only one mechanized division in the entire Iraqi army. They say that the insurgents are particularly afraid of this group. They patrol up and down the main corridor north of Baghdad."

Suddenly a loud explosion ripped through the tank. They had struck a roadside bomb. Both men were hit by shrapnel. Woodruff screamed in excruciating pain. "Don't tell Lee," he cried. His face was covered with blood, and an Iraqi soldier pulled him inside the tank as insurgents opened fire from three directions.

When the attack subsided, Woodruff and Vogt were carried on stretchers to a helicopter and airlifted to a hospital in Baghdad, where they landed thirty-seven minutes after the blast. Then they were flown by helicopter to the U.S. military hospital at Balad Air Base and rushed into surgery.

It was 5 A.M. in New York when a senior producer woke up Jon Banner with the news. Banner, who had been very close to Peter Jennings, could not believe that this was happening again. Neither could David Westin, the ABC News president, when he got the call.

Westin reached Lee Woodruff at a Disney World hotel, where she was vacationing with her four children, at 7 A.M. "Bob has been wounded in Iraq," he said. Lee asked whether her husband was still alive. Westin said he was but had apparently taken shrapnel to the brain.

Elizabeth Vargas was awakened by a phone call from Paul Slavin, ABC's senior vice president. She was utterly stunned. She had been through Jennings's death, her husband's shooting, and now this.

Vargas herself had been in Iraq with the same crew just weeks ago. This just as easily could have happened to her. She rushed into the office, with Marc and their son in tow. With Bob and Doug in surgery, everyone was on edge, awaiting the merest scrap of information about their friends.

The news hit with jackhammer force at the other networks as well. Brian Williams was incredulous when he got the call from John Reiss. "It spooks me," Williams said.

Williams had a Christmas card from the Woodruff family on his desk.

The day Woodruff and Vargas had started as anchors, Williams made sure a note of congratulations arrived at their homes by overnight mail, just as Dan Rather and Peter Jennings had done for him on his first day. Woodruff had called that night to say thanks. They and their wives were supposed to have dinner in a few weeks.

The tragedy reminded Williams of his own harrowing experience in Iraq. In March 2003 Williams had hitched a ride on one of the Army's four Chinook twin-rotor helicopters for a routine mission ferrying steel to a bridge being built over the Euphrates River. Suddenly a man with a pickup truck pulled back a tarp and launched a rocket-propelled grenade at the fleet. The chopper in front of Williams's was hit as AK-47 fire erupted from another direction. The four choppers immediately dropped their load and headed for an emergency landing under hostile fire. A mechanized platoon surrounded the vulnerable helicopters, shoulder to shoulder with tanks and Bradley fighting vehicles, while infantrymen took up positions against Iraqi insurgents known to be in the area. A massive sandstorm blew in, and the fleet was grounded for three days until Williams finally made it to the safety of Kuwait City.

Williams believed that his time in Iraq had been crucial to his understanding the depth and complexity of the war, and he admired Woodruff for being willing to take those risks as well.

He and Reiss agreed that this was the day's big story. But they had to be mindful that some viewers would say that their son or daughter in the military faced the same dangers every day.

Williams called David Westin and asked about Woodruff's condition.

"It will be days," Westin said, "before we even know where we are."

In Washington, Bob Schieffer was at home in his Woodley Park apartment near the National Zoo when his *Face the Nation* producer, Carin Pratt, called him with the news. Schieffer had bumped into Woodruff on the shuttle the previous fall when Woodruff was filling in on *World News Tonight* after Jennings's death but had no idea whether he would be picked as a permanent anchor.

"Have you gotten any word?" Schieffer asked.

"Have you?" Woodruff asked, alluding to Schieffer's interim status.

"I'll tell if you'll tell," Schieffer joked.

Schieffer had an immediate decision to make. *Face the Nation* was set to air in less than two hours. The show was already on tape with an expanded version of the Bush interview that he had done on Friday. He had done his closing commentary about meeting Richard Nixon in a receiving line as a young reporter. But how could they ignore what had happened to Woodruff?

Schieffer called Sean McManus, who was on his way to a corporate meeting in Miami. "Should we dump the program?" Schieffer asked. They both agreed they could not blow off an exclusive interview with the president.

"I think we do it at the end," McManus said. "You absolutely have to take note of this."

The problem was there was no "hot" camera on the set because they hadn't planned on being live. They would have to do it from the newsroom. At 10:30 Schieffer gave viewers the news. Then, as *Face the Nation* rolled the Bush interview, Schieffer banged out a new commentary for the end of the program. He read it to Carin Pratt to make sure it fit the remaining time.

After the last commercial break Schieffer began: "In this electronic age, war has become so familiar that it is easy to forget that it is more than just pictures on television. But the soldiers who fight it and the correspondents who cover it do not forget. They know it is a dangerous business, and yet they are willing to risk that danger."

Elizabeth Vargas tried to concentrate on the Sunday night broadcast. After a long and frustrating day, when she sat down to compose a closing note, it was surprisingly easy to write. She tried to emphasize that the problems in Iraq were far larger than that day's tragedy. "We are all very concerned about our friends tonight and their wives and their children," Vargas said, "and we are once again reminded in a very personal way of what so many families of American service men and women endure so often when they receive news of their loved one being hurt."

No one knew whether Woodruff would live or die. That night Westin talked to Jon Banner about the future of *World News Tonight,* at least in the short term. He wondered whether they should ask Charlie Gibson and Diane Sawyer, ABC's biggest stars, to fill in for the wounded anchor.

"It looks like Bob's going to be out for a while," Westin said. "This is just my gut, but I want you to think about it."

Tom Brokaw was in his country home in New York's Westchester County when he heard what had happened. He and Meredith had gotten friendly with Bob and Lee after David Bloom, the NBC correspondent who was one of Woodruff's closest friends, died during the U.S. invasion of Iraq. Once Brokaw had even tried to persuade NBC to hire Woodruff. Brokaw reached Lee Woodruff on her cell phone and offered to do whatever he could. He also said he was going on *Today* the next morning to talk about the attack.

At 5:30 A.M., Lee and Woodruff's brother, Dave, called from Germany, where the anchor had been taken to a U.S. military hospital, and briefed Brokaw on what they had learned. They told him that doctors had removed part of Woodruff's skull to relieve swelling on the brain—details that ABC News was withholding. They also told Brokaw that Woodruff had suffered a broken collarbone and broken ribs and would have further surgery to remove shrapnel from his neck.

Brokaw felt that he had an obligation to the public to report what he knew. They were journalists, this was what they did, and if they didn't put out the information, the rumor mill would just take over. But he used his discretion and didn't tell the *Today* audience everything he had learned.

On *Good Morning America* Gibson and Sawyer devoted the first seventeen minutes of the program to Woodruff and Vogt. Elizabeth Vargas and David Westin were among the guests. Westin said that Woodruff had wanted to go to Iraq, that he was always anxious to travel where the news was.

After the show Vargas asked to speak to Westin in his office. Amid the chaos of the previous twenty-four hours, she decided that she had no choice but to come clean with her boss.

"I'm pregnant," she said.

Westin burst out laughing. "I think that's wonderful," he said. This was clearly another management headache, but he knew that there was no convenient time to have a child. Westin's first child had been born on the first day of the Supreme Court term during which he was clerking for Justice Lewis Powell. Such events had a way of intruding on your career.

Vargas had been stunned to learn the news soon after she got back from Iraq. She was forty-three and a half years old and simply had not expected to have another child. She had immediately wondered how this would affect the job that she was slated to start in a couple of weeks. The last thing you wanted was to have to take a maternity leave after a big promotion.

As someone who had gotten married and become a mother late in life, Vargas knew what a cataclysmic event having a child was. It forced you to sacrifice, to reshuffle your priorities. You could not be selfish with a child. At the same time parenthood and step-parenthood had also made her more emphathetic as a journalist. It was, Vargas felt, the great equalizer. No matter how famous or rich you were, when your baby had a high fever at three in the morning and was vomiting on you, you coped as best you could. But two small children would be twice as hard.

Her husband was anxious as well. They were barely holding things together with one child. "Don't freak out," she told Marc. "We don't know whether this will be something to freak out about yet." Vargas had already had one miscarriage before Zachary was born, and it was early. She did not allow herself to get overly excited, in case things didn't turn out well.

When she started her coanchoring duties, Vargas felt horrible physically, with morning sickness much worse than the first time around. Her plan was to keep her pregnancy a secret for as long as she could. She would stand with her hands clasped in front of her stomach, just in case she was showing a bit.

But now that Bob had been badly wounded, Vargas felt that her world was turned upside down. She was eleven weeks pregnant. She did not in good conscience feel that she could let Westin and his management team sit upstairs in their offices and make plans to cope with Woodruff's absence and then say later on, "Oh, by the way, I'll be leaving for a while, too." She owed it to herself, and to her unborn child, to be honest.

Vargas had been filled with trepidation as she walked into Westin's office. But she was relieved at how gracious he was. With Bob gravely injured, Westin saw this as a life-affirming event. He was happy for Elizabeth. Westin told her not to worry about her maternity leave, that it would all be worked out.

But if Westin was buoyed by Vargas's personal news, he was furious about something else. Everyone in the office was talking about the front-page *New York Times* headline on the wounding of Woodruff and Vogt. "Field Reports a Ratings Strategy," it said. The two men had risked their lives to cover a dangerous war—and it was being dismissed as a programming gimmick? Were *Times* reporters in Baghdad as part of a circulation strategy? This was nothing short of demeaning, Westin felt. Other network anchors were outraged as well. Bill Keller, the paper's executive editor, called Westin to apologize for the poor choice of words.

Tom Brokaw was stunned to hear that some ABC staffers were spreading the word that he had gone out of bounds by making public a private conversation with Woodruff's family. Brokaw, who felt strongly that he was acting with the family's blessing, called an ABC executive to complain.

During the 9:30 A.M. conference call for *NBC Nightly News,* the talk turned to how much to do that night on Woodruff and Vogt.

"We're all shaken by this," John Reiss said. "It underscores the kind of dangers our journalists face every day in Iraq, and that service men and women face every day. Bob Woodruff is a celebrity, that's the bottom line. It may not be fair that a celebrity gets more coverage than a soldier who's not known, but people want to hear about this."

That evening *Nightly* led off with two stories involving Woodruff and Vogt. Williams offered his prayers in closing the program, saying: "It's a reminder that in our highly competitive business, we are colleagues and we are friends first and foremost."

World News Tonight did four stories, the last of which was Vargas reading from an outpouring of letters from around the world. "I watch Bob every day, and it feels as though a family member has been injured," one person wrote.

In the past the media's narrative would have been the only version of events. The news community had closed ranks around the newly minted anchor. But in a wired world it was no longer difficult for people to talk back to big-name journalists. Some were offended by all the coverage being lavished on Bob Woodruff, viewing it as yet another example of the media taking care of their own. More than 2,200 Americans had been killed in Iraq, more than 16,000 wounded, and the critics wondered why their sacrifices drew so little attention compared to that of a famous television journalist who had chosen to fly into a war zone for a few days. Now these critics had a mechanism, through blogs and e-mail, to make their voices heard.

Williams was flooded with notes, some of them sharply negative.

From Sarasota, Florida: "You have ignored the 'main' reason why so many Americans have become outraged over the Woodruff and Vogt incident, and have elected to once again glorify your profession. The debate is not whether newsmen should have been at the site where the explosion occurred, but the very special treatment afforded Woodruff and Vogt after they were injured."

From Arlington, Texas: "You guys are really impressed with yourselves, always patting each other on the back. You don't do your job for the public good, you do it for yourself and the bucks."

From Wells, Maine: "Why did Woodruff or ABC feel the need to send Woodruff in again? Unfortunately, the answer is, in my view, greed on the part of Disney/ABC. Ratings—the better they are—the more money Disney/ABC makes."

Williams found the outpouring of e-mail sobering. He understood the critics' sentiments, but it was sad nonetheless.

*   *   *

The show must go on, according to the old Broadway adage, so Elizabeth Vargas flew to Washington the next day for Bush's State of the Union address.

The first order of business was the traditional White House luncheon with the top network anchors. As they waited for the president, Brian Williams and Bob Schieffer, among others, offered condolences to Vargas and peppered her with questions about Woodruff and Vogt, who were being flown that day to Bethesda Naval Hospital in Maryland.

The luncheon was held in a small room off the State Dining Room. The ground rules were that everything was off the record, but the anchors could use Bush's comments as long as they weren't directly attributed to the president. It was, in other words, a spin session at the highest possible level.

Bush was wound up about the war on terror and using language that he never uttered in public. "We're not backing away," he said. "We're going after the bastards."

"Mr. President," Schieffer asked, "do we really have a military option on Iran that's viable?"

"Hell yes, it's viable," Bush shot back.

Fox News anchor Chris Wallace asked whether, after a tough year, Bush was trying to restart his presidency. "I'm just trying to lead," Bush said. "I know I'm addressing a nation that is unsettled and somewhat disgruntled. I also know that war is on the minds of many people."

Brian Williams made use of his high-ranking source that night. "The president is known to be very frustrated at what he sees as a large part of the population in the country, and in that chamber tonight, that doesn't seem to agree with his message that this is a nation at war," Williams said. "He's expressed frustration over and over on that."

Schieffer used Bush's comment, without revealing his source, that the president didn't seek congressional approval for his domestic eavesdropping program because he thought it would tip off the enemy.

Elizabeth Vargas was smooth, as usual, on camera, but her lack of political experience showed. She had never anchored a State of the Union address. Vargas noted that Bush "reached out many, many times to the Democrats, reached out with an olive branch," when the more trenchant observation, made by Williams and Schieffer, was that the Democrats had sat on their hands while the Republicans cheered Bush's applause lines. Charlie Gibson, who was coanchoring with Vargas, offered seasoned judgments, saying that these addresses over the years had not been "terribly memorable speeches." Vargas mostly limited herself to asking questions of her guests.

As Gibson's presence suggested, David Westin had taken steps to ensure that Vargas would not be flying solo during Woodruff's recuperation. In Westin's view, Vargas needed help because they had built the vehicle for two drivers. But others in the business believed that Vargas was simply too inexperienced in hard news for ABC to leave her out there by herself. And Westin was well aware that an injection of star power wouldn't hurt as *World News Tonight* tried to maintain its second-place slot in the ratings.

First Westin went to Diane Sawyer's office. He asked whether she and Charlie would help him out by filling in on the evening news, at least for a few weeks, while holding down the fort at *Good Morning America.* Sawyer immediately agreed.

The Gibson situation was more problematic. After all, Charlie had really wanted the evening news job, had worked a backbreaking schedule as a temporary substitute, and Westin had refused to give him a three-year commitment. Westin knew that it had been a difficult time for Gibson, both because of his friend Jennings's death and because he had come so close to getting the job he had always wanted. The two men had been previously scheduled to meet at a restaurant for lunch, but Gibson suggested that he just bring a sandwich to Westin's office.

"I've got to change the agenda here," Westin began. He explained that he needed temporary help on *World News* and that Diane had already said yes. Gibson graciously agreed to do double duty as well. Westin knew that the irony of his having to beg Gibson's indulgence once again was not lost on either one of them.

By tapping his two morning stars, Westin was abandoning, at least for the moment, the ambitious plan to put his anchors on the road. And he was handing ammunition to those in the business who believed that Vargas, with her pleasant manner and feature background, simply wasn't ready to become the sole occupant of Peter Jennings's job.

Gibson stopped by Vargas's office to chat about the temporary arrangement. By the way, Vargas said, there was something that he should know. She was pregnant.

Oh boy, Gibson thought. The situation kept getting more complicated.

The news that Charlie and Diane would be riding to the rescue broke the morning after the State of the Union. When Westin was waiting at National Airport for the shuttle back to New York, he spotted Bob Schieffer and Brian Williams. Bob was kibitzing on Brian's end of the *Nightly News* morning conference call, and they seemed to be having a grand old time.

"You're not going to work my friend Charlie into the ground, are you?" Schieffer asked Westin.

Williams and Schieffer jokingly offered to fill in at ABC, each doing one night a week.

Westin said he appreciated the good wishes but shook his head at the enormity of the past forty-eight hours.

"My mother once said God doesn't give you anything unless you can handle it," Westin told them. "He must think we can handle anything."

CHAPTER 10

Hit or Miss

By virtue of his office, his power, and the media's need to filter compli-cated stories through a single recognizable figure, the president could lead the nightly newscasts essentially by clearing his throat. The challenge for the newscasts was to avoid becoming a transmission belt for White House propaganda. In the post-9/11 climate, television journalists were par-ticularly concerned that they not be seen as undermining the war on terror or disparaging American troops, even as government surveillance and the continued carnage in Iraq became the overriding political issues of the day.

On February 9, 2006, George W. Bush delivered a speech in which he described an unsuccessful al-Qaeda plot four years earlier to fly airplanes into the Library Tower in Los Angeles. The outlines of the plot had been dis-closed by the White House four months earlier. And it was not at all clear that this scheme had ever gotten past the talking stage.

No matter. Bush's remarks were the lead story on the *CBS Evening News,* where Bob Schieffer simply quoted the president. "It has been alluded to in the past, but for the first time President Bush confirmed today that in the months after 9/11, the government broke up another terrorist plot to fly a plane into the tallest building in Los Angeles," Schieffer said. "And he said the plot had been put together by the same al-Qaeda operatives that had planned the 9/11 attacks in New York and Washington. This disclosure came in a speech in which the president said the war on terror is being won but it's far from over." Score one for Bush.

The speech was the second story on *World News Tonight,* where Charlie Gibson, in his first week filling in with Elizabeth Vargas, also played it straight: "We turn next to the war on terror. President Bush today revealed some details of a terrorist plot that was foiled. It was, he says, an al-Qaeda plan in the weeks right after 9/11, to attack the tallest building in Los Angeles."

Just to add an extra shiver, correspondent Pierre Thomas closed his report with this warning: "Police say that Los Angeles, Washington, and New York remain the top targets for al-Qaeda." Score two for Bush.

But the tone was markedly different on *NBC Nightly News*. Brian Williams was in Turin, Italy, preparing to cohost the opening ceremony at the Winter Olympics, for which NBC had bought the broadcast rights. Williams's philosophy was simple: When either party tried to use the terrorism issue for blatant political advantage, they should be called out. Williams had read the president-said-today script prepared by correspondent Kelly O'Donnell and believed that the White House was getting a pass on the motive and timing of Bush's remarks. That, in his view, shifted the burden of skepticism to what he called his good-evening page.

He called Tim Russert in Washington. "What's your take down there?" he asked. "Is this political or what?"

Russert noted that Attorney General Alberto Gonzales had just testified about Bush's domestic spying program amid growing accusations that the warrantless wiretaps violated the law. "I think it's very fair that we mention the timing," Russert said. "The president is declassifying this before our eyes. Why the need to do it today?"

In leading off the broadcast, Williams oozed skepticism about the speech. He was practically waving his arms to call attention to his doubts.

"The White House says it was just a coincidence that during this time while the president is under fire for a program of domestic eavesdropping and while he's been trying to renew provisions of the Patriot Act, he just happened to choose today as the day to talk about a planned terrorist incident in the U.S. that was thwarted and thus never happened," Williams said. He figured he would probably get static from the administration, but that came with the territory.

It wasn't that the other newscasts gave the White House a completely free ride. But only Williams climbed out on a ledge by challenging the story's very premise at the top of the newscast. In doing so, he risked criticism that he was biased against the administration, was belittling the war on terror, or was injecting his own opinions into daily reporting.

The Media Research Center, a conservative advocacy group in Alexandria, Virginia, ran a headline on its Web site: "Brian Williams Calls L.A. Terrorist Plot 'Alleged.' "

The coup de grâce for the Media Research Center was the shocking discovery that, long ago, Williams had "proclaimed his commitment to the 'Democret' party." Of course, it was 1966 and Williams was seven years old at the time. The proof was in the handwritten note he had scrawled to Lyndon Johnson—reproduced in a book of children's letters—signed "One of you'r young Democrets, Brian Williams, 927 W. Church St., Elmira, N.Y. 14905."

The irony was that of all the men and women who had occupied the network anchor chair, Brian Williams, the Rush Limbaugh listener, was clearly the most open to conservative viewpoints. But any perceived deviation from conservative orthodoxy was enough to brand him the stereotypical liberal anchor.

In the eyes of the left, meanwhile, Williams also remained suspect. Media Matters for America, a liberal organization just as determined to detect evidence to support its ideological view, disparaged his recent presidential interview—with its tight time constraints—in this headline: "NBC's Williams Asked Almost No Follow-up Questions of Bush During *Nightly News* Interview."

Williams had called out the president on his use of a terrorism speech, but he was drawing no cheers from the partisans on either side.

*   *   *

A nagging problem was brewing at the *CBS Evening News.*

The staff kept getting beaten on stories.

When Oprah Winfrey eviscerated an author whose book she had promoted onto the bestseller lists, newsrooms across America were buzzing. The controversy had erupted weeks earlier, when the Web site *The Smoking Gun* revealed that James Frey had largely fabricated his memoir of a life of crime and drugs, and again when Winfrey called in to CNN's *Larry King Live* and defended the embattled author. When the talk show queen finally admitted on her program that she had made a huge mistake and berated Frey for duping her, it was a big story on *NBC Nightly News,* a big story on *World News Tonight,* and a front-page story in *The New York Times* and *The Washington Post* the next morning.

Bob Schieffer's broadcast had nothing.

"What's this all about?" Sean McManus asked Schieffer. "Why did we it?"

Schieffer realized that he had dampened the enthusiasm of his colleagues. More than a week earlier, after the *Smoking Gun* exposé, senior producer Reid Collins Jr. had suggested doing a story on the James Frey controversy.

"Horseshit," Schieffer said. "There's not three people in America who know who this guy is. I've never heard of him." Frey's memoir, *A Million Little Pieces,* had sold more than two million copies.

The morning after they missed the Oprah spectacle, Schieffer spoke up at a staff meeting.

"I was right," he said. "There weren't three people in America who knew who this guy was. Unfortunately, those three worked for ABC, NBC, and *The New York Times.*"

Maybe, Schieffer realized, his earlier words had had too much impact. Maybe people were going around saying, *Bob doesn't think this is much of a story.* Schieffer loved to joke around, and sometimes he would say something just to get off a good line. Now that he was the anchor, he realized, he had to be more careful. People hung on your every word.

Sometimes the network newscasts would intentionally blow off a story—particularly if that story had to do with politics. There had been a debate for a quarter-century about how much the public really cared about the twists and turns of Beltway maneuvering. The conventional wisdom at the networks was that viewers would swallow politics only in small doses.

When Bush gave a speech in Nashville the day after the State of the Union, Rome Hartman argued that it would be a snooze: "The president went to another city today, to say much the same thing he said in a nationally televised address eighteen hours earlier, which was fully covered and dissected last night, in this morning's papers and on this morning's TV shows. Here's our White House correspondent to rehash the rehash." Schieffer agreed to forgo the usual piece.

But the broadcast that consistently displayed the least interest in national politics was *World News Tonight.* Perhaps this reflected the fact that Elizabeth Vargas, having spent most of her career as a feature reporter, had never worked in Washington.

ABC's nightly newscast was the only one that refused to report—even in a single sentence—that Congressman John Boehner had won an upset victory to become House majority leader in the midst of a major uproar over the Jack Abramoff lobbying scandal.

Vargas believed that she and her staff had to work hard to make political news understandable to the audience. Instead of talking about a bloated budget bill in Congress, they would focus on the notorious Bridge to Nowhere, the Alaska pork project pushed through by its powerful senator, Ted Stevens. As for Boehner, she felt, no one knew who he was or what he was going to do as majority leader. Her view meshed with that of Jon Banner, who believed that journalists spent an inordinate amount of time covering Washington.

But Vargas's rivals saw it differently. Bob Schieffer led his program that night by talking about the indicted Republican power broker who had been forced to give up the leadership post now claimed by Boehner. "Well, there's just no other way to say it," Schieffer said. "The Tom DeLay era in Republican politics is over."

At NBC, John Reiss called Tim Russert, who said that Boehner's election was important but could be handled as the second story on *Nightly News*. "The way you do it is you say, 'This is Tom DeLay's replacement,' " Russert told him.

On a far more dramatic day, when DeLay, under indictment and battling for his political life, surprised the world by announcing that he would resign from Congress, Brian Williams and Bob Schieffer both led with the news. Vargas's lead story was about child pornography, specifically the congressional testimony of eighteen-year-old Justin Berry, who had performed sex acts for money in front of a Webcam. Berry had been the centerpiece of a *New York Times* exposé more than three months earlier that had led to two arrests, but no matter. Porn trumped politics in the ABC universe. The *CBS Evening News* also did a piece on Berry, but Brian Williams passed. Katie Couric had already gotten Berry for an exclusive *Today* interview that morning.

Vargas didn't care that the news was old. A huge portion of the country didn't read *The New York Times*. Besides, she thought, this kid had been telling an incredible tale up on Capitol Hill, about how he had masturbated for paying Webcam customers without his mother finding out. It was deeply, deeply disturbing. Vargas had two teenage stepkids and was amazed by how much time they spent on the Net. As Vargas saw it, a child-porn exposé beat Tom DeLay any day.

The same ABC tendencies were on display when the indicted former White House aide Lewis "Scooter" Libby, in a letter from his lawyers, said that his superiors had authorized him to leak classified information. Libby, who had been Dick Cheney's vice-presidential chief of staff, had been charged with perjury and obstruction of justice in the leak to the press that Valerie Plame—the wife of prominent White House critic Joseph

Wilson—had been a CIA operative. On CBS, correspondent Gloria Borger said this was "an embarrassment, particularly for an administration that prides itself on keeping secrets." On NBC, investigative reporter Lisa Myers said Libby's disclosure "could be embarrassing to a White House which delights in attacking others for leaks endangering national security."

World News Tonight didn't mention the Libby story.

And when disgraced lawmaker Duke Cunningham was sentenced to more than eight years in prison for accepting a Rolls-Royce, a yacht, and $2 million in other bribes from a defense contractor—the longest incarceration ever imposed on a member of Congress—CBS and NBC reported the news. ABC couldn't find the time.

Sometimes ABC's political antennae just seemed broken. When *The Washington Post* ran a front-page piece on a half-dozen retired generals calling on Donald Rumsfeld to resign, Williams and Schieffer played it up big. "Defense Secretary Rumsfeld has become the lightning rod for criticism of an unpopular war, and the lightning is reaching storm levels," Schieffer said.

"The man in charge of running the wars in Iraq and Afghanistan, Secretary of Defense Donald Rumsfeld, is under fire tonight from within the U.S. military and from a group of men with a lot of stars on their shoulders, retired generals, who say it is time for him to go," Williams reported.

Vargas was AWOL. The next night she had to catch up with her rivals—and virtually every newspaper in America—by leading the broadcast with Bush defending his Pentagon chief against the criticism that *World News* had dismissed earlier.

But every once in a while the networks jumped on a political story so strange, so compelling, and so filled with human drama that it became a virtual obsession. And that obsession could ultimately alienate viewers if it seemed that the journalists had lost all sense of perspective.

When Dick Cheney went quail hunting on a Texas ranch with a seventy-eight-year-old lawyer named Harry Whittington, an unfortunate accident became worldwide news. The mere fact that the vice president of the United States had shot a man was enough to lead the network newscasts for five straight days. But what really fueled the story was Cheney's decision not to tell the national press about the shooting, instead having an owner of the Texas ranch relay the news to the *Corpus Christi Caller-Times* nearly twenty-four hours later.

The White House pressroom erupted with angry questions for spokesman Scott McClellan about why the vice president had felt no responsibility to disclose the shooting himself or to answer questions about how the accident had occurred. The network correspondents led the badgering. And if the reporters' interrogation of McClellan seemed absurdly repetitive, there was a hidden reason: A confrontational question meant that the correspondent might be seen on the air, holding the president's spokesman accountable.

NBC Nightly News used part of a question from David Gregory, the tall, wisecracking reporter who had emerged as the most combative member of the press corps, in the opening headlines, and he was seen again during the newscast, asking McClellan: "The vice president of the United States accidentally shoots a man, and he feels that it's appropriate for a ranch owner who had witnessed this to tell the local Corpus Christi newspaper and not the White House press corps at-large or notify the public in a national way?"

World News Tonight showed its reporter, Martha Raddatz: "What time on Sunday morning did you learn that Vice President Dick Cheney was the shooter?"

CBS Evening News spotlighted Jim Axelrod: "I just want to clarify one thing. Is it appropriate for a private citizen to be the person to disseminate the information that the vice president of the United States has shot someone?" Axelrod also showed up on *Nightly News*.

The next day, as CBS correspondent Richard Schlesinger was finishing a light piece on all the punch lines about the incident, Whittington's doctors announced that he had suffered a minor heart attack caused by a birdshot pellet moving near his heart. Suddenly the accident no longer seemed like a laughing matter.

Sean McManus called his anchor one hour before airtime. "There's no way we can run that piece," he said.

"You're absolutely right," Schieffer said. "We've already killed it."

McManus also sent Jim Axelrod a note, saying that everyone was trying to figure out Cheney's public relations strategy. Cheney didn't seem to care about his image, McManus wrote, because he was the first vice president in recent memory who was not interested in running for president. As a lifelong sports executive, McManus sometimes brought a fresh eye to politics, but this was a fairly obvious point that had been made many times.

Nonetheless, on the *Evening News* that night, Axelrod reported that Cheney "really couldn't care less what reporters think of him now. Unlike the four vice presidents who came before him, Mr. Cheney definitely won't be running for president."

Mary Matalin, the high-profile Republican operative who had worked for

Cheney and was now an informal adviser, could not believe the way the story had spun out of control. White House officials were hammering her, saying that the press was freaking out and they couldn't talk about anything else, while journalists were telling her that Cheney needed to publicly show remorse. But Matalin felt that that would be a losing argument with the vice president, who cared little about his media portrayal. What reporters failed to understand was that Cheney was very emotional, just beside himself over the shooting, and that those around him were in tears. She could not believe all these rumors about how Cheney had been drunk, and how they had migrated from these crazy, vile bloggers to the mainstream media.

Matalin blamed herself for the public relations disaster. After her two daughters had held an all-night sleepover party on the Saturday night of the shooting, she had taken them to a snow-covered park, coordinating strategy by juggling three cell phones. After speaking to Cheney at 8 A.M., Matalin had recommended that they use an eyewitness—Katharine Armstrong, the ranch owner—and the official sheriff's report to get the story out quickly to a local paper that Armstrong trusted. Matalin had failed to anticipate that the White House press corps would see this as a thumb in the eye and was mortified that her strategy had backfired.

As Cheney maintained his silence, the network newscasts trumpeted the story night after night, fueled by a sense of outrage toward a vice president who openly disdained the national media. And no one seemed to take greater offense than Gregory, the son of a Broadway producer and a rising NBC star who often filled in on the *Today* show.

Earlier that day, at the morning White House briefing—an informal session known as "the gaggle"—the thirty-five-year-old Gregory got particularly aggressive in his questioning.

"David, hold on . . . The cameras aren't on right now," Scott McClellan told him.

Gregory erupted: "Don't accuse me of trying to pose to the cameras. Don't be a jerk to me personally when I'm asking you a serious question."

That was a cheap shot on McClellan's part, Gregory felt. He soon regretted losing his temper. But he did not apologize for asking tough questions about what had happened when Cheney shot Harry Whittington. He was in the business of digging out information. The way White House correspondents did their job wasn't pretty, and if people wanted to be critical, he accepted that. But Gregory had no intention of changing his dogged style.

That afternoon, with the cameras rolling, the two men went at it again.

"Don't tell me that you're giving us complete answers when you're not actually answering the question," Gregory told McClellan, "because everybody knows what is an answer and what is not an answer."

"David, now you want to make this about you, and it's not about you, it's about what happened," McClellan shot back.

As the pressure mounted, network reporters had no trouble vacuuming up leaks from White House officials and Bush allies who were distressed by Cheney's refusal to discuss the shooting and concerned that the growing storm was hurting the administration. The willingness of the correspondents to rely so heavily on unnamed sources made it easy for presidential aides, behind a curtain of anonymity, to try to distance Bush from the fiasco.

"Here at the White House," Gregory reported, "aides have done little to hide their disagreement with the vice president and his staff over the handling of this whole matter."

On CBS, Schieffer chatted with Gloria Borger, who cited "one source who's very close to the vice president" as saying "that Dick Cheney has been in what he calls a state of meltdown."

Within hours *The Huffington Post,* the liberal Web site founded by columnist and socialite Arianna Huffington, had a screaming banner headline, "CBS NEWS: CHENEY IN MELTDOWN."

Bob Schieffer had known Cheney since he was Gerald Ford's White House chief of staff, and he liked the man. But he believed that Cheney was just totally mishandling this episode. No one had forced him to run for vice president, and he owed the American people an accounting.

Schieffer had pulled Cheney aside on the day of the State of the Union and asked for an interview. The vice president said he would grant one in the near future. After the hunting accident, Schieffer sent Dan Bartlett a note, reminding him of the Cheney promise. He never heard back.

On February 15, three days after the shooting, Mary Matalin sat down with Cheney and went through a list of options. He could take questions in the White House briefing room, but Matalin argued that the reporters would try to make themselves look good by shouting at Cheney. A one-on-one interview, she said, would be the best forum for putting the mounting questions to rest.

They quickly ruled out the network newscasts because they wanted more than the usual allotment of four minutes. The Sunday shows were out because Matalin was convinced that they needed to do something that day. That left cable news.

Cheney and Matalin settled on Brit Hume, the veteran Fox News anchor, who they believed would be thorough but not confrontational. Although

Hume had been a White House correspondent for ABC News a decade earlier, the choice prompted a wave of derision from most mainstream journalists. They identified Fox with the high-decibel conservatism of Bill O'Reilly and Sean Hannity—both of whom had belittled the importance of the shooting—and concluded that the vice president had opted for a softball interview. Hume had never hidden his conservative views, but he had a reputation in Washington as a solid journalist.

There was a time when a politician in trouble would go to Barbara Walters, Diane Sawyer, or Katie Couric and the mass audience provided by a broadcast network. He would not turn to a lesser-known cable program such as Hume's *Special Report,* which had an audience of just over 1 million viewers. But Cheney and his handlers made the calculation that if he spoke only to Hume, every other network and news organization would have to run excerpts of the Fox interview, sparing the vice president the need to engage what he viewed as a hostile press corps.

Although Hume conducted a serious and thorough, if low-key, interview about the shooting, his rivals couldn't resist taking potshots. "A former White House correspondent," David Gregory said on NBC, Hume "has been outspoken in his criticism of the White House press corps coverage of this story." The vice president had chosen "a broadcast Mr. Cheney sees as friendly and has turned to before," CBS's Jim Axelrod said. Only ABC, where Hume had previously worked, did not disparage him.

World News Tonight was also riding the story hard. Elizabeth Vargas thought that Cheney had turned the shooting into a far bigger story by acting like he had something to hide. The whole episode was a window into the vice president's style, she believed, and highlighted his arrogance in not immediately telling Bush that he had shot someone. Only now, Vargas felt, had Cheney done the right thing by accepting responsibility for his actions.

Diane Sawyer, filling in for Bob Woodruff for the first time, seemed to loosen up Vargas, who came across as a bit chilly when she was anchoring on her own.

"You know, Elizabeth," Sawyer said, "I'm thinking of our conversation in the newsroom today about President Bush and his own hunting mishap."

"That's right," Vargas said. "He wrote about it in his autobiography. In 1994 he shot a rare bird by accident on a hunting trip of his own. He says he didn't know what to do, but then decided to tell every single reporter who was accompanying him on that hunting trip."

When the newscast was over, they high-fived each other. Sawyer felt that they had briefly hijacked the heavily scripted program. It was a small moment, and obviously planned, but Sawyer's morning-show ease had finally allowed Vargas to show a bit of her personality at the anchor desk.

Brian Williams knew, from the blogs and his e-mail and what was on the tube, that plenty of people were tired of the shooting story and regarded it as way overblown, the yammering of a frustrated press. But others were still amazed by the surreal spectacle of a shooting by a vice president, for the first time since Aaron Burr in 1804, and could not get enough. What really bothered him was the partisan venom on both sides.

Much of that poison was aimed at David Gregory. Tim Russert was struck by the way talk radio had made Gregory the poster boy for an obnoxious press corps, and he felt he had no choice but to invite Gregory on *Meet the Press.* Among the other guests was Mary Matalin.

A former cohost of CNN's *Crossfire,* the sharp-tongued Matalin dismissed Russert's question about whether any alcohol had been consumed beyond the one beer that Cheney had acknowledged having at lunch. Gregory apologized for calling McClellan a jerk but said it was odd that Cheney had chosen to disclose the shooting through Katharine Armstrong.

Matalin promptly pounced on Gregory. "It strikes you as odd because you live in a parallel universe. It did not strike Americans as odd," Matalin said. She accused Gregory of going "on a jihad" against the vice president.

Gregory objected to the word and said that Matalin was mistaken if she believed that journalists wouldn't have pressed as hard for answers if Vice President Al Gore had accidentally shot someone.

After the show Gregory was angry. How could Matalin have accused him of being on a *jihad*? Matalin said that she used the word all the time. She thought journalists had completely lost their minds. "As if the Secret Service would have let Cheney go out drunk, even if you think Cheney would be that irresponsible," she said.

Gregory kept after her.

"This is a parallel universe," Matalin said, and she walked away.

Williams was glad that Gregory had acknowledged going too far. But he remembered full well from his White House days the importance of an aggressive, loudmouth correspondent like Sam Donaldson. The country hadn't really had one since then, someone who would push the boundaries in trying to hold the president accountable. Every press corps needed a Sam, he felt, and David Gregory was filling the role nicely.

CHAPTER 11

Fake News Rules

The networks were being squeezed from every possible direction.

Newspapers were deeper. Web sites were faster. Bloggers were more opinionated. And Jon Stewart was funnier.

As they struggled to carve out a comfortable niche, the evening newscasts tried to lift a page from their new-media competitors. Rather than be seen as hopelessly staid, *they* would display a sense of humor. *They* would check in with bloggers. *They* would critique the news business, just like the online opinion-mongers.

"Why don't we do one about us? Shine the light on ourselves for a change?" Rome Hartman asked his deputy, Bill Owens, early in 2006.

Thus it was that the *CBS Evening News* aired a segment on journalistic credibility, focused in part on how bloggers had helped bring down the program's former anchor, Dan Rather. One of those interviewed was Jeff Jarvis, the cofounder of *Entertainment Weekly*. But Jarvis felt that CBS had selectively used his comments to make a predetermined point, and he vented on his blog, *BuzzMachine.com*.

"When the producer called," Jarvis wrote, "it's clear they had an angle in mind: citizens' journalism vs. professional journalism. They asked for stories in which I'd gone up against big media. I told him that's not the story now. I said the real story is how, with citizens' help, journalism can and must expand with new ways to gather and share news."

When he tried to make those points, Jarvis said, "they didn't use that, apart from one line about news not being finished when we print it, which is actually a line about Dan Rather . . .

"Now, of course, this happens all the time. This is what sours sources o the news . . . I don't care if they used more or different quotes from me. But I care about getting a story that's not as shallow as videotape. But evening news is the shallowest of news: Give us twenty-two minutes and we can't possibly give you the world."

There were no space limitations in cyberspace, so his rant continued, screen after screen.

"The real story about the state of the media isn't what CBS aired, but what it didn't air: The story of how broadcast TV, without the Web and without the public's help there, will continue to be shallow and shrinking and outmoded. The irony is that CBS News' story about the state of the media is the best illustration of the state of old media."

For John Reiss, the detour into the blogosphere began when he attended the White House Correspondents' Association dinner in the spring of 2006. Stephen Colbert, who played a talk show blowhard on Comedy Central, took some pretty hard jabs at President Bush, but the networks were so busy running clips of a Bush impersonator who appeared alongside the president that they ignored Colbert.

In trolling online, however, Reiss saw that some liberal bloggers were embracing Colbert as a hero, saying that he had displayed the guts so conspicuously lacking among Washington journalists. Several sites had put up video of the routine, which had been carried by C-SPAN. At the same time many conservative bloggers were ripping the comedian for being disrespectful to the president.

What struck Reiss was that this was percolating as a national controversy even though the major news organizations had missed the boat. Why not do a piece, he thought, admitting that his network and the others could no longer control the debate, that other sources could now define what was news?

Brian Williams loved the idea, and *NBC Nightly News* did a segment on bloggers and interviewed one of the most popular practitioners, Glenn Reynolds, a University of Tennessee law professor. He was underwhelmed.

"Well, I watched it," Reynolds wrote on *Instapundit.com,* "and I don't want to be rude to the NBC people, who were quite pleasant. But jeez, that was a 2002 story. If you hadn't heard of blogs before, I guess it was news. Otherwise, not so much."

Bloggers always got the last word.

*   *   *

Jon Stewart was taking questions from the audience.

One man wanted to know about Stephen Colbert, who had been a correspondent for *The Daily Show* and now followed Stewart's late-night program on Comedy Central.

"How big are his balls?" asked the man, clearly still wowed over
Colbert's comedic skewering of President Bush.

"We are now sitting inside them," Stewart said. "Gi-normous balls. Any
other questions?" He then imitated a deep-voiced moronic fan: *"Yeah, how
big are Samantha Bee's breasts?"*

It was show number 11,080, and the nation's premier fake newsman was
warming up the crowd in the studio on Eleventh Avenue, a stone's throw
from the Hudson River.

Against the left wall just below the balcony, unnoticed by the 216 audience members, was Ben Karlin, a bearded man with sandy-colored hair,
wearing a navy shirt, jeans, and sneakers. Karlin was the show's executive
producer, and they had just completed their nightly ritual, a last-minute
rewrite session. They also had to trim the script, which was three minutes
and fifty-six seconds too long.

The idea for the first segment had emerged when the staff noticed the
cable news networks going wild over the latest round of arrests in the war on
terror. Seven suspects had been picked up in Miami, and the Bush administration had put out the word that they were plotting to blow up the Sears
Tower in Chicago.

But when Alberto Gonzales held a news conference to tout the arrests,
and a reporter asked whether any of the seven men had ties to al-Qaeda, the
attorney general had paused, consulted with his team, turned back to the
mikes, and said, "The answer to that is no." As the day wore on, it became
clear that the men had no money, no weapons, and no equipment, just
some military boots supplied by the federal informant who had infiltrated
the group.

The central paradox of *The Daily Show* was that Jon Stewart regularly
covered the same ground as the evening newscasts, but, for all his fakery,
regularly managed to outclass the networks. His deft use of satire made the
television journalists look as clueless as the public figures they chronicled.

As a performer, Jon Stewart had won four Emmy Awards, a coveted turn
hosting the Oscars, and a cult following among the young, the hip, and the
deeply ironic. As a bogus anchor, he had conjured up the ideal persona for
mocking the conventions of politics and journalism while pretending to

deliver the news. In the process, Stewart had emerged as the country's most acerbic media critic, a man who used his comedic gifts to expose and humiliate the unintentional inanities of network news.

And yet, like gluttons for punishment, journalists were his most devoted fans. They laughed the hardest as Stewart portrayed them as pretentious pinheads, for they knew that his pointed barbs were right on target. *Newsweek* put Stewart on the cover, *Nightline* had him as a guest, and *60 Minutes* ran a profile. It was a strange spectacle, the media celebrating the man who had risen to prominence by making its members look like clowns.

The second segment on this evening was Karlin's idea, mocking the practice of politicians reciting the same talking points again and again, which were replayed on television without skepticism. *The Daily Show* had a small army of researchers who pored over a vast tape library and TiVo hard drives to find the perfect sound bites. Karlin thought that the Republicans were unbelievably disciplined when it came to staying on message, so when dozens of them started accusing the Democrats of wanting to "cut and run" in Iraq, the show would highlight how scripted it all seemed by running the clips rapid-fire. This time Karlin had noticed that Bush, Secretary of State Condoleezza Rice, and Defense Secretary Donald Rumsfeld had all said it was too soon to evaluate the situation in Iraq and that history would judge the final outcome. Karlin pitched the idea to actor and commentator John Hodgman, who wrote a draft for the segment.

Now it was showtime, and the crowd roared—having been prompted to yell as loud as possible—when the music came up and Stewart introduced himself. He tossed to a tape of Gonzales saying at the news conference that the seven men arrested were planning on "waging a full ground war against the United States."

"I am not a general," Stewart said, "but I believe that if you are going to wage a full ground war against the United States, you need at least as many people as, say, a softball team." After the video of Gonzales's awkward silence, Stewart provided the analysis: "These deadly international terrorists had very slyly disguised themselves as dipshits living in a warehouse . . . no weapons, no actual contact with al-Qaeda, but one of them had been to Chicago."

In a few short minutes Stewart had managed to do what the network newscasts had not, which was make the administration look ridiculous for hyping a sad group of wannabes as a big-time threat.

After the second segment with John Hodgman, who deadpanned that it would take a thousand years to properly judge the war in Iraq, Karlin hustled up to the desk. He said that the show was running a little light, so Stewart could spend more time with his guest, biking champion Lance Armstrong.

Before the show ended, Stewart had a brief video chat with Colbert, who was sitting in another studio, to persuade viewers to stick around for *The Colbert Report.*

"Stephen," he said, "we had a discussion with the studio audience about the size of your genitalia, and there was a question about your sack."

"The balls are getting bigger," Colbert responded. "It's very painful."

It was all a fake-out, just to goof on the audience. They did the real tease, the one that would air, a moment later.

As the audience roared its approval, Stewart thanked the crowd and then retreated to a small, windowless office down the hall. He sat down at a computer and began skimming *RottenTomatoes.com,* a movie industry gossip site. A moment later Karlin arrived for their postgame review and a brief discussion of the next day's show.

Ben Karlin's night was only half over when he finished the meeting with Stewart. He hustled two blocks north to the old *Daily Show* studio and arrived just in time for the start of *The Colbert Report,* where he also served as executive producer.

In playing a fatuous right-wing blowhard whose lack of knowledge did nothing to temper the certainty of his opinions, Colbert took plenty of shots at the press as well. He did a bit about "the yellow journalists over at *USA Today*"—whom he dubbed "the USA Todayholes."

In the midst of a paean to Republican policies that kept many people impoverished—"We need the destitute, they remind the rest of us it sucks to be poor"—Colbert suddenly stopped.

"Fuck!" he declared. "I don't know what to do." He had stumbled over the script a couple of times. The lights went down, Karlin rushed up to the desk, and they worked out a way to edit the mistakes out of the tape. Regaining his composure, Colbert told the audience: "You may have noticed that something went wrong. I sucked!"

And if the *real* journalists on *real* network shows dared to dis Colbert? A couple of weeks later *Today* and *Good Morning America* ran pieces questioning why politicians appeared with Colbert, after Florida congressman Robert Wexler went on the show and played along with a gag about enjoying cocaine. "They think they're being hip, I don't know," Matt Lauer said.

The Colbert Report retaliated by running some of the sillier teases that are staples on the morning shows: "Coming up, the python that ate electric blanket," Lauer was seen saying. Next was a Diane Sawyer come-on: "They call it tanorexia. Could tanning be almost as addictive as heroin?"

Stewart, like Colbert, enjoyed nothing more than tweaking his more serious brethren. But for a guy who earned a nice living denigrating the news business, Jon Stuart Leibowitz had plenty of social connections to the field. Tom Brokaw had met Stewart at the 2000 Democratic convention, was struck by how smart he was, and they had become friends. Brokaw invited Stewart to join in the commentary on NBC during the 2004 conventions, seeing the man as a master satirist, the Mort Sahl of their era. Sure, *The Daily Show* featured fake news, Brokaw felt, but there was an essential truth to what Stewart said.

Brian Williams was perhaps the biggest Stewart fan. They would spend forty-five minutes on the phone at times, chatting about fatherhood, charity dinners, and life in the public eye. Williams saw him as a sharp social critic who held the media accountable by lampooning their excesses. Whenever a guest canceled at the last minute, *The Daily Show* would call and Williams would go running over to Eleventh Avenue. It was a rare opportunity for Williams to showcase a natural sense of humor that he kept well hidden on the evening news.

There was a lot of claptrap in the press about how younger people were getting their news from *The Daily Show,* usually presented with a slight shake of the head, as in, *how sad that this generation knows so little that it has to be spoon-fed by a professional comic.* In fact, Stewart and Karlin knew that the situation was exactly the opposite of the popular mythology. No one would get the jokes they did night after night without at least a passing familiarity with the headlines. A study by the Annenberg Public Policy Center concluded in 2004 that viewers of late-night comedy, especially Stewart's show, knew more about the backgrounds and positions of the presidential candidates than those who did not watch such programs. Even in the late-night audience, the researchers found that *Daily Show* viewers were better educated, more interested in politics, younger, and more liberal than those who watched Jay Leno or David Letterman.

Karlin saw their formula as simple. They used the language of television news—something that everyone understood—as the fastest route to the punch line. They were not on a crusade to reform the media.

The Daily Show had found its voice, Karlin believed, during the 2000 election recount, when reporters would faithfully parrot the diametrically opposite spins of the George Bush and Al Gore camps. News organizations had also failed miserably, he felt, when the Swift Boat Veterans for Truth had torpedoed John Kerry's credibility with cheap, sinister tactics about his war record. Why, he wondered, couldn't journalists call bullshit on people in public life who lied or engaged in distortion? The reporters must be worried to death about being called biased, Karlin believed, or about losing access to the powerful.

Stephen Colbert, who made no secret of being a Democrat, wrestled with the same question. One reporter after another would say to him privately, "I wish I could say what you say." Well, why *couldn't* they say the kinds of things he said, albeit in their own way, and blow the whistle on political hypocrisy? Perhaps, he thought, they felt they would be accused of being too aggressive.

When Dick Cheney was asked on a CNBC talk show about having said it was "pretty well confirmed" that terrorist leader Mohamed Atta had met before the war with an Iraqi official in Prague, Cheney simply denied making the comment, which had been part of an effort to demonstrate a link between Saddam Hussein's regime and al-Qaeda. *The Daily Show* went to the videotape and aired a clip of the vice president declaring on *Meet the Press* back in 2001 that the Atta meeting was "pretty well confirmed." Why, Colbert wondered, didn't others in the press do precisely the same thing? This wasn't some kind of advocacy journalism, it was the rawest form of objectivity: Cheney denied saying X, but in fact he said X on such-and-such a date. Why was it left to a comedy show to demonstrate that Cheney had been flat wrong?

Jon Stewart was obsessed with the question of why journalists couldn't find ways to report the "truth," as opposed to mindlessly repeating the partisan garbage spewed by each side, or staging pointless debates in which Republicans and Democrats traded scripted barbs. How did that help the public understand the issues, if media folks simply handed each side a megaphone without making a real attempt to fact-check the competing claims?

Stewart had one of the fastest wits around, but he was dead serious about how the media were letting down the country. He would spend hours arguing with journalists, away from the cameras, about what he saw as their fundamental failure.

He spouted these arguments again and again, but he really got on his high horse when he appeared on CNN's *Crossfire* in the fall of 2004. He complained that the show's "theater" and "partisan hackery" was "hurting America" and, for good measure, called conservative cohost Tucker Carlson a "dick." Stewart was stunned by the reaction to his appearance, which was downloaded on the Internet 670,000 times in the following days. He viewed it as a moment of honest frustration on his part, and in retrospect he believed that perhaps he had been too harsh. But when CNN announced the program's cancellation weeks later, Stewart looked like he had a giant notch on his belt.

His version of the elusive "truth," however, often resembled a liberal assault on the Bush presidency. Stewart announced that he was voting for John Kerry, was opposed to the Iraq war, and increasingly ridiculed the war effort as a giant "Mess O' Potamia." The show depicted Bush as a tongue-tied cowboy and amateurish bumbler. Stewart would argue that Republicans were running the country and that Democrats, lacking any real influence, were a far smaller target.

The show became a magnet for Democratic politicians. John Edwards announced his presidential candidacy on Stewart's program, and Kerry did *The Daily Show* in the fall of 2004. Stewart went rather easy on Kerry between the jokes, although he was polite to conservative guests as well. He believed that liberal activists who saw him as leading them into battle would ultimately be disappointed. He didn't hide his views, but ultimately, he was paid to be funny.

Denizens of the "real" news operations began taking note of the Stewart style. When President Bush nominated General Michael Hayden to head the CIA, Brian Williams observed on *Nightly News* that Bush's remarks "might have sounded familiar." He played a clip of the president introducing his nominee:

"He's the right man to lead the CIA at this critical moment in our nation's history," Bush said.

Then Williams played a clip of the president nominating Porter Goss, the man who had just been dismissed as CIA chief, less than two years earlier:

"He's the right man to lead this important agency at this critical moment in our nation's history."

The anchor added a "full disclosure," saying: "It wasn't our discovery. The strange coincidence was actually uncovered by the crack staff at Comedy Central, the folks who bring you *The Daily Show with Jon Stewart.*"

Williams had seen the bit on Stewart's show, and he was upset with his staff for not detecting the recycling of presidential rhetoric. It was a small glimpse of the impact that a group of comedians was having on the news business. Everyone, even big-time anchors, wanted to be Jon Stewart now, or at least do a reasonably good imitation.

CHAPTER 12

Terror Watch

Elizabeth Vargas was nervous about sitting down with George W. Bush. That was entirely natural, she felt. Any journalist who claimed not to be apprehensive about interviewing the president of the United States was pulling your leg.

Perhaps the challenge was greater because she had never done such an interview before. And perhaps the hurdle was slightly higher because she was a woman. Vargas had spent some time thinking about how to strike the right tone. She believed it was possible to conduct a tough interview with grace. There was no point in being rude. She didn't want to be seen as obnoxious. This, Vargas knew, was a special problem for women. If she was overly aggressive, she would be dismissed as shrill.

Unbeknownst to Vargas, the first battle—simply getting the interview—had been won when she had attended the State of the Union luncheon. Before the meeting, "I had no read on her at all," Bush told Dan Bartlett, his White House counselor. "But I was very impressed with her. She came very prepared. I thought, 'Is she going to try to come in here and show she can stand up to the president in front of these hotshots?' " Instead, Vargas had asked detailed questions about U.S. strategy on Iran and other subjects.

"That's someone I can do business with," Bush told Bartlett.

Now, on the last day of February 2006, the major problem, as Vargas saw it, was time. If you had more time, you could take more chances, ask riskier questions. You would have enough breathing room to smooth things over if you ruffled some feathers. With a tighter schedule, she would have far less flexibility. Vargas called Bartlett and Nicolle Wallace, the new communications director, and pressed for a session longer than the twenty allotted minutes. ABC had promised that excerpts would also run on *Night-line* and *Good Morning America.*

From the moment Bush greeted Vargas in the Oval Office, her nervousness evaporated. She found him easy to be around. First they made harmless chat as Bush showed her around the office and told her how his wife, Laura, had designed the blue rug. Vargas asked whether one of his "very attractive" daughters might have a White House wedding.

When they got seated, Vargas began with Hurricane Katrina. Did the president agree, as a congressional report had charged, that the administration was "woefully unprepared" for another natural disaster or attack?

The problem, said Bush, is that "we weren't getting good, solid information from people who were on the ground." Here Vargas missed a golden opportunity. There had been all kinds of testimony, from Michael Brown, the former director of the Federal Emergency Management Agency, and others, that the president had been explicitly warned about the catastrophic conditions in New Orleans and the imminent danger to the levees that were holding back the floodwaters. But instead of citing specifics, she repeated her question: "So you don't agree with that report that calls the U.S. 'woefully unprepared'?" She also asked whether Bush was being "well served" by Michael Chertoff, the Homeland Security secretary, and, in a Hail Mary pass, whether he would accept Chertoff's resignation. That simply allowed Bush to express confidence in his appointee.

When the conversation turned to Iraq, Vargas dug in. If the country was sliding toward "civil war"—a possibility that she, Williams, and Schieffer had all raised after terrorists bombed a Shiite mosque—"are you willing to sacrifice American lives to get the Sunnis and the Shiites to stop killing each other?"

Bush rejected her use of the term "civil war."

"But what is the plan if the sectarian violence continues? No matter what happens with the level of sectarian violence, the U.S. troops will stay there?" Vargas followed up again and again.

She then turned to the political uproar over the administration's approval of a Dubai company to take over management of a half-dozen American ports. "Would you be willing to scuttle the deal?"

Bush began giving a long-winded answer: "The security of our ports is managed by the Coast Guard and Customs . . ." Vargas had been warned that the president did not like to be interrupted. But with limited time, she decided to cut in rather than let him give a speech.

"But even—"

"Let me finish," Bush said.

Moments later Vargas interrupted again, but did not shake Bush from his script.

She noted that Bush's approval rating was at an all-time low and asked whether he had political capital. Bush, unsurprisingly, said that he did.

During their walk-and-talk around the White House grounds, she was struck by how blunt and freewheeling Bush was away from the cameras. Vargas felt good about the interview. She felt as though she had passed some kind of test.

*   *   *

On some evenings the anchors seemed to be editorializing as much with their news judgment as with their choice of words. The way they framed a story, defined an issue, pumped it up, or played it down set a tone that had real political impact.

In mid-March, the day after the administration's Dubai ports deal collapsed, *World News* led off with an encouraging employment report.

"We begin with signs of strength for the U.S. economy," Vargas said. "Today the government released employment figures that show the economy added nearly a quarter of a million jobs last month and hourly wages rose by three and a half percent. The growth is a welcome surprise for economists, employers, and workers across the country." It was a perfectly legitimate lead, followed by an upbeat report in which the president was seen saying: "American workers are defying the pessimists. Our economy is strong."

But the fortunes of the Bush administration appeared dramatically darker that evening in the opening moments of *NBC Nightly News*.

"It can now be said with very little debate, this is a very tough time politically for President Bush," Brian Williams began. "And in very blunt terms backed up by some surprising numbers, the American people have lately been telling him just that. The latest Associated Press poll has the president's job approval at thirty-seven percent. For some context here, that matches President Clinton at the lowest point in his presidency. Sixty-seven percent of respondents—two thirds of the people—said the nation is currently headed in the wrong direction. The president today acknowledged the reversal in that deal for a Dubai company to run U.S. ports, and he accepted today the resignation of the secretary of the interior, who insists tonight she is not leaving because of her department's associations with lobbyist Jack Abramoff."

In just five sentences Williams had told viewers that Bush was in trouble, that he was sinking in the polls, that he was as unpopular as his impeached predecessor had ever been, that folks did not like where the country was headed, and that one of his Cabinet members had quit amid a whiff of scandal. After that everything else seemed like mere details, including the positive employment report.

It was true that Bush's approval rating had been dropping. But every time anchors introduced a story, whatever the topic, by talking about the president's bad numbers, they colored that story and made Bush sound slightly desperate.

Williams took the same combative stance in March, when American-led forces mounted what was billed as the biggest air assault against Iraqi insurgents since the 2003 invasion. He was struck by how the cable networks had aired the Pentagon's own footage all day as video wallpaper, using the military's official moniker of "Operation Swarmer." Williams could not believe how little skepticism the reporters were showing. The media, Williams felt, were helping the Pentagon do its business by repeating these slogans, and he refused to follow suit. Williams wouldn't even refer to *our* troops, lest he be seen as part of the American war effort. What was going on in the journalism world? Would they ever snap out of this?

On the newscast that night Jim Miklaszewski told Williams that some Pentagon officials admitted that the mission "may have been overblown a bit." David Gregory began a piece by saying: "At his lowest level yet in the polls, the president is left to wonder, which way is up?"

Days later, when it turned out that just eighty insurgents had been captured, General George Casey, the U.S. commander in Iraq, admitted to Tim Russert on *Meet the Press* that the raid had been in "an almost uninhabited area" and that "frankly, it got a little bit more hype than it really deserved."

*   *   *

ABC made one glaring exception to its lukewarm approach to Washington political stories, and that involved terror warnings. The constant question was whether to pull the trigger.

In March 2006 Brian Ross, the network's chief investigative reporter, appeared with Vargas on the set. "Elizabeth," he said, "Pakistani officials tell ABC News they are now picking up indications of the early planning stages of a new attack against the U.S. They say they have no specific targets or timing, but that something is in the works." Without specifics, though, what meaning did the story actually have, beyond possibly scaring people?

Days later, just before the NCAA college basketball playoffs, Ross was back with another urgent-sounding story: "The FBI and the Department of Homeland Security have issued a terror warning tonight. It says suicide bombers may be planning to attack a major sporting arena somewhere in the country."

Ross added, however, that "the FBI sent this warning out today without saying whether it's credible." And after he explained that information about how to attack a sports arena was being carried on extremist Web sites, Vargas asked: "I know we get a lot of these warnings. How seriously is the government taking this one?"

Federal officials, said Ross, "do not believe any imminent threat exists." With those words he undercut the importance of his own report.

Half an hour before airtime, Rome Hartman saw the terror story on ABC's Web site. He immediately called two of his CBS correspondents: Jim Stewart, who checked with the FBI, and Bob Orr, who called the Homeland Security Department. Both reported back by 6:20 that their sources were discounting the warning as routine. This story was bull, Hartman decided, nothing more than old-fashioned hype. Why report the warning at all if you had to add so many caveats?

At NBC, Brian Williams and his staff had had the information cold all day but decided not to air it. Williams thought the story was cheap. He saw it as a classic scare 'em piece of the kind that Brian Ross was doing too often.

Jon Banner, the *World News* producer, was dismissive of such criticism. If federal officials thought the warning was important enough to put out to eighteen thousand police agencies and sports authorities, ABC had a responsibility to report it. Banner knew that he would feel awful if they held back the information and something happened.

Ross made no apologies for being aggressive and felt that his team was so well connected in law enforcement circles that they were constantly getting an early look at sensitive material. He always tried to figure out which of the warnings were worthless, and at times he had to fight off demands to go with information that he deemed shaky or premature. But sometimes you had to tell the public what you knew. The test, for him, was whether the authorities were actually doing something, and in this case they were. Ross knew that his rivals were sniping at him, and one reason, he concluded, was that they wished they had gotten some of his exclusives.

Weeks later the other networks again went on a Brian Ross alert. Vargas led off with what was billed as a Ross exclusive about an important turn in the high-profile probe of crooked lobbyist Jack Abramoff.

"Elizabeth," Ross reported, "federal officials tell us the congressional bribery investigation now includes the Speaker of the House, Dennis Hastert, based on information from the convicted lobbyists who are cooperating with the government."

He chose his words carefully. Ross said that Hastert was "very much in the mix of the corruption investigation," according to unnamed Justice Department officials. Prosecutors were said to be looking at a letter that the Illinois congressman had written three years earlier, asking the Interior secretary to block an Indian casino that would have competed with gaming operations run by other tribes represented by Abramoff. That letter had been previously reported, along with the fact that it was written shortly after a fund-raiser at which Abramoff and his clients had contributed more than $26,000 to the House speaker.

Vargas's inexperience showed when she told George Stephanopoulos that "the political implications are huge if in fact Speaker Hastert is now a target of this FBI investigation." *Target* is a well-defined term in law enforcement, meaning that the person's lawyer has been notified that he is facing possible indictment. Ross had carefully avoided using the word. Stephanopoulos pronounced the implications "potentially seismic."

In the CBS control room Rome Hartman immediately spotted the story on a monitor and asked Jim Stewart and Gloria Borger to make some calls. Within ten minutes he heard back that the Justice Department was knocking down the story with a hard, on-the-record denial. Hartman again felt that Ross was playing too close to the edge.

John Reiss had the same reaction in the NBC control room, and he ordered Lisa Myers, Pete Williams, and Jim Popkin, the senior investigative producer, to look into the matter. Within fifteen minutes, Reiss heard back that his staff had gotten three different denials, with a senior FBI official telling Popkin that the story was a complete overreach. Reiss believed that it was like a number of Ross pieces, where the basic facts were accurate but the conclusions were overstated.

But Ross was comfortable with what he had reported. Perhaps there was a question of semantics. He had been cautious enough to say that the investigation was "at the very beginning" and that "the allegations could well prove unfounded." But if that was the case, it was hard to fathom why *World News* had elevated the story to the top of the newscast.

The Hastert story quickly vanished into the ether, an ABC exclusive that remained exclusive.

CHAPTER 13

Grudge Match

For Les Moonves, who knew something about keeping television viewers entertained, the lure of Katie Couric was irresistible.

Moonves didn't know whether landing the *Today* star was a serious possibility. But he knew what she brought to the evening news table.

Katie, he felt, was a big personality. Katie was probably the biggest personality in television. She was watched by millions of folks every morning. Whatever she did, people paid attention.

Moonves was accustomed to playing chess with the biggest and richest stars in television. Everybody talked to everybody in this business, trying to steal the other team's best talent. Flattery was the coin of the realm. And you had to be patient. It had taken him eight years to lure actor William Petersen, who became a star criminologist on *CSI.*

The news world operated the same way. Moonves had talked to Brian Williams about the CBS anchor job. When Dan Rather announced that he was stepping down, Moonves was flooded with calls from agents for correspondents at both the broadcast and cable networks: *Are you interested in so-and-so?* Sometimes, it turned out, the journalist's contract had another three years to run, in which case Moonves asked why on earth the agent was calling him. But he knew the answer. It was so the agent could tell the other networks that "Les is interested in my client." Moonves felt that many agents inflated the offers that their clients had supposedly received. If an agent said that NBC had dangled a fantastic sum before his man, Moonves would say, "If I were you, I'd drive to Burbank and get them to sign the contract."

As he climbed the industry ladder—vice president of Twentieth Century

Fox, then president of Lorimar Television, then president of Warner Bros. Television, then president of CBS Television, and now chief executive of the CBS Corporation, which had been spun off from Viacom at the end of 2005—Moonves grew convinced that he had an intuitive feel for what people wanted to watch.

Shuttling between his thirty-fifth-floor Black Rock suite in midtown Manhattan and his Beverly Boulevard office in Los Angeles, Moonves spent most of his time worrying about *CSI* and *Survivor* and *The King of Queens,* the hit entertainment shows that filled the CBS coffers. In fact, given the paltry amount of revenue generated by the news division, he found it hard to believe how much press attention was lavished on the anchor wars.

The television news business, Moonves believed, had lost touch with the audience. Sometimes the personalities just overwhelmed the programming. That was what Moonves kept telling *The Early Show,* where his new wife, Julie Chen, was one of the four coanchors: Don't make it about you, make it about them.

Bob Schieffer understood that instinctively. Moonves marveled at the way Schieffer never saw himself as more important than the story. Schieffer was like a great point guard who was more concerned with getting the ball to his teammates than running up his scoring total. The nice thing about Schieffer's success in his first year, Moonves felt, was that it gave the network more options. When Rather relinquished the chair, Moonves felt like he had a gun to his head. But now that Schieffer had actually increased the *CBS Evening News* audience by hundreds of thousands while the other two newscasts were losing viewers, the pressure was off. If Couric decided not to jump ship, Moonves would be perfectly happy with Schieffer in the chair for another year or two.

One option had already been taken off the table. At Moonves's direction, Sean McManus had told John Roberts that they would be going in a different direction for the anchor job, and that he wasn't sure there would be a place for Roberts on the new team. Roberts figured he had been Rather's heir apparent for so long that he would just be a distraction, a vestige of the past, once a successor was chosen. He soon left to become an anchor and correspondent at CNN.

In a twenty-four-hour world, Moonves felt at a distinct disadvantage by not owning a cable news network. Every time he ran into Richard Parsons, the chief executive of Time Warner, he said that he wanted to buy CNN. But Parsons kept insisting that the channel was not for sale, and repeated negotiations about turning CBS and CNN into a joint venture had foundered over issues of editorial control. But it sure would have made it easier to fix CBS News.

Moonves had been wary of the news division from the start. Shortly after taking over the network, he had sat down with a dozen top CBS News executives, describing his philosophy and explaining that he was a news junkie. By the time he got back to his office—Black Rock was all of ten blocks away—he had six messages from print reporters, asking about aspects of the meeting. This was family business, their first big sit-down. Moonves could understand these executives grumbling to their spouses, but it was inconceivable to him that they would immediately blab to the press.

He had been intimidated at first, but gradually concluded that working for CBS News was like getting a job at the post office, where you got to hang around for thirty years without being challenged. Now he was determined to change that. For a Hollywood guy, Moonves realized, he was shooting off his mouth quite a bit about the evening news, but they were in third place. When you were last, you had to take some risks. The first year he had put on *Everybody Loves Raymond,* it was a ratings disaster. If CBS Entertainment had been in first place, he would have dumped it, even though he loved the show, and Ray Romano never would have had time for the sitcom to become a hit. That was why Moonves had bucked conventional wisdom in insisting that *The Early Show* switch to four anchors after Bryant Gumbel, making his morning-show comeback, proved to be a flop. *Today* already had two great anchors in Katie and Matt, and *Good Morning America* already had two great anchors in Charlie and Diane. If CBS just put on two anchors, unless they were absolutely unbelievable, there was no way they were going to gain on the other shows, Moonves argued. At least by using Harry Smith, Hannah Storm, René Syler, and Julie, they were trying something different.

Pushing the boundaries a bit further, Moonves said that he might put on Jon Stewart to do satire on the evening news, and he jokingly praised the Web site *Naked News,* on which fetching women disrobed as they read the headlines.

One year after Rather's Memogate scandal, the news division hadn't hired one new anchor, one new reporter, one new producer, or one new executive. Not a single thing had changed, and Moonves was frustrated as hell. That was why he had taken the unusual step of putting his sports guy in charge when he gave the top job to Sean McManus. Moonves saw himself as the coach, and when you weren't getting results, you tried hugging your players. If that didn't work, you tried cajoling your players. And if that didn't work, you tried yelling at your players. Moonves was determined to change things, one way or another, and he hoped that change would include Katie Couric.

*   *   *

When Jeff Zucker arrived at his new Burbank office in the first weeks of 2001, Moonves was already the king of Hollywood.

It was Moonves who was quoted most frequently by the press, Moonves who had long relationships with the entertainment reporters, Moonves who had deep roots in the moviemaking world. As a former actor with a full head of dark hair graying at the temples—he had played bit parts in *The Six Million Dollar Man* and *Cannon*—Moonves even looked the part.

Zucker, by contrast, was a fireplug of a man, short and nearly bald, with steel-rimmed glasses and a gruff voice. More important, he had spent his professional life on the East Coast, toiling in NBC's news division. Zucker was an outsider to the insular culture of Tinseltown, and some Hollywood veterans were jealous: Who *was* this little guy getting all this ink, and what did he know about entertainment?

It wasn't long before Zucker and Moonves were on a collision course.

These were two strong-willed Jewish men with brash styles who had rocketed to the top of their respective networks. Each was attempting a crossover move to a different part of the business.

Now that he was in Los Angeles, Zucker began to be quoted by reporters as often as Moonves, especially since NBC's prime-time schedule was strong. He became a valuable source who was quite comfortable chatting off the record. He began to take a few jabs at Moonves, who was quick to jab back.

At times they could seem like preening peacocks, each jealous of the other's plumage. When Moonves declared that CBS was more profitable because NBC had higher programming costs, Zucker called Moonves's assessment "one of the more laughable claims of the year."

As *Variety* put it: "Moonves doesn't hide his distaste for Zucker's management skills, openly referring to the NBC chief as 'Zippy' during conversations with agents and producers. Likewise, Zucker—an ex-newsman who's never met a reporter he can't spin—isn't afraid to play hardball in the scheduling room or to openly dis a rival."

They came from very different backgrounds. Moonves was the son of a Long Island gas station owner. Zucker, who was sixteen years younger, was the son of a Miami cardiologist.

Privately, Moonves would protest that he liked Zucker just fine. In fact, he had once tried to hire him. In the mid-1990s, when Zucker was producing *Today,* Moonves was considering replacing Andrew Heyward as the president of CBS News. Zucker, who was the boy wonder of NBC News, looked as though he might fit the bill. They met for a drink at the St. Regis Hotel. Moonves was impressed by the man's energy and saw that Zucker had limited mobility at NBC, where Andy Lack looked to be running the news division for a long time to come.

Zucker wanted to take the CBS News post but couldn't get out of his NBC contract. Moonves decided to stick with Heyward, and Zucker later signed a new deal with NBC.

Away from the cameras, they would joke that the press loved a good feud and they were providing juicy copy. But perhaps they were too much alike.

Zucker was the person best positioned at NBC to persuade Katie Couric to stay with the network. They had worked together for fifteen years.

Zucker was twenty-six when he became executive producer of *Today* in 1991, just five years after graduating from Harvard, where he had been president of the *Harvard Crimson.* Couric loved his high-energy style. Her image of Jeff was that of a man snapping his fingers, boom, boom, boom, getting things done. He was close to Bryant Gumbel, Couric's cohost, as well.

After his ill-fated ventures as the producer of *Nightly News* and *Now,* Zucker returned to *Today,* where he became so competitive in cutting deals to book top guests and cutting off those who crossed him that he was forced to declare, "I'm not trying to be a bully." And when *Good Morning America* debuted a Times Square studio to try to match *Today*'s street-level Rockefeller Center set, Zucker used his network's rights to a giant video screen at 1 Times Square to ensure that a live feed of the NBC show appeared in the background behind Gibson and Sawyer.

The late 1990s were a difficult time for Zucker. He was diagnosed with colon cancer, beat the disease, and then had to undergo treatment for a relapse. He bounced back, however, and many network staffers were stunned when Zucker was named the president of NBC Entertainment at the end of 2000, since his entire background was in news. Suddenly the man who had spent his career shaping the morning mix of serious news and light features would be green-lighting sitcoms, dramas, and reality shows. But

Zucker brought his customary drive and tenacity to the job, and at the end of 2005 was promoted to chief executive of the NBC Universal Television Group, positioning him as the likely successor to Robert Wright as head of the network.

While all of Zucker's news shows—*NBC Nightly News, Today,* and *Meet the Press*—were ratings leaders, the network had fallen to fourth place in prime time. After the loss of such NBC hits as *Seinfeld, Friends,* and *Fraser,* Zucker had his hands full just when the possible loss of Katie Couric was threatening to damage *Today* and create a formidable competitor to Brian Williams's newscast.

Zucker was also giving advice to Williams about how to jazz up the program. The secret—and Zucker knew it was heresy to say this—was showmanship. You might be doing rock-solid journalism, but you had to entertain people in the way you presented the news.

Cable news, Zucker felt, was the best example. Fox News did a sensational job. He watched Fox because it was entertaining. Bill O'Reilly was an actor. Sean Hannity was an actor. Who gave a shit whether they were conservative or liberal? They were fun to watch. That was the biggest mistake MSNBC had made—that it wasn't particularly exciting. As the cable outpost of NBC News, Zucker knew, most of those who worked at the channel felt that they had to be fair, measured, and middle-of-the-road. Nothing failed faster than that.

Brian was personable, funny, and down to earth, and Zucker felt that he needed to reveal more of himself on *Nightly.* The more that he talked on the air in the breezy way he wrote on his blog, Zucker told Williams, the better the show was.

But Williams was reluctant. He told Zucker that he was dealing with serious news, that he was a guest in people's homes, and that he faced limits on how far he could go. Zucker was insistent. Williams had a winning personality and should not be afraid to display it for the viewers. It was a confidence thing, Zucker believed. When Williams was at the Winter Olympics, he appeared in a coat and tie, while Brokaw had worn parkas. Over time, he felt, Williams would mature and become more sure of himself.

Now Zucker had a new ally in the effort. In the fall of 2005 Zucker had forced out Neal Shapiro, who believed that his low-key approach was never a good fit with Zucker's hard-charging style, and named Steve Capus as the acting president of NBC News. Capus, who knew Williams better than anyone in the news division, agreed that viewers needed to see more of Brian unplugged.

If Williams could be adamant about the seriousness of his mission, Zucker, like Moonves, knew the root of the reluctance: It was harder to make changes when you were in first place. It was human nature to say that things ain't broke and there was no need to fix them. The most fun he had ever had was when *Today* was in second place, because then he could take chances, throw things against the wall, and see what stuck. NBC Entertainment had slid to fourth place, Zucker felt, precisely because its leaders had stood pat when they were in first. He told that to the *Nightly News* staff again and again: Don't make the same mistake. Don't be bound by tradition. Don't remain frozen in place just because you're on top, or before long you'll be sliding down the ratings hill.

*   *   *

It was one hell of a victory lap for Bob Schieffer.

For a man who was supposed to keep the anchor seat warm only for a few weeks, Schieffer was feeling pretty good when he hit his one-year anniversary. While the other newscasts were losing viewers, Schieffer had actually brought the *CBS Evening News* to within 300,000 viewers of second-place ABC. CBS was making the boast in its advertising: "More People are Watching." Of course, more people were actually watching the other broadcasts, since the *Evening News* remained in last place. But at a time when the networks worshipped at the altar of the young and sexy, a white-haired, sixty-nine-year-old man had somehow brought the program up from the depths of Dan Rather's final days.

One reason viewers seemed to respond to Schieffer was that he was relaxed, unpretentious, and as comfortable as an old shoe. After the Cheney hunting accident, he led the broadcast this way: "The question was being asked at gas stations, in offices, restaurants, all across America today, and the question was: 'Did I hear that right? The vice president shot someone?'" When terrorists attacked the U.S. consulate in Pakistan just before President Bush's visit to that country, Schieffer said: "Frankly, this is kinda scary stuff we're talking about."

And after watching an interview with Sir Patrick Moore, an eccentric-looking British astronomer, about whether Pluto should be deemed a planet, Schieffer couldn't help blurting out: "How long has it been since you've seen someone wearing a monocle?"

Schieffer had taken some starch out of the anchor collar. When he chatted with the correspondents, he sounded like your opinionated grandfather holding forth at the dinner table.

But some tensions were beginning to creep into his relationship with Rome Hartman, who would press Schieffer on what questions he planned to ask the reporters. Sometimes Hartman would call the correspondents and ask what they were going to say when Schieffer debriefed them. Hartman explained that he was worried about the chats running too long, but Schieffer wanted to stick with the approach he had developed with Jim Murphy when they launched the broadcast.

"Rome, we've got to keep this spontaneous," he told his producer. "We've got to dance with who brung us."

Friends wondered whether Schieffer might try to make Moonves and McManus forget about courting Katie Couric and keep the job for himself. But the reality was that Schieffer was tired. Commuting back and forth to New York was a terrible grind and had disrupted his marriage. He didn't want to work this hard anymore. These late-in-life accolades were wonderful, but he still wanted to hang it up at seventy. Schieffer loved the attention but didn't *need* to be an anchor, which may be why he wore the mantle so lightly.

When Schieffer received the Fred Friendly First Amendment Award during a luncheon at the Metropolitan Club, Brian Williams pulled him aside and took note of his ratings success.

"It is really fun to watch this race for second developing," Williams said. "And I have a very good seat from my perch high above you."

For Williams, this was clearly the best of times. After being mired at a tiny Kansas station, after pounding the pavement in local news, after serving as Brokaw's understudy for a decade, he finally had the job he had wanted since elementary school, and a firm grip on first place to boot. He was forty-six and wanted to hold on to the anchor chair for two decades, the way Brokaw had done.

But one television producer found Williams rather tightly wound over lunch. The friend told Williams to relax, that he was riding high.

"Everyone's always out to get you in these jobs," Williams grumbled.

Despite his initial success, he could get peeved at a colleague whom he knew had once lusted after the anchor job, even though Williams already had it. He was deeply annoyed by television correspondents he viewed as phonies and dilettantes. Andrew Tyndall, a television industry analyst who was sometimes quoted as criticizing Williams, got under his skin as well. What made Tyndall a certified expert? It was a sign of sheer laziness, Williams felt, that television critics kept calling him.

Williams hadn't forgotten the naysayers who mocked him as he prepared to take over, who depicted him as the kid who couldn't start Brokaw's car. You really had to have your own rudder, your own gyro, in this job. If you were deeply hurt by criticism, you would not be able to make it. Williams was not going to pretend to be someone he wasn't. He was a mild-mannered suburban dad who never touched a drop of alcohol and kept his personality, on camera at least, tightly in check.

Despite his growing stature at NBC, Williams did not always get his way. He was pushing hard, with Zucker and Capus, for the network to launch a rebranded newsmagazine. The *Dateline* image, Williams felt, was too soiled after too many years of too many tabloid stories. The once-vaunted show had fallen on hard times. What Williams wanted was a prime-time program that would be a repository of serious journalism, built around the young turks, people like him and Campbell Brown. It was a tough sell, to be sure, but Williams wanted to take his million-viewer lead out for a spin. What was the point of accumulating the capital that came with anchoring the top-ranked newscast if you never used it?

As he labored to keep up with the demands of the job, working so hard that lunch was often a slice of takeout pizza eaten at his desk, Williams faced his share of personal difficulties. His eighty-nine-year-old father, who had heart problems and was in frail health, fell and broke his hip.

The morning after Williams arrived in New Orleans for one of his periodic visits, Jane called on his cell phone. "Mary Jane didn't make it," she said. Mary Jane Esser, his older sister, had lost her long struggle with breast cancer. Williams hastily arranged to get the next flight back to New York and spent the rest of the week with his family. Weeks later he was still working his way through the mass cards in a box at home as viewers flooded him with condolences after reading about Mary Jane's passing on his blog.

During the mourning period Williams had to deal with a messy affair that had disrupted his small staff. A female producer originally from *Dateline* who was not working out—Williams found her pieces too soft for the newscast—was carrying on with a senior *Nightly* producer, despite the fact that both were married. The result was that Williams had to appoint new senior staff members while trying to deal with the awkwardness in the office. Life felt horrible at the moment.

One day Williams was locked in meetings until 4 P.M., trying to contain the damage, which meant that he could not give the broadcast his full attention. President Bush was in New Orleans that day, making his first visit to the Lower Ninth Ward, accusing Congress of shortchanging the city, and demanding billions more for housing and the rebuilding of the decimated levees. Although New Orleans had long been his signature issue, Williams gave the story just three sentences. Both CBS and ABC did full reports on the Bush trip.

The next day Williams realized that he had screwed up. He had been immersed in the office scandal and had missed the importance of the visit. Williams heard that Dan Bartlett had called Tim Russert from the White House to complain about the lack of coverage. Williams called Bartlett and acknowledged the foul-up. He had made an error in judgment, no doubt about it.

Although his program remained number one, Williams was well aware that he was losing viewers, a fact ameliorated by even greater losses at ABC. At times he would fret about the 800,000 people who had deserted the newscast since he took over for Brokaw. He had a singular strategy for dealing with the gradual erosion of the network news audience. He was *pretending* that he still lived in the heyday of the Big Three networks, when they enjoyed huge ratings. It sounded a bit delusional, Williams knew, but he didn't care. That was his right.

*   *   *

Everyone in the business was gossiping about Elizabeth Vargas's job.

They figured that she was on her way out.

Anchors turned the camera on the rest of the world, but they lived in glass houses, and their difficulties, real and perceived, were always on public display.

Bob Schieffer assumed that once Vargas went on maternity leave, ABC would cook up a story about how she wanted to spend more time with her children and give her job to Diane Sawyer, or maybe Charlie Gibson.

Even some ABC staffers believed that David Westin had sent a message that Vargas couldn't handle the job on her own when he sent in Gibson and Sawyer as temporary coanchors.

Vargas had a serious internal problem as well. A number of *World News Tonight* staffers simply did not like her and felt that she wasn't up to Jennings's job.

In this overheated environment, speculation somehow hardened into fact. "My sources now say that Diane Sawyer has secured the position of anchor of the nightly ABC network news show at 6:30 P.M.," Fox News columnist Roger Friedman declared on the network's Web site. The buzz grew louder after Sawyer anchored the program one night on her own. The real reason for Vargas's absence was that she had taken the day off to have her amniocentesis test.

Much of the criticism in the press was unfair to Vargas. She had been the coanchor for all of three weeks when Woodruff's tank hit that roadside bomb in Iraq. Since then ABC had not been able to put on the kind of newscast it had planned. Vargas could not travel to various hot spots as she had hoped, not with the pregnancy. The West Coast edition, which required her to stay at the office until 10 P.M., was a constant drain. Yet she was being blamed for the program remaining a distant second behind Brian Williams and falling closer to Schieffer's third-place newscast.

Vargas was utterly convinced that the critics and competitors who thought that she would give up the anchor job were wrong. On this point she was absolutely passionate, her determination reflected in her eyes. She loved it too much. She had loved interviewing Bush, loved planning the newscast. People could spin their scenarios, but she was 100 percent committed to the job. It was the last way anyone wanted to get a job, succeeding a legend who had died, but now that she had it, she wanted to fulfill her potential and continue to grow.

Of course, Vargas realized that she couldn't control what ABC did. The network bosses might decide that someone else was a better solution to the anchor puzzle. If that happened, if the decision was taken out of her hands when her second son was born, Vargas knew that the other networks were interested in her. But no way would she voluntarily surrender the anchor chair.

What was particularly frustrating for Vargas was that ABC was unable to promote the broadcast now that it was hers. She felt like she was running a race with a cast on one leg. The mere fact that Katie Couric might become the CBS anchor was generating an avalanche of publicity, while the press had all but ignored the actual fact that Vargas had been anchoring *World News Tonight* on her own for weeks on end.

Vargas had a luminous smile that she rarely let viewers see. But she positively beamed when she reported that Bob Woodruff had been able to exchange a few words with his family, and later that he had been transferred from Bethesda Naval Hospital to a facility in the New York area, and again when he won the David Bloom Award for courageous reporting. But she had not been able to see him. The family was still discouraging outside visitors.

Vargas was convinced that her partner would return to the air. "I just have a very good feeling about it," she told Lee Woodruff. Maybe, Vargas thought, she was being a Pollyanna. Maybe it was just a case of wanting something so badly that you believed it would happen.

Now that Charlie and Diane had gone back to their morning duties, Vargas adored doing the program on her own. She felt a greater level of ownership as the lone star. The only person she had to argue with was her producer, Jon Banner. She was gradually asserting herself more in the daily debate over story selection. "I don't have that gene," she would say, if she didn't see the point of a suggested piece.

When three Duke University lacrosse players were accused of sexually assaulting a young woman who had been hired to entertain the team at midnight, Vargas worried about convicting them on the air.

"Imagine that the DNA tests come back negative," she told her staff. "Are we still happy with every single punctuation mark in the script?" Some changes were made.

When the DNA examination did not produce a match with the players' semen, Banner asked Vargas: "How did you know?"

World News was doing a spate of family-related stories: Overweight babies. Postpartum depression. Protecting kids from hazardous chemicals. Suspect vitamins and supplements.

"If we keep doing these pieces," Vargas complained at one news meeting, "people are going to think it's all me." Still, she set the tone, and family issues kept squeezing out politics.

Whatever the mix, it wasn't working, at least at the box office. There was no getting around the fact that *World News* had lost 900,000 viewers over the past year, and that Schieffer's resurgent newscast was coming closer to knocking Vargas out of second place. As the spring of 2006 began, Brian Williams had 9.6 million viewers; Vargas, 8.6 million, and Schieffer, 8.5 million. It was a major hemorrhaging from the end of the Peter Jennings era.

David Westin, of course, had never planned for Vargas to be the sole anchor. During this period he finally got the chance to visit Bob Woodruff at home. Westin was surprised at how cogent he seemed. It was no longer impossible to imagine Woodruff back on the air.

"I want you to take as much time as you want, knowing there's a chair waiting for you," Westin said. But Woodruff had limited energy and still spent much of his time sleeping. Westin knew it would be a long time before he could return.

Westin felt that Vargas had held things together under difficult circumstances, but he was concerned about the ratings slide. By mid-August
she would be off on maternity leave. With each passing day, Vargas's
growing girth served as a reminder of the decision that ABC had failed to
make.

CHAPTER 14

Mind Games

Brian Williams was at his computer, making last-minute script changes, while John Reiss, at the next desk, was staring at the figures on his screen.

"We won by 370,000," Reiss announced. The Nielsen ratings for the last newscast had just come in. It was an hour before airtime, but nothing could disturb their daily ritual of dissecting the numbers.

Williams looked up. "We started out behind by 100,000," Reiss said. *Nightly News* didn't have the strongest lead-in audience. "ABC went up a little, we went up more, CBS dropped a little, and we won the demo by a smidgen."

Nightly had been number one every week since Williams succeeded Tom Brokaw more than a year earlier, but they all watched the numbers and worried about the demo, the all-important 25-to-54 age group. The pressure from management, which reaped more advertising revenue when the figures blipped up, was quiet but constant. Television was an unforgiving business. What you did last week was old news. You were judged at the box office every day.

Reiss had studied the minute-by-minute ratings and found that very few stories moved the needle. Six in ten *Nightly* viewers were women, the average age hovering around sixty. That dictated how Reiss and his staff promoted the show. They might have a great sports story, but they would never advertise it. A piece on breast cancer, though, would get a big ride. Reiss was always thinking: What do women want to see?

Williams felt rather comfortable with the aging audience. This whole fix-ation on the money demo was bullshit, he believed. Older folks bought the advertisers' products too. Besides, it made Williams feel comfortable to know exactly who he was writing for. He was their grandson.

At the moment Williams and his staff were discussing the crisis in Darfur, the mass genocide being perpetrated by the Sudanese government. The story had received little coverage on the networks, but tonight was an exception. Ann Curry, the news anchor at *Today,* had just returned from the region and had done a piece for the morning show; *Nightly* was running a version of her report. Williams didn't like the ribbon, the on-screen headline they crafted for each segment.

"We have to call this 'The Darfur Crisis,'" he said. "No one fucking knows the story. We have to say Darfur, Darfur."

Williams knew that the networks were way behind on the tragedy, and he didn't like it. He decided to call in some artillery on their own position. "It is," he typed, "a story that has been largely missed by mainstream media in this country. In fact, we've been accused of ignoring it and challenged to cover it: the nearly three-year-long massacre of innocent Africans in the Darfur region of Sudan."

Moments later Ann Curry walked into the newsroom.

"Good on you," Williams said, complimenting her on her reporting.

She said she would kiss him, but she had been wearing the same makeup since the morning show. "What do you want from me, babe?" Curry asked.

"We'll come out and I'll say, 'We're been accused of not covering the story. Part of that is the danger. How palpable was the sense of danger when you were there?'"

Curry nodded. "I'll say it's so dangerous, it's called the no-go area." These were not the unscripted chats prized by Bob Schieffer.

When Curry walked off, the talk in the newsroom turned to what Schieffer and Vargas would lead with.

They played the game every day around this time. All the networks looked for clues about what their rivals might do. And in the electronic age they all dropped hints, through blog postings and e-mail alerts.

John Reiss had learned to read the signals. CBS was pretty straightforward about its intentions, he felt, but ABC kept engaging in head fakes. The folks there would imply they were leading with story A and then switch to story B. Well, they weren't the only ones who could be devious. We need to start fucking with their heads, Reiss decided. At times NBC started being deliberately misleading in its own public hints about what would be the newscast's top story.

At the moment *Nightly* planned to lead with Bush's speech that day on Iraq. Reiss predicted that CBS would start off with the deadly tornadoes that had swept across the Midwest, and that ABC would top the broadcast with a government lawyer's misconduct that had disrupted the trial of Zacarias Moussaoui, the only man charged in the 9/11 hijackings.

"CBS didn't even mention tornadoes in their newsletter," one producer said.

That was meaningless, Williams said. "They do feints. It's all a mind game inside an enigma."

Williams saw himself as above that kind of deception. "I've never lied on my blog," Williams declared. "Sometimes I just won't say." If they had something hot and exclusive, he wouldn't tip his hand.

Williams peered across the cubicle divider. "Have you ever lied in the newsletter?" he asked.

A devilish smile spread across Reiss's face.

"Oh, you bastard," Williams said. "I'm *so* much more intellectually honest than you are."

At 6:30 Reiss was wearing his headset in the control room as Williams's voice echoed throughout the darkened room: "Plea for patience: President Bush tries again to shore up support for the war . . ." But Reiss was watching the row of overhead monitors.

"I had it backwards!" he shouted. "CBS is doing Moussaoui, and ABC is doing tornadoes!"

*　　　*　　　*

The next morning Bob Schieffer was in the Fishbowl, near a wall sign that marked "The Hectoring Chair," as Rome Hartman ran through the lineup. High on the list was the legal chaos at the Moussaoui trial.

"God, what a fuckup," Schieffer said, shaking his head. "Can you imagine?"

The 11:30 daily meeting always took place in the narrow, rectangular, glass-sheathed office just off the CBS newsroom. Twenty people were seated around a conference table, with senior producer Jim McGlinchy joining by speakerphone from Washington. Thirteen television monitors were mounted along the wall.

"For the moment," said Hartman, "it looks like the Hawkins piece on the West Bank is the lead." Correspondent David Hawkins was in Jericho after the Israeli military had raided a Palestinian prison. "It has spawned kidnapping and attacks elsewhere in the West Bank."

"Do we have action photos?" Schieffer asked. No one was sure.

Schieffer noted that the day's death toll in Iraq was about eighty. Another producer said it was up to ninety.

Hartman asked whether the Moussaoui story should be in the first block of the show. Schieffer said that depended on whether the judge issued a contempt ruling against the Transportation Department lawyer who had improperly coached witnesses.

"We shouldn't set the bar too high," Hartman said. "Because we led with this yesterday, we're going to need to take note of it. It might be a Stewart chat."

Next on the rundown was everyone's favorite yarn. Three weeks earlier CBS had dispatched Steve Hartman, who handled offbeat features, to Rochester, New York. A video had surfaced of an autistic high school student who, in his first basketball game after being a benchwarmer, had scored twenty points in four minutes. It was a touching piece about how the community had embraced Jason McElwaine, and the response was so overwhelming that the *Evening News* staged an instant replay, running the piece again the next night. Schieffer later bumped into Bob Wright, the NBC president, who had an autistic child and was heavily involved, with his wife, in fundraising on the issue. "That piece did more for the cause of autism than any single thing that's happened since we've been involved in this," Wright said.

Now Bush had gotten in on the act, meeting with the teenager on a trip to western New York. The baby-faced Hartman had gotten into the White House travel pool and snagged an interview with the president.

"This is a great story," Schieffer said, looking up from the interview transcript. "The president says he saw the piece on TV and wept."

"Want to lead with it?" Rome Hartman joked.

"Your headline could be 'We Made the President Cry,' " said producer Reid Collins Jr.

Other producers ran through a laundry list of potential stories, from possible hearing loss caused by iPods to the first school without chairs, designed to fight obesity.

One producer noted that the Sex Pistols had written a profane letter to the Rock and Roll Hall of Fame after the punk group refused to be inducted, calling the hall a "piss stain" and "urine in wine." Everyone around the table had a good laugh, and no one suggested that this might make an interesting item.

After the meeting broke up, Schieffer still wondered whether they had the right lead. "You really think this Hamas is better than Iraq?" he asked Rome Hartman.

"The problem with Iraq," said Hartman, "is that it feels like more of the same."

"But does that mean we're one day closer to civil war?"

Early that afternoon Pentagon correspondent David Martin came up with information that the military planned to send a battalion with seven hundred soldiers from Kuwait to Iraq. It was a marginal development, but with eighty-seven more bodies found in the country, it was enough to persuade Schieffer and Hartman to flip the lead story to Iraq.

Up on West 66th and Columbus Avenue, at ABC headquarters, Elizabeth Vargas was slipping off a tan blazer, then tying a brown scarf over her plum blouse. Her calf-length boots were out of camera range. A makeup woman hovered on the set, enveloping her shoulder-length hair with aerosol spray, then applying eyebrow pencil and eye shadow. It was time for the Webcast.

Vargas began with the headlines at 3 P.M. and led with the Moussaoui trial, chatting with correspondent Pierre Thomas about the likelihood that the convicted terrorist would receive the death penalty. She read the five most popular Google searches of the day, a new feature that had grown out of a partnership between ABC and the Internet giant.

Soon it was on to the controversy at the Rock and Roll Hall of Fame. The correspondent explained that the Sex Pistols had written a letter telling the award officials that "we're not your monkeys." And there was a clip of Ozzy Osbourne, making a speech in his incomprehensible mumble.

"Come on, I understood every word that Ozzy Osbourne said," Vargas cracked. She looked like she was having fun.

When Vargas returned to the set at 6:30—this time wearing the blazer— she led with the Moussaoui trial, as Brian Williams did, while Bob Schieffer kicked things off with the David Martin report on Iraq. Vargas did death squads in Iraq, the Israeli prison raid, wildfires in Texas, a segment on bird flu, and the presidential visit with the autistic basketball player that CBS had made into a national story. Vargas was crisp and smooth, but it was a very traditional broadcast. She conducted no chats with the correspondents, stuck with the script, cracked no jokes.

And there was nothing about the Sex Pistols.

*   *   *

Every day, through meetings, conference calls, hallway conversations, memos, BlackBerry messages, winks, and whispers, dozens of people at the three networks wrestled with one essential question: What is news?

The definition was as slippery as an eel. News was not merely what was important, for important things regularly happened in Latin America, Asia, and Africa that almost never appeared on the evening news. Important things happened in economic policy, in social science, in state capitals, in sports arenas, synagogues, and churches, yet had no hope of making the cut.

News was inherently new, and yet the day's events played in a constant loop on the cable networks, rendering them old hat for many viewers by 6:30.

News that involved famous people had a major advantage, and news that involved those who lacked name recognition did not, unless the television news machine had conferred celebrity on an ordinary person through sheer repetition.

Complicated news was difficult for television, and news that could be reduced to a simple story line was not.

Sometimes things that were relatively unimportant—a runaway bride, a whale swimming through the waterways of London, a man who recovered a Corvette that had been stolen in 1969—made it to the nightly news nevertheless. It helped if video was available, or if it happened in a major city where reporters were stationed.

And sometimes news was simply whatever the anchors happened to find interesting. Brian Williams was often infuriated by airline delays and hassles, so he loved to include any story that reeked of bad service. As a NASCAR fanatic, he looked for chances to feature car racing. But he didn't care much about soccer and had to be convinced that even stories about the game's highly paid superstars merited a spot on the broadcast.

In early 2006, after landing in New Orleans, Williams called John Reiss and asked if anything had happened while he was in the air.

Reiss ran through the list, adding, "Oh, and the president hasn't seen *Brokeback Mountain.*" Bush, the Texas ranch owner, had divulged his failure to see the controversial film about two gay cowboys after delivering a speech in Kansas. Reiss said that the staff didn't see that as a story.

Williams was in an SUV with four women, one of them his wife. He asked them what they thought. They found the tidbit fascinating. And NBC was too high-minded to mention it? Hello?

"John, that story's going in *Nightly,*" Williams said. The people—or at least the ladies in the van—had spoken.

Williams also felt strongly after seeing the movie *United 93,* about the hijacked 9/11 flight on which the passengers revolted, forcing a crash into a Pennsylvania field. He saw the advance screening with Jeff Zucker and Ron Meyer, the chairman of Universal Pictures, a studio that had been taken over by NBC—and that presented a dilemma.

Over dinner Williams said: "I think I'm going to write about what happened in that room." The invited audience had reacted to the film with stunned silence.

"Do it, absolutely," Zucker said. "And start it by saying how you don't care if anyone sees this movie. Don't let people twist your words into the idea that you're shilling for the movie." Meyer also urged Williams to talk about the film. And Williams did, describing it as an unforgettable experience.

Sometimes Williams ordered up a piece for the newscast just because he got mad. When Ann Coulter, the conservative author who knew that hurling ugly charges made her a magnet for television, was publicizing a new book, she launched a stinging attack on a group of widows whose husbands died in the World Trade Center collapse. She called them "witches" and "harpies" and said that they were enjoying their husbands' deaths. Matt Lauer had grilled her on the *Today* show, and the New York *Daily News* had picked up the story with a screaming banner headline, "COULTER THE CRUEL."

Williams was fuming over Coulter's incendiary remarks, walking around the 30 Rock offices and saying that it was time for some journalist to take her down with the question that Army lawyer Joseph Welch had posed to Joe McCarthy a half-century earlier: "Have you no sense of decency?" But was it the place of a nightly newscast to take such a stand?

After the 2:30 editorial meeting, where no one suggested doing a Coulter story, Williams learned from a source that ABC was planning to examine the controversy on *World News.* There was no way he wanted to be beaten on the fallout from an interview conducted on NBC.

"This is the elephant in the room," he told John Reiss. Society determined its own limits, Williams felt, and it was time to say that sliming the 9/11 widows was simply going too far.

Reporter Mike Taibbi was assigned to crash a piece in three hours, and Williams put the question he had been asking around the office into the headlines at the top of the show: "Have you no shame?"

Williams was deluged with e-mail from angry conservatives. A man named John said that he was "disgusted" by the treatment of Coulter: "You have taken what she said about the 9/11 widows and skewed what was there to meet your own bias. What happened to the notion that the news was supposed to be reported objectively and not reflect the bias of the reporters."

A Virginia man named Christopher wrote that "Coulter's criticism of legacy media outlets like NBC seems to be hitting too close to home, so you're trying to destroy her. Your disgraceful politically motivated attack on Ann Coulter only makes me more admiring of her intellect and poise; thank you for making up my mind to buy her book. You people are jackasses which after all is the symbol of your party, the Dumbocrats. NO WONDER EACH YEAR YOU HAVE FEWER AND FEWER VIEWERS."

Williams had tried to make a case for civility in public debate, but in an age when anyone could unleash a torrent of abuse with the click of a mouse, perhaps it had already vanished.

*   *   *

In its early years television was known for retelling all kinds of tales that had already been published in newspapers, and local stations became famous for their rip-and-read style. As the network operations matured, they came to pride themselves on breaking their own news. But even in the early twenty-first century the evening newscasts still ripped off the morning headlines with stunning regularity, and generally without a smidgen of credit. It was no accident, for instance, that the tale of the stolen Corvette ended up on all three newscasts, since it had been trumpeted that morning on the front page of *The New York Times.*

March 2006 was an all-too-typical month for the migration of news from print to broadcast, which moved along a constant conveyor belt. On March 8 the *CBS Evening News* and *NBC Nightly News* reported that some people taking the prescription sleep medication Ambien were sleep-driving with no subsequent recollection of having been behind the wheel, news that had been in that morning's *New York Times.* ABC was in the slow lane, doing the "Ambien driver" story the next night. Only Brian Williams credited the *Times.*

But *World News Tonight* was quicker to jump on another March 8 *New York Times* story, examining how technical problems with the SAT exams had left thousands of high school students with lower scores than they deserved. *Nightly News* got to the SAT snafu two days later, while CBS warranted a failing grade for waiting eleven days to catch up.

Schieffer was a quicker study on March 9, when he reported that "we're not smoking as much as we used to"—which had been the lead story in that morning's *Washington Post*—and that "we are also drinking fewer carbonated soft drinks," a story from that day's *Times*.

A few days later CBS's Byron Pitts was in Bangor, Maine, where crowds were regularly turning out at the airport to greet U.S. troops returning from Iraq, as *The Washington Post* had reported the day before.

On March 14 *Nightly News* reported on cancer drugs that cost as much as $100,000, putting them out of the reach of many patients—as good a story as when it had appeared in *The New York Times* two days earlier. The same night Brian Williams, saying that it "added insult to injury" for frustrated fliers, reported that Northwest Airlines would begin charging extra for front-row and exit-row seats, news that had been launched that morning in *The Wall Street Journal*. Elizabeth Vargas landed on the same story the next night. The following week Williams reported that the airlines had lost a record 30 million bags in 2005, an eye-popping figure divulged the day before by *USA Today*.

The college basketball playoffs also sent the newscasts scrambling for the papers. On March 15 CBS, which was broadcasting the games, reported on the study of "bracketology," the bracketed matchups for the tournament that had been dissected on the front page of the *Times*. The next day NBC got into March Madness by exploring the lost productivity of office workers watching the action online, a phenomenon that had been splashed on page one of *The Washington Post*.

And on March 20 Bob Schieffer introduced a report on "one spot in nearly smoke-free Chicago" that was bucking the national trend of restricting smoking, a bar that had been sniffed out that very morning in the *Post*.

The copycatting went on. On March 27 Elizabeth Vargas reported that "a memo has surfaced that paints President Bush as eager to provoke Saddam Hussein into war." The memo, involving a meeting between Bush and British Prime Minister Tony Blair, didn't just "surface," it was disclosed by *The New York Times*, as the other networks noted. On March 28 CBS reported that the staid *Encyclopaedia Britannica* was being challenged by Wikipedia, an online compendium assembled by users, a bit of knowledge gleaned from *The Wall Street Journal*. On March 31 *World News* and *Nightly News* both reported on a study concluding that prayer by others did not help patients heal. *The New York Times*, which played the findings on page one, and the *Los Angeles Times* and *Washington Post*, which gave the study prominent display, got no credit.

None of this amounted to grand larceny, in that the newscasts did their own interviews in replicating the longer pieces. And occasionally NBC's

Lisa Myers, ABC's Brian Ross, CBS's David Martin, or other correspondents would break stories that the newspapers would be compelled to follow. But in siphoning news from the morning papers without attribution, the newscasts were trying to give the impression that they were more far-ranging and imaginative than was in fact the case. The anchors were professional copycats, always on the lookout for opportunities. They were content to repackage the news for a broader audience, leaving it to print organizations to do the heavy journalistic lifting.

CHAPTER 15

America's Sweetheart

The celebrities were out in force on January 20, 1989, at a black-tie party celebrating the inauguration of George Herbert Walker Bush as the nation's 41st president. Two reporters for Washington's Channel 4 were stationed on the periphery, trying to flag down anyone who looked famous.

"Mr. Rather, Mr. Rather," said Arch Campbell, the mustachioed entertainment reporter, as the anchor of the *CBS Evening News* walked past without so much as a glance in their direction.

Suddenly a female voice rose above the din.

"C'mon, DAN! Give us a break. You used to be a reporter!" shouted Katie Couric. Rather stopped cold.

No one had any way of imagining that the five-foot-three-and-a-half-inch woman with the huge grin and the slightly hoarse voice would one day have Dan Rather's job.

The secret of Couric's appeal was not that she was the roughest, toughest journalist around, although she could be a pit bull and a dogged interviewer. What brought her international stardom was her Everywoman image, the cheerleader-next-door type who shared her laughter and her sorrow with the television audience. She wasn't afraid of giggling or looking silly, and she didn't believe that her antics undermined her ability to handle serious news. But as she grew richer, more famous, more glamorous, more at home with the trappings of high society, her very success began eating away at the qualities that had endeared her to the viewing audience. No longer the sweet girl who colored her hair at home, Couric was now the ever-blonder fashionista who seemed to live a jet-set life. No longer the brave single mother who had lost a husband to cancer, she was the flashy socialite who was dating multimillionaires. All this, of course, emanated from the gauzy realm of image, but image, in television, was what mattered. For the first time in her life, Katie Couric was getting terrible press. In the popular mind, at least, the dynamo had become a diva.

She grew up in Arlington, Virginia, the daughter of John Martin Couric, a reporter and editor for the Macon, Georgia, *Telegraph, The Atlanta Journal-Constitution,* and United Press International, and Elinor Hene, a Jewish homemaker who worked part time at Lord & Taylor. Couric, who was raised as a Presbyterian, graduated from the University of Virginia, where she was a sorority sister at Delta Delta Delta and an associate editor of the student paper.

Couric soon talked her way into a desk assistant's job at the ABC Washington bureau. Within a year she was an assignment editor in Washington for CNN, the fledgling cable network. She did occasional stints as a correspondent until Reese Schoenfeld, the network's president, called the control room and said he never wanted to see her on the air again.

After moving to Atlanta for an assistant producer's job, Couric hired a voice coach to shed her squeaky sound and again made occasional on-air appearances. But when that assignment expired in 1984, the woman who signed off as "Katherine Couric, CNN" was not offered a permanent reporting job. She had, in effect, flunked the screen test.

Determined to make it in front of the camera, Couric moved to Miami, where she spent two years as a general assignment reporter for WTVJ, covering crime and immigration. Two years later she landed the job at WRC, the Washington station owned by NBC.

The station's news director, Bret Marcus, agreed to allow Couric to do the morning news cut-ins. She was a nervous wreck about reading the short headlines, and with good reason: She was horrible. Couric had to run her own teleprompter and time the brief segments herself, with the result that she kept talking long after the station had gone to commercials. The experiment didn't last long.

"Could I do that again?" Couric asked.

"Only if you go to a really, really small market," Marcus replied.

As a reporter, though, Couric was dogged in developing police officials as sources, and she invited one of them to her wedding to attorney Jay Monahan. She won her first Emmy Award for a piece about a dating service for the handicapped.

Couric caught the eye of Fred Francis, NBC's Pentagon correspondent.

He needed a backup and told Tim Russert that it would be a good idea to hire a woman.

"Let's face it, guys in uniform respond well," Francis said.

Russert made the hire, and during her first week at the Pentagon, in early 1989, Couric got lost in the parking lot and was befriended by two women. One of them, a military lawyer, called Couric the next morning and offered her exclusive information about an Air Force captain arrested in Berlin on suspicion of spying on behalf of the Soviet Union.

"Do we do espionage stories?" Couric asked Francis. After being assured that they did, the pair managed to get two confirming sources, and Couric's scoop led *Nightly News* that night.

At 7:15 CBS's David Martin, whom Francis considered the best Pentagon reporter ever to work the beat, came out of his booth and approached his rival. "Tell me you gave her that story," Martin said. The officer, as it turned out, was never charged.

Francis was impressed with how Couric roamed the Pentagon's endless corridors day after day, trolling for stories. She had a glow about her, he believed, that induced high-ranking officials to tell her things. He was a friend of Bryant Gumbel, the veteran *Today* host, who was depressed over how badly things were going with his cohost, Deborah Norville. When Gumbel was in Washington to play golf, Francis invited him to dinner at the posh Italian restaurant I Ricchi and asked if he could bring along his partner. He briefed her on how to handle Gumbel. After three bottles of wine, Couric and Gumbel were finishing each other's sentences.

The next day Francis called Don Browne, who was running the news division. "I think this is a marriage," he said.

NBC began asking Couric to fill in occasionally on the *Today* show, as the news reader or even cohost. One morning when Couric was substituting, Gumbel reported a story about a lost skier who was discovered after setting her money on fire. "With my luck, I'd only have change," Couric joked.

Within a year of joining the network Couric got word that she would soon be named *Today*'s national correspondent. While she and Jay were at the University of New Mexico for his sister's graduation, she got an urgent call from an NBC executive, telling her to return to New York. It seemed that the network brass was going to dump Norville after a year on the job and give her cohost's seat to Couric. Thanks to NBC's bungling, Deborah Norville had been lambasted in the press as the pretty young thing who forced out the much-beloved Jane Pauley, and *Today* had fallen behind *Good Morning America* in the ratings.

But the executives apparently got cold feet. When Couric arrived, all they did was offer her the national correspondent's job. What, then, was the great urgency of summoning her back to New York?

When Saddam Hussein invaded Kuwait, Couric was shipped to Saudi Arabia. The problem was that she kept throwing up. She was pregnant and didn't tell anyone. But Couric was learning the art of the "get," snagging the first interview after the Persian Gulf War with General Norman Schwarzkopf, the commander of the American forces, and chatting up Jordan's King Hussein the next day.

Couric was soon named to fill in for Norville when the cohost went on maternity leave. The ratings instantly jumped with Couric in the chair, and when Norville posed for *People* while breastfeeding her infant son, NBC executives seized on the incident as an excuse to buy out Norville's contract. On April 4, 1991, Katherine Couric was named the cohost of *Today,* joining the team of Bryant Gumbel and Joe Garagiola. She was said to be making about $500,000, half the salary of the woman she replaced. Within weeks, she was just Katie.

As Couric saw it, she commanded automatic respect because she had a track record as a reporter. She wasn't some local weathergirl arriving from a small market. Couric was grateful, in a way, to the local news managers who had kept her in her place until she was ready to move up. But the real secret of her appeal, she believed, was that she was comfortable with herself. Couric had considered watching tapes of Jane Pauley and decided against it. On television, people could spot a phony a mile away. It would be a mistake to try too hard.

Jeff Zucker, who had been Couric's traveling producer when she was national correspondent and soon became executive producer of *Today,* thought that she got by with raw talent and a natural sense of humor but that her lack of hosting experience showed. He coached her to stop trying to imitate what she imagined a network anchor must sound like, and just talk the way that came naturally to her.

The critics, who could be so mercurial, quickly accepted Couric. "She has a comfortable, easy-to-live-with look, pretty without knocking you off the chair," said *The New York Times.*

Couric got a chance to prove her mettle during the 1992 campaign, when the presidential candidates seized upon talk shows as a novel forum for getting out their message. Ross Perot, the quirky billionaire, made what was scheduled as a one-hour appearance on *Today,* and Couric repeatedly pressed him on his folksy generalizations. When he dismissed opinion polls as "goofy," she asked why he had commissioned a $180,000 survey before declaring his independent candidacy. When Perot said that he would ask "people who can afford to give it up" to relinquish their federal benefits, Couric asked: "Who are those people, Mr. Perot?" He said a computer would have to determine that. Things got so hot that Zucker, in the control room, made a snap decision to keep Perot for the program's second hour. Perot later grumbled that Couric, along with NBC correspondent Lisa Myers, were trying to "prove their manhood" by aggressively questioning him.

Three weeks before the election, Couric scored again. Barbara Bush was showing Couric around the White House as part of the mansion's two-hundredth anniversary, and when her husband walked into the Blue Room as the tour was winding up, Couric drew him into the conversation and wound up with a nineteen-minute live interview, ranging from Bush's criticism of Bill Clinton's character to his past comments on the Iran-contra scandal.

The audience clearly liked Couric, but her relationship with Gumbel soon turned sour. As the senior cohost, Gumbel felt that he should continue his longtime role, steering the show in and out of commercial breaks and conducting many of the major newsmaker interviews. He knew Couric was hungry for a larger role, felt that NBC had promised her a larger role, and thought network executives, who were well aware of her popularity, wanted to appease her.

While Couric and Gumbel were careful to remain cordial, they were barely speaking to each other away from the cameras. Gumbel was stuck in his ways after more than a decade on the job, but he also grew frustrated by what he saw as Couric's lack of commitment to the job, the way she would show up shortly before the program started and sometimes seemed unaware of what was coming up in the next half hour. The situation, he felt, was insane.

Andy Lack, the news division president, took Gumbel to lunch and said that he wanted Couric to be a fully equal cohost, sharing even the traffic-cop duties welcoming back the audience in different portions of the show. But Gumbel had no interest in changing. He had been in that situation when he first teamed up with Jane Pauley on *Today,* and it had proved to be unworkable. He was in the final stretch of his contract and doubted that he would continue as Couric's partner.

Their on-screen chemistry may have been of the manufactured variety, but that, apparently, was enough. At the end of 1995 *Today* finally overtook *Good Morning America* in the ratings.

By then, however, NBC management had made clear that Katie was the future of *Today,* and Gumbel had always promised himself that he would quit when he was no longer having fun. A few weeks later Bryant Gumbel announced that he would be leaving the show within a year.

When Matt Lauer, the program's news anchor, was tapped to take Gumbel's spot, he and Couric developed a good rapport, and *Today* held on to its ratings lead. In Zucker's view, Katie was the girl next door, and Matt was the hunk next door. Such were the casting requirements of morning television.

But the year of Lauer's arrival—1997—was also the year that Jay Monahan, who had been enjoying a run as a legal analyst for NBC, fell ill from colon cancer. He died on January 24, 1998, leaving his wife with their two young daughters. It was hard for Couric to believe that the same fate could befall two well-educated men who took pretty good care of themselves: Jay was forty-two, and Zucker had gotten colon cancer a year earlier, at thirty-one. She soldiered on, not just because Ellie and Carrie needed her, but because it helped her to focus on their happiness more than her sadness. Putting her head under the covers wasn't an option. Every day was hard, but Couric was buoyed by the ten thousand condolence cards and letters she received.

After a month off she returned to *Today,* thanking viewers for their compassion and wearing Jay's wedding ring on a chain around her neck. She appeared to be sharing her grief, but there was so much that she kept private.

Couric dived back into the job, interviewing William Ginsburg, the lawyer for Monica Lewinsky, the former intern whose relationship with Clinton had been exposed three days before Jay's death. Working, Couric found, was cathartic. For two hours a day she could distract herself. And she was determined not to lose touch with the real world. Despite signing a new $7 million-a-year contract, Couric kept buying some of her clothes at the Gap.

Still, her emotions remained raw. Once, when Lauer was narrating a story about cancer, she burst into tears. Couric decided to channel her grief into a public awareness effort, producing a five-part series about colon cancer. When someone you loved was dying of cancer, you felt powerless, paralyzed, yet here was something positive, the purest thing that she felt she could do. The segments prompted a flood of calls to doctors' offices and a surge in testing. Two years later Couric underwent a televised colonoscopy, again baring her own life as an example for the audience.

On several occasions Couric was tapped to fill in for Tom Brokaw on *NBC Nightly News.* She had found it easy, pretty much reading intros to the correspondents' pieces, and rather formulaic. Anchoring an evening newscast wasn't on her radar screen. Brian Williams was the heir apparent at NBC, and Dan Rather and Peter Jennings were firmly ensconced at the other networks. In any event, she just didn't find the job appealing.

On the personal front, things began to pick up in 2000 when Couric started dating Tom Werner, the wealthy coproducer of *Roseanne, Third Rock from the Sun,* and other hit shows. But just as her life was stabilizing, Couric got a fateful call from her sister, Emily, a Virginia state senator, with whom she was very close. Emily Couric said that she had been diagnosed with pancreatic cancer. She died the following year.

Despite her personal grief, Couric's professional star was shining more brightly than ever. At the end of 2001 she signed a four-and-a-half-year contract with NBC for more than $60 million, a staggering sum that stirred talk of a new pay structure throughout television news. Couric was making more than Rather, more than Brokaw, more than Jennings, but then, her program was a far bigger moneymaker than any of the evening newscasts.

By now Couric had lived through plenty of history with *Today.* She had gone to Oklahoma City after the bombing of the federal building there. She had conducted what turned out to be the last television interview with John F. Kennedy Jr. before his death. She had been live on the air that fateful morning when she told the audience, "A plane has just crashed into the World Trade Center here in New York City." It was through the accumulation of such moments that a bond developed between an anchor and her viewers.

But the fame and the money that followed also spawned a constant flood of gossip that Couric believed had gotten out of control. The stories spread like wildfire, thanks to the Internet, and came to be accepted as fact, even when they bore no resemblance to reality. People would read these items in two or three places and assume that they must be true. Couric was dumbfounded, and greatly irritated, to learn that some people in the business didn't care if what they wrote was wrong.

Women's Wear Daily had called about an item that Couric was preparing to have a laparoscopic brow lift. She didn't even know exactly what that was. The *Today* publicist dismissed the item as laughable, but the newspaper ran it anyway, and some of Couric's friends heard about it. Couric called the publisher and said that the item was crazy. She was told that it came from a very reliable source. Who, Couric asked, could be a more reliable source than she when it came to her face? After a lawyer friend wrote a letter on her behalf and *Women's Wear Daily* agreed to a correction, Couric tried not to sound defensive. "I can think of a couple of things that could use lifting," she said, "but my forehead's not one of them."

Such was Couric's popularity that she was able to pull off a ratings stunt with Jay Leno, hosting *The Tonight Show* while Leno sat in for her in the morning. In one bit, workers ripped off the bottom of the host's desk to reveal her much-admired legs.

Today was increasingly Couric's show, but over time that became a problem. Katie, and not the news, often seemed to be the star. To some viewers, her antics, which had long been so cute, began to appear cloying. And that provided an opening for *Good Morning America,* which had been rejuvenated under Charlie Gibson and Diane Sawyer.

The morning of July 1, 2004, crystallized the shift in *Today*'s focus. Couric was playing badminton with members of the U.S. Olympic team while Saddam Hussein was being brought into a Baghdad courtroom to hear the list of criminal charges against him. *Today* chose to stick with Couric's athletic adventure rather than cutting away to the breaking news, a decision made worse by the fact that Peter Jennings had gotten into the courtroom for ABC and Christiane Amanpour for CNN. Couric had no way of knowing it at the time, but the image of her wielding a racket while a toppled dictator was facing justice reflected a monumentally bad call by NBC.

The problems, Couric believed, were far worse than anyone realized. *Today* was losing its way, losing its identity. They were dumbing down the program. They weren't chasing stories with their usual aggressiveness.

Couric suggested doing more stories on wounded soldiers returning from Iraq. Nothing happened. Soon afterward *The New York Times* did a front-page piece on the subject. Couric, recalling her time in Miami, proposed an ambitious plan for marking the twenty-fifth anniversary of the Mariel boatlift from Cuba, by chronicling what three refugees had made of their lives. Again, nothing happened.

What was the problem here? Was she crazy? Couric kept hearing that the program didn't do *those kinds* of stories. But they weren't covering politics much either. Friends in Washington told her that *Today* was slipping, that they no longer felt they had to watch the first half-hour, the fast-paced, news-packed portion that had always been the program's signature.

There was no getting around it: The executive producer, Tom Touchet, a former ABC producer who had been hired in 2002, simply wasn't on the same wavelength as Couric.

She called Bob Wright, the NBC president.

"I'm concerned about the quality of the show," Couric said. "It may not show up next week or next month. But if we don't start doing things of the quality that made us number one, we're going to be in double trouble."

Couric complained as well to Jeff Zucker, who was now overseeing all news and entertainment for the network. He was sympathetic, but nothing seemed to change. She complained repeatedly to Touchet, to no avail.

After more than a dozen years with the program, Couric had never been more unhappy. She was frustrated at her inability to make any headway in changing the show's direction. They were shying away from the substantive stories that had always made it the go-to breakfast program. *Today* was losing its soul, and it was her face that was out there every morning.

To make matters worse, the show seemed to be increasingly tabloid. There were times, Couric felt, when they had done the Laci Peterson murder and the Michael Jackson child abuse case ad nauseam. And why was the program wasting its time covering Britney Spears's Las Vegas wedding and her pregnancy?

As Couric had predicted, the ratings soon started to slip. Gibson and Sawyer edged closer, sometimes coming within 350,000 viewers of overtaking *Today.*

Couric saw nothing strange about taking the leading role in trying to fix the program. For one thing, she had seniority over Lauer. She had a stronger journalistic background, since Lauer had come out of local TV. As a former producer, she was much more into the guts of the show, and Matt, by temperament, was more of a go-along, get-along guy. Couric understood that there might have been some lingering resentment over the fact that she and Jeff Zucker were so close and shared the same vision. Perhaps Lauer liked having a producer who was not part of that alliance.

In the spring of 2005, Jeff Zucker approved the firing of Tom Touchet as *Today*'s executive producer. Touchet had been the third man to hold the job in five years. Zucker was also frustrated with Neal Shapiro, the news division president, for not moving more aggressively to revive a program that had grown stale.

Couric protested that she had not gotten Touchet canned, that people were attributing to her a power that she really did not possess. But it was clear to everyone that she had wanted him gone. When Lauer organized a farewell dinner for Touchet, she did not show up.

Four days after Touchet's ouster, Couric was sliced up by *The New York Times* in one of the toughest pieces ever written about a major anchor. Television critic Alessandra Stanley showed no mercy: "Lately her image has grown downright scary: America's girl next door has morphed into the mercurial diva down the hall. At the first sound of her peremptory voice and clickety stiletto heels, people dart behind doors and douse the lights."

But it was Stanley who was wielding the stiletto: *"Today* has turned her popularity into a Marxist-style cult of personality. The camera fixates on Ms. Couric's legs during interviews, she performs in innumerable skits and stunts, and her clowning is given center stage even during news events."

Couric called Jim Bell, the new executive producer, from her car. "I can't believe this story!" she said. "I'm gonna drive off the road. This is unbelievable!"

The review seemed to Couric to be filled with rage and nastiness. If people wanted to criticize her interviewing technique, fine. But why was the focus always on her hair, her legs, and her shoes? If she put too many blond highlights in her hair, did that mean she was a lousy journalist? This was fashion magazine stuff, not worthy of *The New York Times.*

The Stanley piece had rendered some legitimate complaints against Couric. She had, for example, gone through a number of personal assistants. Like most successful network journalists, Couric was demanding and sometimes clashed with people on the staff. But other colleagues and former colleagues spoke of her helpfulness and generosity.

Couric felt that gender stereotypes were a factor in her portrayal. Would a male anchor have been depicted so harshly? How come you never read about the prominent men on television who dyed their hair or went to tanning salons? And some people in the business, she believed, were just jealous of her.

What Touchet's dismissal had done, in Couric's view, was provide an opportunity for all the people who thought she was too involved in micromanaging the show to trash her. *She's lost her mojo. Her hair and clothes are wrong. The show is too Katie-centric.* That last charge, she felt, wasn't true, for she and Lauer had always divided things up. Her biggest frustration was that this was all being attributed to her raging ego. She loved the show. She was proud of the show. If she didn't push everyone to maintain the highest possible standards, what was the point? She might as well be anchoring *A Current Affair.*

Couric had never viewed herself as a quitter and was determined to beef up the program. Jim Bell, a former sports producer, was struck by how tightly scripted the conversations between Couric and Lauer had become. He tried to loosen the reins while cutting some of the fluffier segments. But the run of bad publicity continued, and sometimes NBC did little to help Couric.

When *New York* magazine began working on a "dueling divas" piece about Diane Sawyer and Katie Couric, Sawyer cooperated, and Couric did not. In fact NBC not only refused to make executives available for interviews—except for a single phone conversation with a top producer—but a spokeswoman told author Meryl Gordon that she would be reduced to talking to "disgruntled ex-employees."

The result was an admiring portrait of Sawyer and a less-than-flattering glimpse of her rival. "Couric lost credibility with middle-class viewers . . . Without Zucker around, *Today* hasn't had a leader powerful enough to either make Couric happy or rein her in," the magazine said.

Couric began stewing over the negative stories. When she was in a self-flagellating mood, she would Google herself online and scan the worst stuff. She was disappointed that NBC wasn't responding more aggressively on her behalf. Just out of sheer loyalty, she believed, it would have been nice if NBC executives had publicly gone to bat for her, rather than just giving her private reassurances. Couric felt that she couldn't speak out in her own defense. What was she going to say: *I'm really not a bitch*?

This was a miscalculation on Couric's part. A passive NBC press office could not muzzle her. She had been a journalist long enough to know that if she remained silent, her detractors would fill the void. So everyone was talking about Katie Couric at a time when she wasn't talking very much about herself.

Sometimes Couric bought herself a spate of bad publicity. Two months after the Stanley piece, she devoted an hour-long prime-time special to an interview with Jennifer Wilbanks, known to cable news viewers as the "runaway bride," and her temporarily jilted husband. Wilbanks had gained notoriety by concocting a plot about being abducted by two Hispanic men, when in fact she was simply fleeing her expensive wedding, and television had gone wild over the sociological implications of a woman who had merely gotten cold feet. Couric, who beat out Diane Sawyer for the exclusive sit-down, defended the special, but it was basically exploitation of a media-created tabloid melodrama.

Of course, Couric, like Elizabeth Vargas, had long specialized in stories with a strong emotional component. Couric had interviewed the parents of six-year-old murder victim JonBenet Ramsey; Trisha Meili, the assault victim known as the Central Park Jogger; and the parents of Matthew Shepard, the gay Wyoming student who was killed in a notorious hate crime. Sometimes such stories could be stellar journalism. After the Columbine high school rampage Couric anchored two days of coverage from Colorado and won plaudits for her sensitive interviews with the father of one victim and the brother of another. But it was a résumé quite different from that of most potential evening news anchors.

Once, Couric had been bored by the notion of fronting a heavily scripted half-hour news show. But the battles at *Today* were taking their toll, and she knew that CBS was looking for a permanent replacement for Dan Rather, the man she had chased down at the inauguration party so many years ago. What she didn't know was whether this was a leap that she was really prepared to make.

CHAPTER 16

The Courtship

Les Moonves poured the white wine and began the seduction.

Katie Couric, seated on the living room couch of his Upper East Side apartment, took a sip and listened intently.

"You have two roads," he said. "You stay there, you have a great life, they've treated you great, it's your family, you'll never lose and probably be in first place forever."

He let his words sink in.

"Or," he said, "we have something no one else can offer you."

But Couric was not so easily swept off her feet. She was full of questions.

"Are you guys really committed to doing this right?" she said. "Are you committed to changing the news? To spending the money?" Couric had other concerns: She wanted to bring with her a group of people from *Today*: a few producers, a makeup person, a personal booker.

The woman was nothing if not deliberate. Clearly, Moonves thought, this was going to be a long courtship.

It was the summer of 2005, a few short months after Dan Rather had relinquished the anchor chair, and Moonves badly wanted Katie Couric. In fact, he had wanted to hire Couric for years. The last time her NBC contract was expiring, in 2001, Moonves and Don Hewitt, the septuagenarian producer of *60 Minutes,* had tried to lure her to television's oldest newsmagazine. Couric was clearly flattered by the attempt.

"The only thing I would ever consider leaving the *Today* show for would be to do *60 Minutes,*" she told them in a room at the Regency Hotel rented by her agent, Alan Berger of Creative Artists Agency. "I watched it growing up. Those guys are my idols."

But Couric was not quite ready to give up her morning show perch. Moonves had stayed in touch with Couric, seeking her out at various social events. Moonves was also close to Alan Berger, a friend from Los Angeles whose children had grown up with Moonves's kids.

Once Bob Schieffer took the helm on an interim basis, Moonves began weighing his anchor options. Could he steal Charlie Gibson, or even Diane Sawyer, from ABC? Should he go after Bob Woodruff, who was temporarily filling in after Peter Jennings's death? What about Anderson Cooper at CNN? Or even Matt Lauer? Moonves needed to find out whose contracts were coming up for renewal.

But Couric was his first choice. She was part of the television culture, part of people's lives.

Couric was pondering her choices. For nearly fifteen years she had been getting up before dawn and showing up at Studio 1A, standing outside with the crowds at Rockefeller Plaza, and dutifully performing all the rituals of morning television. Each time her contract was nearing an end, she asked herself: How uncomfortable would she feel *not* doing the show? How much would it bother her to see some other woman take her place on *Today*? And then she would sign up for a few more years.

This time she felt that her expiration date was slowly approaching. She was almost fifty and feeling antsy. And if she was going to make a change, she had to jump off the high-dive and into the water.

In the spring of 2005 Alan Berger had floated the idea in a phone conversation with Moonves. If Couric happened to be available when her contract expired, he said, would you be interested? Moonves said he loved the idea.

In that first session in Moonves's new apartment, near Park Avenue in the East 60s, the couch they sat on was the only piece of furniture in the place. Unpacked boxes were stacked everywhere. The meeting was low key; Moonves told Couric and Berger that he was ready to beef up CBS's news division, which had just been through such a traumatic period, and that Katie would be a great fit.

When the two men chatted privately, though, Moonves did not seem to believe that he could pry Couric away from NBC. After all, Moonves said, if the shoe were on the other foot, he would do whatever it took to keep her.

Couric later met with Moonves and Andrew Heyward, who was still running CBS News. She mostly listened as they talked about how journalism could be made more compelling, more invigorating. Couric came away thinking that she and Moonves were on the same wavelength in believing that the news did not need to be delivered by a patriarchal authority figure from high on a mountaintop.

Her subsequent meetings with Moonves usually took place around six o'clock, in his living room, and lasted more than an hour. Each time Moonves would open another bottle of white wine, serving it in glasses that he and his wife had bought in Venice, and put out a bowl of blue tortilla chips.

"You've won ten years in a row. What else can you do?" Moonves said. "If you do that for five more years, that won't change anything. But if you take CBS and make it a winner, that would be something. They'll never take that away from you."

At every session Couric had more questions. She wanted to know how many *60 Minutes* stories she could do, how many prime-time specials.

"Katie, you can do as much as you want to do, but you're not going to have time to do it," Moonves said. "A *60 Minutes* piece takes a chunk of time. You can do twenty *60 Minutes* pieces, five specials, and the *Evening News,* but we're going to have to slow you down."

At other times Couric worried aloud about the constant demands of being the top network anchor. She had made her peace with the lifestyle at NBC, getting up at an ungodly hour—although she was known for showing up as close to seven in the morning as possible—but being free in the late afternoon and evening. How would she cope with being on call for breaking news around the clock?

"Katie, you're talking out of both sides of your mouth," Moonves teased her, recalling her earlier insistence that she wanted to be involved in every aspect of CBS News.

"Look, I have two daughters and I'm a very active mother," she said. "If there's a story in Iraq, I may not be the one who flies over there."

"You're right," Moonves said. "You shouldn't have to, and that's fine. We have other people who can do that."

During their first half-dozen meetings, no mention was made of money. Since Couric was still under contract to NBC, that was considered out of bounds. Moonves had consulted his corporate lawyers before the first meeting about precisely what he could and could not say. But he knew what Couric was making at *Today,* and there was an unspoken understanding that CBS would have to be in the same ballpark.

Time and again Couric returned to the sizable sums that she believed CBS needed to invest in its news division. CBS News had grown too stagnant, too accustomed to being mired in third place. The whole place needed a face-lift, she thought.

"You can't expect one person to make massive changes," she told Moonves. "You cannot just rely on me. I'm flattered you think I have some talents, but it's really about the operation."

Couric wondered whether she should suggest a figure, a specific budget that would be needed for a serious news upgrade. But she decided that would be crazy. She had to trust these people, or she shouldn't take the job.

She did ask, however, how much CBS was willing to spend to promote her newscast.

"You don't have to worry," Moonves said. "Everyone in America is going to know when you're premiering."

There were little bumps along the way. Couric once surprised Moonves by saying: "I heard a rumor you were moving *60 Minutes.*"

Remove television's most successful newsmagazine from its Sunday night home of nearly four decades? "Katie, you have my word—as long as I'm here, *60 Minutes* is not moving."

Jeff Zucker, meanwhile, had a pretty good sense that he was going to lose the services of his old friend. No one in the world, he felt, knew her better. In the early fall they met in the living room of her apartment, in the East 90s off Park Avenue, whose most luxurious feature was a Steinway grand piano. They sat down in front of the fireplace and talked about her options.

Zucker told Couric that she was chasing a dream that existed ten years ago. If, a decade earlier, she had wanted to jump from a morning show to the evening news, he said, that would have made sense. But not now, not in the new television universe. The morning shows were the big draw, the major moneymakers, and the evening news had declined in importance and was losing viewers. *Today* had made Couric a superstar. Why give up her perch at the premier morning show to join a last-place nightly newscast? He was there both as a boss and as a friend, but it soon became clear that Couric wanted to do something else.

Zucker would do his best to talk her out of leaving, but he understood her desire to blaze a new trail, to get off the arduous morning shift, even when everything was going well. After all, he had left *Today* after eight of the show's most successful years, before returning later on. How could he sit there and argue *why would you ever leave* when he had done the same thing himself?

The *Today* show, Zucker believed, had been the best job he would ever have, despite the fact that he was a top executive. It was the best job Katie would ever have. *Today,* he told her, affords you the opportunity to run the gamut of life. You helped get the country through the Columbine school massacre. Nothing that Rather, Brokaw, or Jennings did was as important. You and Matt helped get the country through one of the worst days in its history during that six-hour show on 9/11.

Television critics, Zucker felt, tended to dismiss the morning shows because of the Halloween costume contests and other silly stuff. But that was the thing about *Today*: You were also allowed to have a good time. Brian Williams would probably disagree, but the morning show was a broader stage on which to roam. It was, Zucker thought, the perfect fit for Katie's personality. And the *CBS Evening News* would be a much more constricted closet.

Still, Zucker had to act as if Couric were leaving, to protect himself and the franchise. In October he called Meredith Vieira, the cohost of *The View,* the all-women chat show launched by Barbara Walters at ABC. Could he meet her after a taping and take her to her next appointment, as ringmaster of the game show *Who Wants to Be a Millionaire?* Zucker picked her up in an SUV with tinted windows and, as they sat in the backseat during a ride of just a few blocks, broached the possibility of Vieira succeeding Couric if she left *Today.* He later arranged for Vieira to have dinner at Matt Lauer's apartment in what both regarded as a blind date. The search for Couric's successor was on, even as her future remained unclear.

A few weeks later Jim Bell asked Couric to lunch at the Harvard Club. He raised the subject directly.

"I need to know because I need to know," the producer said.

Couric didn't play coy. "I think you should prepare for me leaving," she said.

In November Couric went to Zucker's spacious fifty-second-floor office, with its sweeping views of the Manhattan skyline, for a formal presentation of the best package that he could assemble. The man who was always downright cocky seemed slightly nervous. Couric found that touching.

The original offer, the previous spring, had been little more than keeping the status quo: still doing *Today,* with a couple of specials thrown in. Couric had been disappointed. Was this the best NBC could come up with?

This time Zucker pulled out the stops. More money. A four-day work week. Entire summers off. Her own Sunday night magazine show.

It was a good try. But why should she launch a startup magazine show on Sundays, Couric thought, when she could join an institution like *60 Minutes* the same night, and maybe just once get to say, "Those stories and Andy

Rooney, next." And Couric didn't really want summers off, since her daughters spent the season in camp.

She appreciated Zucker's efforts. At times they would talk about the situation as old friends, but she felt that Jeff never really took off his NBC hat. Besides, with Brian Williams firmly ensconced in NBC's anchor chair, what opportunities did the network have, really, that could match the CBS offer? Ultimately, Couric realized, she would regret *not* doing it more than taking the plunge.

The meeting broke up. Nothing was definite, but Zucker was convinced. She was gone.

Couric decided to consult her small circle of advisers. She arranged a conference call with Alan Berger; her friend Lisa Gregorich; Wendy Walker Whitman, the executive producer of *Larry King Live*; her lawyer, Craig Jacobson; and her newly hired personal spokesman, Matthew Hiltzik. They kicked around the Zucker offer, and the consensus was that she should probably go to CBS.

Couric also consulted Andy Lack, who had run NBC News for nearly a decade before becoming the chief executive of the Sony-BMG Music Group. She told him about her conversations with Moonves.

"Katie, you know what? You've got to like the people you're working with," Lack said. "Do you like this guy? Do you think he'd be fun to have as a colleague?"

As the autumn leaves fell and the weather grew colder, Moonves's assessment of the situation waxed and waned. After one meeting at his apartment, when Couric's questions and concerns seemed more pronounced than usual, he told his wife, Julie Chen: "I don't think she's going to do it."

But in the wake of a better meeting a few weeks later, Moonves told his wife that he thought Couric would jump to CBS after all.

Friends also detected several mood swings. Couric would seem excited about the CBS anchor job, but after meetings at NBC she would no longer be so sure.

Within the ranks of CBS News, a significant faction strongly opposed the move. Schieffer was getting the numbers up, these staffers said, and everything was clicking—why switch horses now? What made Katie Couric the great savior? What changes would CBS make to accommodate her? Bob's great success, many at the network felt, was in making the newscast about the correspondents. There was concern that the new show would be more about Katie and less about the reporters.

Moonves was fully aware of the dissenters. He was enormously grateful to his interim anchor, feeling that Schieffer had saved the news division and restored its credibility after the Rather debacle, but Couric was clearly the best choice for the future. Moonves also felt that newsrooms were places of endless disgruntlement. You could put Jesus Christ in the chair and some folks would say, gee, what a bad choice.

The biggest factor working against him, he believed, was Couric's strong sense of loyalty to NBC. He admired that, to be sure. When stars from other networks told him how badly they were being treated, Moonves figured that in a couple of years they would be complaining about CBS as well. He knew how close Couric was to Zucker and wasn't sure that, in the end, she could cut the cord.

"That's going to be a hard walk for Katie, to walk down that hallway and knock on Jeff's door," Moonves told Alan Berger.

Couric began to wonder whether she would be comfortable working with the other top executives at CBS. She asked Jeff Fager, who had succeeded Hewitt as executive producer of *60 Minutes,* to visit her.

"I haven't had so many men in my apartment since my husband died," Couric told him.

Fager reassured Couric that he was committed to having her on *60 Minutes* but said there were some things she needed to understand. This was an ensemble program. There was no star system. Fager did not think that had been a comfortable situation for Diane Sawyer when she had worked for the show. Perhaps the only star, by virtue of longevity, was eighty-seven-year-old Mike Wallace, the only correspondent who could grab your story and get away with it. Otherwise, *60 Minutes* was a team effort.

"I respect that, and I want to be part of it," Couric said.

In December CBS moved the first chess piece. The network's attorneys had concluded that it was legal under Couric's NBC contract to send her an offer letter—as long as she didn't respond. *That* would be a negotiation, and she was barred from negotiating. So Moonves had a letter sent to Berger, outlining a five-year deal.

Jeff Zucker, naturally, was anxious to know whether one of his company's biggest assets was going to defect. "I need to know what's going on," he told Berger.

"I can't tell you what's going on unless you let us negotiate with CBS," Berger responded. But Zucker refused.

In January Couric began meeting with Sean McManus at her apartment. He struck her as very serious, very earnest. At first, Couric thought, he had a bit of a deer-in-the-headlights look about the enormity of their discussions.

But even though he was a stranger to the news world, she liked the fact that he had run a sports bureaucracy.

Couric repeated her pitch about the importance of spending money. "I don't want to do this unless you're really investing in the news division," she said.

McManus said he hadn't taken his new job to lag behind the competition. "My ass is on the line too," he said.

Their conversations would stretch for two hours at a time. McManus was immediately drawn to her. There was no facade to the woman. The courtship reminded McManus of the way he had lured Dick Engberg from NBC Sports seven years earlier. Fortunately, since CBS had won back pro football, he could offer Engberg the one thing that NBC could not, and that was broadcasting National Football League games. This time the trump card was the anchor job.

McManus quickly became convinced that Couric was going to make the leap. She had all these specific ideas about what she wanted to do with the *CBS Evening News* and with her role on *60 Minutes.* She told him that she was determined to be a regular presence on the network's Web site and to get involved with CBS radio as well.

The more they talked, the more excited Couric seemed. Her major concern was the news budget. McManus assured her that CBS would step up to the plate, that the resources would be there for a truly competitive show.

Couric also invited Rome Hartman, the *Evening News* producer, to her apartment for a series of meetings. She had known Hartman slightly since she was NBC's number-two reporter at the Pentagon in the late 1980s and he was the White House producer for CBS. Couric and her husband Jay had gone out to dinner a few times with Rome and his wife.

Over tea, Couric was brimming with ideas. What if, on slow news days, they did broadcasts devoted to a single subject? What if they gave names to regular segments? What if they let some interviews run as long as five minutes? Hartman said that was hard to pull off, because other pieces would have to be killed, but it could be worth doing if the story was compelling enough. They were feeling each other out, trying to envision what a *Couric Evening News* would look and sound like.

These meetings with the executives were crucial. Couric felt that she needed to get inside their heads, to understand their vision and figure out how she fit in.

Couric turned over the options in her mind again and again. These opportunities, she realized, didn't come up very often. She had done the *Today* show for fifteen years and been on top for a decade. What else was there left to prove? She wanted to leave the job while she still loved it.

If she went to CBS, Couric thought, she would be surrounded by new brains, new people. It was like going to a new school and encountering new teachers and classmates. She would feel reenergized.

Matt Lauer wondered whether Couric would really walk away. When *Good Morning America* was threatening to overtake their show, he figured that Couric might stay just to prove that she could catapult them back to unchallenged supremacy. But when Jim Bell helped *Today* widen its ratings lead again, Lauer figured that Couric was likely to jump ship. Whether that was a good idea was another question. Lauer told a friend that he did not think Couric would succeed at 6:30 because the format didn't play to her strengths.

Tom Brokaw sounded a cautious note, telling Couric that she would feel greatly constrained by having to pack everything into a half-hour program.

For all the talk about the decline of the evening news, Couric felt, it was still an incredibly vital outlet for information. But it was time for some retooling. The format seemed so stale: a minute-thirty package, a voice-over. A minute-thirty package, stocks. A minute-thirty package, today at the White House. There was no reason the evening news couldn't have more four-minute pieces. It was mostly about storytelling, just like in the morning. Everyone was bombarded with information: cable, the Internet, iPods. They had to figure out something different, forge some new tributaries to get people to take a dip.

Couric had to laugh when she read all these ridiculous analyses of how she might do at 6:30, how she was a lousy news reader and so on. It was so easy to pigeonhole someone who worked in morning television. One friend had told her, "The fundamental problem, Katie, is that you're really good at the light stuff too." The people who groused that she didn't have the proper news background clearly didn't watch the *Today* show, especially the first half-hour, when she and Lauer did most of their newsmaker interviews.

What the naysayers didn't understand was that she wouldn't go to the *CBS Evening News* if she was just going to sit in front of the prompter and read, *"Tonight in Iraq . . ."* She wasn't going to deliver the news in stentorian tones. That wasn't her style. People wanted realness and authenticity. You had to take complicated stories, such as the Valerie Plame leak investigation, and explain why they mattered, not just serve up alternating spin from each side. They were going to experiment, to play with the guts of the newcast. Some things would work, some wouldn't, but they were not going to stand pat.

As for the lighter side of *Today,* you had to perform on morning television, you had to be a personality. Making pizza with a famous chef, talking fashion with a famous designer—she had never felt above that sort of thing. Viewers lived vicariously by watching you rub shoulders with the famous. There was nothing wrong with showing different sides of yourself. Even Dan Rather had fun on the weekends, didn't he?

By early February McManus had concluded that Couric was going to be his new anchor. In their conversations she stopped using the word *if* and started talking about *when.* "When we come on in September," she asked, "are we going to anchor from New York that week or go on the road?" Katie was ready. He could see it in her eyes.

Couric was reaching the same conclusion as she prepared to head off to Italy for the Winter Olympics. Moonves, on the other hand, worried that three weeks in the snow with her longtime NBC family might cause her to get cold feet.

During the Olympics Couric sought out Brian Williams, and they had a long talk over a couple of burgers. Couric asked about his schedule as an evening news anchor. They ranged widely over television and cancer and life. Williams said it was sad that they hadn't spent more time together. But he also served up a half-joking warning: "You know, I'm gonna come after you. I feel awful about it." In other words, if Couric left, he wished her well, but not too well.

Couric, for her part, told him: "You know what the honest-to-God answer is? I don't know."

Back home after the Olympics, Couric wanted to make sure that her family was comfortable with the move. During a dinner-table meeting with her daughters, Ellie, who was fourteen, and ten-year-old Carrie encouraged her to take the job. Couric was sad to leave her television home and couldn't stand the idea of the final negotiations degenerating into a harsh competition for the "talent." She had seen plenty of bad transitions and knew how disastrous they could be.

In early March Berger asked Zucker yet again whether his client could begin formal talks with CBS. Zucker faced the prospect of going to the May upfronts—the big New York meetings where the networks pitched the upcoming season to advertisers—without being able to say whether Couric would remain at *Today.* It was time to bite the bullet.

In a meeting in Zucker's Burbank office, Berger and Craig Jacobson sat down, along with Mark Graboff, an NBC executive vice president. Zucker agreed to give Couric a one-week contractual window to cut a deal with CBS.

From that moment the negotiations went surprisingly smoothly. "This is not going to be a choice about money," Couric told Moonves.

Her side asked for a huge sum of money and substantial perks, but Moonves dismissed that approach as the usual negotiating tactic. Over the next three days, with Berger communicating by phone from a corporate retreat at the Ojai Valley Inn in northern California, the details were hammered out, mainly with Sean McManus.

CBS eventually offered Couric $75 million for a five-year deal, slightly less than she was earning at *Today*. Both sides knew that she could probably win a bigger package by staying at NBC. After all, according to estimates by one industry group, *Today* had generated $600 million in advertising sales in 2005, compared to a relatively paltry $156 million for the *CBS Evening News*. But Couric was more interested in tackling a fresh journalistic challenge than in squeezing a few more dollars out of her new employer.

Late on a Friday afternoon in mid-March, Berger called Couric to say that the final points had been resolved and the deal was done. When Couric went to Zucker's office with the news, it almost felt pro forma.

It was a bittersweet moment for Jeff Zucker. Katie was his friend, they had essentially started out together at *Today*, and he was happy for her. Professionally speaking, Zucker hated to see her go, but he thought that Meredith Vieira, whom he was on the verge of signing, would make a very strong replacement. This really had nothing to do with him, *Today*, or NBC. Zucker had known all along that he would probably lose Katie. The position she wanted already belonged to Brian Williams.

Now the only challenge was keeping the secret. Couric didn't want to announce the CBS deal until her fifteenth anniversary at *Today*, in early April.

As confident as Couric was, she felt a certain amount of trepidation as well. Could she really pull this off? Would a new audience accept her as the face of CBS News? There was no turning back now.

After so many meetings at his place, Moonves went to Couric's apartment for the first time to celebrate. They drank a toast, this time using her wine.

Moonves was told that Couric would make the announcement that Thursday. Then he got a call saying that the date had been moved up to Wednesday. "You know what this means? They have their deal done," he told a colleague. Zucker, Moonves figured, must have come to terms with Meredith Vieira as Couric's replacement and wanted to hold a news conference the day after Katie went public. Since no one liked making major announcements on Friday—the Saturday newspapers had the lowest readership of the week—Zucker was changing the schedule.

Moonves had told almost no one about the state of the negotiations, figuring that once the word got beyond a tiny inner circle, it was almost certain to leak out.

The uncertainty presented Schieffer with a dilemma. He was scheduled to leave town on Wednesday for a speech at his alma mater, Texas Christian University, at the journalism school that had been named for him. There was no way he could cancel. What if CBS announced that day that Couric would be taking over his job? In today's world, without bothering to call him for comment, some blogger would write that Bob Schieffer got pissed off at Katie's hiring and had walked off the set. It didn't matter how obscure the blogger was, Schieffer thought, it would get picked up by the *Romenesko* media news site or *Media Bistro* and ricochet around the world. It would take months to repair the false impression.

Schieffer told Hartman that he should make a videotape congratulating Couric, and if the deal was announced, they could play it on tomorrow's evening news.

He went into the studio and read his lines: "Well, the news is out that Katie Couric is coming to CBS News, and I for one could not be happier."

That night Schieffer was having dinner at the Union Square Café when his cell phone rang. It was Katie. She wanted him to know that she would be announcing her new job the next morning on *Today*.

"I just want to tell you," Couric said, "I don't think this would have happened had it not been for you. I'm really excited about doing it. I really appreciate the nice things you've said. You've made me feel welcome."

The word was quietly spreading. Jeff Zucker called Brian Williams at home to warn him that Couric's departure was about to become official.

Jeffrey Immelt, the chairman of General Electric, summoned Couric to his office and was gracious about her plans. "I know you're doing this for the right reasons," he said. "I'm really sorry you're going to be leaving NBC, but I get it."

Immelt strongly hinted that he did not want Moonves to be able to use the situation to trash Zucker for losing her. Couric, too, was mindful of the history of verbal sparring between the two men. There was no reason for everyone to get into the sandbox. She did not want to be seen as a piece of property being sold from one corporate boss to another. She made clear to Moonves and Zucker that she wanted them on their best behavior.

Over the next few hours there was a flurry of phone calls between the NBC and CBS press offices and Matthew Hiltzik, Couric's spokesman. NBC executives felt that they had been magnanimous in allowing Couric to negotiate early for the CBS job, and Couric had agreed to serve out her last two months at *Today.* Zucker didn't want CBS doing any kind of victory dance in the end zone. CBS could not trot Katie out at a press conference, NBC insisted. She could not grant any on-the-record interviews, and neither could top CBS executives. Moonves, not wanting to upset Couric, agreed to the conditions. He believed that as long as he didn't speak to any reporters on the record, Zucker would be mollified.

At 7:30 A.M. on April 5, 2006, Katie Couric, sitting next to Matt Lauer, announced what she called "the worst-kept secret in America."

"It was really a very difficult decision for a lot of reasons," she said. "First of all because of the connection I feel with you." She closed by offering "a heartfelt thank you for a great fifteen years." Couric never got around to saying that she was going to CBS; Lauer had to prod her into mentioning it.

It was a watershed moment. Nearly sixty years after the first network newscast flickered on black and white sets across America in the wake of World War II, a woman would now be the solo anchor of one of the prestigious evening programs. No network had ever trusted a female to be anything more than part of a boy-girl team.

CBS was offering reporters all kinds of interviews. Sean McManus, Rome Hartman, Jeff Fager, and Lesley Stahl would all be available, and Moonves would talk on a background basis. But in mid-morning Hiltzik called Sandy Genelius, the top spokeswoman for CBS News, and complained that the media blitz was violating the agreement the two networks had worked out the night before. Moonves agreed to back off, and Genelius called reporters back to say that the interviews were being canceled, with only a few CBS executives available on a not-for-attribution basis.

Inside the CBS newsroom there was a celebratory feeling. McManus was in the midst of a whirlwind—he had just gotten back from college basketball's Final Four a few days earlier, and he was leaving in a few hours for the Masters golf championship. McManus told the staff that this was his most exciting day at CBS since he'd won back the rights to carry the NFL eight years earlier. Getting Couric was a game-changing event that could have an enormous impact on a network, and such events were rare indeed.

McManus reassured the staff that they would not turn the newscast into

Entertainment Tonight, with forty stories a night and lots of upbeat music, in an attempt to persuade thirty-year-olds to watch. He said he was not going to obsess over the ratings and conclude that Couric's hiring was a disaster if they weren't number one after a month, or four months, or six months. It was all about building a better newscast, he insisted. Then Schieffer appeared on videotape, a longer one than he had made for the broadcast, and said he had known Couric since she was a Pentagon reporter, that he admired her, and that her hiring showed that CBS was playing to win at the highest level.

Now that it was official, Les Moonves called Jeff Zucker to thank him for allowing the early negotiations. "You guys handled this like real gentlemen," Moonves said. "You were really classy."

Moonves also congratulated him on snagging Meredith Vieira, who had worked for CBS back in her *60 Minutes* days. "We were not happy about that," Moonves allowed. "That was a great get." Zucker was gracious and wished Moonves good luck with Katie.

Moonves also tried to score points at home. "See, Jules, I did this for you, to help *The Early Show,*" he teased his wife, meaning that a major rival had been removed for Julie Chen's low-rated morning program.

He knew that there would a huge debate in the press: Katie will be great, Katie will be terrible, Katie is a breath of fresh air, Katie can't handle the job. He had warned Couric as much. Indeed, the avalanche of press coverage was remarkable, even by the media's usual standards of self-absorption. Cable chat shows argued over Couric's suitability to be an evening news anchor. *The New York Times* ran five stories in one day. The Associated Press and *TV Guide* took a poll (49 percent had wanted Couric to stay at *Today,* while 29 percent favored the jump to CBS). And the television critics were locked and loaded.

"The woman who dressed in Marilyn Monroe and SpongeBob Square Pants outfits on Halloween and gave viewers a tour of her colon will take the position once held by the iconic Walter Cronkite and the ousted Dan Rather," wrote the AP's David Bauder.

"Star power is the reason CBS is hiring her . . . Gravitas is a non-factor, because she doesn't have it," said Tim Goodman in the *San Francisco Chronicle.*

"I've seen Katie Couric swoon and giggle far too many times from her *Today* show perch . . . The nightly news isn't banter from your girlfriend," groused Florangela Davila of *The Seattle Times.*

And that wasn't all. The Web site *Jossip.com* ran a high school photo of Couric in a cheerleading outfit. *Star* magazine did a spread on "Katie's Amazing GLAMover," with before-and-after shots and scribbled notes about her "more feminine" hair and "longer, fake eyelashes."

The moment was revealing. Almost no one really talked about what kind of broadcast the *CBS Evening News* would be under Couric, except in mocking tones. Her plans for the program were essentially deemed irrelevant. It was all about Katie: her personality, her wardrobe, her legs, her hair, her laugh, her sincerity, her morning show antics, her degree of gravitas or lack thereof. This was driven in part by her high-octane celebrity, the way her every date or charity endeavor showed up in the gossip columns. And, Couric believed, it was driven in part by envy, particularly among men who were miffed that she was commanding $15 million a year.

The notion that a woman in a dress would be delivering the news challenged a cultural assumption deeply embedded in the country's psyche. *What if there was another terrorist attack? Another killer hurricane? Would America really turn to . . . Katie?* Yes, Couric had done some silly things before morning show audiences. But she had also interviewed presidents and world leaders and business titans, had interviewed grieving families in times of tragedy, had been on the air on 9/11. Tom Brokaw had endured some of the same razzing when he jumped from *Today* to *Nightly News,* but nothing like this. Even in 2006 the country was conflicted over a woman taking a seat that had long been reserved for the other sex. And a few of the critics at CBS could not restrain themselves.

"She doesn't fit the image that we have of ourself as a hard news operation, a Walter Cronkite kind of news operation," said Andy Rooney, the curmudgeonly *60 Minutes* commentator.

Bob Schieffer was excited about Couric's hiring. But he did get a word of advice from an old friend.

"Wait'll you get a load of this," Tom Brokaw told him. "She's got all these people around her telling her how great she is. She's behind this wall."

There was considerable grumbling in the hallways at CBS. What happened when the novelty of having Katie in the chair wore off? What if she turned out to be another Geraldine Ferraro, who had been a bust as a vice presidential candidate?

Rome Hartman wondered how Schieffer really felt about it all. This had to be hard for Bob. There was no way to calculate how much he had loved sitting in the anchor chair, much more than he had originally expected. Schieffer had been amazingly gracious, but when it finally came down to it, giving up such a coveted post wasn't easy.

Schieffer would never say so publicly, but he did feel a twinge of regret. He had never expected his anchor stint to last as long as it did, and he was extremely proud of what he had accomplished. He had finally gotten a chance to put his ideas about news into practice. If pressed, he told McManus, he would have agreed to stay through the 2008 election. But Pat was thrilled at the prospect that her husband would no longer have to commute to New York every week, and he had to think about his health. He had survived his cancer scare, and his diabetes was under control at the moment, but he was sixty-nine years old and it was time to step back. He didn't want to kill himself. Schieffer was telling the skeptics at CBS that trying to torpedo his successor wouldn't help anyone. It was in their self-interest to make Couric a success.

Schieffer planned to return to his old role as chief Washington correspondent. There was some talk at the network about him doing three commentaries a week for the evening news, but he wasn't sure he had quite that much to say. Plus, he had to talk to Katie. She might not want him in that role, and it would be her broadcast now.

At 6:15, nearly twelve hours after the announcement on *Today,* Brian Williams was editing his last couple of scripts when his phone rang.

Katie Couric apologized for not calling him the night before. She had woken up Ann Curry, the *Today* news anchor, with her bulletin and was wary of calling too late.

"You know," Williams said, "it's just a matter of personal preference, but I choose to write at this time."

"This is a bad time?" Couric asked, playing dumb. "Okay, so you air at what time?"

"As you'll find out, six-thirty Eastern, although we're on at seven o'clock in D.C. . . ."

Williams had only a couple of minutes to get into the studio. "Listen," he said, "let's have lunch in a very public place, like Michael's, and get everyone talking. If this is what you want, mazel tov. Let's have at it."

Twenty-five minutes later the newscasts took note of the Couric announcement.

"This is a very big day for us here at CBS News," said Russ Mitchell, filling in as *Evening News* anchor, before tossing to the Schieffer tape.

"It is great to welcome another woman to the evening news," Elizabeth Vargas said.

Williams opted for subtlety. "Our friend Katie Couric is about to become competition officially," he said. Then he deadpanned, "And we wish her the very best—right up to a point."

Vargas thought some of the criticism of Couric, who had been kind to her when she nervously filled in on *Today,* was rather sexist. Katie was a tough interviewer; she would do a great job for CBS and become a fierce competitor. But Vargas much preferred to keep a lower profile. She had been a jock in high school, a gymnast and a skier, and had learned that you never won by watching the other guy while you were competing.

Moonves and his wife decided to take Couric out for a celebratory dinner at Elio's, an Italian eatery on Second Avenue. When the couple arrived, Tom Selleck, whom Moonves had dealt with in Hollywood, was at the table they had reserved, and he politely got up to finish his coffee at the bar. When Couric arrived, she started laughing uproariously. Matt Lauer was sitting at the very next table.

"I just signed him, too," Moonves joked.

Brian Williams was bemused by all the media chatter about how Katie was going to revolutionize television news. But he was disturbed by one of the details of Couric's contract that had leaked out: CBS would pay her more money if the broadcast hit certain ratings targets.

That had to be a first, a sad first, for an evening news anchor. That would beckon the *CBS Evening News,* the broadcast he had once considered taking over, down a very dangerous road. It might even lead to stories about spring break, live executions, cash giveaways, and baby pandas. It was playing with fire in the House of Murrow. If you won the night with a car chase on Tuesday, wouldn't you scan the satellite feeds for another good chase on Wednesday? The temptation would be to chase any subject that would move the needle. This clause, he felt, was the equivalent of crack cocaine.

Williams wondered how all this information about anchors' contracts made its way into the press. Everyone kept reporting that he was making $4 million a year. In fact, Williams was earning considerably more. How could people make up these numbers? What if he just guessed at stuff in his job?

He wasn't especially worried that Couric was far more famous than he was and making a far bigger salary. He had married a modest woman, and they couldn't believe how much money they already had. He had stopped his last negotiation with NBC when he felt that his compensation was more than adequate. In private, Williams made a bold prediction. He told friends that Bob Schieffer's core audience, the hard-core fans devoted to hard news, wouldn't dig Katie Couric.

Sean McManus was worried about the media feeding frenzy that would undoubtedly surround Couric's debut: Would they show her legs? Would she wear a more mature hair style? Would her clothes be more subdued? Of course, McManus figured, it was better than the opposite: no one writing about you at all.

The week after the announcement Bob Schieffer had lunch with Katie Couric at Michael's, the media world's see-and-be-seen midtown eatery, as a public show of support. Barbara Walters, who was dining with Tipper Gore, stopped by their table and talked about how much more positive the reaction to Couric's move had been than when she had been installed as ABC's coanchor three decades earlier.

Once Couric's chicken salad arrived, along with Schieffer's twenty-eight-dollar rib-eye burger, she asked him about the major players at CBS. The talk turned to the conversational format that Schieffer had adopted when he succeeded Rather. "What will make this work is if you do it my way plus one," Schieffer said. Chat up the correspondents, he said, but don't be afraid to hold a piece to make room for a hot interview with a major newsmaker.

Couric said she was worried that the anchor's office was on the second floor. "I want to be closer to people," she said. Schieffer said that she would come to appreciate the solitude of the office.

One other thing was bothering Couric.

"Does Andy Rooney really reflect how some people feel over there?" she asked.

"We love Andy, but he doesn't reflect a majority opinion," Schieffer replied.

But Rooney's impolitic remarks did represent a minority attitude that Couric would have to confront. Schieffer, for his part, felt that Couric didn't have anything to prove. She didn't have to put a scowl on her face just to show she was a serious person.

As NBC played up Couric's final weeks on *Today,* with endless tributes and highlight reels, even the departing star was a little embarrassed by what she called "a celebration of moi, ad nauseam." Jeff Zucker found it a bit awkward to be showering publicity on a woman who was about to become a CBS star, but he felt that Couric deserved a grand send-off, and besides, the long goodbye was good for ratings.

But the cumulative effect was over the top, an orgy of self-congratulation more fitting for the retirement of the queen mother than the migration of a journalist to another network. The continuous loop of images of Couric the performer—singing, dancing, leaping, ice skating, mugging for the cameras—seemed to underscore what troubled the skeptics about the prospect of Couric the serious evening anchor. Even she sensed the disconnect. One morning, after a series of clips showing her dressed up as Sponge-Bob SquarePants, Mary Poppins, and Marie Antoinette, and then soaring through the air in a silly green Peter Pan costume, the camera turned back to Couric. She told Matt Lauer the first thing that popped into her head.

"CBS just called and retracted their offer," she joked.

CHAPTER 17

Back to New Orleans

The siren was blaring as the white sheriff's car picked up speed and the Superdome receded in the rearview mirror.

"That's where we saw the first body," Brian Williams said. He was in the passenger seat and staring at the underpass beneath Interstate 10, the sight of which was bringing back a flood of bad memories.

As Matt Pincus, an officer with the Jefferson Parish sheriff's department, raced along the street in the shadow of the elevated highway, Williams stared at the rows of abandoned cars, caked with dirt and mud, their trunk lids flipped open, many stripped of their tires, block after block of crippled vehicles that would never be reclaimed.

"It's been eight months," Williams told Pincus in a tone of disbelief. Eight months since he had covered the awful aftermath of Hurricane Katrina. Eight months since New Orleans had suffered the worst natural disaster in American history. Eight months in which, as Williams surveyed the damage from the squad car, almost nothing had changed.

Here, just a couple of miles from downtown, were houses that had been battered or smashed by the wind and the rain, most of them with visible lines showing how high the floodwaters had risen. There were piles of rubble everywhere, sprawling heaps of plywood planks, sodden mattresses, rotting refrigerators. And something kept drawing Williams back.

Katrina had left an indelible mark on Brian Williams. It was the story that defined him as a network anchor, the story that he was determined to own, the story that haunted him in ways that were impossible to explain to anyone who had not seen the devastation firsthand. After making several trips to New Orleans, he had insisted that his wife, Jane, come along. "If you're going to live with me," Williams told her, "you're going to live with this story."

This was his eighth visit to Louisiana since the storm. Some viewers, Williams knew, were sick of the story, sick of the way he insisted on including a report on "The Long Road Back" in almost every broadcast. He didn't care. A major American city, one with a unique culture and cuisine and musical heritage, had been under water, and a quarter of a million people were still displaced.

In a six-hundred-channel universe, what chance did journalists have to make a difference? How often, in a business that thrived on the new and the novel, did reporters stick with a story month after month? Here, Williams felt, was his chance to have an impact. Without sustained attention from the national media, he believed, New Orleans would never recover.

*   *   *

He had spent that first night in the Superdome, with no power and no air flow, when it had turned into a squalid and dangerous hellhole for the thousands of hungry and desperate people who sought refuge inside. He had slipped and hit his head on the Astroturf and seen that the roof was starting to leak. He had gotten out the next day and then watched the city drown as the levees broke. He had seen the dead bodies and the women clutching their babies and the people scrounging to stay alive. He had watched the unbelievable scenes of looting. He had asked the state troopers to cover him and his crew as they left in a car, carrying cans of Vienna sausage that he planned to offer in exchange for his life if someone tried to steal the car.

He had seen for himself, and had told the world, that the Bush administration's assurances that help had arrived were nothing but fiction. On September 1, 2005, Williams had begun *NBC Nightly News* this way: "People are dying inside the city of New Orleans today, and that city has descended further into chaos tonight . . . They feel forgotten, and the people inside the city of New Orleans are asking repeatedly to people in Washington, 'Are you watching? Are you listening?' "

He had asked Michael Brown, the hapless FEMA chief, why no aid had arrived at the Superdome. "The federal government just learned about those people today," Brown had replied, a stunning admission in light of the constant television coverage.

Williams was filled with anger at the failure of federal officials to drop food and water from helicopters as New Orleans descended into chaos. It was hard to believe that this was happening in America. He was an eyewitness and would never forget, could never forget, what had transpired.

Brian Williams was a hero in New Orleans. He had been touched by the scrawled letters that schoolchildren wrote him, thanking him for his concern. He was accustomed to getting the shit kicked out of him by e-mail, but he had been swamped with warm messages from the Gulf region.

For all his undeniable passion about Katrina, there was, of course, an ancillary benefit. The hurricane had provided a great way for Williams to market himself. He had won a George Foster Peabody Award and a George Polk Award for his coverage of the storm. An NBC advertising campaign touted favorable press comments like movie blurbs, such as *Vanity Fair* calling his performance "Murrow-worthy." Katrina was a way of showing off his anchor chops.

Elizabeth Vargas believed that she had snagged the first network interview with Brown after President Bush had fired him for doing less than a heck of a job. She had Brown booked for *World News Tonight* and *20/20*. But the talks had broken down.

Williams, for his part, recalled Brown telling him weeks earlier that he would get the first interview. There had been more cajoling over the phone. Brown finally accepted when Williams offered him a three-part series on *Nightly*.

NBC shamelessly hyped the interview as a major exclusive, even though Brown had said many of the same things in Senate testimony and in newspaper interviews. Williams warned viewers that Brown had used a crude term—"balls to the wall"—to describe the Katrina rescue efforts, but those words, from his Capitol Hill appearance, had already been played on *World News Tonight, Good Morning America,* and CNN's *Anderson Cooper 360*.

Still, even as Brownie tried to deflect blame to the White House, Williams demanded answers with a righteous indignation rarely seen on network news:

"A lot of people down in the Gulf region feel that a lot of you have blood on your hands."

And: "People were left in that Superdome for a week. It was an awful situation. Who bears the responsibility for this?"

And: "Why weren't you people watching the television coverage that was on around the clock of the biggest natural disaster in American history?"

And: "Were you truly qualified to run FEMA?"

And: "How did your years as the head of an Arabian horse association prepare you to deal with eighty percent of the city of New Orleans under water?"

This indignation was no act. While Williams was not unaware of the publicity dividends of making Katrina his niche, anyone who talked to him for five minutes came away convinced that his passions about New Orleans were not of the manufactured variety. A searing moment of tragedy was indelibly imprinted upon him, and keeping the spotlight on the battered city was now his mission.

His chartered plane had landed at two in the morning on this warm Thursday in the spring of 2006, a last-minute scramble prompted by the fact that President Bush was returning to New Orleans as well. Williams had called Dan Bartlett at the White House and asked for a chance to talk to Bush. It wouldn't be a formal interview, Williams insisted—he did not want this to count as NBC's "turn" in the network rotation—just a little walk-and-talk at a location of the president's choosing. Bartlett thought it over and concluded that talking to Williams would be a good way for the president to reach 8 million viewers with his message of concern for New Orleans.

Matt Pincus, whom the sheriff's department had assigned to chauffeur Williams around whenever he was in town, eased his squad car toward a huge field partially covered with gravel and dirt. The area was surrounded by damaged houses, some abandoned, some still inhabited. They passed a blue frame house on the corner.

"Oh my God, I interviewed him," Williams said, spotting A. J. Perkins on the porch. "He was the nicest man. We were all so touched by him."

When Williams arrived at the field, he assumed a spread-eagle stance as Secret Service officers checked him, and then his producers, with magnetic wands. Once cleared inside, he watched as a couple of dozen Habitat for Humanity workers hammered away at wooden frames that formed the foundation of a row of new houses. The area was called Musicians Village, the land bought by a group headed by Wynton Marsalis and Harry Connick to provide homes for displaced musicians. Williams could see the skeletal frame of a house being financed by NBC's Bob Wright.

Williams was dressed in traveling anchorman garb: a blue button-down shirt, sleeves rolled up, over a dark T-shirt, white pants, and brown loafers. He had a sudden jolt of nervousness: What if Bush showed up in a suit and tie?

The answer would have to wait, for Bush was running an hour late. "Is he helo-ing here?" Williams asked Bob De Servi, a former NBC staffer who was now a White House advance man.

"This particular location will be a vehicular movement," De Servi said.

"I had one of those once—very painful," Williams said.

Pincus noticed a bug on Williams's backside and brushed it off with a yellow Taser gun, surprising several onlookers.

The minutes dragged on. Williams, working a wad of chewing gum, started to pace. He had to get into presidential interviewing mode. He was one of those television performers who needed to talk things out to get his rhythm.

He asked his veteran producer, Jean Harper, to check on ExxonMobil's just-reported quarterly profit—over $8 billion—and how it compared to the gross domestic product of various countries. She got the answer on her BlackBerry: Exxon's haul was bigger than the economies of the United Arab Emirates and Sri Lanka. Williams mulled it over.

"I might just say, 'Last night we did a piece from Houston on parents in a carpool line, paying three dollars a gallon for gasoline. People are going to find these figures obscene. You are from oil country. What do you have to say to these people?' "

Williams walked across the grassy field, sat on a pile of wooden beams, and made himself some notes on a small reporter's pad. By the time he returned, Bush had arrived and, wearing shirtsleeves, gray work gloves, and a carpenter's apron, was helping the Habitat workers carry roof beams to one of the houses under construction. Williams began pacing again.

"This is going to be a four-question gig," he said to no one in particular.

Finally Bush, who was already outfitted with a wireless lavalier mike, walked over and greeted Williams. Dan Bartlett, wearing an earpiece so he could hear the interview over the construction noise, stood to their right.

About forty yards away, two older women were using an electric saw to cut wooden blocks. An NBC producer asked them to stop, since the piercing sound might interfere with the interview, but they said their instructions were to keep working. They were, however, aware of the nearby cameras.

"Look good, suck it in," the woman in a tank top said to her friend.

Williams began by asking Bush about a Senate committee report calling for the abolition of FEMA as "discredited," "demoralized," and "dysfunctional." Bush said that he wanted to improve the agency.

They walked a few steps as Williams, looking at his pad, read Bush a few quotes from his televised speech at a floodlit Jackson Square the previous September, the one in which he vowed that "this great city will rise again."

"Do you still stand by those words," Williams asked, "and are you confident the levees are going to be here for the start of hurricane season?"

The second part of the question allowed Bush to simply express confidence that the levees would be ready.

The Exxon question came next. Bush gave a boilerplate answer.

Williams couldn't resist asking a poll question. "In the history of our polling you're at a low number," he said. "Does this weigh on you, considering you will need popularity to get what you want in your second term?"

The president ignored the question, reciting the latest positive statistics for economic growth.

Williams tried again: "But you'd rather not go into a second term at thirty-six percent approval." The president said he would work his hardest.

That was it, and they began chatting; Bush, as he often did, switched to more profane language than he would employ on camera. The discussion turned to books they had read, their children, and other topics that they had chewed over at their last meeting.

Williams seized the opportunity to make a serious point. Whenever Bush was asked about American troop levels in Iraq, he usually replied that such matters were up to the generals. As a student of history, Williams felt that was intellectually dishonest.

"You know, Mr. President," he said, "if Lincoln had done that, we'd all have southern accents like you."

Despite his outward persona as a cool and unflappable anchor, Williams was amazed that he had this kind of personal rapport with Bush, much as he had enjoyed with Bill Clinton. The idea that he could talk to presidents this way was absolutely mind-blowing. Williams still had in him a bit of the elementary school kid who had scrawled a letter to LBJ and somehow gotten a response.

Williams was not surprised that Bush had finessed every question. The president, he had learned, was quite disciplined at message control.

It was time to take stock. Williams talked about what they had with Bob Epstein, the newscast's second-ranking producer, and Subrata De, the young field producer who accompanied him everywhere and seemingly did everything, even though she had been born without a left hand.

"It didn't break any new ground," Epstein said.

"I quoted him back from his Jackson Square speech," Williams said. "He had to stand there and take it."

"When you went back at him about the poll numbers," De said, "he didn't answer."

"There was no major headline," Epstein said.

"Except he feels confident the levees will be ready," said De.

Williams thought about which excerpts they would use on *Nightly*. "I'd like my peeps to help me decide what the best sound is," he said.

It was almost 1:30 Central time, so Williams and his producers got on their cell phones for the 2:30 editorial conference in New York. John Reiss said that the lead story would be Chip Reid's piece on the Senate committee calling for FEMA to be dismantled. Williams said he could set that up by invoking the Bush interview.

There would also be a piece by Martin Savidge, the correspondent who spent much of his time in New Orleans, on whether the Army Corps of Engineers could repair the city's busted levees before hurricane season began in a few weeks. Williams said he would frame the question this way: " 'Marty, plain English. You've been living here. Are they going to be ready? Any way they can be ready?' And let him have at it and be as strong as he wants."

Reiss loved when Williams was on the road because it clearly energized the anchor. The producers in New York would talk about Inside Brian and how to get him to be Outside Brian. The difference was striking. Inside Brian was the polished, composed, slightly formal man who read his lines in the studio. Outside Brian was the engaged and enthusiastic correspondent who wasn't afraid to let his emotions show, and the witty, irreverent man who emceed awards dinners and charity events. There was even talk of building a new anchor set that would force Williams to move around and loosen up.

What was behind the great disparity? Reiss believed that Brian secretly wanted to be Walter Cronkite, sitting at a desk with a picture over his shoulder and tossing to a correspondent standing in front of the State Department for a forty-five-second report. That was the broadcast he had grown up watching, and that was the old-fashioned model they were trying to get him to relinquish.

Airtime was less than four hours away. Williams wondered whether he had enough time for his next interview, with a fire department captain named Ruel Douvillier who was heading up the city's search and rescue effort. "He won't be offended if I say I need to do this quickly?" Williams asked.

Subrata De said that would not be a problem. She briefed him, rapid fire, from a typed pre-interview sheet: He's fifty-two. His wife is a nurse. Army veteran, Vietnam and Desert Storm. He's able to deal with the nature of this recovery because of all the violence and death he's seen.

Pincus pulled the squad car in front of the fire station. Williams had to double-check: "First name?"

"Ruel," De reminded him.

Douvillier was wearing a blue uniform, black work boots, and a helmet. "I'm very sorry to impose on you," Williams said. "I was once a volunteer fireman."

The cameras rolled as Douvillier and a colleague waded through the waist-high weeds, cinder blocks, and rusty pipes in front of a rickety wooden house on Lizardi Street and began searching inside. They also searched the white house next door, which had collapsed like an accordion, with the roof caved in on one side, the screen doors off their hinges. An enormous, uprooted tree lay in the side yard.

"When I heard you were a vet," Williams said, "I understood why this gets to you the way it does."

There was a problem with the shot, so Williams repeated the line.

Just the other day, Douvillier said, he had found two brothers in the same house. He was surprised that they were not finding more bodies, since more than a thousand people were still missing.

"There is a smell here that you know instantly," Williams said. "Is it what we think it is?"

"It's the scent of decay," Douvillier said. "There is human remains and animal remains all over the place." The worst thing about making a discovery, he said, was that you found yourself visualizing the person's final moments.

Williams seemed deeply affected by the interview. "How do you keep your sanity?" he asked.

"My God-given family," Douvillier replied. "The other family is the firefighter family."

They were finished. The two men shook hands. "Can I get a wide shot?" Williams asked his cameraman.

Returning to the squad car, Williams used his BlackBerry to send an entry for his daily blog while Pincus drove him across town to the London Avenue levee, one of those that had failed during the storm.

Williams and De, wearing protective orange vests, made their way onto a rocky strip of light brown dirt that stood atop an enormous pit. To their left a wall of corrugated steel was holding back the water that had burst through the previous summer. Below, a giant crane, twelve stories tall, groaned as it lifted a large piece of equipment. An earth digger was scooping up dirt below, while a Caterpillar tractor was depositing massive steel beams.

It was, Williams thought, a spectacular spot on which to open the program. Here was an image that captured the race against time. But the staff in New York was nervous about Williams doing a live shot from such a precarious perch, and Subrata De was openly skeptical of how it would look.

"When you're here, it's just a wall with a dirt pile," she said.

"But that gives me such writing texture at the top of the broadcast: *Behind us was where the London Canal breach took place.*"

The producer was unconvinced.

"We can pan left or right, and we've got a house in ruins," Williams said. "By moving me four feet, you've got a second shot."

She said it would take two hours for the cameras to set up.

They decided to investigate a second possibility back on the street, between two abandoned houses that sat in front of the construction site where the levee repair work was taking place. The roof of one of the houses had collapsed.

The exterior wall of the house on the right had been ripped away, exposing what appeared to be a child's bedroom. Williams and Bob Epstein looked at the possessions peeking out from the rubble inside: A single sneaker. A cardboard box for a Wilson NFL football. A fashion magazine. A compact disc. A package of unused batteries. Nothing, apparently, had changed since the day the hurricane struck.

"This is like Pompeii," Epstein said, as if volcanic dust had frozen everything in place.

"It *is* Pompeii," Williams agreed. He was always in the market for a good metaphor.

"Brian," De said, "we need to give the *Today* show an answer." The morning show wanted him to talk about his Bush interview, but that would require him to show up before 6 A.M. local time. Williams remained undecided.

It was just before 3 o'clock, giving them two and a half hours until the broadcast began at 5:30 Central time. The Louisiana sun had grown quite hot. They piled into one of a pair of white, air-conditioned RVs that served as their office during the trip. There was a television, café-style seats with Dell laptops on the tables, and a kitchenette with a counter full of muffins, cinnamon rolls, and Doritos, plus a small bathroom and a back room with a king bed. Williams was annoyed that no food was waiting, forcing them to send out for Subway sandwiches.

Once they got settled, Bob Epstein wanted to talk about the top of the broadcast. Bush had gone on to Mississippi after the stop in New Orleans, and they had no mention of that. "Are we burying the lead?" he asked.

"We don't need his day," Williams said. "His day is the V/O lead to our interview." Williams wanted to do a voice-over while they showed footage of the president's Gulf tour.

The question now was how to introduce their lead story on the Senate proposal that FEMA be replaced with a larger agency.

Williams took a stab at what the script would sound like: "Back home in Washington, while he was in the air—"

"That gets you to Chip Reid," Epstein said. Once his anchor made that geographic transition, they could run their piece from Capitol Hill.

What about Williams's toss to Martin Savidge, who was on the scene? "Is it whizbang cooler to have him at a second location, even if we're a hundred yards apart?" Williams asked. They decided that Savidge could just stand next to the anchor.

Subrata De was thinking about how to promote the interview. "I think we should give the polling SOT to the affiliates," she said. If local newscasts played the sound bite—or sound-on-tape, in television jargon—of Williams asking Bush about his low approval ratings, it might draw a larger audience to *Nightly.*

Williams signed on to his laptop to work on scripts, but something was nagging at him. It was the pile of e-mails next to his computer mouse, complaining about his Katrina coverage.

"Stop making 'news' of what isn't news anymore—Hurricane Katrina," a California woman wrote. "It's not interesting. It comes off as an excuse to bash Bush. Enough is enough."

"Has it occurred to you that people could be sick and tired of your constant stories about Katrina?" a Massachusetts man asked. "Time to give it a rest, Brian."

"I'm so sick of hearing about Katrina," a North Dakota man said. "I'm sick of my tax money going to these people who are too lazy to take control . . . When will you stop going on and on about it."

These missives came in day after day. Williams knew that he was alienating part of the audience with his nearly obsessive focus on New Orleans, but he was determined to make people see why the whole country should care about the partial destruction of an American city. In the past an anchor would never have acknowledged negative mail, but in an age of digital communication, Williams felt that he needed to respond. He planned to close the show by reading some of the e-mails on the air and challenging his critics.

They all watched a tape of the stroll with Bush on a Sony Betamax. Williams was surprised by how close Bush had gotten to him, giving the interview an intimate feel.

Williams hadn't eaten since breakfast, but he ignored the late-arriving subs. He popped a B-12 vitamin, grabbed a plastic-wrapped cinnamon bun, headed outside, and slipped into a Grand Caravan. Using a handheld mike, he began recording the headlines that would play at the top of the show: "Tonight, here in New Orleans, eight months after Katrina, is FEMA beyond repair?"

The Dodge deposited him at the location up the street, between the two hollowed-out houses in front of the levee wall, where he would anchor the show. The dull roar of a bulldozer, working on the levee behind the homes, filled the air. A makeup woman spread her wares on a makeshift table, but Williams did not utilize her services. Instead, he peered back inside the exposed bedroom, then approached his two cameramen.

"Can you go off sticks just to go here if I come walking at you?" he asked. Williams wanted to make sure the men could move their camcorders off the tripods as he came out of the abandoned house. This reminded him of all his years in local news: You go to the scene of a story, find the best backdrop, and start walking.

Returning to the cameras to tape some promos, Williams looked into the monitor and saw a high-angle shot being transmitted from another camera atop a large cherry-picker across the street, rented by NBC for the occasion. "Holy God! Wow, that is fantastic." He decided to rewrite the script to reflect the view.

A large white screen, surrounded by four lights mounted on tall blue poles, had been set up to block the sun. It was time for the busters, as the staff called the promo spots.

"Coming up here tonight, we're back in New Orleans. We'll have our conversation here today with President Bush and the rest of the day's news . . ."

Williams did several versions for local stations, then was ready for the *Today* show tease.

"Thanks, Ann, and we are back in New Orleans . . ." His rhythm was off.

"Thanks, Ann . . ." He stumbled again.

"Wow, the wheels are falling off today," Williams said.

There was one last intro to read. "A special good evening to our online viewers. I'm Brian Williams . . ." The Webcast version was longer, since there were no time limits.

It was 4:15, just over an hour to airtime. Williams walked back to the trailer, sat down at his laptop to finish polishing the scripts, and slipped on his iPod. He often did this as a way of zoning out, grabbing a bit of solitude while focusing on the task at hand. Williams tapped his left foot as he typed.

Bob Epstein had a question. "A minute lead-in to Marty?" he asked. It sounded long.

"I'm just going to give a little tour of the house," Williams said. He slipped the earpiece back in. "I'm going back to the Rolling Stones," he announced. "Goodbye, everybody." The broadcast began in twenty-two minutes.

With nine minutes to spare, Williams walked back to the camera location and practiced reading the introduction.

"A minute and a half," the director said.

It was showtime. "And good evening from the Lakeview neighborhood of the city of New Orleans," Williams said. "And we can show you exactly where we are by using a high shot of this very location tonight, and if we pull back with that camera, we can show you how close we are to the levee. Beyond that is the water. Of course, the water has since receded. They have rebuilt this levee with corrugated steel. This is right where it broke, right where the water came in. This very spot is actually well known to millions of Americans, whether they know it or not. They have seen it on the air and from the air. We have pictures of this very location, back when the water was high, and we watched the helicopter sandbagging effort at this levee break during the height of the aftermath. President Bush visited this city today and made a second stop next door in Biloxi, Mississippi, thanking volunteers at each location."

For all their careful planning, Williams had a big problem. The teleprompter was running about two lines behind him, slowing him down and forcing him to try to remember what he had written next. The prompter operator in New York was supposed to be listening to his voice over an open phone line, but he was hearing the anchor instead on the satellite feed, which had a built-in delay.

Williams struggled on, setting up his Bush interview: "I asked the president about this proposal to kill FEMA."

During the first break Williams walked to the exposed back bedroom of the crumbling house to begin his walking shot. He borrowed a line from Bob Epstein: "A member of our traveling party today who hadn't visited New Orleans since Katrina today called this city Pompeii, meaning that everything is as it was the morning the water came up. Life stood still. The debris has stood still, untouched for now eight months."

After Savidge's piece, Williams said: "Martin, this calls for a judgment, but you've been covering this story nonstop. Are the levees going to be ready anything close to the start of hurricane season, and how much faith will the people here have?"

"They'll be ready, but just barely," Savidge said.

After reports on a nationwide roundup of sex offenders and a letter from the sole survivor of the West Virginia mine collapse, Williams read a few of the e-mails from viewers telling him that they were sick of him going overboard on the Katrina saga.

"But look what happens here in New Orleans every day," he said. "Today we went out with a body recovery team. Last week they found two brothers, together, undiscovered for eight months. They are still finding bodies, in houses, and we'll show you what their jobs are like when we join you from here tomorrow night. Meantime, a huge area in this region is still very much broken and not at all ready for the next hurricane."

He had both teased the next broadcast and told the critics to stuff it.

While Williams waited another fifteen minutes to do a live shot for CNBC, he got a BlackBerry message from Steve Capus: *"Nightly* is about as good as it gets."

Another e-mail arrived, surprisingly, from CBS News. "Good get," Sean McManus wrote of the Bush interview. He also lauded Williams for reading and rebutting the negative e-mails. For the president of another news division to lavish such praise on a competing anchor was a rare occurrence.

The CNBC anchor, Melissa Francis, was ready. Williams set the scene and then tossed to Bush's answer on gas prices, which had been cut from the evening news for time reasons. Once the live shot ended, he sat down with Jefferson Parish's Chinese-American sheriff, Harry Lee, reading some of the negative e-mail and describing his response with an obscene gesture.

As Williams walked toward the trailer, a woman named Heather Wright, in a white peasant blouse and sandals, came running up to greet him.

"I just wanted to tell you, thank you so much and keep up the great work," she said. Suddenly she dissolved into tears. Her home in Metairie had been deluged by two and a half feet of water. Williams put his arm around her and tried to console her.

A second woman, Cris Sewell, wearing a camera around her neck, approached with a warm smile. "There's a special place in heaven for you," she said.

Williams returned to the trailer, clearly touched. In a city that felt abandoned, he was, by virtue of his periodic visits and his television celebrity, seen as a lifeline.

"It's like you're all they have," he told his staff.

Within minutes a colleague told him that an elderly woman had walked a great distance to find him. Williams ambled back out of the trailer.

"I'm Carmen Morial," she said in a thin voice. "I'm ninety-one years old. I lost my home, all of my clothes, my car. I'm so happy to see you."

"How about a hug?" Williams said, as seamlessly as any politician. "God bless. Things are going to get better. We're trying to keep everyone's attention on you."

The next morning Brian Williams faced a far more difficult interview subject than the president of the United States.

After getting up early for the *Today* interview—he had chatted with Matt Lauer, not Katie Couric, who was now his rival-in-waiting—Williams found himself at Tipitina's, a landmark French Quarter bar that had a worn and faded feel. He was on a stage, leaning against a black piano, and talking to a musical legend.

The problem was, he couldn't get Fats Domino to say anything.

Williams, a jazz aficionado, had been warned that the reclusive singer would be difficult. Domino was an eccentric character, and he had threatened to cancel the meeting when Williams was running late because the anchor was watching Bush hold an impromptu news conference at the White House. Subrata De persuaded him to change his mind by promising to order some Popeye's Fried Chicken.

Williams told Domino, who owned a home in the Ninth Ward, that the whole country had been worried about him when he was nowhere to be found after Katrina. Was he angry about what happened in the aftermath of the storm?

No, Domino said.

"A lot of newspapers said you were missing. Where were you?"

"I went to Baton Rouge."

When did he see what had happened to his house?

"A few days later."

Williams shifted gears, tried talking about New Orleans. "What was special about that place that gave birth to so many talented musicians?"

"I don't know."

"What influence has New Orleans had on music in the U.S.?"

"I don't know."

It was hopeless. Williams leaned in, smiled broadly, oozed charm, rephrased the questions, but Domino seemed uninterested in conversing.

Finally Williams pleaded: "Are your fingers feeling it today? Could I talk you into just a few notes?"

Domino broke into a refrain of "Walking to New Orleans." When he was finished, Williams clapped his hands. "That was beautiful," he said.

Domino seemed to come to life as he continued to play. Williams, pretending the interview was over, kept chatting with him, getting him to say just enough that he could stitch it together with the music to make a closing piece for *Nightly.* Finally, Domino got up, retreated to the bar, and opened a Heineken.

An hour later Williams was staring in disbelief at a white van that was wedged into the roof of an abandoned home, jutting out toward the sky at a forty-five-degree angle. He was in the middle of St. Bernard Parish, in an upscale enclave of ranch houses that had been so totally submerged that seaweed still clung to many of the damaged roofs. There was no sign of human life for miles around, just pile after pile of rubble in the front yards, sometimes with a recognizable item or two—a black shoe, a red bathing suit—serving as a reminder that, eight months earlier, the area had been a thriving suburb.

"This is hell on earth," Williams declared.

Subrata De had found the perfect backdrop for the newscast: a white shrimp boat, called the *Dolphin,* that the fierce floodwaters had carried out of the Gulf, three miles away, and deposited here among the brick houses, listing to its left. Williams went up in the cherry-picker, surveyed the scene, came down, and began talking out the opening of the broadcast. He could describe the van that had attached itself to the house, the seaweed on the roofs, the marooned boat that a furious Mother Nature had ripped from the water.

As a hot sun in a cloudless sky bore down on the eerily quiet neighborhood, Williams's thoughts turned to the longtime colleague who would soon be his rival. If Katie Couric ever asked him for advice, he had plenty.

This, Katie, was what the job was all about. If she was going to be managing editor of the *CBS Evening News,* these were the kinds of disasters she would have to cover, these were the kinds of trips she would have to make, this was the kind of grueling work she would have to do. There was no easy path to being a network anchor. It was all or nothing.

CHAPTER 18

The Endless War

As the American occupation of Iraq stretched into its fourth bloody year, the media coverage was turning increasingly negative.

The network newscasts had become a nightly tableau of death and destruction, and whether that was an accurate picture of Iraq had become a matter of fierce political debate. Certainly the constant plague of bombings, explosive devices, sniper fire and, occasionally, the massacre of large numbers of civilians played into television's need for dramatic events and arresting visuals. Certainly it was easier for the anchors and correspondents to offer a skeptical vision of the war, now that a majority of the country disapproved of the conflict, than it had been in the heady days after the toppling of Saddam Hussein seemed to strike a blow for democracy in the Middle East. By training their powerful spotlight on the chaos gripping Iraq, the anchors were arguably contributing to the political downfall of a president who had seemed to be riding high when he won his second term.

Through the routine decisions of daily journalism—how prominently to play a story, what pictures to use, what voices to include—the newscasts were sending an unmistakable message. And the message was that George W. Bush's war was a debacle.

When Brian Williams thought about Iraq, he thought about his visits to Walter Reed Army Hospital. He was tortured by these trips to the medical center in Northwest Washington to comfort the veterans being treated there. It was hard to look at their wounds. One soldier had five titanium pins sticking out of his toes. His heart ached for these brave men and women who had been to Iraq, the worst place in the world, on orders from their commander in chief.

For Williams, it all went back to 9/11. As a citizen, he had thought on that fateful day, thank God that Dick Cheney and Donald Rumsfeld and Colin Powell were on this team. How together we all seemed. In Williams's view, there was something about the murderous attacks on the World Trade Center and the Pentagon that, in the eyes of the White House press corps, gave Bush a stature that could not be violated. And that, Williams believed, was no accident. The administration's deft use of 9/11 to neutralize its critics had created an impenetrable shield. It was political magic.

Some people, Williams knew, believed that the administration was jonesing for a fight, exploiting September 11 as an opportunity to launch a war in Iraq. Whatever the truth, he had to admire, in a clinical sort of way, the political management of the press during what came to be known as the war on terror. It was truly remarkable.

Williams did not enjoy looking back on the run-up to war, knowing what he knew now about the media's flawed performance. He did not want to look back on this period with the same sense of regret. No one in their right mind, he believed, would want America to pull out tomorrow. He did not want America to withdraw from Iraq. But he recognized how deeply the war had divided the country.

Every day Williams asked the question: Did Baghdad correspondent Richard Engel have any news other than another twenty Iraqi civilians killed when an IED detonated, leaving the same smoking carcasses and pathetic scenes of loved ones crying? That, Williams felt, was the problem: the horrible had become utterly commonplace. To most Americans, he believed, the war could not be more ephemeral. It was half a world away, and it required no sacrifice by those who did not have a family member in the armed forces.

Williams had his own private intelligence channel on the war. He had formed e-mail relationships with a number of military men—some still on active duty, some who had returned from the region—and they were candid about the conflict in a way that top generals were not. These informants alerted him to a wide range of problems with IEDs, armor, and morale. But they never spoke on the phone, which would be too dangerous, since they were barred from talking to journalists. Private e-mail was the only safe form of communication.

If Iraq was more accessible—if he didn't think he was going to get killed—Williams would have regularly taken the show there. But he saw what had happened to Bob Woodruff. As important as he believed the story to be, the safety questions were daunting.

As chief of the news division, Steve Capus was also frustrated by the sameness of the coverage. Why, he asked, couldn't they just put Richard Engel on the air, without videotape if necessary, and let him explain what it was like to live in Iraq?

Finally Engel—who had overcome childhood dyslexia, gone to the region as a young freelancer, learned Arabic, and bribed his way into Iraq just before the war—did just that. He used portions of a video diary he had been keeping with his own camcorder. "I've seen so many ugly things," the thirty-three-year-old reporter said, "so many memories I'm not sure that people are equipped, and images people are equipped to handle, that—you know, two weeks ago, I was walking around Latifiya in the south of Baghdad. I was watching stray dogs eat a dead body and just picking it to pieces." There was footage of Engel hitting a punching bag, unloading with all the pent-up anger of a man who had lived too long with the horror of war.

Bob Schieffer was also a regular at Walter Reed, having been persuaded to start visiting by John McCain. Schieffer struck up a friendship with a vet named Brent Jurgensen, a man who had lost his tongue in combat—it was later reattached—then returned to Iraq a second time and lost a leg in a rocket attack. Schieffer often gave him front-row tickets to Washington Nationals games.

Three years earlier Schieffer had believed that Bush was doing the right thing in going to war. He believed that Saddam indeed had weapons of mass destruction, as the administration contended. He argued about the situation with his wife Pat.

"If this guy has a nuclear weapon or some kind of weapon of mass destruction and he uses it, and this president or any other president knew about it, he would be impeached," Schieffer told her. "That's an impeachable offense."

Pat had argued that invading Iraq was the worst thing the country could do and that we would regret it. And now, Schieffer felt, she had been right and he had been wrong.

Schieffer had been appalled by the administration's incompetence in mishandling the war. The United States, he believed, had never sent enough troops to Iraq to get the job done. Rummy had just wanted to prove that he could do it with a small mobile force. The result, in Schieffer's view, was that we never had enough troops to keep the peace. No one in the administration would acknowledge this basic point, and yet everyone knew that it was true.

"What must stop is the ongoing government effort to sugarcoat it, trying to blame it on the media, or saying it's all going very, very well," he said on *Face the Nation.*

The never-ending violence reminded Schieffer of his time as a correspondent in Vietnam. Once he had been riding along on a bombing mission on the last propeller plane that the Navy flew off carriers; the aircraft was hit three times by 50-caliber machine gun fire. But in Saigon, except for the occasional hand grenade tossed into a restaurant, Schieffer had felt safe. That was hardly the case for his colleagues in Baghdad.

Schieffer was particularly worried about his top reporter in Iraq. Lara Logan, a stunning thirty-five-year-old South African who had grown up during apartheid and worked a series of freelance television jobs before becoming a CBS radio stringer in Afghanistan, was taking all kinds of risks as she spent time with American troops. On one mission, as Logan's Marine unit was returning to base in the Iraqi town of Ramadi, they were caught in an ambush, and the soldier walking in front of her was shot. Undeterred, Logan videotaped a stand-up moments later, even as the gunfire continued. During the same period Logan was crouched on the floor of a building with a group of Marines as a rocket-propelled grenade hit their observation post, and they exchanged fire with insurgents in an abandoned building nearby. Schieffer thought Logan would be the next Diane Sawyer or Barbara Walters—if she lived that long.

Logan was accustomed to hearing demands for good-news stories from her bosses. They were tired of gloom and doom all the time. She would hear about it from Sean McManus and Rome Hartman, or she would get a note from the foreign news desk: "Sean is interested in a reconstruction piece."

In a meeting in New York, McManus told her: "It doesn't have to be all serious hard news. You could do other things." He suggested she do a piece on the Baghdad soccer team.

The next day, in her e-mail, was a *Los Angeles Times* piece on the soccer team: A nineteen-year-old player had bled to death after heading the ball and, before he hit the ground, taking a stray bullet in the throat. Logan didn't mind nice features, but this was yet another indication of how the security situation affected everything in Iraq. Kids couldn't go to soccer practice because their parents were afraid they would die.

Logan felt that it was her mission to dig behind the statistics. The previous fall, when the bodies of thirty-six Sunni men turned up in a dry riverbed, she was able to track sixteen of them to a single street in a Baghdad suburb. Logan closed her piece by talking about a "climate of fear" in which "no one is being held responsible. What's worse is no one seems either capable or, more importantly, willing to stop these murders from escalating into an all-out civil war."

Jeff Fager, the *60 Minutes* producer who brought Logan to the network, took issue with her approach. "I didn't like that piece," he said. "You were over the top. You have to be more subtle."

Now, with the violence in Iraq spiraling out of control, Logan went back to Fager. He admitted that she had been right.

Logan was acutely aware of the administration's accusation that journalists were painting an unduly negative portrait of Iraq by focusing so heavily on the violence. She thought the charge was complete nonsense. She would tell American commanders: When we can get in our cars and drive to the opening of a store and interview people on camera without fear of being killed, or getting everyone involved with us killed, then the positive stories would be told. Logan was equally impatient with the notion that Americans were suffering from Iraq fatigue. These brave soldiers were risking their lives, watching their friends burn to death in front of them, and she was going to pretend that the story didn't matter anymore because people were tired of hearing about it?

Elizabeth Vargas had an instinctive feel for military life because she had grown up as an Army brat. When her father, Ralf, had served as a colonel in Vietnam, he had narrowly avoided having his helicopter shot down, and after that he had considered retiring, in part out of disillusionment with the war effort. This was not some foreign culture in her eyes.

When ordinary people were getting killed every day, she thought, it was unfair for a network to minimize that as just another bombing. Imagine the reaction if a suicide bomber had blown up innocent people in the middle of an American city. She had been to Baghdad, had seen how difficult the conditions were there. Journalists were not just deaf, dumb, and blind bystanders, Vargas felt. They had to hold the administration accountable. Otherwise they would be shirking their duty.

While the networks brought the war into American living rooms, they rarely broke new journalistic ground. In the middle of March 2006, *Time* magazine reported that a group of Marines were under investigation for killing two dozen unarmed Iraqi civilians, including women and children, in the town of Haditha. CNN had aired a report on the probe first, then *NBC Nightly News* and *World News Tonight,* and the *CBS Evening News* the night after that. But the story quickly faded from view.

CBS's David Martin had an update on the Pentagon probe in late April, and in the middle of May, NBC's Jim Miklaszewski covered accusations by Congressman Jack Murtha, a former Marine, that the unit had "killed innocent civilians in cold blood."

It wasn't until a week later, when more details of the investigation leaked out and politicians started weighing in, that the Haditha slaughter became the lead story on all the networks. Suddenly, some observers were comparing Haditha to Vietnam's infamous My Lai massacre. Conservative critics accused news organizations of making too much of an isolated incident, but the truth was that the media, especially television, had largely shied away from the story for two and a half months. Accusing American soldiers of atrocities was a risky business, and gathering evidence of such incidents was extremely difficult. As every reporter there was acutely aware, roaming around Iraq was growing more dangerous by the day.

On the night of Sunday, May 28, Rome Hartman's deputy at CBS, Bill Owens, got what appeared to be a routine e-mail from one of his correspondents.

"Hey, Bill—

"Gotcha a Memorial Day pitch . . . spending the morning with a 4th ID joint US-Iraqi patrol in Baghdad (some of which will likely end up in the *Early Show* offer) . . . then interviewing a decorated Purple-Heart medevac guy who got injured three weeks into duty . . . then insisted on coming straight back, the moment he got his medical all-clear. A kind of 'fighting on in memory of those who have fallen' piece. Kd."

It was from Kimberly Dozier, proposing an *Evening News* piece for the holiday that would give precious airtime to a once-wounded soldier. Dozier had spent three years in Iraq, had done every conceivable kind of story there, and knew that Americans were tuning out of the war and that her bosses wanted less coverage of the conflict. Two months earlier, in the Iraqi town of Dura, a car bomb had gone off near Dozier and her cameraman, Paul Douglas, and her story wound up getting held. "Don't risk my life if we're not going to get on the air," Douglas told her. But she was determined to find new angles, new characters, new ways of capturing the conflict.

On Memorial Day, Dozier set out in an armored Humvee with Paul Douglas and her sound man, James Brolan, wearing flak jackets, helmets, and protective glasses. The crew got out of their vehicle to examine an Iraqi Army checkpoint. Suddenly a powerful car bomb exploded. Douglas and Brolan died in the street. Dozier was taken by helicopter to an emergency room in Baghdad's Green Zone, one mile away, and rushed into surgery with shrapnel in her brain, her legs badly crushed. Her heart stopped twice as she hovered between life and death. Titanium rods were inserted in her legs. Dozier was soon moved to a second hospital for more surgery. She was listed in critical condition.

Once again, the war had hit home for the networks. Once again, journalists came to symbolize the carnage in Iraq and drew the kind of heightened media attention that was rarely bestowed on anonymous soldiers.

Sean McManus got the call at 5:20 A.M. Linda Mason, a senior vice president at CBS, told him that Douglas and Brolan appeared to be dead, although this was unconfirmed, and that Dozier might not survive.

McManus didn't want to overdo the coverage just because three of their own had been hit. That, he felt, might appear self-serving. At the same time the wounding of a prominent correspondent and the killing of two crew members was a major story. On the *Evening News* that night Bob Schieffer noted that the blast that hit the CBS team was only one of eight that day, and at least thirty-three people, most of them Iraqis, had died in the attacks.

Schieffer kept thinking about how Dozier had just been in New York the week before, had moved her parents into an assisted living home, and was feeling good about herself. Schieffer had teased her about her new haircut, and she was anxious to get back to the story in Iraq.

Brian Williams had spent several hours chatting with Dozier in Mosul, during his last trip to Iraq, and came to admire her reporting skills and her network of sources in the U.S. military. Williams had also shared a couple of military flights with Paul Douglas, whom he viewed, along with James Brolan, as part of the "standing army" of tenacious crewmen who made it possible for the images of anchors and correspondents to be beamed back home from war zones.

For Rome Hartman, the irony was that Dozier and her colleagues were attempting to do exactly what the critics had accused the media of failing to do. The next time he heard some fat and comfortable pundit bitch about how reporters didn't get out of their protected enclaves to tell the "good news" stories about Iraq, he wanted to punch that person in the nose.

It was a miracle that Dozier was alive, given that she had lost thirty pints of blood. McManus flew to Germany, where he arrived at the U.S. military hospital in Landstuhl at midnight. After meeting her parents and brother, he was led into the room. Kimberly was lying in bed, hooked up to various machines, her legs elevated under sheets that had been fashioned into makeshift tents. Blood was encrusted under her fingernails.

McManus decided to test her mental capacity. She had tried to arrange a meeting with him the previous week, but the scheduling hadn't worked out.

"You didn't have to go through all this just to meet me in person," he said.

"It would have been a whole lot easier just to have that drink in New York," Dozier replied.

That was a good sign. Her memory was intact.

McManus got very emotional. If Kimberly had been a few inches to the left or the right, he realized, she might well be dead.

"Don't you ever tell anybody that you saw the president cry," he said.

"That's in my next negotiation," Dozier said.

On his way out McManus saw a large group of soldiers standing around, wearing surgical gowns and gloves over their khaki uniforms. He asked what they were doing there so late. One of them said they had gotten a call and were expecting two dozen casualties to be arriving at the hospital any minute. The war kept grinding on.

McManus was introduced to Michael Potter, a specialist who had been in a nearby Humvee when the bomb went off. He looked like a kid. The young man had minor burns on his face and hands.

"We'll never be able to repay the debt of gratitude to the military for what you did for Kimberly," McManus said.

"We think of her as one of us, sir," the soldier said.

CHAPTER 19

Pregnant and Powerless

By the time the 2004 election passed, Charlie Gibson had resigned himself to never becoming an evening news anchor.

For years, the reality at ABC was staring him in the face: Peter Jennings was anchor for life. Gibson used to tease him about how much older he was—actually, the gap was just five years—but Jennings was the most energetic sixtysomething man that he had ever seen. Occasionally Jennings would grouse about the negative aspects of the job and how long he had been doing it.

"I'm getting into the end game," Jennings would say. "But it's not going to be in time for you," he would add as a friendly taunt.

Their relationship was complicated. In Gibson's view, Jennings was a demanding, nettlesome, difficult man, tough to get along with. He always had to be the smartest guy in the room, and Gibson had drawn more than his share of zingers.

Gibson had regularly filled in on *World News Tonight,* but it was like being a grandfather. You would come for a couple of weeks, play with the kids, and then leave, but the kids weren't really yours. Jennings *was* ABC News, he clearly wasn't going anywhere, and Gibson began to think about retirement.

Indeed, Gibson looked like a genial granddad, with his crinkly eyes, flat brown hair graying at the temples, and the hint of jowls. His wife, Arlene, ran the Spence School on East 91st Street, an exclusive private girls' school whose students had included Katie Couric's daughters. After more than thirty-five years of marriage, Arlene was getting ready to retire, and she wanted a playmate. At a reception at the 2004 Republican convention, Gibson had told David Westin that he planned to hang it up in June 2006.

"Let's not talk about retirement," Westin said. "I'd like to have you in some role."

"No," Gibson said, "I really think it's time to retire." But Gibson allowed that he might be willing to stay an extra year, and later signed a contract to keep him at *Good Morning America* until the spring of 2007.

When Jennings was diagnosed with lung cancer, Timothy Johnson, the physician who was ABC's medical correspondent, told Gibson that the odds for survival were small, given the advanced state of the disease. Gibson began to wonder whether he would be in the running for the anchor chair if his old friend didn't make it. The truth was, he wanted the job. He was, at the moment, already doing the job, alternating nights with Elizabeth Vargas while continuing to work the morning shift.

After Jennings succumbed to cancer, Gibson reached the impasse over whether he would serve two or three years as the anchor. It had been a mistake on his part, Gibson realized, to get into a squabble over the timing, but the bottom line was that the coveted assignment had gone to Vargas and Bob Woodruff. Gibson was greatly disappointed, but he resigned himself to finishing up at *GMA* and then bidding ABC farewell.

After Woodruff was nearly killed in Iraq and Gibson had spent a month filling in as Vargas's coanchor, Westin summoned Gibson to his sixth-floor office, nestled in the corner of a huge corporate reception area.

Westin, who had the easy manner of a politician taking someone into his confidence, was candid. He said he had three possible choices.

"What I'd like to do is pair you up with Elizabeth," Westin said. He repeated, as he often did, like a mantra, "I believe in the two-anchor format."

Or, Westin said, he could leave Vargas in place as the solo anchor.

What he couldn't do, Westin said, was put Vargas together with Diane Sawyer. "I don't think two women on the broadcast would necessarily work," he said. But he could decide on a third option: handing *World News* to Sawyer alone.

Gibson responded by addressing the only scenario that involved him, teaming up with Vargas. "I don't think that'll work," he said, "because I don't believe in two people sitting next to each other on the set." He would not be on the road constantly the way Woodruff was, not at his age. The thing would look like a local news show, he said. With only nineteen minutes of airtime, what would be the purpose?

"You have to make me believe that one plus one equals more than two," Gibson said. Westin mostly listened.

During the same period Westin had a similar conversation with Diane

Sawyer. He had to be especially solicitous of her feelings, because Sawyer was famous for being resentful if she felt that she wasn't being treated properly. More important, if Gibson agreed to sign on as Vargas's coanchor, Westin would be taking away her trusted partner at *GMA*.

Westin outlined his three options. Did Diane want to leave the morning show and take over *World News*?

"If one of us has to go," Sawyer said, "it should be Charlie."

"Are you sure about it?" Westin asked. "I'm not saying you get it if you want it, but do you want it?"

"I would love to do it," Sawyer said. "It would be great. I love hard news. But I can't. I cannot do it if it's taken away from Charlie. That's just not going to work."

Sawyer gave the situation some serious thought. She would not snatch the job from Charlie, but what if he bowed out? Deciphering what Charlie wanted was like reading shadows on the wall of a cave.

In the weeks that followed, Gibson and Sawyer talked about the situation a number of times. They had grown close over the years since making the joint leap into morning television.

"If you want to do it," Gibson said, "you certainly have my blessing."

But Sawyer demurred. "I'm really burned out," she said. "I'm whipped. I don't have the energy to do *Good Morning America*."

"Then go do *World News Tonight*," Gibson said.

"No, no, no. *You* have to do it."

"Okay," Gibson said, "but there's no offer on the table."

Reading Diane was not the easiest thing in the world, Gibson felt. She had one of the fastest minds of anyone he had ever met, an intelligence that operated almost at warp speed. She was like a chess grandmaster, always nine moves ahead of him. She could claim to be burned out and then be a ball of fire the next day.

Gibson was sure that Sawyer had entertained the possibility of doing *World News*. She liked to try on an enormous number of clothes and figure out which outfit felt most comfortable. Perhaps she still wasn't sure about this journalistic suit.

But having Diane's approval was tremendously important to Gibson. They were a team, and he did not want to do anything that would make her feel that he had abandoned the morning show.

Sawyer grew upset that no one was thinking about her long-term interests. She could well have won the *World News* job, but that would have been suicidal, Sawyer concluded, because Gibson would retire and she would be responsible for his leaving ABC.

Sawyer told Westin that *GMA* could not compete with *Today* if Gibson took over the evening news. "David, I know this better than you know it," she said. Charlie was the core of the show. Charlie was the reason she came back to mornings, the reason the viewers came back. Westin disagreed, but she did not believe she could make it work on her own.

She talked to Robert Iger, the Disney chief executive, about her career. How much longer could she keep getting up at 4 A.M. to do cooking segments while also flying around the world to interview foreign leaders? Sawyer was throwing her weight around. She wanted to hear from the top of the company that she was valued for more than just light morning chat.

A couple of weeks later Sawyer had a brainstorm: She and Charlie should do *World News* together, just as they had taken on *GMA* nearly eight years earlier. They both liked to do reporting on the road. Charlie could do the majority of the show, and she could be a subanchor. She could come on in the third block, she didn't care, and bring her signature pieces to the broadcast. They could tackle the big, hard subjects and continue their relationship on the air.

"It'll be fun," Sawyer told him.

Gibson didn't get it. Hadn't they agreed, when he had brought up the possible pairing with Vargas, that a coanchoring situation made no sense?

But with them it would be different. "You could do the top half, I could do the back half," Sawyer said.

When Diane spoke, you had to listen, and Gibson knew that management must be listening as well. But he soon realized why the concept wouldn't fly: ABC undoubtedly would not want to pay two enormous salaries—especially Diane's, which had to be several times larger than his—for one show. And of course, the network would never allow *Good Morning America* to be crippled by having both its stars leave at the same time.

Although they had become good friends over the years, sometimes there were strains in their relationship. Sawyer felt that he could be an absolute bear in the morning, difficult to deal with. Gibson often joked about how his role was to fetch Diane's coffee, and Sawyer's velvet-gloved maneuvering, coupled with her celebrity status, could be wearying. Anchoring on his own, without his famous costar, would be liberating.

It seemed to Sawyer that Gibson was looking ahead to retirement. His brother had recently died, he had moved to a new apartment, he was taking vacations on Cape Cod, and he kept claiming that not taking the anchor job the previous fall was the best thing that had ever happened to him. Gibson's friends knew that he was literally counting the number of shows he had left until his *GMA* contract expired in 2007.

It was so tempting. The rhythms of the evening news were so familiar to people after all these years, Sawyer believed. This is where the sound bite comes, here is the stand-up. As the anchor, you throw to the piece, then throw to the next piece. Sawyer wanted to mix it up, to get away from the survey of the day's news and jump right to the burning questions. That was what Fox News had done, and it was what she could do in a very different way.

But as the delicate dance with Gibson played out, Sawyer reached a decision. Even if Charlie bowed out, she would not make a play for *World News Tonight*. And the reason was Katie Couric.

It had been clear for some time that Couric was headed to CBS to take over Dan Rather's old job. If Sawyer were to take the plunge as the second woman to be the solo anchor of a nightly newscast, she realized, all the press coverage would be about dueling divas. Never mind that they knew each other only slightly. It would be like that *New York* magazine cover every day, a relentless focus on what they were wearing and similar trivia. It would be like every movie that featured two women battling it out. Women made great copy, that was the way the popular culture worked. Sawyer herself wasn't above that sort of thing; they all loved reading the gossip columns.

Westin told her that that sort of coverage would be temporary, that she could ride it out, but Sawyer disagreed. She did not want her evening news tenure to be viewed through that prism. If she went to Darfur, the stories would be all about how she was trying to demonstrate that she was more interested in the plight of refugees than Couric was. She would be cast in a catfight. Couric would be the featured player, and her role would be to juice up the story. No matter what she did journalistically, everyone would suspect her motives. No, it just wouldn't work. This was Katie's moment. Sawyer would not thrust herself into that particular spotlight.

*   *   *

Elizabeth Vargas was feeling nauseous every day.

This was an exceedingly difficult pregnancy, far more taxing than her first one. She was headed for a scheduled cesarean section in mid-August, and she felt awful. But day after day, as she dragged herself through the afternoon Webcast and the evening newscast, Vargas tried not to let it show.

The situation was enormously frustrating. She was the anchor of *World News Tonight.* She wanted to shine, to be her best. Yet at times she felt that she had fallen short of her own standards.

Vargas had gotten a jolt in February when David Westin had spoken with her about the three scenarios he was weighing. There was Elizabeth on her own, Elizabeth with Charlie, or Diane anchoring.

"What do you mean?" Vargas asked. "With me?"

"No," said Westin. "You and Diane would switch jobs."

Vargas was stunned. He wanted to ship her to *Good Morning America*?

"Well," Westin said, "you've always said you loved doing morning news."

At another point in her career, Vargas might have jumped at such a move. She had been all but run off the show a decade earlier. But at the moment, she was ABC's top news anchor.

"You can't do this to me now," Vargas said. "It will look like I've failed."

Westin said he didn't want to do anything that would damage her career. But the fact that she was a mother—unlike Sawyer, he might have added, or Robin Roberts, the third cohost—would hold great appeal for the morning audience.

"I have to be honest with you, David," Vargas said. "I think *GMA* is unwatchable. If you send me to that show, you're going to have to blow it up." She said the program wasn't tightly focused enough on the news and ran too many freakish segments about strange people and strange diseases.

Still, the news flash was that Sawyer, the biggest star at the network, seemed to be in play for *World News.*

"Does Diane want it?" Vargas asked.

"I don't know," Westin said. "I can't even tell what Diane wants. I think she wants it, but I don't know how much."

With that, Westin let the job switch drop and did not bring it up again.

As the weeks dragged on, what was most infuriating to Vargas was having to stay until 10 o'clock each night because of Westin's innovation, the West Coast update. There was exactly one market, Los Angeles, that took the 9:30 feed. They were barely updating the broadcast at all, just making small changes for the sake of making changes. Meanwhile, she was not able to be home with Zachary, who insisted on staying up till she got home and was having serious sleeping problems. The situation was ludicrous. She had to find a way she could do her job and still be a moderately decent mother.

When her doctor urged her to cut back her workday, at least to ten hours a day instead of the twelve-and-a-half-hour marathons she was putting in,

Vargas went to see Westin. They had to drop the West Coast updates, she said.

"David, I'm the mother of a three-year-old," Vargas said. "I cannot be away from home all these nights."

Westin knew how hard Vargas was working and that she could be putting herself in physical jeopardy. But he believed strongly that ABC should not be broadcasting a show in the West that was three hours old. What's more, Robert Iger, at Disney, and Anne Sweeney, the network president, both loved the updated newscast and, from their California perspective, considered it a huge deal. Westin refused to change the schedule.

The impasse over coanchoring was keeping everyone on edge. Sawyer could not believe that Gibson's dream job was slipping away again. She marched down the hall to his office, walked in, and began lecturing him.

"Don't do this to yourself again," Sawyer insisted. "If you want this, go get this. If you coanchor with Elizabeth, you're going to be the driving force because of your seniority with the show."

Gibson was so stunned by her performance that he didn't know what to say.

Later that morning Gibson came padding down the hall and stuck his head in Sawyer's office.

"Thank you," he said. No further words were needed.

Gibson never changed his stance, but perhaps his opposition no longer seemed quite as rigid. Westin was telling Vargas that he believed Gibson was close to agreeing to serve as her coanchor. That would take some of the burden off her and would solve the problem of what to do during the two months that she planned to be on maternity leave.

Westin was under considerable pressure. The press was constantly highlighting the fact that *World News* had lost 900,000 viewers during the season, while Bob Schieffer had picked up almost as many and was pulling closer to Vargas in the ratings.

On May 16, Westin asked Vargas to come to his office. The situation, he said, was still unsettled. But he was concerned about her maternity leave.

"I'm worried that you won't want to come back," Westin said.

How likely was *that*? Vargas sensed that the ground was beginning to shift, that Westin's promises to her over the past few months were no longer quite so ironclad. Vargas suddenly wondered whether this was the real reason that ABC had never run a single commercial touting her as the evening news anchor.

"Your lack of promotion of me is now beginning to feel like a lack of confidence," she said.

Westin assured her that he had enormous confidence in her. But her maternity leave loomed large. Gibson had not agreed to serve as her coanchor, Westin said, and would not be able to fill in for her while she was off. The other alternatives were Dan Harris, an ABC correspondent, and Terry Moran, one of the new *Nightline* anchors. But the ratings had dipped when they substituted in the past.

"Dan or Terry filling in for you would kill the show," Westin said.

Vargas looked at him. "What are you going to do if Charlie doesn't sign?"

"I don't know," he said.

When she got home that night, Vargas told her husband Marc that she believed a power play was in the works. "Charlie's pushing to get this by himself," she said.

Westin had become increasingly concerned that Elizabeth didn't fully understand just how big a commitment it was to anchor *World News Tonight.* When she came back from having the baby, there would be a whole new set of demands on her, including plenty of travel for the newscast. How could she handle that, and *20/20,* and deal with her child and a new baby?

In part, Westin was reflecting the worries communicated to him by some of the *World News* staff. Some of the reporters and producers did not consider her a strong leader or someone with a vision for the newscast. While Woodruff had been a correspondent for the program, Vargas had always been an outsider.

As he edged closer to making up his mind, Westin decided to visit Bob Woodruff at his home in New York's Westchester County, where he was recuperating from his injuries.

The recovery had been slow and frustrating. After Woodruff had awakened from a thirty-six-day coma, he could not remember his brothers' names, or the fact that he had six-year-old twins. The rocks and shrapnel that had penetrated his face had damaged the part of the brain that controls speech. When he listened to television news reports, he could not understand a thing. He struggled to recall the most common words. Woodruff's children helped him with flash cards and practice sessions. His wife, Lee, who had once feared that he would emerge from all the surgery blind and deaf, alternated between joy at his gradual recovery and anger at the ordeal he had inflicted on the family.

When Westin arrived, he found Woodruff in good spirits. His black hair had been trimmed to a buzz cut, and the scars from his surgery were visible on the top of his head. He clearly tired easily. But he was able to carry on a conversation, even as he occasionally grappled for the right word.

Westin explained the problem facing the broadcast.

"I feel really badly that you're in this jam," Woodruff said.

"Let's just see you get well," Westin said. No matter how long it took, and even if he could work only a few hours a week, Woodruff would have a place waiting for him at ABC.

But Woodruff knew that there was something unspoken between them. Westin, he felt, must be wondering whether there was any job that Woodruff could do, whether he could ever appear on television again. Woodruff did not know the answer to that question. He knew only that he wanted to get back to some form of journalism.

Westin had gone back to Diane Sawyer several times, just to make absolutely sure that she didn't want to throw her hat into the evening news ring. He wanted to play his cards face up with everyone. But Diane, however ambivalent she might have felt, was still backing Charlie.

It was time to make another run at Gibson.

"I really want you to do this," Westin told him. "But you've got to be prepared to do it with Elizabeth."

"Sorry," Gibson said. "I know you believe in it. I backed you the last time," when Vargas and Woodruff had been named. "But I just don't believe in it. I just don't believe it's a two-anchor job."

Gibson wanted the job but wouldn't be crushed if he didn't get it. He was perfectly comfortable serving out his remaining time at *GMA,* which had been his plan before Jennings got sick.

He had been discussing the situation with his wife. "I want what you want," she said. "Please understand that if you do this, I'm fine. I will not be bored. I will not complain that you're spending time at work or away."

Westin would always believe that he had done the right thing in teaming Elizabeth Vargas with Bob Woodruff. But forcing Gibson into a shotgun marriage made no sense. The truth was, he just didn't have the perfect person to pair with Vargas, and he no longer believed that she could handle the workload on her own. Westin felt especially bad because he was the one who had talked her into taking the job. But the maternity leave problem was insurmountable. He couldn't very well ask Gibson, after passing him over last time, to fill in for Vargas for two months and then go back to *GMA.* It would be too much of an insult.

The problem, Westin knew, was that Katie Couric was making her CBS debut in September, and Brian Williams was still leading the field at NBC. At precisely the time when *World News* needed to be competitive, he couldn't go to a second-string lineup.

Westin had to face the facts. Charlie Gibson was the best person he had to anchor the newscast, and Gibson would do it only on his own. Westin had pushed as hard as he could push. Gibson was an incredibly experienced newsman, someone in the Peter Jennings mold. He could bring to the broadcast a strong editorial voice. Westin concluded that he could no longer keep his promise to Vargas. He had to do what was best for the news division. He summoned Gibson to his office.

"I want you to do *World News,* and I want you to do it solo," Westin said.

Gibson thanked him. Now all that remained were the negotiations with his agent. "I hope we can work this out," Gibson said.

He asked about Vargas. Westin said that she would take a longer maternity leave than she had planned and then return to *20/20.*

What about Bob Woodruff? When he came back to work, would Westin want him back on the broadcast, perhaps with Elizabeth?

"That's way down the pike," Westin said.

Gibson felt like he was in a daze, but he had to know about the future of *GMA.* Westin said that Sawyer and Robin Roberts, the former ESPN sportscaster who had been elevated to a cohost spot a year earlier, would carry on without him.

The negotiations continued over the weekend, eased by the fact that Gibson had decided not to ask for another cent beyond his multimillion-dollar *GMA* salary. On Saturday night Gibson ran into Bob Schieffer in a front-row seat, to the right of the home dugout, at a Washington Nationals game. The two were old pals, having spent years covering Capitol Hill.

A few weeks earlier Schieffer had run into Vargas at Gabriel's restaurant on the West Side of Manhattan and asked how her pregnancy was going.

"How long are you going to work?" Schieffer had asked.

"I'm going to work right up to the last minute," she said. "I'll be there to the end."

But Schieffer had always believed that Vargas wouldn't last, and that Charlie or Diane would probably get the job.

Now he asked Gibson: "Well, what are y'all gonna do?"

"God only knows," Gibson said.

"My guess is they're gonna give you that job," Schieffer said.

Gibson said he honestly wasn't sure what would happen. But, he said, "I think there's going to be some sort of announcement this week."

On Monday Gibson agreed to a three-year contract that would carry him through the 2008 presidential campaign, the very issue that had derailed his candidacy the previous fall. But both he and Westin understood that, as long as he wasn't a total flop, he would continue in the chair beyond then. Money was not a factor: Gibson did not ask for one dollar more than he was making at *GMA*.

Now Westin had to tell Vargas that his previous assurances to her were no longer valid. This, he knew, was an inescapable part of his job, and when he no longer felt able to deliver bad news to employees, he should quit.

The meeting, like the rest, took place on the couch in his office.

"Elizabeth, I just think this is not going to work," Westin said. "I think it's best to just put in Charlie."

Vargas didn't say much. Gibson had played hardball, and he had won. The irony was that Westin had coaxed her into taking the job in the first place. All of her instincts had been to wait. She had believed the previous fall that Gibson had deserved a turn at the job, should be allowed to do it for two or three years, and then she would have her turn. Now Westin had taken away her dream job after just five months.

But Vargas did not blame him. Westin had made the decision with a gun to his head. Who would have thought that Charlie, who was universally regarded as a nice guy, would play such a tough hand? She believed that he had gotten the job by threatening to quit, although he was simply promising to stick to his previously planned retirement the following year. She also believed, wrongly, that Gibson had refused to substitute for her during the maternity leave as a way of ratcheting up the pressure.

How could this possibly be fair? Bob Woodruff had been bombed and she had gotten pregnant, and now, because Gibson wanted to be a solo act, she was out? Gibson, she felt, had blatantly taken advantage of the tragedy and her family situation. Looking back, one of the turning points had come after Bob was injured in Iraq, when Westin had installed Gibson and Sawyer as her alternating coanchors for the month of February. Vargas had really felt jerked around by the move. That had been an announcement to the world that management felt she couldn't handle the job on her own, and it had reignited all the talk about how unfair it was that Charlie had been passed over. It gave the pro-Charlie agitators at ABC a chance to renew their campaign against the woman they viewed as an interloper, to whisper that she wasn't up to the task.

But Vargas said none of this. She didn't believe in getting mad or yelling in meetings. What would that accomplish? Women had always been taught, don't get emotional, gather yourself, leave the room. Vargas ended the meeting in less than ten minutes and returned to her office.

The next morning, May 23, Gibson went to see Vargas.

For months he had been tempted to approach her. He had felt terrible about what was happening. He knew what it was like to have your job openly shopped in the press, an experience he had been through before he left *GMA* the first time. But he felt that he could not approach her—her first question would be, "What do you know?" And at the time, he didn't know anything. He read the same gossip as everyone else, but didn't have a clue whether he or someone else would get her job. So he said nothing.

Now the time had come.

"I'm sorry," Gibson said. "I know what you've been going through. I hope you're satisfied with what you did. You were a creature of circumstance. Bob's injury hurt you worse than anybody. This was not the situation you were hired for."

Gibson found Vargas to be extremely gracious. When they were finished talking, he gave her a big hug.

Vargas didn't like confrontations. Maybe Charlie had rationalized the whole thing to himself. What was she supposed to do: Convince him that he had been a jerk? Point out that his own daughter had just given birth to his first grandchild? What would that buy her?

Gibson made sure to talk to Woodruff's wife, Lee. He told her that as every clause of his contract was being negotiated, he had discussed with ABC how this would affect Bob. The network had been patient, he said, and Bob would always be welcome at the newscast.

Moments later, ABC News announced that the new anchor of *World News Tonight* was Charles Gibson.

To Vargas and her allies, Gibson had trampled her while bulling his way into the job. From Gibson's perspective, he had merely set the conditions under which he would and would not take over the evening newscast and let Westin make the decision.

What Vargas found exasperating were the other concessions that Gibson had extracted. Westin had agreed to drop the West Coast updates, and it was understood that at sixty-three, Gibson would not be parachuting into war zones. That was the job she had wanted, had begged for, and could easily have handled. All those nights when she had been stuck at the office until ten, and now Charlie wouldn't have to do any of that. This was hard to fathom.

The one person who was upbeat about the turn of events was Marc

Cohn. It had been difficult for Vargas to come home late every night and deal with her husband's unhappiness. He, at least, had gotten his wish.

Bob Woodruff felt guilty over what he had done to Elizabeth. By getting himself injured in Iraq, he knew, he had blown up their partnership. There was no way that one anchor could handle the kind of travel and long hours that their arrangement had required, and her pregnancy had sealed her fate.

Vargas now had to weigh how candid to be with the press. She decided to be a team player. She would emphasize what was true, that the pregnancy had put a great strain on her and that she was relieved, on one level, to be freed from an impossible workload. Of *course* she had felt conflicted over that. But in claiming that she had made the decision, rather than acknowledging that her coveted anchorship had been snatched away from her, Vargas was playing along with an ABC cover story that bore no resemblance to what had actually happened.

That Friday, preparing for her final newscast, Vargas wrote her farewell: "It's been an honor and a privilege to share the news with you these past months." Two hours before airtime Cathie Levine, the spokeswoman for *World News,* told her she needed to respond to a letter that the National Organization for Women and two other women's groups had written Westin. The letter called Vargas's job change "a clear demotion" and "a dispiriting return to the days of discrimination against women."

Vargas had to make a choice. She could be the poster girl for NOW for a couple of months and make things ugly and uncomfortable for ABC. But then she would be labeled a troublemaker, and she had four years to go on her contract. What was the upside of playing the role of the victimized pregnant woman? She held her tongue.

Westin was furious about the letter. Hadn't he given Vargas the anchor job in the first place, despite the fact that she had a young son? He fired off an aggressive response to NOW. "Your letter is contrary to the facts and to common sense," Westin wrote. "No one has 'demoted' her, much less shown 'discrimination' against her as a woman or because of her impending maternity leave."

But it was too late. A backlash against the dumping of Vargas was building in the press. Despite the fact that she had not uttered a peep of protest, Vargas had become a national symbol of the professional hazards facing pregnant women.

The *St. Petersburg Times* said that the move was "reinforcing many women's fears that the family card will reshuffle their careers to the bottom of the deck."

"Elizabeth Vargas did not deserve to be kicked to the curb. It appears she is being punished for becoming pregnant," said the *South Florida Sun-Sentinel*. Andrew Tyndall, the television industry analyst, declared that Vargas had suffered "the worst workplace nightmare" of the pregnant employee. Carol Rivers, a journalism professor at Boston University, said that Vargas's replacement sent "a message to all women taking maternity leave that you missed your shot."

Vargas was flabbergasted by the number of calls and e-mails pouring in from working mothers at the networks, expressing sympathy for her plight. Clearly, her ouster from the newscast had touched some kind of exposed nerve.

When she talked about the situation with friends, Vargas wondered what ABC executives had bought themselves, other than several years of a status quo newscast until Gibson eventually retired. When she and Woodruff had been chosen, at least the network was making a statement that it wanted a bold new program. Gibson was palatable to most people at ABC, Vargas told her allies, precisely because he didn't augur any big changes that would shake things up.

Days after the decision was announced, Diane Sawyer walked into Vargas's office and shut the door. Sawyer felt that Vargas had been a wonderful team player, very confident on the air, and she wanted to vent for a moment.

"I would like to come back in my next life as Charlie Gibson," Sawyer said. "We have both sat next to this man when he's thrown temper tantrums on the set. That never gets written up. Why is it we get written about and speculated about so much?"

They both agreed: because Charlie was a man. Gender still played a huge role in how network anchors were portrayed in the press. A male journalist might be viewed as demanding, while they were dissed as divas. It was a complaint with which Katie Couric was intimately familiar.

What Vargas had to decide in the coming months was how much of a career remained for her at ABC. She would see how much she could accomplish at *20/20*. But that was a taped weekly show, and she loved hard news, daily news, live broadcasting. The day after the announcement, executives from the other networks had been on the phone to her agent. If ABC couldn't find something fulfilling for her, she would get management's permission to put out some feelers. Vargas had never set out to become the anchor of *World News Tonight,* but losing the job, after so briefly tasting its fruits, had been a bitter experience indeed.

CHAPTER 20

Morning Man

Brian Williams had just gotten back from vacation, had dragged the suitcases up the stairs, and was out of breath when he got a phone call telling him that Peter Jennings had died. He had watched ABC that night and was struck by the way Charlie Gibson handled the sad news, calm and steady with just the right dollop of emotion.

Gibson, he thought, had struck all the necessary notes. He had always projected a comfortable, old-shoe feeling and was easy to watch. Charlie would be formidable competition if he got Jennings's chair, Williams felt.

Williams and Gibson were similar in many ways: solid newsmen, not particularly flashy, with more than a touch of the traditionalist. Both were dogged competitors who kept their ambition safely tucked beneath a nice-guy aura, family men with all-American names who wore reading glasses, had married young, and each had two kids. Gibson hailed from an older generation, of course, and sported a middle-aged paunch. But Williams clung to a courtly belief that fierce television rivals—and they would be locked in a battle for survival—could also be friends.

When Gibson finally got the anchor nod, Williams sat down and typed him a congratulatory letter, continuing the tradition that Dan Rather and Peter Jennings had followed when he was named to succeed Tom Brokaw. Williams apologized for being slightly late with his note, but said he had just gotten back from a three-day trip to Africa with the singer and AIDS activist Bono—and had to attend his daughter Allison's high school graduation and sweat out prom night.

"While the circumstances could not be stranger or more bittersweet,"

Williams wrote, "your ascension to this job is a terrific development for the news business and for what we do each night."

He was just warming up.

"From the moment of Peter's death (as I need not tell you), you have been the class of a vastly altered news division. You are one of a select few veterans in our business with no known enemies. You have gingerly navigated the unique tragedy of Bob's injuries, and you have always been kind to me. I know we will have fun at this while competing against one another . . . You have raised our game by joining the field."

John Reiss, the *Nightly* producer, had once been Gibson's producer at *Good Morning America* and liked him enormously. Charlie was smart, hardworking, the best ad-libber in the business and, in his sixties, closer to the average age of the evening news audience. Reiss dashed off a congratulatory e-mail.

Gibson sent back a note of thanks, adding: "Now explain to me why the hell you went to Africa with Bono."

Reiss found the line about Williams's trip puzzling.

Gibson had simply been expressing his curiosity. The idea of the anchor of a network newscast traveling with a rock star seemed strange to him. Maybe there was something he didn't get.

Later in the day Gibson was giving an interview to Joe Hagan, a reporter for *New York* magazine, and recalled the e-mail he had sent Reiss. When the article came out, Gibson was quoted as addressing the question of why Williams had taken the trip: "That's because of Katrina, you saw him going down there. Now he's in Africa. I don't know why you do that. Why the hell do you go to Africa? It's certainly an interesting choice. We'll do travel, when it warrants."

When Gibson saw the quote on a media Web site, he thought: Oh damn. The guy had left out two critical words: *with Bono.* This was why Gibson often avoided reading what was written about him.

Cathie Levine, the *World News* spokeswoman, marched into Gibson's office.

"You can't ignore this," she said.

"Yeah, I can," Gibson said.

"No, you really can't," Levine insisted.

She was right. The comment was beginning to reverberate. A black radio station in Chicago was ripping Gibson for appearing indifferent to African poverty and disease.

Gibson spoke to AP reporter David Bauder and said he had just been jesting, but more important, that he certainly wasn't questioning the importance of reporting in Africa. He also got on the phone with Roland Martin, the host of a talk show on Chicago's WVON.

"This guy, who I will never talk to again, from *New York* magazine, who is something of a snake, he took my quote and I think perverted the meaning of it to indicate in some way that I was insensitive to news from one of the five major continents in the world," Gibson said. Hagan, for his part, stood by his story.

When Reiss told him about the quote, Williams figured that Gibson just didn't understand Bono's importance as a global activist, as someone who had met with President Bush, as one of *Time*'s persons of the year. Williams also surmised that Gibson must feel like an idiot, having delivered that slap so soon after receiving his congratulatory letter.

Gibson regretted that his comment had been misconstrued. He also felt it was a mistake to have called Hagan a snake. The truth was, he was not accustomed to the white-hot spotlight that came with being an evening news anchor. Morning television was a more freewheeling atmosphere, and besides, Diane Sawyer had soaked up most of the publicity. Now he had to watch his words more carefully.

After thirty-one years with ABC Gibson had great confidence as a broadcaster, but in some ways he was wary of the challenge in taking on *World News*. He was rock solid on American politics, which he loved, but what about areas like the Middle East? Gibson was worried that at some point he would demonstrate how much better Jennings had handled that story.

When Yitzhak Rabin, the Israeli prime minister, was killed in 1995, Gibson, who had been at a college football game in Chicago, flew to New York and caught the last El Al flight to Tel Aviv, where he was stuck in a middle seat between two women. One was clearly crazy, babbling to herself. When he expressed his condolences to the other Israeli woman, she said, "I wish they'd killed the bastard years ago." Gibson pored over his briefing books on the long flight and performed credibly for *GMA*. But when Jennings came on the air, he began a disquisition about the cedar trees that surrounded the cemetery where Rabin was being buried and the meaning of the trees. Where the hell had that come from? How did Peter do it?

Of course, Jennings had had twenty-two years to grow into the anchor job. Gibson had slipped into the chair six days after the announcement that he was replacing Elizabeth Vargas. He didn't really know what they should do about covering Iraq. Was it fair to ask correspondents to risk their lives there? Maybe they could give video cameras to ordinary Iraqis to get footage of what life was like, but would that be putting them at risk? He had not had a chance to think these things through.

Gibson was in some respects a reluctant leader. Although he had been raised an Episcopalian, he had received a Quaker education and became enamored of the philosophy that there was a little bit of God in every man. He still occasionally attended Quaker gatherings, where questions were hashed out through quiet deliberation until a "sense of the meeting" was achieved. But at a network newscast, where dozens of decisions had to be made under the tyranny of a ticking clock, there was no time for such niceties. People would turn to him and say, *Okay, what are we going to do?* And Gibson was expected to have the answers.

*   *   *

After years in the minor leagues, Charles DeWolf Gibson had finally become a national reporter. Roger Ailes had to decide whether he got to keep the job.

It was 1975, and Gibson had signed on with an outfit called Television News, which had grand ambitions of becoming the nation's fourth network. With a handful of crews in New York, Washington, Chicago, and Los Angeles, and a blueprint for using new satellite technology to beam material to local stations across the country, TVN was a major experiment in providing an alternative to ABC, CBS, and NBC. It was also bankrolled by Joseph Coors, the conservative beer magnate in Colorado. Coors, who considered Walter Cronkite a leftist, said that he was putting his company's money into the operation "because of our strong belief that network news is slanted to the liberal, left side of the spectrum and does not give an objective view to the American public."

Much of the service's Washington reporting was straightforward, and that included Gibson's—he covered the congressional hearings on Watergate, where he sat next to ABC newsman Sam Donaldson, and the trials of top Nixon White House officials. But some of the one hundred local stations that subscribed to the service later dropped it, in some cases questioning its objectivity, and TVN went deep into the red. At that point Coors brought in Ailes, who had been a young media adviser in Richard Nixon's 1968 campaign, to save the operation. And Ailes, in turn, summoned Gibson to his office.

"Given what this place is trying to do," Ailes said, "I should probably fire you." Gibson took that to mean that Ailes did not believe he was conservative enough to fit in with an avowedly conservative operation.

"But," Ailes said, "you're pretty good on the air." Gibson got to hang on to his job.

The reprieve, as it turned out, was temporary. Television News, an early precursor of Fox News in the pre-cable era, soon went belly up, but not before Gibson, based in part on Donaldson's recommendation, had been hired by ABC.

Gibson was, on many levels, a creature of Washington. He grew up in Evanston, Illinois, watching *The Huntley-Brinkley Report* on NBC every night with his father, and the family had moved to Washington when he was twelve. Gibson's dad had gotten a job at the Commerce Department, and Charlie attended Sidwell Friends School, an exclusive Quaker institution with a well-tended campus that educated many of the offspring of the city's elite. The capital was an ideal location for a teenager who liked to pore over *Congressional Quarterly.*

Gibson went off to Princeton, where he met his future wife, Arlene, and when Yale Law School rejected him, he returned to Washington and landed a $325-a-month job as a producer for the RKO radio network. He was fired four months later, when the local union insisted that he be paid the same wages as its members. With the Vietnam War escalating, Gibson enrolled in the Coast Guard reserve to avoid the draft and, by lying about his meager radio experience, landed in a training program at Washington's ABC affiliate, Channel 7. The work was rather menial: cutting down B-movies that the station aired on Sunday afternoons; keeping score at a bowling show taped in the alley downstairs; and cleaning up after Coco, the French poodle on the children's show *Claire and Coco.* But he did well enough that the station shipped him to another company property, WLVA in Lynchburg, Virginia, for seasoning.

Gibson was so absorbed by politics that he paid his own way to the 1968 Republican convention in Miami. When he walked into the area where the *Today* show had set up its live location, he thought how glamorous it must be to have the politicians come to you for interviews, rather than prostrating yourself for access, as he and other local reporters routinely did.

Gibson grew utterly absorbed by the desegregation battles in Lynchburg, which had one white high school and one black high school. He was appalled by the *Lynchburg News and Daily Advertiser,* which he considered to be racist, a newspaper in which black people essentially did not exist, except for those Negroes who were convicted of crimes. He was so transfixed by the racial issues that he became too much of a civil rights advocate at WLVA. Gibson and his colleagues at the station found themselves denounced by the paper's editorial page. In retrospect, Gibson would come to feel that he had been a young punk who came in thinking he knew everything. When he was about to leave town in 1970—his wife had already returned to Washington—he discovered that all four tires on his car had been slashed.

Gibson became a reporter and weekend anchor back at Channel 7, now called WJLA, where the news director, Leonard Deibert, found him savvy and confident, just this side of cocky, and curious about nearly everything. He never turned down an assignment. When a hurricane struck Washington, Gibson was out on Chain Bridge, describing the dangerously rising waters of the Potomac River below. But the general manager, Tom Cookerly, was never enthusiastic about Gibson.

"He'll never make it in television," Cookerly told Deibert. "He looks too preppy."

When Cookerly tried to transfer him to the company's radio station, Gibson quit. He obtained a journalism fellowship at the University of Michigan and tried to figure out whether he had a future in television. He asked Arlene whether he should try again to go to law school.

"I'm probably never going to hit it in this business, and I'm probably never going to make a lot of money," he said.

Arlene asked what he loved doing.

"I love this," Gibson said.

He gave it one more shot, with Joe Coors's fledgling operation, and became a general assignment reporter for ABC News in 1975. Gibson was soon promoted to cover the Ford White House, and after the 1976 election he was shifted to the House of Representatives, in an era when the networks had a correspondent assigned to each chamber. He loved the debates and political intrigue of Congress, but the challenge was getting on the air from an institution where legislation seemed to progress one inch at a time.

Roone Arledge's philosophy, as Gibson saw it, was to throw staff members together and make them compete. ABC's man in the Senate was Brit Hume, and Gibson felt that Arledge wanted them to go at it hammer and tong and see who emerged. Gibson took the gentlemanly approach instead, inviting Hume to lunch and offering a nonaggression pact, even though *World News* would generally take only one piece a night from Capitol Hill. After Ronald Reagan was elected, Gibson felt ideally positioned because Tip O'Neill, the House speaker, had become the leader of the Democratic opposition, and the House was the only chamber that allowed television cameras.

After spending nearly a decade on the Hill, Gibson realized that he had to find something else to do or he would be stuck there forever. He had been substituting periodically for Ted Koppel on *Nightline* and soon began coanchoring a 6 A.M. newscast, with Kathleen Sullivan, called *World News This Morning.* He could do it from Washington, and no one else wanted the gig because ABC had made it an extra responsibility, to be followed by a full day's work. The show had trouble attracting advertising, but Gibson's role drew the interest of Joan Lunden.

At Lunden's urging, the network began using Gibson to substitute for David Hartman, her longtime cohost on *Good Morning America.* That was a big break, because Arledge didn't particularly like Gibson and would never have pushed to give him a tryout.

Arledge was not pleased. After a few of Gibson's appearances, he called Rick Kaplan, the producer who ran the news side of *GMA,* and started yelling at him.

"Charlie's not an anchor," Arledge declared.

Kaplan insisted that Gibson was actually quite strong, and Arledge gradually came to agree.

In 1986 the network asked Gibson to take over for Hartman for a week. It was a measure of Gibson's ambivalence about the show that he decided to go skiing with his family instead. He watched *GMA* every morning during the vacation, and realized that he had probably doomed his chances of moving to the morning. His ambition was to succeed Steve Bell, the program's news reader, who was based in Washington. Gibson and his wife had a nice life in Washington and weren't wild about moving to New York.

Before long Phil Beuth, the executive in charge of *GMA,* was asking to speak to Gibson in the company cafeteria.

"What you don't know is that on Tuesday it's going to be announced that David Hartman is quitting," Beuth said. "You're very much in my mind."

Gibson said he wasn't sure he was right for the job.

"I'll make you a deal," Beuth said. "If you decide you don't want it, you'll call me. If I lose interest, I'll call you." That call never came.

There was, however, a major problem. Arlene was a candidate to head the Holton Arms School, a prestigious private school in Bethesda, Maryland, where she was in charge of the lower grades. They talked about the possibility of moving to New York.

"If you get it, I will turn down *GMA,*" Gibson told her. His friends all said that he was crazy, and Gibson himself wasn't sure whether he was telling her the truth. As it turned out, Arlene was passed over for the post, and ABC offered David Hartman's prized chair to Gibson.

Still, he hesitated. What if he bombed? "I'm worried about taking *GMA* because it may not last," he told Kathleen Sullivan. But the job was too tempting to pass up, and the deal was made.

Gibson's promotion on January 29, 1987, was not a big story—the press in those days did not obsess over each morning show move—but there was some chatter about whether he was the right choice. Hartman had once been an actor, and his successor was anything but. Gibson had "the dogged, authoritarian air of a political reporter," *The Washington Post* observed. He was a "Washington reporter who has demonstrated a hard-edged toughness," said the *Los Angeles Times*. But Gibson found that he enjoyed the cooking segments and some of the lighter features, that they enabled him to show more of his personality.

Still, despite his years in television, Gibson realized that almost no one in the country knew who he was. In fact, people who stopped him on the street often confused him with Brit Hume. At times he felt like an impostor. What was he doing with two hours of national television every morning? He also had trouble getting up at 3:20, in the middle of the night, and was dragging by the time he reached the studio.

The art of interviewing celebrities did not come naturally to Gibson. When he chatted with Vanessa Williams, who had been dethroned as Miss America, he asked how she felt about being equated in the public mind with the sexually explicit photographs that had been published of her with another woman. Williams froze and said she dealt with it by hoping that people like him wouldn't continue to bring it up. A more adept host might have handled the matter more smoothly, Gibson felt, but he was a newsman at heart.

No matter. Joan Lunden was now the star. He did the heavy news lifting—when the Persian Gulf War erupted, Gibson went to Saudi Arabia to report from the region—and the audience grew comfortable with him. *Good Morning America* remained a strong second in the race to overtake Bryant Gumbel and Jane Pauley at *Today*.

Gibson liked Lunden and was grateful to her for helping him get the job, but he was not above making a joke or two at her expense. One day Sam Donaldson, who had recently started coanchoring *Primetime Live* with Diane Sawyer, was in a sedan on Columbus Avenue, waiting for a red light, when he saw Gibson in the next car. They both rolled down their windows.

"Charlie, guess what," Donaldson shouted. "Now both of us are teamed with beautiful blondes."

"Yeah, but you got the smart one," Gibson cracked.

It was, by any measure, a successful partnership. Gibson and Lunden caught a break when *Today* imploded over the hiring of Deborah Norville, who was replaced by Katie Couric, and *GMA* surged into first place. Over time, Gibson learned to balance the tension between the fluffy aspects of the show and the demands of the news division, which eventually gained control of the program from ABC's entertainment unit.

When major news broke, Gibson was generally the one hopping on airplanes. He flew to Oklahoma City right after the federal building there was bombed, and he went back after Timothy McVeigh was convicted in the murderous attack.

GMA held on to its ratings lead for six long years until 1995, when *Today,* like *NBC Nightly News,* was playing up the O.J. Simpson case day after day. Gibson was surprised that the press didn't criticize Couric and Gumbel for their obsessive focus on the sensationalized case, and was glad that he and Lunden had not exploited the double murder to the same degree.

He soon had other things to worry about. On the morning of July 31, 1995, Gibson sensed that something big was brewing because the studio next door was being readied for a news conference, apparently by ABC's owner, Capital Cities.

At 7:25, a *GMA* producer, Bob Reichblum, told Gibson in his earpiece that the Walt Disney Company had just announced that it was buying ABC. An hour later, without benefit of preparation, Gibson was conducting a live interview with Michael Eisner, the Disney chairman, and Thomas Murphy, who ran Capital Cities, about the $19 billion blockbuster deal.

The encounter was nothing if not awkward. Gibson asked the obvious journalistic question: What would be the impact on ABC News of a takeover by one of the world's largest entertainment conglomerates? When the bosses asked how *he* felt, Gibson replied: "I never thought I'd work for a guy named Mickey."

Murphy put Gibson on the spot, asking: "Wouldn't you be proud to be associated with Disney?"

Gibson stammered for a moment. "Yes, sure," he replied, but said he had to remain an "objective interviewer."

A year later, he appeared less than objective. *Good Morning America* did a broadcast from Disney World, devoting the program to praising the park on its fiftieth anniversary. "Probably the greatest man-made vacation center that has ever been built," Gibson said. Maybe so, but his presence was embarrassing.

While the acquisition by Disney had no immediate impact on Gibson's career, declining ratings most assuredly did. Joan Lunden left the program in the spring of 1997 and was replaced by Lisa McRee, an anchor from ABC's Los Angeles station—a move that also led to the departure of Elizabeth Vargas as *GMA*'s news reader.

Gibson blamed ABC management for destroying the program's sense of family, a crucial ingredient when you were guests in people's homes at such an early hour. He felt strongly that *Good Morning America* was being dumbed down, that there were too many pointless segments along the lines of "fun things to do with raisins." And maybe, after eleven years, he had grown stale as well.

The next few months were particularly awful. Gibson saw that his job was being openly advertised in the press, but no one in management said a word to him. Even before Lunden's departure, there were stories like the one in *USA Today* that said: "ABC executives are scouting around for someone to replace Gibson at some point and hope to find someone to help No. 2 *GMA* pull ahead of *Today.*" Everyone in the business was gossiping about his future. After a decade in the penthouse of morning television, Gibson knew that his elevator was headed down. Perhaps it was time to get off.

In the final weeks of 1997 Gibson began negotiating with the A&E Network to become the host of the series *Biography.* He decided to stay with ABC, though, and in March 1998 the network announced that Kevin Newman, who had become the show's news reader five months earlier, was taking over Gibson's job. Gibson was shifted to *20/20,* cohosting an hour before *Monday Night Football* with Connie Chung, and occasionally filling in for Peter Jennings.

Friends viewed this as a difficult period for Gibson and tried to boost his morale. Sam Donaldson saw a parallel to Jennings when he was dropped as anchor after his first stint in the 1960s. "Charlie, you're good," Donaldson told him. "You've got it. Remember how Peter got thrown out and had nothing to do and went overseas? I'm sure they'll find a job for you."

At *GMA,* meanwhile, the ratings were plummeting, from 4.1 million viewers to 3.1 million, and the reviews were awful. No one knew who Newman and McRee were, and there was no way that they could compete with Katie Couric and her new partner, Matt Lauer.

David Westin was desperate to save the show. He began a series of conversations with Diane Sawyer, who had once done the CBS morning show and now co-hosted *20/20* two nights a week, about moving to *GMA* as a temporary measure. This would be a radical step for Sawyer, but she liked the notion of being a savior and was drawn to the idea of working with an old pro like Gibson. Westin approached Gibson as well. Would he, out of loyalty to ABC, return to the show with Sawyer, at least for a few months?

Gibson had first become aware of Sawyer back when he was a student at Princeton. Bill Bradley was the basketball phenomenon and biggest star on campus, and Bradley, Gibson knew, was dating America's Junior Miss, a beauty queen named Diane Sawyer.

Gibson had followed Sawyer's career when she became a press aide in the Nixon White House and after that when she joined CBS News. The first time he saw her in person, Sawyer was standing in front of him at a news event and taking notes with four different colored pens. The woman, apparently, was well organized.

Neither of them, for the moment, was ready to take the leap. They wanted assurances that Westin would pour more resources into *GMA* and that they would be able to shape it into a newsier program. Salaries were not an issue: Sawyer was already making $7 million a year, and Gibson about $3 million. Neither asked for an extra nickel.

On Christmas Eve Gibson and Sawyer sat down for a heart-to-heart talk in her tenth-floor office. Gibson allowed that he was ready to return to his old show if Sawyer would be his partner, and she agreed that the only way it made sense was for them to do it together. They would give ABC a few months to find a pair of permanent anchors.

The interim team was announced on January 4, 1999. Gibson got anguished phone calls from a number of friends: "This is going to be a disaster." "She's going to eat you alive." "She's a viper." Only one person called with a different message: "This is going to be the best working relationship you'll ever have." It was Barbara Walters, who was constantly depicted in the press as feuding with her supposed ABC rival.

Within weeks about 1 million viewers returned to *Good Morning America.* Gibson seemed rejuvenated by Sawyer's presence, and they quickly developed an on-air chemistry. Sawyer often looked to Gibson for guidance when she lost her place in the show and papers were being thrust at her from every direction. Gibson was dazzled by the quickness of her mind. He felt that they had forged a mutually dependent relationship. They were, in fact, sharp and funny together, but just as important, they were familiar figures for the audience. The hotly competitive arena of morning television was no place for obscure rookies.

The new team was such an instant success that the length of their tenure became a murky question, even to them. Gibson was a little anxious about when the "handoff," as they called it, would come. He could see sticking around for a year, two at the most, but definitely not beyond that.

Westin secretly hoped that they would gradually decide to work the morning shift indefinitely. But he would not force the issue. Gibson and Sawyer would make sacrifices out of loyalty, but they were stars, and you didn't try to break their elbows.

As it turned out, Gibson and Sawyer settled into their morning routine, and talk of a handoff gradually faded. Charlie Gibson had been bounced out of his job, then begged to return, and now was back on top of the world, if not the ratings game. Sawyer was unquestionably the bigger celebrity, with Gibson basking in the reflected spotlight, but that suited him just fine.

The problem, for Gibson, was the predawn schedule and the sheer physical exhaustion. Every few months he would sit down with Sawyer and ask: "Are you having fun?" Once they agreed on that, they would resolve to stay with the show a few more months. If you thought about doing it for longer, Gibson felt, you would jump off a bridge. They kept enjoying themselves, though, and the months stretched into years.

Gibson conducted hundreds of interviews with newsmakers—from a half-dozen American presidents to Tony Blair, Nelson Mandela, Mikhail Gorbachev, and Yasir Arafat—and the focus was almost always on their answers, not his questions. He was not a prosecutorial interrogator, which helped explain why guests felt comfortable with him. But in the spring of 1999, in the wake of the Columbine high school massacre in Littleton, Colorado, Gibson went at Bill Clinton on the subject of gun control.

Starting off with a congressional proposal to modestly tighten the regulation of guns, Gibson told the president: "You and I know, don't we, really, that it's not going to make a damn bit of difference, only on the margins, in the way kids get guns."

When Clinton said that progress had been made with background checks, Gibson countered that many people were still getting guns through the "back door." He quoted a friend of Clinton as telling him, " 'The president had a chance to roar on gun control and he meowed.' . . . We register every automobile in America. We don't register guns. That's a step that would make a difference."

Clinton turned angry, scowling at Gibson. "Look, let's join the real world here," he said. "Now, you want to have an honest conversation?" Gibson said that he did, and Clinton pronounced himself the first president ever to take on the National Rifle Association.

Conservative detractors said that Gibson was crusading for gun control, but Gibson felt it was less predictable to ask Clinton about criticism from the left than from the NRA. He viewed himself as agnostic on the issues, with one glaring exception: tobacco. Smoking had killed his father, his mother, and his sister, and there was no way he could be objective about that.

Breaking news always lurked as a possibility on a two-hour show. Gibson and Sawyer were on the air on the morning of September 11, 2001, when they suddenly switched to a picture of smoke rising from the twin towers of lower Manhattan. "This is at the World Trade Center," Gibson reported. "Obviously a major fire there. And there has been some sort of explosion. We don't fully know the details. There is one report, as of yet unconfirmed, that a plane has hit the World Trade Center."

During the 2004 presidential campaign Gibson was invited to host the second debate between Bush and John Kerry, a town hall session in St. Louis that would feature questions from the audience. Gibson was surprised, and made sure to ask the debate commission whether the Bush campaign knew that he had a family connection to the Democratic Party. Gibson's son-in-law had once worked for Bill Clinton and had become the political director for Ted Kennedy. Bush strategists told the commission that they still had no objection to Gibson.

When the debate ended, Gibson walked up to the podium to shake hands with the candidates.

"You did a pretty good job," Bush said. "I didn't think you were going to."

Gibson wanted to ask what the president meant—was this related to his son-in-law?—but Laura Bush walked up at that moment and he never got a chance to follow up. The president later sent Gibson a letter, saying that the debate had been the most illuminating for the public. Soon afterward Gibson was invited to Bush's Crawford ranch for a *Good Morning America* interview timed for the campaign's final days. Here was Gibson's chance to be as aggressive with a Republican president as he had been with Clinton.

Gibson took an unexpected tack, pressing Bush on the subject of gays. The president allowed that homosexuals might have been born that way.

"If that's the case, just for sake of argument, that's an unalterable characteristic for them," Gibson said. "That's like being black or being a woman.

So, how can we deny them rights in any way to a civil union that would allow, give them the same economic rights or health rights or other things?"

Bush said that the states had the power to allow civil unions.

"But the platform opposes it," Gibson said, referring to policies adopted months earlier at the Republican convention.

"Well, I don't," Bush said, although he acknowledged supporting a constitutional amendment against gay marriage that would override the states.

A moment later Gibson moved on to religion: Was God on America's side in the war on terror? Did Christians and Muslims pray to the same God? Would that include Abu al-Zarqawi? Did Christians, non-Christians, and Muslims all go to heaven?

As an interviewer, Gibson didn't have the strongest fastball in television, but he had the knack for throwing a great curve.

For all the serious moments, Gibson had, if not let it all hang out, at least let some of it hang out. He had played guitar, dodgeball, and paintball. He had danced with Whoopi Goldberg. He had donned a baseball uniform and a bellman's uniform. He had gone bungee-jumping. He had had food fights, snowball fights, and watergun fights with Diane Sawyer. And yet his demeanor was such that no one raised the questions that were constantly hurled at Katie Couric, about whether his behavior had been too frivolous and had diminished his sense of gravitas. He was Charlie, the avuncular newsman, and somehow, that was enough.

Whatever fantasies he had once entertained of being an evening news anchor had long since vanished. Gibson was perfectly content to wrap up his career on *Good Morning America*. And then, while Gibson was in Rome, covering the funeral of Pope John Paul II, Peter Jennings told the world that he had lung cancer.

*   *   *

It was a brilliant spring day, and waves of yellow taxis were cruising down Broadway as Charlie Gibson stood on a traffic island, microphone in hand, and watched twenty young women throw themselves into an oversize vat of vanilla frosting.

They were wearing long white dresses topped by white helmets with blue horns, like a horde of overweight Vikings, and they scrambled over an eight-foot wall of frosting, covering themselves in white goo. One woman was the first to grab a bouquet from inside the vat, and Gibson, beaming with good cheer, presented her with an oversize $25,000 check for winning the "Bridezilla" contest.

Gibson hated the segment. He could not understand why people degraded themselves in this fashion, even for money. But *Good Morning America* was a smorgasbord of the serious and the silly, and he rarely made a fuss about the show's content.

It was one of Gibson's final mornings on *GMA*, three weeks after he had started the *World News* job, doing double duty on the evening shift. Moments after his driver picked him up outside the Times Square studio, where Gibson finished every show by patiently posing for pictures with members of the audience, his cell phone rang. It was Jon Banner.

"Hello, Jonathan." Gibson had a habit of using full names as nicknames. Banner briefed him on the progress of Tropical Storm Alberto, then heading for Florida's west coast.

"In your mind," he asked, "does this trump Camp David?" Bush had gathered his war cabinet at the presidential retreat for discussions of the situation in Iraq. But Banner explained that opportunities for the press—and particularly for television, which needed pictures—were limited.

"So we've got no access to anybody on conclusions reached or thoughts expressed?" Gibson asked. "And the president won't say anything until tomorrow?" Perhaps they would need to find a different lead story.

Inside the offices on West 66th Street, a dozen *World News* staffers were sitting shoulder to shoulder around a long conference table in a cramped room, their new home while their offices one floor below were being renovated. On a television set in the corner, the U.S. team was losing to the Czech Republic in the World Cup. Gibson tried to tamp down the enthusiasm about Alberto.

"For a storm that hasn't even hit yet and is less than seventy-five miles per hour, you don't want to do three pieces," he said.

The producers ran through the day's other stories. A pair of Supreme Court decisions on the death penalty. The shooting of a Nevada judge. Pittsburgh Steelers quarterback Ben Roethlisberger, riding without a helmet, badly injured in a motorcycle accident. Gibson recalled that his station manager at Washington's Channel 7 had forced him to sell his motorcycle on grounds that it was too dangerous for a television reporter.

There were new details about the U.S. bombing mission days earlier that had killed Abu al-Zarqawi, the Iraqi terrorist leader. Contrary to the Pentagon's initial report, Zarqawi had lived for fifty-two minutes after a pair of five-hundred-pound bombs devastated his hideaway.

"How the hell could he survive?" Gibson wondered.

There were other odds and ends. Phil Merrill, owner of *Washingtonian* magazine, had disappeared from his boat on the Chesapeake Bay and was presumed dead. Gibson found the story interesting. "The problem is, nobody knows who he is," Gibson said.

The television in the corner, now turned to Fox News, showed Bush in a cabin at Camp David with Dick Cheney, Donald Rumsfeld, and Condoleezza Rice.

"Does this purport to be some of the meeting?" Gibson asked.

"It's a photo op," Banner said.

The gathering in the conference room broke up after one o'clock, with all the major decisions yet to come. Two hours later Gibson walked onto the set for the 3 P.M. Webcast. As when Vargas had anchored the online edition, he seemed looser and the interviews had more vibrancy.

On the teleprompter, the questions for Jake Tapper, the correspondent stationed outside Camp David, and Miguel Marquez, reporting from Baghdad, were scripted.

"Jake: why president call this meeting?"

"Miguel: If you were at meeting what would you say are biggest challenges?"

But once the Internet show began, Gibson largely ignored the suggested queries. "I'm tempted to ask whether this is PR or substance," he told Tapper.

"Are people more worried about the security situation, or is it daily life, like having water and electricity?" he asked Marquez.

Then the fun began. Gibson picked up on a *New York Times* piece about a new ring tone for cell phones—a mosquito sound—that supposedly could be heard only by teenagers. The control room played it.

"If you heard nothing, you heard what I heard. But we checked it out with our twenty-one-year-old intern, and she assured us she could hear it."

Reporter David Muir walked around the Upper West Side as he described a new technology that allowed users to track their friends' whereabouts through their cell phones. The Webcast ran two minutes and thirty-two seconds long, but no one seemed to care.

Back at the conference table, the din of overlapping conversations grew louder and the arguments sharper. Gibson and Banner were dissecting reporter John Cochran's piece on the Supreme Court rulings, one of which gave death row prisoners more leeway to object to lethal injections as too painful. "I want to know what the ruling said today. He's way into the interpretation before he tells me what it did," Gibson said. He looked at the justices' language. "How do they know that twenty-one out of forty-nine people—since they're dead—endured suffocating and a burning sensation? I do find it passing strange that we have to deny them pain, but we can kill them."

At five o'clock Gibson slipped onto the set to anchor ABC's daily radio news feed, using a more booming voice than he did on television. When he returned to the airless conference room, Gibson began mapping out the tropical storm coverage. Every discussion revolved around him. He even suggested that a "but" be added to one reporter's script. Gibson was quietly taking charge of the newscast in ways that Vargas never had, choreographing each step in the upcoming performance.

When he tossed to Mike Von Fremd in Cedar Keys, Florida, Gibson explained, "He just says to me, 'Charlie, this isn't even a Category One hurricane, although it might be by dawn.' He can give me the numbers of people being evacuated and the geographic area, and you put up a chart. Then I say to him, 'Do you think a year ago they would have been evacuating this quickly for what is not even a Category One?' Then we do a line about how it's the first hurricane to hit in June since da da da . . ." Unlike Bob Schieffer, Gibson was leaving nothing to chance.

With less than an hour to air, they decided to make Ben Roethlisberger's motorcycle accident a "Closer Look" segment, and Gibson said he wanted to tout it in the show's opening.

"I don't know how you do the headlines," he said. "Do I need a two-word stinger?" This was the punchy subject line that all the newscasts used before summarizing each top story. No one had an idea, so Gibson decided to forgo it.

As he walked down the hall to the anchor set, Tom Nagorski, the number-two producer, raced after him and shouted: "Gibson! Quarterback Crash!"

Gibson slipped on his mike and read: "Quarterback Crash: The winning Super Bowl quarterback is injured in a motorcycle accident—he was not wearing a helmet."

Now the major question was whether to air a video package by Jonathan Karl, the diplomatic correspondent, or Pierre Thomas, the law enforcement reporter, since they didn't have time for both. Karl's report involved conditions at the U.S. detainee prison at Guantánamo Bay, but he also had exclusive information about the Iraqi government about to take the lead in launching a security crackdown in Baghdad. The problem, Banner said, was that Karl only had one source. The Thomas piece was a story that everyone had, the FBI releasing figures showing a significant rise in crime in many parts of the country.

They concluded that Thomas's story would be old news by the next day. "You could probably hold Karl," Gibson said. That was the tentative plan.

Mike Von Fremd called in from Florida, and Gibson grabbed the phone.

"Hi, Michael," he said. "I want you to tell me about the evacuations first: 'I'm right smack where it's coming ashore, Charlie, it's a low-lying area.' Then I'm going to say to you, 'Mike, this isn't even fully a hurricane, would they have done this last year?' And you're going to tell me, 'Not on my life.' "

With twenty-one minutes to go, one producer realized that they had forgotten to include the day's stock prices. Gibson said they would have to kill the twenty-second item on Phil Merrill, the publisher who had died at sea.

"Let's do stocks *and* Merrill," Nagorski said.

"How are we going to do that?" Banner asked.

"I'll just lie about the times," Nagorski cracked.

At 6:27 Gibson was miked and on the *World News* set, and Banner was in the control room. They were leading with the tropical storm.

"Jon, tell Mike I'll start him off by saying I understand they're moving people out of there," Gibson said. With thirty seconds to go, he began practicing the opening lines to himself.

Once on the air, Gibson went to Von Fremd, standing on a Florida beach in a blue windbreaker, but the audio was very scratchy so the control room quickly moved on. Jake Tapper introduced his taped report from outside Camp David, but the producers felt that he had read his lines too quickly.

Everything else went as planned: the Zarqawi autopsy; al-Qaeda naming a new leader in Iraq; the Supreme Court rulings; the wounding of the Nevada judge; and Pierre Thomas's report on increases in the murder rate. This was followed by Roethlisberger's motorcycle crash; the U.S. loss in the World Cup; Robert Byrd becoming the longest-serving senator in American history; and activists complaining about elephants in captivity after one died at the Los Angeles Zoo. There were no mosquito ring tones or other light elements. It was a meat and potatoes broadcast, which very much reflected Gibson's preferred diet. He was a hard-news guy and didn't want to waste precious airtime on frothy features.

As Gibson remained in the chair for the beginning of the second feed at 7, the producers talked about fixing some glitches. David Muir had said it was six months since Roethlisberger had won the Super Bowl; he would track that line again, since it had only been four months. They decided that Tapper should record his script again at a slightly slower pace.

"It'll be five or ten seconds more, and we kill a swoop if we have to," Nagorski said. The swoop was a Roone Arledge creation, a quick promotional pop, such as "More Americans get their news from ABC than from any other source"—a claim that was possible because it included radio.

Suddenly an announcer's promo was on the air: "Tomorrow, a *Good Morning America* wake-up call." Gibson laughed, since he would be waking up for that show as well.

The next day, shortly before noon, Bob Woodruff walked into the ABC newsroom for the first time since he had left on his fateful trip to the Middle East more than five months earlier. Wearing an open-necked blue shirt and a baseball cap over his buzz-cut hair, which hid the scars on top of his head, Woodruff and his wife, Lee, were surrounded by well-wishers, 150 in all, as word quickly spread around the building. Clearly moved, he addressed the crowd.

"Man, it's good to be here," Woodruff said, beaming. He recounted the tale of how he had been injured. "I woke up in this hospital. And I looked up and I just thought about you guys. And I thought about everything that I wanted badly to come back to."

A wave of emotion swept over the room. Had Woodruff not stuck his head out of that Iraqi tank, he would still be the coanchor of *World News Tonight.* Instead he was embraced by a man two decades older who, by a twist of fate, was now settling into the job that Woodruff had expected to hold for a long time. It was Charlie Gibson's newsroom now.

The two men had lunch, and Gibson assured Woodruff that his place was secure. "You can come back at whatever pace you want," he said. "If you come all the way back, I would be delighted to hand the job off to you."

Outside the public spotlight, Brian Williams was also spending time with Woodruff. His wife, Jane, had started lunching and e-mailing with Bob's wife before ABC gave him the anchor job, and she reached out to Lee Woodruff after the injury. Appallingly enough, the Woodruffs had to worry about paparazzi trying to get an unauthorized picture of him that could be sold to a magazine or a tabloid. Bob would not go to the door if there was a package delivery or pizza takeout man for fear of encountering a photographer.

During a Saturday night visit, Williams came bearing a gift, a baseball cap emblazoned with *NBC Nightly News* and the peacock symbol. Williams put on a *World News Tonight* cap, and they got ready to pose for pictures in the kitchen, each wearing the other's logo. To put on the cap, Woodruff had to remove a helmet that he had been wearing to protect himself against a brain injury. Because he had lost small pieces of his skull in the explosion, there was no skin to protect the nerves under his cranium if he were to fall, and his balance left something to be desired. Woodruff was in good spirits, though, and they both mugged for the camera. Williams suggested that Woodruff do his first interview with Jon Stewart on *The Daily Show* as a way of easing back into the public eye.

Despite the display of friendship, this was still a game of hardball. NBC soon put out an in-your-face press release crowing: "Charlie Gibson's second week in the anchor chair marked ABC *World News Tonight*'s lowest delivery since . . . September, 1987." *Nightly* had averaged 7.8 million viewers for the week, 769,000 more than ABC. Williams was pleased that Gibson was off to an anemic start. His staff had studied the ratings, and he believed that several hundred thousand women, mostly younger ones with kids, had abandoned ABC because they were pissed off about the treatment of Elizabeth Vargas. Or maybe they thought that Gibson looked too much like a sixty-three-year-old man. Whatever the reason, Williams was happy about the defectors. Charlie was a fine fellow, but business was business, and his business was to whip his rivals and stay on top.

CHAPTER 21

Fall of an Anchor

Dan Rather ambled slowly into the Madison Avenue diner and took a seat in the back. He did not look like himself, or at least like the televised image that was fixed in the national consciousness after his nearly quarter-century in the anchor chair.

His slate-gray hair, which he had dyed jet black until recent years, when friends persuaded him to move to a salt-and-pepper hue, was mostly hidden by a baseball cap. His jowls were pronounced, making him look every one of his seventy-four years. But more startling than the ravages of time was the slow and deliberate way he talked and the wounded look in his eyes, depression seeming to ooze from every pore.

Rather looked like a beaten man. His friends were worried about him. In several recent public appearances he had gotten weepy as he talked about journalism. He would invoke the legacy of Edward R. Murrow and choke back tears.

He kept falling back on the same defiant-sounding phrases. He would not back up or back down. Aggressive journalism was in his bloodstream, but his enemies had tried to paint him as a Bolshevik for political reasons because he wouldn't report the news the way they wanted. Rather seemed not to understand the gravity of his mistakes on the National Guard story, relying on suspect documents from an eccentric man with an agenda and then rushing the story to air. When pressed, Rather would say that he still believed the Bush story was true. But he had not proven it to be true.

CBS News no longer wanted him. After forty-four years of intense pursuit of news—from the Kennedy assassination to the jungles of Vietnam to the final sit-down with Saddam before the Iraq war—his services were no longer required. This was apparent to everyone around him, to everyone in the business except, perhaps, Rather himself. He was still pitching stories to *60 Minutes,* still hoping to salvage some kind of contract extension.

But that was not in the cards. Les Moonves liked Rather but didn't see him as part of the new CBS team. Rather had a big salary, there was no slot for him at *60 Minutes,* and no role that Moonves could envision, since they rarely did specials anymore. Sean McManus had refused to meet with him. McManus knew he would bear the brunt of considerable criticism for letting Rather go, but he felt that the network needed to move on.

Jeff Fager, his boss at *60 Minutes,* who had been the executive producer of the *Evening News* in the mid-1990s, had the closest bond with Rather, but the relationship had been badly strained. Months earlier, when Rather had been assigned to the Sunday show, after the demise of *60 Minutes Wednesday,* the two men had sat down.

"Dan, let's make this work, but you know it can't be a full-time job," Fager said. He understood that Rather blamed him for the frustrating situation, but he had no alternative if he was going to keep Bob Simon, Scott Pelley, and others from the defunct Wednesday program gainfully employed.

Rather wound up getting nine pieces on the air for the season, about half a regular correspondent's workload. Some of the assignments seemed quite pedestrian for a journalist of his stature, such as a profile of stockpicker turned CNBC commentator Jim Cramer or a look at the Whole Foods grocery chain. There were no blockbuster investigations. And there was plenty of internal competition as well. Katie Couric would soon be contributing a half-dozen stories a year.

From the moment Rather moved to the *60 Minutes* offices, across West 57th Street from the Broadcast Center where he had worked as anchor, there was an open revolt at the program. The fabled corps of correspondents— Mike Wallace, Morley Safer, Lesley Stahl, Ed Bradley, and Steve Kroft— had filed into Fager's office. Some vehemently protested the move, while others said Rather's presence might hurt the program. Wasn't there some way for Fager to block it?

As the correspondents saw it, Rather had tarnished their brand—the name of the program that they felt symbolized journalistic quality—by reporting an obviously shoddy story. And now, having tainted them all, he was being shipped to their offices to work among them? How could this be happening?

Fager explained that there was nothing he could do. Rather's contract required that once he was no longer anchor, he was guaranteed a spot on *60 Minutes.*

The open hostility permeated the hallways. Mike Wallace had told Rather, and proclaimed publicly, that he should have resigned in solidarity with his troops after the National Guard story was officially discredited. Andy Rooney complained that Rather had hurt his own cause by making his views so obvious, unlike Walter Cronkite, who was even more liberal but had kept his opinions under wraps until his retirement years. Morley Safer had been mad at Rather for three decades for bad-mouthing him to a group of Marines in Vietnam.

To make matters worse, some *60 Minutes* producers sensed that Rather was phoning it in. He had been pampered as an anchor for so long, they believed, that when it came to rolling up his sleeves and slogging away at a story from scratch, his skills had atrophied. His report from North Korea had been terrific, they felt, but some of the other stories had been relegated to the Christmas and New Year's weekends.

Outside the network, as Rather's days seemed numbered, much of his support seemed to melt away. He had been on Don Imus's radio show dozens of times and enjoyed bantering with the sometimes caustic morning man. But Imus appeared disgusted by his longtime acquaintance's conduct: "What they found was that Rather had no integrity or character and was gutless. If you're Rather, you had to resign. You can't let them blow out your staff. He went and locked himself in his office and hid under his desk. This is a guy who was saying 'courage,' and he had none."

McManus had the lawyers offer Rather what the network called a "Cronkite deal"—a permanent office, title, assistant, and perhaps an occasional assignment or two—but Rather was resisting that.

Friends could not understand why he hung on at CBS, why he allowed himself to be humiliated in this fashion. On many days Rather stayed away from the office. He had been to see *Good Night and Good Luck,* the George Clooney film about Murrow, five times, sometimes sitting in the darkened theater by himself. But Rather seemed to have trouble envisioning himself apart from CBS. He had taken long walks at the vacation retreat where he loved to fish, in New York's Catskill Mountains, and decided to fight for his job. He kept repeating, like a mantra, "My best work is still ahead of me." At the same time, Rather was deeply wounded by the dismissive attitude of the network he had served for so long.

He knew, of course, that he was a lightning rod. He knew that he had flaws as a journalist. He also believed that there was considerable jealousy toward him within the news division. When you had been where he had been, had done what he had accomplished, not everyone was going to love you. He knew, too, that Jeff Fager was under pressure to attract younger viewers at *60 Minutes,* and he found the atmosphere at the show, with so many correspondents jockeying for airtime, absolutely toxic.

Despite his decades of service, Rather had no real friends at CBS. He had always been something of a loner, and a strange one at that. Some colleagues, who revered his independence and toughness, felt sorry for him. Others believed that he had badly damaged CBS with the Guard report and were relieved that he seemed to be on his way out.

Most disconcerting of all for this proud man was what seemed to be almost a loss of identity. He had created a character called Dan Rather, one friend said, and now, without a network outlet, that character no longer existed.

CBS was promising him a substantial severance package if he would sign a nondisclosure agreement, promising not to disparage the network. Rather was offended by the demand and refused to sign.

The industry that had once waged a fierce bidding war for his services was treating Rather as if he were radioactive. He was about to accept a job offer from Mark Cuban, the billionaire businessman who owned the Dallas Mavericks basketball team and who wanted Rather to create and host a weekly show for his high-definition satellite and cable channel, HDNet. The channel reached just 3 million homes, a significant comedown for an anchor known around the world. Like a ballplayer past his prime, Rather still needed to walk into the stadium, even a tiny one, and hear the cheers.

Many people, he knew, believed that he was seeking to salvage his reputation in this new job, but he didn't see it that way. Rather believed that his long record at CBS was clear and that he didn't need redemption. He wasn't perfect, but who was? Rather felt that the current crop of CBS executives wanted to break with the Murrow tradition, the Murrow legend, and that was their prerogative, but he didn't want such a break.

On June 19, 2006, word began circulating around CBS that this was the day that Rather's departure would be announced. Rome Hartman, who had worked for him at the *Evening News* and sat in the office next door during the final months of *60 Minutes Wednesday,* called him at home.

"Listen, Dan, I hear it's going to be official today," he said.

"Well, I don't know if it's today," Rather said cryptically. "I really don't know anything." CBS executives had drafted a three-page statement announcing the separation, larded with praise for Rather's career, but Rather decided that he wanted to sleep on it.

Bob Schieffer was struck by how tense things were around the office. *Was Dan going? Was he refusing to go?* It reminded him of the drama that had often surrounded Rather in his anchor days.

The next morning the CBS press office put out the release, and Hartman called again. He explained that the *Evening News* would be doing a piece on his departure.

"I want you to have an opportunity to be in the story if you want to be in it," Hartman said.

Rather was polite but firm. "Listen, I've thought a lot about it," he said. "I appreciate the fact that you're doing it on the broadcast. I've just decided I'm not going to do any interviews today. I just feel like today's a day I don't want to be talking about myself."

It was, in a way, remarkable. Dan Rather was telling his old newscast that he would have no comment.

But in the battle to define what had happened between him and CBS, Rather had plenty of comment. He put out a statement announcing that his departure "represents CBS's final acknowledgement, after a protracted struggle," that network executives had not "lived up to their obligation to allow me to do substantive work there . . . As for their offers of a future with only an office but no assignments, it just isn't in me to sit around doing nothing."

It was a measure of Rather's frustration that he could not resist these parting shots. Instead of expressing satisfaction with his long career and looking forward to new challenges, he had refused to play along with the polite corporate fiction that was customary for such occasions. Rather wanted the world to know that CBS had given him the boot.

There was a significant irony in the network's decision that, at seventy-four, Rather's usefulness had come to an end. Back when he had assumed the anchor chair, in 1981, Rather had all but ensured that Walter Cronkite, then sixty-five, would no longer play an on-air role at CBS. Now Rather was the aging warhorse who still wanted to strut his stuff in front of the cameras, only to be put out to pasture.

Schieffer, for his part, was trying to put out a small brushfire. CBS management had asked him to tape a couple of promotional spots heralding the arrival of Katie Couric, in essence to give the incoming anchor his official blessing. Schieffer had hated the ads, which called for him to praise her qualifications and call her "the real deal." That, he thought, was condescending. He had gone to see Sean McManus.

"People are going to say, 'Who thought she *wasn't* the real deal?' You don't want to do this," Schieffer said. He rewrote the copy so that he was calling her tough and straightforward. Now the network wanted to run the first of the spots tonight—the very night that they would be reporting that Dan Rather was leaving CBS.

"Guys, let's think this through," Schieffer told his staff. "I'm going to say, *Goodbye, old friend,* and thirty seconds later we run this?" The promos were delayed.

On the *Evening News* that night, correspondent Anthony Mason reported a piece that was mainly a tribute to Rather's long career. The story glossed over the fact that the network had essentially fired its longtime anchor, saying only that the two sides "could not come to terms." Mason abandoned any effort at objectivity when he said, "For those of us who've had the honor of working with him . . ." Mason felt that he was writing the piece for CBS management, for the critics, for his colleagues, and for Dan, when his first allegiance should have been to the audience.

Schieffer followed with some closing remarks, saying that Rather had become a part of his life and he would miss him. But Schieffer, who had made no attempt to defend the horribly botched Guard story, cleverly signaled that he did not approve of everything Rather did: "His way was not always my way and we did not always agree, but we became friends along the way because we shared a great love for news."

After the broadcast Rather called to tell Schieffer how much he appreciated the comments. It was the first time the two men had spoken in months.

Brian Williams felt badly for the man whose job he had once secretly negotiated to assume. Rather had had a remarkable career. Yes, he had made a very big mistake with the Guard story by mishandling such an explosive topic—especially with this president, in the wake of 9/11, in the middle of a war. But should that blunder overshadow the rest of his career?

The two men had met for lunch a few weeks earlier, and the talk had turned to Katie Couric. Rather struck a note of skepticism.

"I just want to know: Will she defend the news?" he asked. "Is she passionate about it? That's what I don't know."

Now, on the day of Rather's ouster, Williams went to his computer and tapped out a letter. They should have lunch, he wrote, perhaps in the front window at Michael's restaurant. "I am also willing to have lunch on the front steps of the New York Public Library, on the bow of the Circle Line, or behind home plate during a Yankee game. Read into that whatever you want, but I'm tired of watching adults behave badly." Williams closed by recalling Rather's old sign-off. "To quote something I once heard a great man say: Courage."

Rather thanked him in a handwritten note. Civility was important to Williams. Life was short, and there was nothing wrong with being nice to people who were on the way down as well as on the way up.

The next day Sean McManus sat down for lunch with Rather at Gabriel's restaurant near Columbus Circle. It was the first time the two men had exchanged more than a few words.

"If you're mad, I'm the guy," McManus said as they both tucked into plates of ravioli. "I thought it was for the best. With the level of work, it didn't make sense for you or me. Whether it was right or wrong, I made the decision."

The question about assignments was a sore point for Rather. "There were certain promises I thought were made to me about the level of work," he said.

McManus noted that he had not been at CBS News at the time. "My understanding is, the problem with that was when *60 Minutes II* went off the air," he said.

They eventually moved on to talk of fishing, vacations, and family. After two hours of chatting, the encounter ended amicably enough.

Three weeks later Rather went on *Larry King Live* and complained sharply about "a contract which went unfulfilled."

"I never heard the other side of the story, which is to say that I never heard from the top of the corporation or the top of the news division," Rather said.

Never heard from the top of the news division? Sean McManus could only shake his head.

*   *   *

When war broke out in the Middle East that summer, it was one of those moments when the anchors rush to the airport and plant their network flag in the soil of the world's most volatile region.

Once Israel was attacked and retaliated against both the Hamas government in the Gaza Strip and the Hezbollah guerrillas in Lebanon, Charlie Gibson, who had been off on vacation, flew to Tel Aviv, his first trip as the new face of ABC News. Gibson felt that his presence would call more attention to the story, but he was mindful that the beat reporters knew the region best, and he did not want to preempt them by parachuting in. He still thought like a correspondent rather than a star anchor.

Brian Williams went to Israel as well. He thought the decision was a no-brainer. His chief frustration was that he could report only from the Israeli side of the border, and with the cooperation of the Israeli military. To take his crew to Beirut, where bombs were constantly dropping and there was no military to protect Western journalists, would have been too dangerous.

Bob Schieffer told his bosses that he wanted to go, but was turned down. Instead Sean McManus decided that Schieffer should remain in New York and Lara Logan should coanchor the newscast from Israel. Schieffer was glad to see Logan, whom he had worked hard to promote, get the added exposure, but he was badly disappointed by the decision.

The changing of the guard was clear. Schieffer had only a few weeks left in the anchor chair; Logan was the rising young star. And Katie Couric, now the subject of an intensive advertising campaign, was the anchor-in-waiting.

As part of that campaign, the network announced that Couric would contribute to a new CBS News blog—a cool idea that just happened to emulate what Brian Williams had been doing online for fifteen months. But Couric would go further, CBS said, by appearing on video early in the day to casually chat about what stories the *Evening News* was working on. Anchor wars were fought not only on foreign turf but in cyberspace.

Sean McManus had to laugh when he saw Williams trying to one-up his new rival the next day. From Israel, Williams began posting his first video blogs, a new morning feature dubbed the *Early Nightly,* with NBC maintaining that the plan had been in the works for months. One two-minute clip consisted of a tour of NBC's Tel Aviv bureau, and it ended with Williams opening his bag and pulling out his body armor. The sound was spotty and the lighting dark, but the footage was compelling nonetheless. In another, while riding in a car, Williams said softly: "I'm not in this job to take undue risks. We've seen that happen before. I'm not in it to leave NBC without an anchorman, leave my wife without a husband, or my children without a father. We are here though because there's no substitute for covering the story. For being here, seeing it, touching it, and smelling it."

In a written post, he described watching the launch of a Hezbollah missile from Lebanon as he flew with an Israeli military officer in a Black Hawk helicopter at fifteen hundred feet. Williams was breaking down the barrier between himself and the viewers, using jerky video and evocative language to convey a sense of what it was like to be on duty in a war zone. After taking the most tentative baby steps, television was beginning to explore the power of the Internet.

ABC, which still had the only daily Webcast, also made a show of joining the blogging arms race. But Gibson's posts and video footage from Israel were just snippets and transcripts of what was on the air, as opposed to fresh contributions for the online audience. The network tried a semantic switch as well. After twenty-eight years it dropped "Tonight" from the broadcast's name, to signify that this was no longer an evening newscast but part of a round-the-clock operation. The program would now be known as *World News with Charles Gibson.*

On the day he left Israel, Williams saw a man in a blue blazer and yellow shirt at the gate at Ben Gurion Airport, nodding off with his mouth open. It was none other than Charles Gibson. Williams grabbed his cell phone camera and took a picture. It was too good to pass up. Besides, you never knew when you might need a deterrent under the doctrine of mutually assured destruction.

Once Gibson woke up, they began to chat. He brought up the interview about Williams's Africa trip.

"I'm sorry if I screwed that up," Gibson said. "I wasn't being critical of you traveling with Bono. I was questioning whether this was the new paradigm. My point was misunderstood."

Williams told him not to worry. "It's always going to be my philosophy in these jobs, Charlie, to say nice things about my competitors."

The talk turned to the nature of their careers. Gibson marveled that they got to fly around the world and go to fascinating places. "Aren't these jobs great?" Gibson said.

*   *   *

Tom Brokaw was back on *Nightly,* talking about his recent interview with Al Gore for a special program on global warming. Jeff Zucker had made clear that he wanted to see Brokaw sitting next to Brian Williams more often. Zucker felt that enough time had passed since the former anchor stepped down, and Williams was now successful enough, that no one would view Brokaw as overshadowing his successor. ABC, sadly, had lost Jennings, and CBS had now dumped Rather. Brokaw was an asset that the competition didn't have, and a link to the days when the newscasts commanded a far bigger audience.

He was grayer now, and wore a hearing aid in his right ear, the result of too many years of listening to program after program through an earpiece. But although Brokaw was spending a bit more time at his Montana ranch, he still had a full journalistic plate, reporting documentaries for NBC and for the Discovery Channel. He had trouble saying no to all the requests that came in. He had worked his whole life and couldn't shake the feeling that he had to work to justify his existence. When a *Fortune* reporter asked to include him in the magazine's upcoming retirement issue, Brokaw dismissed the idea as absurd.

He was making his presence felt behind the scenes as well, calling Williams and John Reiss with a steady stream of ideas. Brokaw suggested that they examine an effort in California to build an attachment for a Toyota Prius so that the hybrid car could be plugged into an electrical outlet and recharged. Months earlier he had urged Lisa Myers to devote more time to the congressional lobbying scandal swirling around Jack Abramoff. And after Zarqawi was killed, Brokaw told Reiss that the most underreported part of the Iraq war was the impact of American air strikes.

Williams, meanwhile, had been lobbying both Jeff Zucker and Steve Capus on the need to launch a magazine show as a hipper alternative to the increasingly tabloid *Dateline.* Williams actually couldn't stand doing long-form programming. He wasn't wired for it; he needed a daily deadline to prod him into action. But with Katie Couric heading to *60 Minutes,* Williams felt that he needed a foothold in prime time.

Capus, whose wife was a *Dateline* producer, could not green-light the project. Williams was running smack into the economics of television. An additional hour of news would mean one less reality show, drama, or sitcom that might pull better ratings for NBC. In the brutally competitive world of network television, anchors, even top-rated ones, didn't get everything they wanted.

There was rarely a moment when Williams wasn't thinking about the newscast. On a Sunday night in late June, when he learned that investor Warren Buffett was making the largest charitable contribution in history to the foundation run by Buffett's pal Bill Gates, Williams took out his Black-Berry and started tapping out a message to Reiss and the other producers. He sent the e-mail at 12:20 A.M.

"The question is, does anybody want to go large?" he wrote. "I don't think this will motivate Applebee Americans," but might the richest 1 percent be inspired to give away more money? "Is there room for a history lesson?" How rich had Andrew Carnegie been, anyway? How many Americans knew that Buffett owned Fruit of the Loom, See's Candies, and Netjets? "I think there's no more interesting story out there. I say we go large."

Reiss didn't see the e-mail when he woke up the next morning. Williams, in a takeoff on the title of their periodic segment on people making a positive contribution to society, had written: "Talk about Making a Fucking Difference."

The F-word, thanks to NBC's filtering technology, sent the missive straight into Reiss's spam file.

CHAPTER 22

White House Spin

If it were up to him, Katie Couric would not have been Dan Bartlett's first choice to anchor the *CBS Evening News.* Or his second, third, or fourth choice.

The relationship with the *Today* host had turned sour two days before Bartlett moved into his new White House office. During the countdown to the president's 2001 inauguration, Bartlett, as the new communications director, had helped arrange for Couric to sit down with Laura Bush.

"Do you personally believe women in this country should have a legal right to an abortion?" Couric asked.

The incoming first lady said that everyone should work to reduce the number of abortions in America.

"But having said that, Mrs. Bush, should women, in spite, because they're not mutually exclusive, even if you do advocate those things, do you believe that women in this country should have the right to an abortion?"

Bush gave the same answer about reducing the number of abortions.

"Should *Roe v. Wade,* for example, be overturned?" Couric asked.

Bartlett was appalled. For her to grill Laura Bush on this controversial issue near the top of the liberal agenda, on a celebratory day when partisanship is briefly put aside, was just stunning. So this was Couric's approach, he thought, combative and confrontational.

Couric also asked about Bush's plans as first lady, her love of books, and her strategy for protecting her daughters from the glare of publicity, but no one in the White House remembered any of those things. President Bush was angry as well. The relationship had gotten off on a bad foot. Over the next several years, *Today* staffers complained that they weren't getting their fair share of top-level administration guests. And Couric was never granted an interview with the president or another sit-down with his wife.

Couric was taken aback by the White House reaction. She hadn't badgered Laura Bush, she had been politely persistent. And it wasn't like she hadn't done plenty of tough interviews with Democrats. Days before the 2004 election she had asked John Kerry whether he was trying to scare people by warning that Bush might impose a military draft and might change Social Security in a way that would force seniors to work into their seventies and eighties. Couric viewed herself as an equal opportunity annoyer. Asking follow-up questions was what she was paid to do. What this was really about, Couric felt, was the Bush administration trying to control the message. White House strategists, she believed, were determined to bypass the mainstream media and go straight to the most sympathetic outlet, Fox News.

The tensions with Couric left *Today* in an awkward position. Matt Lauer called Bartlett before the 2004 campaign, after seeking advice from Tim Russert. Lauer visited Bartlett at the White House.

"I've talked to Tim, and he says you're a straight-up guy," Lauer said. "Why can't we have a good relationship?"

Their twenty-minute talk produced a thaw in the frosty relations, and the president had Lauer on his campaign bus for an interview a few weeks before the election.

When Couric was considering jumping to CBS, she went to see Bartlett as well, and they talked through some of their differences. But Bartlett was still wary of her.

Such tensions were typical for network journalists, who were paid to be aggressive, and instinctively wanted to hold top government officials accountable, but also needed the access required to book big interviews. A total freeze-out, the ultimate weapon available to any administration, was unusual, since both sides benefited from a productive relationship.

Bartlett did not underestimate the importance of the nightly newscasts and the morning shows. He would watch from the desk of his second-floor West Wing office, on a television monitor that allowed him to split the screen into four boxes, monitoring all the newscasts at once and flipping among them as needed. During the day he would put Fox News, CNN, and MSNBC in the boxes. If he missed any of the network shows, he would watch them on Shadow TV, an online subscription service that recorded every minute of network programming. And since the big network shows had the largest audiences, Bartlett made sure to brief the president on what they were reporting. Each morning he would watch the opening segments of *Today, Good Morning America,* and *The Early Show* at seven, then report at the 7:30 senior staff meeting on how the media day was shaping up. Sometimes he already knew what the day's television angle was, because the morning show bookers would begin calling for guests at 10:30 the night before, as soon as *The New York Times* posted the following day's articles on its Web site. It was uncanny, Bartlett thought, how slavishly the news shows followed the *Times*'s lead.

While other White House officials had higher profiles, Bartlett, an even-tempered Texan who had started working for Bush when he was governor, wielded substantial influence behind the scenes. He was the traffic cop for news organizations looking to score big interviews, and he wasn't shy about blowing the whistle on those he felt were treating the administration unfairly. Bartlett would regularly call or e-mail the anchors, correspondents, and executive producers to object to stories that he found inadequate or misleading.

In Bartlett's view, Bush was a feel player who fed off interviewers with whom he felt comfortable and was not as strong with those he regarded skeptically. Whether Bush personally liked an anchor was a key factor in how much access he or she would receive.

During Bush's first term, the only network anchor with whom the White House had a solid relationship was Tom Brokaw. Bartlett considered the interview that Brokaw did with the president during the 2004 campaign to have been brutal, but Bush said afterward that it had been fine.

Bartlett had little personal contact with Peter Jennings, although Jennings did meet with him, in pursuit of a presidential interview, a couple of months before he was diagnosed with lung cancer. Instead, Bartlett dealt mainly with Jon Banner, George Stephanopoulos, and the ABC correspondents.

He and others at the White House had written off Dan Rather almost from the beginning. Bartlett felt that Rather's broadcast seemed to decide in advance on its story lines, which were frequently negative toward the administration. And it was Bartlett who had examined the purported National Guard memos about Bush, and given an interview to *60 Minutes Wednesday,* on the morning of the broadcast that led to Rather's downfall.

Once Bob Schieffer took over, the tensions quickly dissipated. Bush had enjoyed the walk-and-talk interview they did on the White House grounds. The president told Bartlett he knew Schieffer would ask him tough questions but felt that he respected the office and was never overly harsh.

Brian Williams had followed in Brokaw's footsteps in developing a good rapport with the White House, as was clear when Bush granted him an interview in New Orleans. Bartlett recognized that Williams often said far more provocative things about the administration at the top of *Nightly News* than the other anchors, but that was Williams's style, and Bartlett complained only when he thought that something was egregious.

The president had instinctively liked Elizabeth Vargas, but their dealings turned out to be brief. Bartlett had a decent relationship with Charlie Gibson from his years at *Good Morning America,* and Bush felt reasonably comfortable with Gibson, especially after the 2004 debate he had moderated. After Gibson was tapped for *World News,* he and Jon Banner went to see Bartlett at the White House. Gibson explained that he was a Washington news junkie, having spent his teenage years and the early part of his career in the capital, and that he hoped the two sides could work together.

There was one other network big shot whom Bartlett treated as an eight-hundred-pound gorilla, and that was Tim Russert. Unlike the other Washington bureau chiefs, Janet Leissner at CBS and Robin Sproul at ABC, Russert was constantly on the air, both as a political analyst and, of course, as the host of *Meet the Press,* and he was always calling and trying to get tidbits that he could use. Bush liked and respected Russert, having granted *Meet the Press* his first live Sunday interview as a presidential candidate in 1999 and appearing as the incumbent in 2004. Bartlett felt that Russert was important for another reason: He heavily influenced Williams on political coverage, as he had earlier helped shape what Brokaw reported. And lately, Bartlett believed, that had been a problem. He felt that Russert had turned against the Iraq war toward the end of 2004, and that his hardening attitude had spread throughout 30 Rockefeller Plaza.

That, in Russert's view, was ridiculous. He was dealing with objective reality. If things turned more violent in Iraq, they covered that. If 60 percent of Americans now opposed the war, they covered that as well. Russert didn't remember hearing these kinds of complaints from the White House when Bush was at 80 in the polls. Besides, there was no big meeting where he determined the official position for everyone at NBC. Network television didn't work that way.

Bartlett was mindful that the White House correspondents for the networks worked incredibly long hours and logged hundreds of thousands of miles, yet got bigfooted by their anchors whenever there was an opportunity to talk to Bush. During a trip to Arizona, near the Mexican border, Bartlett arranged for each of the five correspondents for the broadcast and cable net-

works to be granted five minutes with Bush as a way of highlighting his pro-
posals on illegal immigration. Face time with the president, he knew, would
produce longer stories on the newscasts.

When NBC's David Gregory sat down with Bush, he had another subject
in mind. After posing a question about immigration, Gregory said: "Let me
ask you about your leadership. In the most recent survey, your disapproval
rating is now one point lower than Richard Nixon's before he resigned the
presidency. You're laughing . . ."

"I'm not laughing," Bush said.

"Why do you think that is?"

"Because we're at war," Bush said. "And war unsettles people."

Bartlett couldn't believe it. Given a precious few minutes with the president to explore a substantive issue, Gregory had used part of his time to talk
about polls. Bartlett complained to Gregory and groused to Bush about the
interview as well. But the president dismissed Bartlett's concern. Bush
liked Gregory and had posed for a picture with him after the interview, rib-
bing the reporter about his safari hat.

What was most frustrating, in Bartlett's view, was that journalists often
criticized Bush for seeing the world in stark, black and white terms, but then
turned around and did the same thing. They had no time to go into detail on
the nightly news, so everything had to be boiled down to thirty seconds,
forty-five seconds, or one minute. And even that minute tended to reflect a
horse-race view of the presidency in which Bush couldn't possibly be succeeding, at anything, if he was down in the polls. That was the narrative, and
the newscasts were sticking to it. With Bush's domestic agenda stalled, his
party split on key issues, and the war in Iraq turning more violent, Dan
Bartlett was searching for a way to change the storyline as the campaign
heated up.

*   *   *

Seven months before the 2006 elections, Brian Williams served notice that
President Bush and the Republicans were facing a very tough season.

"There is concern the coming midterm elections this year could spell
colossal defeat for his own party," Williams declared in mid-April.

His evidence? The president's poll numbers had hit an all-time low; he
had hired a new chief of staff, who was replacing other White House officials, including the press secretary, Scott McClellan; and some Republicans
on Capitol Hill were complaining about the administration.

Was that enough to justify a loaded phrase like "colossal defeat"?

Williams felt perfectly comfortable, since he had prefaced it with the word "concern." After all, Bill Clinton had suffered a colossal defeat in the midterm elections of 1994, and Ronald Reagan had met the same fate in 1986, so if the Democrats captured one or both houses of Congress, that would be a cataclysmic event for the Bush presidency.

For much of 2006, the network newscasts simply did not cover the midterm campaign. Four hundred and thirty-five House races and thirty-three Senate contests were too much of a blur, and far too local, to warrant much airtime on national programs. But the newscasts played a vital role by promoting the notion that the Democrats might well regain power on Capitol Hill after losing three straight elections. The anchors and correspondents also pounded the drums of GOP vulnerability by constantly reminding viewers both of Bush's depressed approval ratings and of congressional preference polls showing the electorate leaning Democratic. While opinion surveys were nothing but snapshots, each new one created a story for the broadcasts that financed them, giving the anchors the chance to float their own political theories. And they missed few opportunities to tie the mess in Iraq to Bush's fading political fortunes, and by extension to the Republicans' chances of holding the House and Senate.

"What are we finding driving the numbers these days?" Williams asked Tim Russert when an NBC poll showed Bush with a 37 percent approval rating.

"Iraq, Iraq, Iraq," Russert said.

"For months," correspondent Chip Reid reported on *Nightly News*, "the drumbeat of bad news coming out of Iraq had congressional Republicans in a defensive crouch, fearful that growing opposition to the war could cost them control of the House or Senate in November's elections."

And what did the public think? CBS correspondent Sandra Hughes filed a rather one-dimensional report from San Mateo, California. To illustrate the argument that so-called "security moms" were defecting from the Republicans, she aired an interview with a grand total of one such mom, Julee Floyd, who said she wanted to hear a plan from someone in the midterm campaign to get out of Iraq. The only other person in the piece was a Democratic pollster. Did Julee Floyd really represent every security mom in the country? Was there no mother in San Mateo who still believed in Bush and the GOP?

NBC's David Gregory reported from a suburban Philadelphia district. He interviewed three Republicans, none of whom were supporting Bush, and a Democratic House candidate—not exactly a balanced roster.

Williams was particularly influenced by retired general Barry McCaffrey, a gruff, hard-nosed Gulf War commander who had become an NBC consultant. In the summer of 2006, after returning from a visit to Baghdad, McCaffrey told the news division in a briefing that an American driving through the city for twenty-four hours, without security, would have no expectation of surviving. Williams was deeply affected by the downbeat assessment and had McCaffrey on as a guest.

The anchor asked a question to which he knew the answer: "Fair to say an American unguarded, a Westerner walking, driving the streets wouldn't last very long?"

"You're a dead man," McCaffrey replied.

Soon afterward General John Abizaid, the head of the U.S. Central Command, told a Senate committee that sectarian violence in Iraq had gotten so bad that it was possible the country could move toward civil war. Williams saw this as a turning point, believing that the administration was very careful about trotting out such terms. Bob Schieffer thought the average viewer didn't know who Abizaid was and that they had to hammer home what had happened. Diane Sawyer, filling in for Charlie Gibson, described the "stunning admission today from the American generals running the war in Iraq . . . The next stop could be all-out civil war."

For more than three years the Bush administration had been arguing, often quite vociferously, that news organizations were devoting too much attention to the violence in Iraq, while ignoring important signs of progress. Now, in a change of strategy, American military leaders were acknowledging that matters in Iraq were pretty awful and could get worse—admitting, in effect, that the pictures appearing on television screens night after night were an accurate depiction of the carnage in that country. No wonder the anchors had seized on the shift in semantics.

If any further proof were needed that Iraq would be a dominant issue in the campaign, it came on August 8. Joe Lieberman, who had come within a hair of being elected vice president, was defeated in the Democratic Senate primary in Connecticut, in large measure because he had been a staunch supporter of President Bush's war effort. Suddenly, local politics was leading the nightly news.

"It might go down as the political shot heard round the world," Brian Williams announced with great fanfare. "There has been an earthquake in the Democratic Party," Charlie Gibson declared.

But if this was such an earthquake, why had it not registered on their Richter scales until late in the game? After all, it had been evident since early June that an obscure Greenwich millionaire named Ned Lamont, fueled by his antiwar stance and the ardent backing of a coterie of liberal bloggers such as Markos Moulitsas of *Daily Kos,* was a very real threat to knock off Lieberman in the primary. It was all over the newspapers and a constant topic of discussion on the cable news channels.

And yet, other than a brief report on NBC in early July that Lieberman planned to run as an independent if he lost the primary, *Nightly News* did not cover the Lieberman race until July 24, when Bill Clinton campaigned for the embattled senator. The *CBS Evening News,* aside from one story on its Saturday edition, did not report on the race until July 31. And *World News* did not weigh in until August 4, four days before the primary.

The answer was simple: the anchors and producers feared that their audience was not that into politics. Rather than spotlight what had become the most fascinating political contest in the country, heavy with implications for Iraq, the role of partisan bloggers, and a battle for the soul of the Democratic Party, television's top journalists worried about getting out front too soon.

Charlie Gibson had planned to run a Lieberman piece earlier—he was troubled by the way political centrists were getting punished into a polarized climate—but kept bumping it for other news. Bob Schieffer had pushed the idea of covering the Lieberman race earlier but couldn't find much enthusiasm among the *Evening News* staff. Chris Dodd, Connecticut's other Democratic senator, had told him before an appearance on *Face the Nation* that his friend's campaign was dead in the water. Schieffer concluded that they had made a mistake by waiting.

Brian Williams grew so excited about the race that on the day before the primary he asked his top producers if they should broadcast from Hartford that night. They debated whether they were overly excited about the contest and whether geography was a factor, since Williams lived in Connecticut. They decided to nix the idea.

Williams felt that the midterm elections were damned important but at the same time that network journalists had to be generalists. At the afternoon editorial meeting the day before the primary, Williams asked his staff: If you asked one hundred people at a shopping mall in St. Louis who was running in the Connecticut primary, how many would know the answer? Their job was partly civics, he felt, but they had to respect their viewers' interests and what was important in their daily lives.

Of course, one reason people tuned in to the evening news was to get a sense of what was going on beyond their shopping malls. Had the anchors cared a bit more about being on the cutting edge, they could have framed the fading fortunes of a nationally known senator as a referendum on the Iraq war. But as repackagers of the news, they were perfectly content to wait until the story had been so widely reported elsewhere that it had already congealed into conventional wisdom.

Soon afterward Virginia Senator George Allen was embarrassed by a video that his Democratic opponent had posted on *YouTube*. The footage showed Allen mocking an Indian-American volunteer for his Democrat opponent, Jim Webb, by calling him "macaca"—a racial slur meaning monkey in some European cultures—and declaring, "Welcome to America." Even as Allen apologized, the video was downloaded on YouTube more than 150,000 times, *The Washington Post* and other newspapers ran pieces on how online video sites were transforming gaffes by a number of candidates into an endless feedback loop, and the macaca flap was debated on every cable news channel. But the *Evening News* and *World News* did nothing, and when Brian Williams got around to the use of *YouTube* as a political weapon—belatedly, in light of an NBC partnership with the Web site—the story was more than a week old and had been thoroughly rehashed just about everywhere else. Once again the nightly news didn't mind being late to the party, or was unaware that there was a party going on at all. The anchors were in possession of the biggest megaphone in the media world, yet they were rarely the first voices to be heard.

CHAPTER 23

Listening Tour

Katie Couric had just finished holding a town meeting at the Minneapolis Central Library when a woman in her twenties intercepted her at the door and said, "You're a dear friend of mine. You don't know that, but you are."

It had been like that at every stop on the six-city swing across the country, with women approaching Couric and thanking her for being in their lives.

"It's because you've seen them naked," Rome Hartman told her. By coming into people's homes at an hour when they were getting dressed and having their cornflakes, he believed, Couric was viewed more like a member of the family than a typical evening news anchor.

Hartman was chaperoning his new star on what the press had dubbed her "listening tour," in part because Matthew Hiltzik, her PR man, had worked for Hillary Clinton when she had conducted such a tour during her first Senate campaign in New York.

Bob Schieffer told colleagues that it was a mistake for Couric to exclude the press from her meetings with invited guests in Tampa, Denver, Dallas, and other cities. Was there a better way to piss off reporters? Schieffer had quietly made a very different proposal. Why not send Katie to Lebanon to cover the fighting between Israel and Hezbollah? She could talk to him every night from the war zone and burnish her international credentials for her new audience. But the proposal was declined.

Instead, Couric, Hartman, and seven other staffers were flying around in a chartered jet, which was so packed that some of the luggage had to be shipped separately. A nationwide tour in which working reporters had to stand outside the meetings, waiting for a few comments from the star attraction, reinforced the image that she was inaccessible. Schieffer was troubled by the jealousy toward Couric in the news business. While reporters viewed him as one of them, Schieffer concluded, they looked at Couric as a celebrity.

Couric had suggested the trip to Hartman at one of their first meetings, and she wanted the sessions kept private so they wouldn't seem like a publicity stunt. She knew that there would be some criticism, and she was willing to take it. Inevitably there were embarrassing moments, such as when the CBS affiliate in Minneapolis tried to eject a blogger who had been invited to the meeting, and wound up confiscating his pen. The listening tour, said *Orlando Sentinel* columnist Kathleen Parker, merely confirmed what Americans "already dislike about the media—and especially about media personalities on the celebrity level of a Couric. That is, Couric and others who decide what Americans should know are out of touch."

Toward the end of the tour Couric spoke to the semiannual convention of television writers in Los Angeles, and was asked whether she would be willing to go to the Middle East to cover Israel's war against its neighbors. Couric said that she would want to be there but would have to make such decisions on a "case-by-case basis."

Soon, however, the *Drudge Report, Media Bistro,* and other online sites were posting a very different story, that Couric was balking at going to the Mideast. "I think the situation there is so dangerous, and as a single parent with two children, that's something I won't be doing," Couric was quoted as saying.

It was a setup job. The quote had come from the Web site of *Access Hollywood,* the syndicated entertainment show that had in fact spoken to Couric on the subject. The problem was that the interview had taken place two months earlier, right after two CBS crew members were killed and Kimberly Dozier badly wounded in Baghdad, and Couric was talking about Iraq, not Israel. Of *course* she didn't want to take unnecessary risks when she was the only surviving parent for her two daughters, but this had nothing to do with whether she would go to Israel, where journalists faced considerably less danger. Couric was really steamed about the screwup. The only thing she gave a shit about was accuracy. What bothered her was the sloppy reporting, the gross misrepresentations, and the viral mistakes that spread across cyberspace before anyone bothered to ask for her side.

Matthew Hiltzik smelled a rat. *Access Hollywood,* which apologized for the misleading account, was, after all, owned by NBC. How was Couric's old remark, which had never even aired, suddenly resurrected into this hit-job of a story? This was nothing but an old-fashioned smear. The tactic reminded Hiltzik of a political campaign, where the other side would throw out something questionable and make you deny it. Some henchman at NBC, he believed, was trying to cast Couric as a weak woman, a diva who wasn't tough enough to be a network anchor, by using her motherhood against her. There was a media double standard: If she was too strong a personality, she was seen as overly harsh. If she showed emotion— and that was what people liked about Katie, that she was real—she was too weak, not up to the job.

Part of Rome Hartman's job was to figure out how to transform Couric's brainstorming sessions into television form. She had one idea that she called "Left Turn, Right Turn," which involved turning advocates into reporters. Activists on both sides of an issue would be given producing help to make a case in ninety seconds, and the newscast would run their reports on successive nights. Viewers were sick of pundits screaming at each other on cable shows, Couric felt, and this could be an antidote.

At the same time they had to find a place for Schieffer's weekly commentary. Hartman gradually decided that they should combine all these ideas in one branded segment. The next question was what to call it. They settled on "Voices" as a working title but soon concluded that the name was too generic. McManus suggested "Heard in America." One producer came up with "Thinking Aloud." Finally, they settled on "Free Speech."

Hartman sat down and wrote a memo outlining the blueprint for the new program. The first section of the show would feature "the big story of the day, the smart and original bounce piece that we want to have EVERY day, and other first block day-of-air enterprise offers. We also expect that Katie will do regular newsmaker interviews in the first section . . . whether live or pre-tape."

The second section would have "the longest and most ambitious stories in the broadcast," including foreign affairs, health, medicine, investigative, business, pocketbook, education, politics, and culture.

The third block would be the "Free Speech" segment, and the goal in the fourth, Hartman wrote, was "making sure we have a steady supply of the most memorable, timely, and uplifting 'signature' stories to end our broadcast."

The buzz in the CBS corridors was about whether this format was too rigid, whether fewer pieces by the correspondents would make it to air, and whether there was simply too much Katie. There was a growing sense in the newsroom that there was the CBS team and the Katie team, which included a number of the people she had brought over from NBC, and a palpable anxiety among some veterans that their jobs might be in danger. A new anchor, after all, tended to get her way.

And with Couric making $15 million a year, who was going to tell her what to do? Sean McManus seemed to sense that this might become a problem. "She has to understand that I have a boss, and she has a boss, and I'm her boss," McManus told a colleague.

The other networks were paying close attention. Brian Williams scoffed at the "Free Speech" idea. Every time a commentary segment aired, a news story had to be dropped. What news, or even feature story, would he kill each night to make room for pretaped opinions? Besides, commentary was available everywhere. That was what Bill O'Reilly did, and Rush Limbaugh, and Al Franken, and Jack Cafferty, and on and on. The media world was hardly suffering from a shortage of opinions.

What CBS was really planning to sell was Couric's personality, the bubbly woman with the infectious sense of humor. She was determined not to change the way she communicated with people, not to lapse into the sort of anchor-speak she called "Newsak," just because she was moving to an evening time slot.

But Couric's popularity had an undeniable flip side. Many viewers loved her, but others couldn't stand her. The Gallup organization felt compelled to wade into the anchor wars. Couric led the nightly news anchors with a 60 percent approval rating, compared to 55 percent for Gibson, 50 percent for Schieffer, and 47 percent for Williams, although this may have been largely a reflection of name recognition. But Couric's disapproval rating was 23 percent, about triple that of the others, who were in the single digits. In the argot of the political trade, she had high negatives.

At the moment Couric was focused on the positive. Viewers, she believed, wanted more positive stories, more hopeful stories, more stories that dealt with solutions. They were tired of all the gloom and doom on the evening news. This was what she had picked up on her listening tour, and what she wanted to deliver. How Couric would reconcile that approach with the steady diet of war, terrorism, natural disasters, crime, and social problems that tended to dominate the news agenda remained to be seen.

When it came to ushering in the new era, no detail was deemed too small. The set was being completely rebuilt for Couric, relegating the entire news staff to the clatter of the cafeteria, which was dubbed the Newseteria. The network hired James Horner, the Academy Award–winning composer who did the score for *Titanic,* to write some new theme music, and when Couric didn't think it was quite right, Horner was told to revise it.

And then there was the opening. McManus was determined to get it right. His research showed that people switched to other evening newscasts if the first few seconds didn't grab them. Should Couric be standing or seated? Or should she be in motion? Should she do the voice-over on the headlines or leave that to an announcer? Should the correspondents be featured at the top, as Schieffer was doing, or should it be all Katie? The opening had to be dynamic. They had to get it right, and then hone it during the week set aside for rehearsals.

Hartman had his hands full planning the new show, but he still had to get Schieffer's broadcast on the air every night. It was like trying to drive a car and tinker with it at the same time. It was as though he could hear the *60 Minutes* clock ticking in his head, growing louder every day. Finally Hartman handed off the newscast to the weekend producer so he could concentrate on developing the Couric show. The Hartman team worked in the Fishbowl, while the weekend crew camped out in the makeshift newsroom, which they christened the Outhouse Fishbowl.

Bob Schieffer offered to let Couric take early possession of his huge second-floor office, the one he had inherited from Dan Rather, but she declined. The only physical sign of her impending arrival was the dozen clothing racks, each festooned with ten to fifteen hanging bags of designer outfits, that now filled the large back room of his suite.

Couric used the transition to meet some of Washington's premier power players. During a blitz of the capital she sat down with the new chief justice, John Roberts, and with Michael Chertoff, the secretary of Homeland Security. She met with several women who had worked for the Clinton administration, including Madeleine Albright, Carol Browner, and Wendy Sherman. And she chatted with Tony Snow, the Fox News talk show host who had recently taken the White House press secretary's job, in an effort to smooth her tattered relations with the Bush administration.

As she labored on the new broadcast, Couric seemed not to grasp the degree to which she was in the eye of a media hurricane.

"Shouldn't we be out there publicizing the launch?" she asked Sandy Genelius, the chief spokeswoman for CBS News.

"Katie, every newspaper in America is going to write about your debut whether we talk to them or not," Genelius said.

What was strange was that after fifteen years as a huge star at the *Today* show, Couric had no real relationships with veteran television writers, most of whom had never interviewed her more than once or twice. Hiltzik believed that NBC had sheltered her over the years, and that she had not fully understood the importance of dealing with the press. One of the first things that Hiltzik had done was to set up meetings for Couric with Col Allan, the Australian-born editor of the *New York Post,* and Richard Johnson, who ran the gossipy Page Six. If a reporter had met you, had seen your face, he would find it a little bit harder to slam you the following week.

As the debut drew closer, some of the media coverage seemed to sink to the level of Page Six. *The Wall Street Journal* devoted a story to the alleged changes in Couric's wardrobe, noting that in recent promos she was "dressed in a black suit, with a double strand of pearls around her neck—a more serious look than the colorful, trendy outfits she often wore to cover light topics for many years on the *Today* show." The newspaper declared, with no trace of irony, that "how Ms. Couric looks will help shape her image as she discusses weighty topics like the Middle East."

But that article was worthy of *Columbia Journalism Review* compared to one in *USA Today,* which devoted itself to these pressing national issues: "The problem of Katie Couric's hair color (too brassy) and cut (too long). Then there's her makeup (too dark), her clothes (too glam) and her skin (too tan)." Rick DiCecca, an Estée Lauder makeup artist, said that her look had become "distracting," and that she needed to "lighten up the bronzer and lay off the black eyeliner, softening up with plums or grays." It was a descent into utter triviality that seemed oblivious to the fact that Couric was a seasoned journalist who should be judged on more than jewelry and mascara.

When a *Parade* magazine writer, in the summer of 2006, pressed her about her husband's death, Couric began to cry. "My kids are thriving," she said, "but when I see a father walking down the street with a little girl and holding her hand, my feeling of loss is palpable. I'm so envious. We were ripped off." She didn't hide her emotions. That, for the entertainment press, was part of her appeal.

If she bought a seven-bedroom home in East Hampton for $6 million, it was news. If she dated, or stopped dating, trumpeter Chris Botti or Washington beer distributor Jimmy Reyes, it was news. Couric did her best to tune out all the chatter. Otherwise, she felt, it would drive her absolutely out of her mind. "Can you just tell people to stop talking about me, please?" she asked a friend.

Couric believed that there was plenty of residual sexism in the country, and a female network anchor was still a rare species. Besides, women were just more interesting than men. They were less guarded, more comfortable talking about their lives.

But she couldn't stand the way the press invented a shorthand for you, a Velcro label that you could never peel off. The joke among her friends was that Katie had decided what she wanted chiseled on her tombstone: "Don't Call Me Fucking Perky."

*   *   *

Charlie Gibson was in a meeting with his political unit, talking about election coverage, and out of the corner of his eye he was watching Condoleezza Rice on a wall monitor.

She was, in a major policy shift, offering for the first time to hold direct talks with Iran about its nuclear enrichment program if certain conditions were met. But the sound on the monitor was off.

Two minutes after Rice left the State Department podium, a staffer walked into the meeting and told Gibson: "Secretary Rice is on the phone for you."

"For me?" Gibson was stunned.

He picked up the phone.

"Were you watching what I just did?" Rice asked.

"I was watching but not listening," Gibson said. "We were having a meeting. I apologize."

Rice briefly described the diplomacy surrounding her offer to Iran. On an off-the-record basis, she talked about the Chinese interests in the region and what Russian President Vladimir Putin had told President Bush about the situation. Rice then asked whether Gibson had any questions.

"Yeah, I have one question," Gibson said.

What was that?

"Why the hell are you calling *me*?"

Rice laughed. "There are just people we like to keep apprised of what we're doing," she said.

Gibson asked if he should expect such calls with some regularity.

No, Rice said, but she was always happy to talk whenever he had questions.

When they hung up, Gibson couldn't help but think: A kid who damn near didn't graduate from college just finished a private conversation with the secretary of State. Son of a bitch!

He wasn't accustomed to this sort of high-level attention. When Gibson covered the House, he had avoided socializing with lawmakers, preferring pizza and a movie with his wife and kids. But being a nightly news anchor, he was coming to realize, provided admission to a very small club. Peter Jennings had traveled very comfortably in those circles, thought nothing of picking up the phone and talking to Yasir Arafat. Gibson, though, had never quite gotten it into his head that he was on television screens from Boston to Seattle.

Morning television might be the big moneymaker for the networks, but when you got the evening anchor job, the doors of power just swung wide open. When Jon Banner suggested that he pay courtesy calls on Bush administration officials, they had no problem getting time with Josh Bolten, the White House chief of staff, and Tony Snow. Donald Rumsfeld even invited Gibson to the Pentagon for lunch.

That, in itself, was remarkable. Gibson had been on Rummy's shit list for years. In the fall of 2002, as the administration was gearing up for the invasion of Iraq, he had cohosted *GMA* from the Pentagon and as part of the deal got a ten-minute sit-down with the secretary of Defense. Gibson was openly skeptical about the rationale for war that the Bush team was advancing, and he let that show.

"Can you say this morning, with certainty, that Saddam Hussein has weapons of mass destruction, nuclear, chemical, biological?" he asked Rumsfeld.

"Well, he certainly has chemical and biological weapons, there's just no question about that," Rumsfeld replied. There was no way to know for sure about nuclear weapons, he said.

"But do you think Americans are prepared to send sons and daughters to war on the belief that he might have nuclear weapons?"

Rumsfeld described Iraq as "a terrorist country that has weapons of mass destruction already."

Gibson kept pressing: Did Rumsfeld have "direct evidence," as when President Kennedy had shown the country satellite photos of Soviet missiles in Cuba? This was no "court of law," Rumsfeld said, it was a matter of "self-defense."

The interview was turning into a debate. "But you can't go to war without American public support," Gibson said.

"The evidence is certainly there," Rumsfeld countered. And the goal, he said, was regime change.

"With all due respect, then isn't it a bit ingenuous to say that, that we haven't made the decision whether or not to go to war yet? Because absent our going in there and kicking him out and getting a regime change, we don't expect him magically to step aside, do we?"

"Well, you never know," Rumsfeld responded.

Rumsfeld clearly did not like Gibson suggesting that he had been disingenuous; it was, Gibson believed, as though he had called the Pentagon chief a liar. Gibson could never get another interview with him. Now all that was apparently forgotten as Gibson was escorted to Rumsfeld's office for lunch.

"I haven't watched an evening newscast in five and a half years," Rumsfeld said. Gibson wasn't sure whether that was a screw-you remark or just meant that he was too busy. But he found Rumsfeld quite candid on all the questions that he could not answer about the sectarian violence in Iraq. Rumsfeld did not evince the utter certitude about events that he usually displayed in public.

Gibson was a product of the Vietnam War era. When he was a television reporter in Lynchburg, he had driven to Washington on weekends to march in antiwar demonstrations. To this day, he did not know what American soldiers had died for in Vietnam. He had the same feeling now about Iraq.

How should they cover the damn thing? Gibson had not been to Iraq in three years and felt that he should go back, to get a better feel for the situation. Some generals had invited him to make the trip and promised that the military would keep him safe. He brought it up at a lunch with David Westin.

"Not on my life are you going," Westin said. "Not with my track record." After what happened to Bob Woodruff, Westin felt that he couldn't take the risk of losing another anchor.

Gibson wished that he could just sneak off to Iraq on his own. The problem, even if Westin were to acquiesce, was that the press would make the mere fact of his trip a bigger story than any reporting he was able to carry out. And Gibson had no desire to go to Baghdad as a PR stunt, not in light of the danger involved. When he was in Israel, the police had caught a suicide bomber, with explosives in his backpack, two blocks from his hotel. Flying into war zones was risky business.

Despite his strong views about the apparent senselessness of American kids dying in a war whose premise had been faulty, Gibson tried his best to remain agnostic on that and other issues. He had decided to stop voting. Gibson felt terribly guilty about it—voting, he felt, was a basic civic obligation—but he also believed that the process of making up his mind in elections could influence his judgment as a journalist.

In the weeks after Gibson took over *World News,* David Westin kept asking him: What will you do to put your stamp on the program? Westin believed that Gibson had experience, warmth, and an Everyman quality that enabled viewers to identify with him. But he had to put more Charlie into the program, to smile more, as he did off camera.

Jon Banner had the same question for Gibson: How are you going to make it *yours*? He wanted his anchor to do more pieces for the broadcast. Gibson had been a reporter his whole life, Banner figured. It had taken Jennings years to become comfortable with an expanded role, but this was a different time, and viewers expected the anchor to be a major presence.

"We owe it to the audience to have you on more than just anchoring the show," Banner said.

But Gibson was reluctant. He was very conscious of not crowding out the reporters in the field, having toiled in that vineyard for so long. He clung to the old-fashioned view that the broadcast should not revolve around the anchor. You were fronting a great news division; you should never delude yourself into thinking you *were* the news division.

That seemed to be the direction CBS was going with Katie Couric. Gibson thought that it would be a mistake to make the *Evening News* all about Katie. She was an outsider; it was difficult to ask the people of CBS News to buckle down for old K.C. when they didn't really know K.C. If he were Couric, he would do the straightest newscast he could for a year and then figure out what changes to make.

Gibson was gradually giving *World News* a harder edge. Gone were the Vargas days when they would put a child porn case that had broken three months earlier at the top of the show. It was a broadcast with very little spice. Gibson rarely smiled, keeping the playful side of his personality under wraps. A *Chicago Tribune* columnist accused him of having no "on-air charisma" and said that he needed to show "a little leg." But news, in Gibson's view, was serious business, and without Diane Sawyer to bounce off, he was dead serious. Even some of his friends thought that he needed to lighten up.

But sometimes he had the perfect touch. After a story on pending surgery for a pair of four-year-old conjoined twins, Gibson added: "Say a prayer for those kids. We'll let you know how the operation came out tomorrow." When was the last time, Banner thought, that a network anchor had asked the country to pray?

Where Gibson was clearly lacking was in the publicity department. *Newsweek* had put Katie Couric on the cover but had given his promotion one measly paragraph. New York City buses carried placards with Couric's picture, while Gibson's photo might as well have been on milk cartons. With every publication on the planet writing about Katie, ABC executives wanted to get his voice into some of those stories, so that he could remind people that *World News* had a new anchor too. But Gibson disliked talking himself up and turned down many of the interview requests. He even hesitated to call in to the Don Imus radio show, a rite of passage for media elite types, although he joined in the banter just fine when he did appear.

In August, Diane Sawyer filled in for Gibson on *World News*. She thought of offering Charlie some advice on running the broadcast but decided against it. He didn't need to hear from the bossy former cohost. He was free at last, and probably thrilled about it.

When Gibson returned, he noticed some changes in his second-floor office. Sawyer had left a throw pillow emblazoned with a picture of her poodle. There was a photo of her husband, director Mike Nichols. And there was a large framed poster of Michael Jackson, with the inscription: "Thanks for all the great coverage. Love and Kisses, Michael."

Gibson loved showing off the gifts. Diane could always make him laugh. And that, at the moment, was what was missing from the new anchor's performance.

CHAPTER 24

The Handoff

The Continental Airlines jet was cruising at ten thousand feet, beginning its final descent into Edinburgh, Scotland, when Brian Williams felt his Black-Berry vibrate.

He had forgotten to turn it off when they left the night before from Newark Airport. Williams was still wearing his suit from *Nightly News,* having rushed to meet his family in the airport lounge for a long-planned vacation, built around his daughter Allison's appearance in a theatrical production in Edinburgh.

Williams took the device out of its black holster and read the e-mail: British authorities had foiled a plot to detonate liquid explosives on as many as ten airplanes in midair from London to the United States.

Holy fuck! This was a rather unnerving message to receive while still in the air over the United Kingdom. He did not want his fifteen-year-old son, Douglas, to see the e-mail. In fact, Williams didn't tell his wife until the plane's wheels hit the ground, when he handed Jane the BlackBerry.

There was a huge crowd at the airport, with virtually all flights delayed. As the family piled into a minivan that was providing shuttle service to the hotel, Williams asked the driver to turn on an all-news radio station.

"I think people on holiday should be able to relax and not have to listen to the news," the man said in a thick Scottish brogue.

"You don't understand. I'm a presenter in the States. I need to hear this."

"Are ya sure?"

At the hotel Williams called NBC, did a phone interview with the *Today* show about the "absolute bedlam" at British airports, and began talking to his office about flying to London. There was never any question that he would go. His family, which was accustomed to ruined vacations, understood that the news came first.

An NBC crew met Williams at Heathrow, where he changed his tie so he wouldn't look like a carbon copy in the same navy suit and white shirt he had been wearing the night before. A live shot was set up in front of a runway, and at 12:30 A.M. London time he began: "Tonight, a security clamp has come down upon air travel as investigators here in London say they have busted up a plot to blow up commercial airliners."

After the newscast there was no quick way to fly back to Edinburgh for Allison's play, so a driver took him on the six-hour ride, with Williams sleeping in the back seat.

The following week Williams was in an HMV video store in London, looking for a movie to rent, when he saw a television tuned to Sky News. The channel was airing a replay of the *CBS Evening News*. Williams was stunned to see that the lead story was the arrest of a suspect in the decade-old murder of six-year-old JonBenet Ramsey, the child beauty queen whose killing in Colorado had triggered a massive media frenzy.

Oh my God, Williams thought. If Schieffer was leading with the Ramsey case, it must be a huge story in the United States.

"Thank God you're on vacation," Jane told him.

Williams hated these tabloid melodramas, and everyone around him knew it. They were like cotton candy, he felt. There were so many other important issues to talk about. He believed that the sensational soap operas—Chandra Levy, Laci Peterson, killer sharks—were driven by cable's twenty-four-hour noise machine.

What Williams didn't know at the moment was that all the network newscasts, including *Nightly,* had led with the bizarre spectacle of John Mark Karr, who had twice taken teenage brides, claiming that he had been at the Ramsey home in Boulder on the night that JonBenet was killed. The next night they all led with the story again, even as conflicting accounts by relatives raised serious doubts about whether Karr had even been in Colorado at the time.

When Williams returned to New York the following Monday, he told his producers that John Mark Karr was a cable story. But they insisted that there was considerable public interest in the Ramsey case. Like Dan Rather at the height of the Chandra Levy media circus, Williams could have dug in his heels and refused to allow any further mention of Karr on *Nightly News.* But Williams relented, as he had when his MSNBC show had gone through its tabloid phase in the late 1990s. And there was an unspoken pressure—everyone *else* was doing it.

There were times when you couldn't be above the news, Williams felt, and besides, Jane had told him that she was interested in knowing more about Karr. *Nightly* did a story on the case that night, and another one the next night. "Why do so many doubt that John Mark Karr is guilty of murder?" Williams asked. A better question might have been: Why do we keep covering this oddball who so many doubt is guilty of murder?

Within days the networks all looked silly: A DNA test proved that John Mark Karr was a fraud. The newscasts had allowed themselves to be hijacked by the self-delusional claims of a certified creep.

Williams was far more concerned with his trip to New Orleans for the one-year anniversary of Hurricane Katrina. When he heard that Bush would be there as well, he asked the White House for an interview, even though it had been only four months since they had strolled around Musicians Village, and Dan Bartlett agreed.

It was now clear that Williams had become the president's favorite anchor. Whenever they got together, Bush would pepper him with questions about his background. He viewed Williams as a regular, plain-spoken guy. "I can do business with him," he told Bartlett, bestowing his highest compliment for a journalist.

When the president arrived where Williams had gathered with his crew, an hour ahead of schedule, he didn't bother with a formal hello and handshake. "Brian," he said, "do you mind doing this thing outside, because it's hot and these people have been waiting for a jazz band." Bush was to address the sweltering crowd after the interview. Williams said that they could get miked up and start right away.

Laura Bush said that the last time she saw Williams she had been looking for a bathroom, and now she was looking for one again.

As the president and the newsman began their walk-and-talk in the midday sun, there was an unusual air of informality: just two guys on the move in sweaty shirts. Bush was doing what Williams regarded as his LBJ thing, putting his face very close to the anchor's in a subtle effort at establishing dominance. It was very important, Williams felt, not to give ground.

Williams began by asking whether Katrina had been the low point of his presidency, and he used a word that the Bush family had always deemed insulting. Employing his favorite technique of attributing strong criticism to others, Williams said that Michael Eric Dyson, an African-American professor and author, had said on *Nightly* that the disastrous response to Katrina "was because of your patrician upbringing. That it's a class issue."

The president said he didn't know Dyson but insisted that he had "delivered" for New Orleans.

Williams cited some e-mail that he had received about Iraq. "Do you have any moments of doubt that we fought the wrong war?" Bush was quick to play the 9/11 card, saying, "We were attacked."

"But those weren't Iraqis," Williams fired back. After Bush conceded the point, Williams raised the criticism that the president hadn't asked Americans to sacrifice after the September 11th attacks. Bush, clearly off his game, ventured that "we pay a lot of taxes"—an odd example for a president who prided himself on cutting taxes.

The interview seemed to get more personal. Williams asked Bush whether he felt a "palpable tension" with his father, noting that Bill Clinton had lately been to the family compound at Kennebunkport more often than the president. Williams also asked about a recent report that Bush had read *The Stranger,* by the French philosopher Albert Camus. That was quite a change, Williams noted, from his earlier books on Joe DiMaggio and Teddy Roosevelt. Bush said his wife had recommended Camus and that he had also recently read three works by Shakespeare.

The question seemed natural to Williams because he and Bush always talked privately about what they were reading. This time, in fact, Williams had recommended a new LBJ biography. But to some of those watching, it sounded as though Williams was playing off the president's reputation as an intellectual lightweight by skeptically challenging his interest in Camus.

When the twenty-six-minute encounter was over, Bush seemed pumped up and in good spirits. But Williams was concerned about Bartlett's reaction.

"Are we fine?" he asked.

"Yeah, the president can handle anything you throw at him," Bartlett said.

But Bartlett was not happy. Those questions about Bush's book-reading habits, and about his relationship with his dad, they just seemed totally out of left field. Bartlett understood that the president liked to get into the physical space of a questioner, so the nose-to-nose aspect didn't bother him. But of all the interviews that Bush had done, this one stood out as the oddest.

Once it was broadcast, the interview touched off a storm of criticism, especially on the right. Rush Limbaugh took to the airwaves.

"We like Brian Williams here," Limbaugh said. "But I mean, some of these questions that he asked President Bush in the interview last night were downright insolent, disrespectful, and rude, quoting some wacko professor from Princeton . . . This guy Dyson was out there saying, well, the aftermath, you know, Bush, he didn't care what happened down there, didn't care if people lost their homes, didn't care if people lost their lives. It's just typical, Bush and his family being a bunch of East Coast patricians."

Williams got a torrent of negative e-mail.

"I'm a Democrat and am against many of Bush's policies—but I feel that questioning Bush about his reading habits was an attempt to put him down," said a woman in Washington State.

A woman in St. Louis wrote, "It was like watching a 'bully' in the schoolyard. Brian's face was too close to the president's and seemed extremely disrespectful. Condescending is another way to describe Brian Williams's way of speaking to Bush . . . The slant is evident in his voice and in the entire newscast."

"It was very threatening and disrespectful to the president," one man wrote. "Brian was in Bush's face with his arms crossed and appeared angry. At one point he made a quick gesture with his hand by the president's face as if he was trying to get him to flinch . . . What a crock. At least quit pretending to be unbiased."

"In the future I intend to watch Fox News exclusively," another man announced. "They're not such snobs."

Some viewers had the opposite reaction toward the encounter with Bush. Williams "was soft on him and did not confront him," an Illinois woman complained. But the most biting letters portrayed the anchor as dissing the president.

Williams was totally taken aback by the reaction. Disrespectful? There was nothing he respected more than the American presidency. Williams believed that it made some viewers uncomfortable to see him walking alongside Bush, up close and personal. They were accustomed to formal sitdowns in the Blue Room, two men in suits on wingback chairs. To some Americans in the post-9/11 world, Williams felt, simply asking tough questions of the president made you seem unpatriotic. In his mind, he had just been quoting a professor in suggesting that Bush was a patrician. Still, he had to know it was a loaded word when it came to his dad, George Herbert Walker Bush, especially in the context of failing to rescue drowning neighborhoods that were heavily poor and black.

Williams defended himself on his blog and read a sampling of the e-mail on the air. He called Dan Bartlett and told him that the critics would get some rebuttal time on *Nightly*.

On a personal level, it had been a tough week. While he was talking to Bush, his eighty-nine-year-old father, Gordon, who already had a replacement hip, was undergoing surgery for congestive heart failure. There were times when he wanted to go on the air and say, *Folks, I've got my dad in the hospital, I'm about to put my daughter in college, there's a lot going on, go easy on me.*

As he walked around the city—he had recently bought an apartment in the East 50s, a few blocks from Rockefeller Center, for nights when it was too late to return to Connecticut—Williams was struck by the number of ordinary folks who were wishing him good luck. He had to stop and think before realizing that they were talking about the challenge he was about to face from Katie Couric, whose beaming face now adorned every bus in New York City.

Although they had been colleagues at NBC for more than a decade, Williams had never forged much of a relationship with Couric. After her first big fund-raising gala for colon cancer, in memory of her husband, Williams had sent her a note. He said he was sure it was just an oversight that he wasn't invited, that he and Jane would love to be active in supporting the charity. He never heard back.

The last time Williams had cohosted *Today,* filling in for Matt Lauer, they had just wrapped up the program at 9 A.M. when the producer asked them to stick around for a possible news bulletin. NBC had picked up a rumor that William Rehnquist might be stepping down as chief justice. Couric ordered up some research on the Supreme Court.

As the chatter turned to possible replacements, Williams overheard her telling a producer: "You can't be appointed chief justice unless you've been a justice."

"You know what, that's not correct," Williams said. He rattled off the examples of Earl Warren and Salmon P. Chase.

"Oh, everyone," Couric announced, in a tone that he deemed sarcastic, "we have a Supreme Court expert on our hands."

The rumor turned out to be a false alarm, and Williams thought nothing more about the incident. Maybe Katie just didn't like him. But friends had heard Williams go on about how the best evening news anchors were the ones who had dedicated their lives to pursuing the job. He referred to those who had lucked into such jobs—which would include Couric, Elizabeth Vargas, even his pal Bob Woodruff—as "accidental tourists." There was nothing accidental about Williams's lifelong quest for the post he now held.

Williams had his share of detractors, who kept noting that he had lost half a million viewers since Tom Brokaw vacated the chair. Why, they asked, had Williams barely tinkered with the newscast? Why was he being so cautious? He was so decorous that he still insisted on introducing each correspondent by saying "good evening."

Katie Couric admired Williams but did not understand why he did not let more of his terrific sense of humor show on the air. Diane Sawyer also thought Williams should be funnier, and that as a strapping young man he should be constantly taking the program to far-flung places.

The critics missed some of the subtler changes—Brokaw had never read negative letters on the air or attempted a daily blog, and Williams had utterly owned the New Orleans story—but more important, what Williams was doing was completely by design. He believed in a traditional broadcast, believed that the news was too serious for him to joke around the way he did with Jon Stewart.

If Gibson managed to beat him, so be it. Charlie was a newsman's newsman, Williams felt, an older version of himself. There was no shame in losing to Charlie. But he felt very differently about Katie Couric.

It wasn't that Williams was jealous of her fame, her huge salary, or the enormous wave of coverage surrounding her ascension. But Williams and others at NBC believed that Katie was in something of a bubble, living a wealthy celebrity lifestyle that set her apart from her viewers.

What was central to Williams's conception of himself was that he was the down-to-earth journalist, the NASCAR fan, the onetime volunteer fireman, the guy who shopped at Price Club and watched *American Idol*. One recent Sunday his in-laws' basement in Connecticut flooded and he spent four hours cleaning the gunk out of their sump pump. He was not above grunt work, either at home or in the newsroom, where he insisted on writing every word of his own copy. Let Katie take her best shot. Brian Williams was convinced that when it came to news, people would see who eats it, sleeps it, and breathes it.

*   *   *

Bob Schieffer strolled into the gleaming new studio, checked the cameras, and looked at his mark on the floor.

"She's going to stand here," Rome Hartman explained, pointing to a spot a couple of steps away. "You've got a fair amount of copy to read. I think you should figure out when you should start the walk so the reveal happens at the right time."

The floor director suggested that Schieffer turn to Camera 2, to his left. "That feels natural," Hartman said.

It was a few minutes past three o'clock on Schieffer's final day as anchor of the *CBS Evening News,* and they were choreographing the changing of the generational guard.

Schieffer had planned it differently. While the multimillion-dollar set, with its huge, horseshoe-shaped anchor desk of polished teak, was being constructed, he was doing the news in a small, dingy room with a green curtain hung up with steel clothespins on the wall behind him. A chroma-key machine projected a picture of the old newsroom onto the curtain, the same technology that created a virtual map of cold fronts and rain clouds for local weathermen.

Schieffer wanted to drop the effect to show that it was just a cheap curtain—to let the viewers in on the joke—and then have the cameras follow him as he walked into the new studio and welcomed Katie Couric to CBS. But Sean McManus had second thoughts.

"Last week I thought it was funny," McManus said. "But maybe this week it'd be best if we didn't do that. Maybe we shouldn't be leaving the impression that we go around phonying up stuff all the time."

A few days earlier CBS had become a national laughingstock over the case of the Incredible Shrinking Anchor. Someone in the publicity office had released a photo of a very svelte Couric—so svelte, in fact, that the *TV Newser* blog discovered that it was a digitally altered version of the actual photo. The *New York Post* picked up the story without credit, with a front-page headline blaring: "How TV Queen Katie Lost 20 Pounds." Other newspapers, cable television shows, and Web sites had great fun with the before-and-after shots. Couric, who had known nothing about the stupid stunt, was understandably annoyed. The news operation looked as though it was willing to manipulate the truth to produce a sexier anchor.

Schieffer was now ready for the more straightforward version as Couric walked into the studio in a black dress, white blouse, and black heels. When Schieffer, after announcing his return to Washington, delivered his line—"Here is someone who will be a permanent fixture, my friend Katie Couric"—she oozed warmth as she addressed him.

"Well, thank you so much. I can't imagine following in the footsteps of a kinder, more gracious per—" Couric stopped. She had blown the line.

One producer said, "Bob, you need to get closer."

"Don't invade my personal space, please," Couric warned mockingly.

They tried it again, but Schieffer started his walk too early. On the next take he botched his line. "If we did this live, we'd have just done it," Schieffer grumbled.

In the fifth and sixth take, Schieffer again started the walk too early and reached Couric before he was ready to introduce her. "Rehearsed spontaneity, I love it!" Couric cracked.

She tried to refine the last part. "After Bob chats with me," Couric said, "I'll say, 'Thank you, Bob, the floor is yours.' I'll say something like, 'That's so sweet.' Does that make sense, Rome?"

On the eighth take they nailed it. Schieffer introduced his friend. Couric thanked him for his graciousness. Then she tossed to a taped package that she had narrated, which included a light-hearted look at Schieffer's career, including his long-forgotten stand-up at the National Putt-Putt Championship. In the taped interview, he choked up as he talked about what his mother and his wife meant to him. Couric had had her way with another interview subject: She had made Bob Schieffer cry on camera.

They would do the last part live. In the hallway Hartman told them that he wanted to cut a line about how Katie would like CBS and CBS liked her.

"That's okay," Couric said, touching Schieffer's arm. "This is about you."

Schieffer turned his attention back to the newscast. Their lead story was Bush launching yet another defense of the war on terror.

Now that Schieffer sat down and read an account of the speech, he was struck by the stridency of the rhetoric. He sat down and typed his lead: "The security of the free world depends on an American victory in Iraq. That's what President Bush said today, and that's where we'll start tonight."

But he kept getting distracted, for this was a day of handshakes and hugs. Ed Bradley of *60 Minutes,* looking rather frail, came by to bid Schieffer farewell. "I'm having withdrawal symptoms, Bob," said Pat Shevlin, one of his longtime producers. Schieffer did interviews with the CBS stations in New York and Washington and with *Inside Edition.* And his relatives kept arriving: Pat, his daughters Susan and Sharon, and his brother Tom, who had left his ambassadorial post in Tokyo for the occasion.

At 5:25, as Schieffer returned to his computer, the staff had arranged to get a live feed of a *Late Show* taping on a large monitor next to his desk. They had heard a rumor that David Letterman might do a bit about Bob. Schieffer felt that Letterman didn't like him—the comedian had never invited him on the show, not after any of his three books—but was curious about becoming a punchline.

Suddenly Letterman was hailing Schieffer for his "tremendous career." Then he tossed to a fake promo for the *Evening News*: "And because it's his last night on the air," the announcer intoned, "Bob's gonna show his deal!" The screen filled with what purported to be a picture of a nude Bob Schieffer, with an electronic checkerboard hiding his groin. Schieffer threw back his head and roared.

He was so delighted that he ran to get Pat and had the bit replayed. "That's not him," Pat deadpanned as everyone laughed. Soon he was dragging other staffers to the monitor for a viewing.

Seemingly oblivious to the impending deadline, Schieffer gathered his family in his second-floor office. At 6:12 the phone rang. It was Brian Williams.

"I just want to tell you I'm going to miss you," Williams said. "You are a good guy."

"Well, that's mighty nice of you to say," Schieffer replied. "I'm going to miss you too. It's been fun to compete against you."

As he took his family down to the Fishbowl to watch the broadcast, Schieffer steered Couric toward Sharon. "This is the new kid we've hired," he told his daughter.

While Schieffer was in the anchor chair, Couric and the producers helped arrange the family, friends, and staff members in a semicircle on the periphery of the new set. Les Moonves and Sean McManus were there. In the taped interview, Couric was describing how CBS had turned to Schieffer "in one of its darkest hours," when "Dan Rather stepped down eighteen months ago, following the National Guard document scandal."

After the taped piece Schieffer thanked the viewers for inviting him into their homes, and the relatives and well-wishers mobbed him as the cameras rolled.

Afterward, Couric presented Schieffer with a newspaper cartoon in which his caricature was seen grousing: "Nobody ever talks about my legs!"

CHAPTER 25

Celebrity Anchor

It was opening night, and the Fishbowl was packed.

As the minutes ticked down to Katie Couric's debut, Les Moonves was in the glass-sheathed rectangle along the newsroom's far wall, playing the role of chief cheerleader, feeling as though he were witnessing a bit of history. Rome Hartman's wife was there, and deputy producer Bill Owens's wife, and James Horner, the composer, and Tom Friedman, the *New York Times* columnist who had just pretaped an interview, and a number of others who were milling about.

Man, who are all these people? Hartman wondered. Why don't they get lost so we can get some work done?

Hartman had been tense for days, and it showed. He had been working virtually around the clock for three months, despite an accident in which his teenage son had broken his neck, and had spent Labor Day weekend in final rehearsals with Couric. Suddenly it dawned on him that they were attempting all kinds of new things at once: music, graphics, technical changes. Maybe it was simply too much. Boy, he thought, I wonder if this place is going to blow up.

At least they would have a good introduction. Couric had approached Walter Cronkite, who at eighty-nine was hard of hearing but still had the same growl of an anchor voice, about recording a few opening words for her. Cronkite had a good deal of respect for Couric, dating back to her days as a reporter, and after being frozen out during the Rather years, he was delighted to be asked.

On the Saturday before the debut, they sat around—McManus, Hartman, Couric, and Bob Peterson, the newly installed "creative director," who had come with Couric from NBC—and listened to the tape. The vote was unanimous. The old man would be vouching for the new gal.

They had spent hours running through the opening seven seconds—McManus had listened to eight different mixes—before settling on the final version. Now, in the final moments, Sean McManus, who had produced Super Bowl games, was nervous. How could you *not* be nervous with the kind of relentless publicity buildup they had all been through? Katie had never anchored the evening news before, other than as a substitute. There was so much weight on her shoulders.

Couric seemed outwardly calm, reviewing her copy as airtime approached. But she had woken up several times in the middle of the night, she had raced through a day of meetings and interviews and still more rehearsals, and she had more than the usual butterflies before a big broadcast. For the first time in years, her heart was pounding so hard she thought it might jump out of her chest.

She felt like she was under a high-powered microscope. All the hype, all the attention, it was far more than she had wanted. Couric knew that a lot was riding on her performance. CBS had made a huge investment in her. She had come to personify the shifting epicenter of network news. No matter what she did, Couric felt, she would be picked apart. This was a brand-new venture at a new network. Of course she had jitters. She did not have ice water in her veins.

Dressed less than glamorously in a white jacket over a fitted black dress, Couric was determined to come across as real and warm, not as some kind of anchor-robot. She had already decided to dispense with the two words—"good evening"—that seemed grafted onto the front of every nightly newscast.

"Just have fun," Hartman said shortly before she went on.

The new score by Horner came up, followed by Cronkite's voice-over. Couric took one step, to create a sense of motion, and recited the headlines before a large video screen. Then it was time to dive right in.

"Hi everyone," Couric said. "I'm very happy to be with you tonight." She was the audience's friend.

The lead story was a ten-day-old piece by Lara Logan from Afghanistan—with compelling footage of Logan with gun-waving, tough-talking members of the Taliban—that had no connection to any breaking news. Putting it at the top—rather than leading with President Bush ratcheting up his rhetoric with a speech comparing Osama bin Laden to Lenin and Hitler—was a declaration that this was a different kind of newscast, one that would play up magazine-style journalism as well as the day's events.

After Jim Axelrod's report on the Bush speech and the Tom Friedman interview, Couric offered a "briefing," ticking off items that Brian Williams and Charlie Gibson were covering with full stories. Two sentences on William Ford stepping down as chief executive of the troubled automaker bearing his family name. Two sentences on a study showing that seven of ten workers at Ground Zero had developed lung problems. This was the sort of news that CBS would sacrifice to make room for the new features.

Next came another story that had been in the can for two weeks, Anthony Mason reporting from a Shell oil rig. They had put a new top on the piece after Chevron announced a major oil discovery in the Gulf of Mexico, even though the two stories were unrelated.

Soon Couric was touting "an exclusive first look at *Vanity Fair*'s newest cover girl. She's Suri Cruise, daughter of Tom Cruise and Katie Holmes. After much speculation about why she's been undercover so long, this is proof-positive that, yes siree, she does exist." Couric attempted to justify the harmless bit of tabloid voyeurism by playing a 1949 clip of anchor Douglas Edwards showing a picture of nineteen-week-old Prince Charles.

After the "Free Speech" segment—a weird rant against media polarization by filmmaker Morgan Spurlock—Couric turned to the pressing question of how she should close the show.

"All summer long people have been asking me, how will you sign off at the end of your broadcast? I've wracked my brain and so far nothing has felt right."

So she played a montage of anchor sign-offs—Murrow, Huntley and Brinkley, Cronkite, Rather—followed by the buffoonish Ted Baxter, from the old *Mary Tyler Moore Show,* and the even more outlandish Ron Burgundy, played by Will Ferrell: "You stay classy, San Diego." There it was, actual humor on an evening newscast. Couric closed with the gimmick of asking viewers to go to the CBS Web site and suggest a parting slogan. She was perched on the edge of the horseshoe-shaped anchor desk, her legs dangling in front of her. "Thank you *so much* for watching," she purred.

Seconds after the sign-off, people poured onto the set to congratulate Couric. A bottle of champagne emerged. McManus offered a toast, as did Hartman, and Couric toasted the staff. A friend handed her a martini. She had survived her first night without a major flub.

Or had she? CBS badly miscalculated by loading up the first broadcast with so much softer material—for which the Cruise baby pictures became an irresistible symbol—that Couric conveyed the impression that the format would no longer include much breaking news. Hartman had reasoned that there weren't many important stories on the day after Labor Day, but he somehow forgot that this was like a glittering Broadway debut, with a packed house full of critics, and what might be excused as a slow-news day any other time would on this night be perceived as a bold statement. And that theme ran through even the favorable reviews, of which there were not many.

It was "cuddly news," said *The Hollywood Reporter.*

"Her presence actually gave weight to a blab-filled report that threatened to float away on a cloud of tepid air," said *The Philadelphia Inquirer.*

"If this is the new direction of the *CBS Evening News,* you might want to start watching *Entertainment Tonight,*" sniffed *The Miami Herald.*

The Washington Post said that the program seemed in need of a name change: "Maybe *The CBS Evening No-News.* Or *The CBS Evening Magazine.* Or *30 Minutes.*"

In the *New York Post,* Andrea Peyser bared her claws: "Her face was Botoxed beyond normal human endurance, proving that even pampered, overpaid news babes possess the courage to suffer for their art . . . The best that can be said about Katie Couric was that she did not trip over her 5-inch stiletto heels when she toddled across the floor of the set, crossing her bare legs like some ridiculous tramp."

Cattiness aside, most of the critics missed, or glossed over, the fact that the traditional model had been hemorrhaging viewers for a quarter of a century. What Couric and CBS were groping toward was an alternative format, friendlier and deeper and more textured. Couric was being judged almost as a performance artist, which was hardly surprising in light of her superstar salary and celebrity press coverage. But while the new *Evening News* was clearly about her ability to connect with the audience, it was also the most audacious attempt yet to redefine what a news-saturated audience might fancy at 6:30.

Couric found some of the jibes laughable. Her much-mocked outfit was a winter white Armani jacket. How clueless some of these critics were. She was embarrassed for their lack of fashion sense. The newscast, she felt, hadn't been soft at all. The Tom Cruise baby pictures were an exclusive, and every newspaper in America had run the *Vanity Fair* cover the next day. It must be frustrating, Couric thought, to make a living criticizing other people's work and never doing anything on your own that warranted a critique. Some of the detractors clearly got vicarious thrills by unleashing their slings and arrows. Outside the media circles in New York, Washington, and L.A., they just didn't matter that much. They had a heightened sense of their own importance. The people who mattered, the people she was playing to, were in living rooms across the country.

At NBC and ABC, executives breathed a sigh of relief after seeing what they considered a fluffier, and inferior, newscast.

Brian Williams took a DVD home that night and told colleagues that he didn't think much of the Couric broadcast. Where was the news? The taped pieces were old. The Suri Cruise pictures were a free advertisement for *Vanity Fair* that had no place on a nightly newscast.

Couric was not an anchor, Williams thought. She had never been trained as an anchor. She was trained as a host, and there was a difference. She had plowed through the brief items without pausing, without allowing a beat for transition.

Some at NBC were struck by the choice of guests. Couric, they said, already wore the liberal tag, like it or not. So she has on Tom Friedman, the reliably liberal *Times* columnist who constantly blamed Bush for screwing up Iraq, and Morgan Spurlock, who made the anti-McDonald's film *Super Size Me,* ranting about the media while CBS showed pictures of pro wrestling? And few failed to notice that the Friedman interview, conducted on the periphery of the set, had showed off Couric's legs.

A veteran newswriter at NBC sent Williams a long note about the broadcast, which he called "a perfect example of Katie Couric unleashed with no one to say no to her on air." The result was "all the goofy distractions, including the faux-populist commentaries. No one in the world hates reading copy more than Katie, and it shows. All it is is a bunch of bad ideas we tried long ago and rejected."

Steve Capus thought Couric was an incredibly talented communicator, but that she and CBS were desperately trying to be different. Shedding hard news would hurt them over the long run. It seemed to Capus that Couric's program was trying for a *USA Today* sensibility, while his newscast and ABC's were more in the mold of *The New York Times* and *The Washington Post.*

At ABC, David Westin thought the Couric style didn't make sense. People who watched the evening news at 6:30 wanted a well-produced summary of the day's events. "This is golf, not tennis, ladies and gentlemen," Westin told his staff. "Let's not spend all our time worrying about what others are doing."

Charlie Gibson was aghast at Couric's approach. It was one thing to reinvent the wheel, he told a colleague, but there was no wheel there. No news in Lara Logan's piece. Anthony Mason's oil-rig story was old. He gave CBS credit for rolling the dice, but he was still amazed. What could all the terrific, hardworking people at CBS News possibly think of the format? Maybe, Gibson thought, this was what the public wanted. Maybe he and ABC dismissed this new approach at their peril. But Gibson didn't think that it would last. He believed that CBS would have to pull back.

*　　　*　　　*

Dan Bartlett vividly recalled the conversation with the president.

Couric's appointment as the new CBS anchor had just been announced, and Bush, who had not forgotten her interview with his wife just before he took office, was teasing his White House counselor in front of the staff.

"I can hear it now," Bush said. "Bartlett's going to come in in August or September and say we've got to do the Katie Couric interview."

"No, I'm not," Bartlett protested lamely.

But now CBS had made its pitch, for Couric to talk to the president for a prime-time special on the fifth anniversary of the September 11th attacks that would also be excerpted on the *Evening News*. Bartlett felt that he had opened a channel with Couric in their sit-down a year earlier. Sean McManus had also persuaded him that the network would take a fair approach to the news.

The White House team had decided to have Bush talk to all the networks as part of a two-week media blitz to put the terrorism issue front and center before the midterm elections, as the anniversary of that awful day approached. The networks would all be doing their special programs and live shots from Ground Zero whether the president participated or not, so Bartlett saw this as a prime opportunity to shape the national debate.

Besides, Katie Couric was now in charge of news for a major network, whether they liked it or not. In the end, Bartlett figured, it would be a bigger story if the White House stiffed her than if they held their collective noses and did the interview.

Bartlett talked it over with Tony Snow, and they agreed. Couric had met Snow for coffee at the Hay-Adams Hotel and they'd spent an hour and a half getting acquainted. The White House, he believed, couldn't be nursing grudges about old *Today* interviews.

"What?" Bush said, with exaggerated effect, when Bartlett told him that he should talk to Couric. The president gave his longtime aide some grief but went along with the decision.

Couric and a handful of producers had flown to Washington on a chartered jet right after her debut broadcast. The next morning, as Couric prepared for the interview, they faced what Rome Hartman regarded as a potential trap. Bush was going to deliver what was billed as a major speech on terrorism that afternoon, and unless Couric knew what he was going to say, they could be stuck with an outdated interview by the time it aired at 6:30.

Bartlett realized that he would have to get CBS up to speed. At 2 o'clock the president planned to announce in the East Room that he was transferring fourteen terror suspects held in secret CIA prisons overseas—the first time he would confirm a months-old *Washington Post* report about the existence of the facilities—to Guantánamo Bay, Cuba, and wanted congressional approval to give them military trials under new rules. But first the information had to be declassified, a formal process in which documents had to be signed by John Negroponte, the director of national intelligence. Bartlett and Snow delayed the interview until they finally got Negroponte's approval, in the late morning, to brief Couric and her team on what the president would be disclosing.

When Bush arrived, Bartlett could tell that Couric was nervous. She had decided in advance that she would be respectfully challenging. Couric did not want to go into the interview with a gotcha mentality. She wanted to give Bush a chance to say what was on his mind.

Once they got started, it looked as though Couric was trying too hard to be on her best behavior. Bush seemed stiff as they walked, his lips often pursed in a quizzical expression, and Couric was polite and noticeably restrained.

She began with Bush's plan to transfer the accused terrorists to Guantánamo Bay, where he wanted their fate decided by military tribunals. "Is this a tacit acknowledgment at all, Mr. President, that the way these detainees were handled early on was wrong?" Couric asked. Bush denied that it was.

Several of her questions were open-ended, allowing Bush to recycle some of his standard responses.

"You have said we can't cut and run on more than one occasion," Couric said. "We have to stand till we win, otherwise we'll be fighting the terrorists here at home on our own streets. So what do you mean exactly by that, Mr. President?"

She also asked: "When you think about the threats out there, what is your biggest fear?"

The interview was flat and produced little news. It did not even yield an interesting personal moment of the kind that Couric was so skilled at eliciting. Bush was too guarded and Couric too cautious.

When it was over, the president posed for a photo with Couric and her producers, asked about her new job, and poked fun at Matt Lauer for having been photographed shirtless in *People.*

Couric found Bush to be pleasant but businesslike. He probably figured that she would come in loaded for bear. Instead, she felt, she had pretty much been loaded for squirrel.

The encounter may have lacked drama, but Couric was pleased that it had taken place at all. She had never interviewed Bush before. Her five-year freeze-out at the White House was finally over.

Charlie Gibson had also been pushing hard for a presidential interview during the week of the 9/11 anniversary. He and ABC had thought they were close until, at the last moment, the White House sent word that Couric would get the first sit-down—on the day of her second newscast—and Gibson could see Bush the following day.

"This is ridiculous," David Westin said. "We're not going to just take leftovers."

But they were mollified when Bartlett agreed that Gibson could spend the day with the president as he made a trip to Atlanta. That would allow ABC to develop a narrative and give the broadcast a different feel.

The first part of their talk took place in the small office installed on *Air Force One.* Gibson was the only one of the anchors who was older than Bush, and he spoke to him, in conversational tones, almost as an equal. Gibson's view was that while you had to be respectful toward the president, you also had to point out the weaknesses of his argument, just as in any other interview.

He began with something that had long bothered him, and that was the polarization that was tearing the political culture apart. "Mr. President," he said, "five years ago after the attacks of nine-eleven, we had unprecedented compassion for this country. We had support for this country all over the world. On Capitol Hill, we had Democrats hugging Republicans. We had Republicans hugging Democrats. How did we lose all that?"

Bush gave his stock answer about how 9/11 was a terrible moment for people overseas, but a change of life for Americans.

Gibson wasn't buying: "But isn't the simple answer to that question really one word? What divided the world against us and what's divided us politically? That word being Iraq."

Turning to Bush's core argument, that Iraq was a central front in the war on terror, Gibson did not employ the interviewer's usual dodge of "critics say," as Brian Williams often couched things. Instead, he challenged the president on his own.

"And that's the one thing that I question, whether people do have any sense of. For as loathsome as he may have been, Saddam Hussein was not connected to al-Qaeda and he was not behind nine-eleven."

Bush conceded that Saddam did not order the attacks, but said "the enemy" believes, and Osama bin Laden believes, that Iraq is part of the war on terror.

Gibson had expected Bush to try to morph the two, and tried again to pin him down on the impact of the U.S. invasion. "But the point that I make, and many of the critics make, is that it wasn't a part of the war on terror until we went in there."

Bush bristled at being challenged. "Now, Charlie, I just told you. The president's job is to confront a threat."

As the plane ride continued, Gibson personalized the conversation. When Bush talked about working toward long-term victory, Gibson said: "Tell me what long-term means. I just had a grandson. He's five months old. When he graduates from high school? From college?" Bush said that an ideological struggle would take time.

When Gibson had been covering the Middle East war weeks earlier, he interviewed the Israeli defense minister, Tzipi Livni, who brought up 9/11. Within three sentences Gibson realized that he was crying. It was just so close to the surface with everyone.

Gibson figured this next one would be a dead-end question. Bush wasn't very self-analytical, and you didn't get much emotion from him. But he tried anyway.

"In these five years," Gibson said, "I have found, at times, it's overwhelming what happened. And I find myself crying. Does that happen to you?"

"Yeah," Bush said. "Of course, generally, it's triggered when I meet somebody who lost a loved one. And that happens fairly frequently."

A male anchor had admitted weeping, and had gotten the president to do the same. It was the kind of moment that viewers might have expected from Katie Couric, and Charlie Gibson had pulled it off without embarrassment.

CHAPTER 26

The Katie Surge

Katie Couric and Rome Hartman were having some laughs.

"I just snorted, sorry," Couric said.

"That's Wendy's thing," Hartman said, grinning.

"I know. We have a mutual friend, Wendy, and she snorts all the time."

It was an utterly unremarkable scene, except for the fact that it was on camera. Couric, wearing her glasses, was in the Fishbowl, chatting up the staff about the stories they were developing.

It would all be posted on the CBS Web site, a daily peek at the process of newsgathering, five or six minutes of Couric schmoozing, free-associating, or acting downright goofy. She would hand out chocolates, or kiss the "Employee of the Week," or talk about how she should be committed for getting a third dog. This was Katie unfiltered, sharing herself with the audience in a way that no evening news anchor had ever done, unconcerned with projecting a traditionally serious image. Brian Williams's video logs, dimly lit and shot at his desk, were drab by comparison.

Couric teased senior producer Bill Owens about his close-cropped hair, saying he was using too much "product."

"Rome, whaddya eating?" she demanded. "That cookie is five thousand calories."

Couric quizzed a staffer named Melissa, who said she was looking for "quirky videos" on *YouTube* that they might be able to play on the air.

"My favorite is the guy stomping grapes who falls out of the vat," Couric said.

Couric also talked up a segment in which Steve Hartman went fishing without a pole, and was attacked by flying carp, as perfect for the video Web site. *"YouTube* people, wherever you are, in your garage or whatever, please watch the *CBS Evening News,"* she said. "We're desperate to be on you, so to speak."

Her freewheeling style was, well, different than that of Cronkite, Rather, and Schieffer. She could be funny or frivolous but always seemed to radiate enthusiasm.

In a blog posting after interviewing Condi Rice for *60 Minutes,* Couric wrote: "This is a woman who is 'scary smart'—so intelligent, it's scary. She seems to have a photographic memory. She can tick off events and dates in a way that made my head spin . . . She's much warmer, more 'girly' and fun than the disciplined, controlled stateswoman you see on the world stage." It was impossible to imagine a male anchor gushing over a secretary of State in that fashion. But Couric was not concerned about coming off as bubbly or naïve, as long as she felt that she was being herself.

The same approach applied, in smaller dollops, to the newscast itself. Introducing a piece about a blind teenager who makes his way by clicking his tongue, Couric declared, "I really think this next story is going to knock your socks off." She talked about her teenage daughters during a story on a vaccine for cervical cancer, and when her medical correspondent, Jon LaPook, said there was a 50 percent chance that a seventeen-year-old girl has had intercourse, Couric replied: "Well, you've just ruined my day."

There were brief bursts of pop music to set up stories, and a weekly review of what was hot on the Internet, from a four-year-old drummer to a young man named Noah who photographed himself every day and posted the pictures online. Both light features had been suggested by Couric, who often talked like the producer she had been when she started out in the business. Some of the lighter, hipper fare that might be jokingly mentioned at the other networks' editorial meetings, or slipped into ABC's Webcast, was actually making it onto the air. Couric's program had a baby-boomer sensibility.

But the rebranded *CBS Evening News* was different in more fundamental ways as well. Time and again the broadcast chose to blow off significant news stories, or make just a glancing reference to a roiling political controversy, while stuffing the allotted nineteen minutes with softer pieces and chatty asides. More often than not, these were family-friendly features about mothers, children, or health care that would undoubtedly appeal to a segment of the audience. In her own way, Couric was moving toward the model briefly championed by Elizabeth Vargas.

On September 8 Brian Williams led off with a newly declassified Senate report about the run-up to the Iraq war and served notice—without the usual caveats—that he saw it as evidence of deception by the administration.

"According to an opinion poll just released this week, forty-three percent of Americans believe Saddam Hussein was personally involved in the nine-eleven attacks," Williams said. "That is almost half the country. Linking Iraq and al-Qaeda has been a tricky business. Some in the administration have made the tie. Tonight, the notion of any link between the two has been shredded by a big new report issued by the Republican-controlled U.S. Senate Intelligence Committee. It finds no link between Iraq and al-Qaeda. In fact, it says the two have very little in common. There's even evidence Saddam Hussein used to criticize Osama bin Laden . . . It will be seen as proof that there was a whole lot of bad intelligence floating around, some of which was used to launch a war."

Charlie Gibson also played up the report, and also framed it as exposing untruths by the administration during the prelude to the war in Iraq: "For a long time afterward members of the administration, including the president, have maintained there was a link between Saddam Hussein and al-Qaeda. Today a declassified Senate report said that was not true. That, in fact, Saddam Hussein mistrusted al-Qaeda and thought it a threat to his power."

Katie Couric had nothing, not a word about the findings. Her lead story was about an escaped murderer in upstate New York who was caught about ninety minutes after the broadcast. Sharyl Attkisson had produced a package on the Senate intelligence report, but Rome Hartman killed it, saying that they didn't have room.

What made the decision particularly hard to fathom was that Attkisson had gotten a stunning interview with Democratic Senator Jay Rockefeller, who accused the White House of "absolute cynical manipulation" in the handling of prewar intelligence and said that the world would be better off if the invasion had never happened, even with Saddam Hussein still in power.

The next day, on the Saturday edition of the *Evening News,* weekend anchor Russ Mitchell led off by saying: "A newly released report on prewar intelligence about Iraq is still spreading shock waves this evening and moving a key Democratic senator to make a dramatic claim." The Attkisson package remained powerful enough to lead the broadcast twenty-four hours later, after everyone else had covered the issue. Couric had missed the shock waves.

Couric finished one newscast—the one with Steve Hartman and the carp leaping into his boat—by reading some of the nearly forty thousand suggestions for her signoff slogan ("We share so you're aware"; "Don't blame me, I just work here"), followed by a David Letterman routine on the subject.

Still, Couric had support at the highest levels. Les Moonves was pumped up about the new broadcast. He kept calling Sean McManus with suggestions for minor tweaks, but Moonves felt that Katie brought personality and strong interviewing skills to the job and a work ethic that was just phenomenal. The broadcast was different, he believed, and yet if you were a diehard news junkie, you would not find it jarring. He had urged every television writer he encountered to wait a few weeks before judging Couric, but of course, nobody had listened to him. Moonves had read some of the negative pieces and concluded that some writers had agendas, that some were just rooting against Couric, while others were cheering for her. The press coverage was a runaway train, and there was nothing that anyone could do to stop it.

But while Moonves and McManus were riding high, some in the news division thought the new program was a disaster. They were puzzled by the shrinkage of hard news. They were appalled at some of the blowhards on the "Free Speech" segment. They said that Couric's lead on the escaped killer was one step above a car chase, ripped from the playbook of morning television. Instead of seven pieces by the correspondents each night, there were often four or five, which was making some of the reporters nervous. Was this, they asked, what Moonves really wanted? To them, it was making the newscast optional viewing: you didn't *have* to watch.

Bob Schieffer said nothing in public. He was determined not to sound like an old fart, talking about how much better the news was in *his* day. But he told colleagues that he was very disappointed by how soft the broadcast was becoming and said that despite Couric's obvious talents, the show was making her look like a lightweight.

On Schieffer's next trip to New York, Sean McManus asked him what he thought.

"I think Katie's doing well," Schieffer said, "but I think you've got her in the wrong format. You've just got to find a way to put in more news."

Schieffer said that it made no sense to run the "Free Speech" segment every night—even though that was the vehicle for his weekly essay—on a broadcast where time was at such a premium. Maybe they should air it twice a week at most.

"You may be right about that," McManus said. "We're still fooling with this."

The behind-the-scenes squabbling over content was matched by the public jousting over ratings.

In normal times the networks received the Nielsen ratings once a week, on Tuesdays, and touted them in their press releases. But executives at all three networks knew that there would be enormous media scrutiny of Couric's debut, so for the first week they each paid $12,600 to order a daily Nielsen fix called the "Fast Nationals." When CBS ordered the daily figures the second week, and then the third week, NBC and ABC felt compelled to do the same. Rival executives felt that they could not allow Couric's operation sole possession of the information while they had no statistical ammunition to use with reporters. To opt out would amount to unilateral disarmament.

Everyone had expected Couric to do a huge number on her first night, and she delivered. It was the first time the *CBS Evening News* had bested its rivals in a decade. The question had always been: Would the viewers come back?

For the rest of the week, they did. Couric racked up four consecutive first-place finishes, although the numbers, not surprisingly, came down from the stratospheric levels of her opening night. It set the stage for all-out guerrilla warfare, as the network publicists tried to spin the figures to their advantage.

CBS trumpeted the entire week in a release: "THE 'CBS EVENING NEWS WITH KATIE COURIC' FINISHES ITS DEBUT WEEK NO. 1 WITH AN AVERAGE OF 10.16 MILLION VIEWERS." The boasting came easily when the numbers were good.

ABC countered with a bit of creative math: "WORLD NEWS WITH CHARLES GIBSON PLACES 2ND IN KEY DEMO RATING FOR WEEK OF SEPT. 5TH / CBS'S LEAD OVER ABC SHRINKS BY 81% FROM TUESDAY TO FRIDAY." The network was scrambling to take its ratings lemons and make lemonade. What's more, the second-place finish touted in the statement was actually a tie with NBC.

But the Couric surge seemed to end the following Monday. When the networks got hold of the Fast Nationals, Couric's rivals could barely contain their glee: She had slipped to third place. Brian Williams, who was accustomed to unchallenged possession of first place, had told only his wife and close friends when he expected Katie to fall to third. It had now happened three days earlier than he predicted.

NBC and ABC bombarded reporters with Nielsen research. "With last night's broadcast devoted to coverage of the 5th anniversary of 9/11," said the ABC release, *"World News with Charles Gibson* finished second among

Total Viewers and Adults 25-54, beating Katie Couric and the *CBS Evening News* by 380,000 Total Viewers."

This time it was CBS's turn to make the best of the situation: "THE 'CBS EVENING NEWS WITH KATIE COURIC' TIES FOR SECOND PLACE IN HOUSEHOLDS, ADULTS 25-54 AND ADULTS 18-49." But it wasn't really a tie: *NBC Nightly News* was back in first place with 8.3 million viewers, *World News* was back in second with 7.9 million viewers, and the *CBS Evening News* brought up the rear with 7.5 million viewers.

One executive after another at the rival networks, as if in unison, practically cackled: "Fifteen million dollars a year for *that*?"

Couric bounced back the next day and won her second week, then slipped to a strong second place the following week, about a half-million viewers behind Brian Williams. Viewers were still flipping around, still checking out the new lady on the block and measuring her against the men. And unlike in the age of Dan, Tom, and Peter, one of those newscasts, at least for the moment, was markedly different from the rest.

Schieffer's contract did not expire until the summer of 2007, but he told McManus that their current agreement should last only until February of that year, when he would turn seventy. "You all may decide you don't want me, or I may decide I don't want to do it," Schieffer told him. McManus was determined to sign Schieffer at least through the 2008 election. But an unexpected development prompted him to reexamine Schieffer's future.

George Stephanopoulos wanted to see him.

It seemed like an unusual gambit. Stephanopoulos was already ABC's chief Washington correspondent and hosted its Sunday morning show, *This Week*. His contract was expiring, but why would he want to abandon the network that had hired him from the Clinton White House and helped transform him into a journalist?

When they sat down, it became clear that Stephanopoulos felt underutilized by ABC. McManus was definitely interested in stealing him. He offered Stephanopoulos the job of Washington bureau chief, as well as chief Washington correspondent, and a huge increase in salary.

"You'll be our go-to guy," McManus said.

But there was a problem. Stephanopoulos wanted to take over *Face the Nation* as well.

"I don't want to give up a one-hour show on Sunday if I don't have a show to go to," Stephanopoulos told him.

McManus said that could not happen right away. He hoped that Schieffer would remain at *Face* for another couple of years. George could take over the show right after that, but probably not before.

"I don't think it would be good for you or Bob," McManus said. "You'll be perceived as the guy upstaging Bob Schieffer."

That proved to be the deal-breaker, especially when ABC matched the money that McManus was dangling. The network also promised to boost Stephanopoulos's role, in part by allowing him to fill in as the *World News* anchor—the first time a former White House operative would sit in that coveted chair.

Dan Bartlett was visiting family in Texas when someone at ABC told him what was going on. He felt that Stephanopoulos, despite his Clinton credentials, had proved to the White House that he was a fair interviewer. Bartlett gave him a call.

"You jumping ship?" he asked.

"How'd you hear about that?" Stephanopoulos asked. "I turned it down last night."

*   *   *

It was, by all rights, a story that CBS owned, but Brian Williams was determined to get a piece of it.

Bob Epstein, the number-two producer at *Nightly News,* was the first to notice the press release. It was early on a Thursday afternoon in late September, and *60 Minutes* was touting its upcoming interview that Sunday with Bob Woodward. The Watergate sleuth was about to publish his third book on the inner workings of the Bush administration, and, as usual, Mike Wallace had the television exclusive. Woodward's newspaper, *The Washington Post,* and its sister publication, *Newsweek,* would be publishing excerpts on Sunday. But the mere title of the book—*State of Denial*—practically screamed that this volume would be far more critical of the White House than Woodward's two previous efforts, which many critics had derided as too favorable to President Bush.

At the two-thirty meeting John Reiss called up the CBS release on his computer. "Veteran Washington reporter Bob Woodward tells Mike Wallace that the Bush administration has not told the truth regarding the level of violence, especially against U.S. troops, in Iraq," it said. "He also reveals key intelligence that predicts the insurgency will grow worse next year."

Williams instantly knew that it was a big story. This was Bob Woodward, after all, and if he was turning on a president who had granted him extraordinary access, they had to find a way to get it on the air. At the same time all they had were the tidbits that CBS was handing out, while the *Evening News* would undoubtedly have a much richer piece.

Reiss called Andrea Mitchell, NBC's chief diplomatic correspondent, in Washington. She had gotten an advance copy of *State of Denial* in exchange for a promise that she would not break the embargo set by the publisher.

"I can't help you guys," Mitchell said over the speakerphone. She agreed, however, to call Woodward.

"A confidentiality agreement is a confidentiality agreement," Woodward reminded her, and Mitchell agreed. She would not get involved in the reporting.

The staff meeting dragged on for two hours. Williams didn't care about promoting *60 Minutes*. He didn't believe in the old-school prohibition against mentioning the other team on the air. Besides, they often had to credit *60 Minutes* because, as the most influential newsmagazine on the air, the program kept scoring big "gets" of major newsmakers.

Reiss argued that anyone who wanted to watch Woodward on *60 Minutes* was going to do so, whether they did a story or not. With Woodward accusing the administration of deception on Iraq, this book would be making headlines.

As the meeting dragged on, Epstein made a key discovery. CBS had put a couple of short video clips of the Woodward interview on its Web site. If *Nightly* did the story, they could actually show some pictures rather than just having their anchor read the quotes. Williams felt that they could use a bit of the footage under the "fair use" doctrine, since it was now in the public domain.

They asked Jim Miklaszewski to check with his Pentagon sources on Woodward's charge that the administration was hiding the fact that there were now eight hundred to nine hundred attacks each day against U.S. forces in Iraq. Mik reported back that military officials were saying they had acknowledged such figures all along.

Andrea Mitchell checked back with the *Nightly* brain trust. She had known Woodward for a long time, she said, and he was warning that if they went too hard with the Pentagon's denials, they would look pretty silly on Sunday when he released confidential documents to back up his book.

"Let's be careful," Mitchell said. "Let's make sure we don't go on the air and knock down a book based on what the Pentagon is putting out."

It was 4:30 now, they didn't have a rundown for the show, and someone had to make a decision. Reiss decreed that they would lead *Nightly* with the Woodward book.

Williams went with a hard-edged "good evening" script: "An explosive new book, now just days away from store shelves, is tonight making news even before arriving on the market. It is the work of journalist Bob Woodward. And according to advance publicity materials released to the news media, it alleges that attacks by insurgents on coalition forces in Iraq are worse than Americans have been led to believe. It also alleges a kind of campaign of deception on the part of the Bush administration."

They credited *60 Minutes* and played a clip from the show. "There's public and then there's private," Woodward was shown saying. "But what did they do with the private? They stamp it secret. No one is supposed to know."

In the control room, John Reiss kept glancing up at the CBS monitor but didn't see Katie Couric doing anything with the Woodward book. He found that greatly amusing.

At CBS, Rome Hartman's initial reaction was that *Nightly News* had flat-out stolen their story. This kind of thievery was outrageous. He had no idea that his own network had posted the clip on its Web site. He was angry about the whole episode, and Sean McManus had let him know that he was unhappy as well.

Hartman later told Couric that through a series of miscommunications, he had never been told that *60 Minutes* was posting a portion of the Woodward interview online. He had assumed that they would run a story about the book on Friday's newscast, as they often did to promote the show. Hartman had worked at *60*, after all, so he knew the drill. By a stroke of bad luck, Hartman had left early to catch the 3:30 Delta Shuttle to Washington so he could be at his son's high school soccer game, after having missed most of the previous games. But there were thunderstorms in the region, and he sat on the tarmac for an excruciating three and a half hours. The result was that he never had his usual conversation with Jeff Fager, the executive producer of *60*, about how to handle the week's upcoming stories. Hartman hated these book deals, where the morsels were doled out in spoonfuls. This was not the way news was supposed to work.

Brian Williams felt that they had pulled off a bit of a heist. It wasn't exactly like scoring a touchdown on your own, more like recovering a fumble by the other team and racing into the end zone.

NBC's touchdown looked even better the next morning, when *The New York Times,* having obtained an advance copy at a bookstore, splashed a big piece about the Woodward book on its front page, sticking it to the rival *Washington Post.*

Woodward called Brian Williams. "I was amazed that you would lead with a *60 Minutes* story," he said. It was as though NBC were using Mike Wallace as "kind of a surrogate correspondent."

"It was obviously the lead story," Williams said.

But still, Woodward said, it was highly unusual to run another network's scoop.

"When you're number one," Williams said, "you don't have to live in fear."

Now, with the *Times* story out, CBS really looked out of the loop. Katie Couric led her newscast that night with the Woodward bombshell and how it had become "Topic A at the White House"—which, of course, was in reaction to the NBC and *Times* reports on a story that CBS thought it had under lock and key. *World News* played catch-up as well on the book. And Williams got to preen a bit by saying, "As we first reported here last night, the book paints a picture of dysfunction and deception at the highest levels."

There was nothing like rubbing it in.

*   *   *

As the sinking ratings produced a spate of negative stories on what had gone wrong, turmoil was growing within the ranks of CBS News. In whispered hallway conversations, staffers wondered why the hugely hyped broadcast seemed to be floundering. Katie Couric was now in third place.

The consensus was that Couric and company had hogtied themselves with a format that seemed to squeeze out news even as it made room for lighter items and the odd assortment of opinion-mongers featured on "Free Speech."

Some of the correspondents were barely getting on the air; they were wondering what was expected of them and growing nervous about their jobs. Meanwhile the man universally referred to as "Katie's doctor," Jon LaPook, was getting all kinds of airtime. LaPook had arranged Couric's famous on-air colonoscopy at *Today,* and the Jay Monahan Cancer Center, named for her late husband, was affiliated with LaPook's department at Columbia University Medical Center. To make room for the gastroenterologist, CBS dumped medical correspondent Elizabeth Kaledin, a ten-year veteran. LaPook had no experience as a journalist, and his segments generally had to be taped in advance because of his repeated stumbles.

While staffers saw that Couric was working morning, noon, and night, they grew to resent her micromanaging style. She didn't seem happy with anything—the writing, the stories, the ideas that bubbled up from the staff. Some even questioned whether Rome Hartman was truly in charge.

Much of the staff hated "Free Speech," as Hartman was acutely aware. It was, in fact, a strange and uneven pastiche. Sometimes the segment provided a forum for new or interesting voices. But other speakers included Rush Limbaugh, Sean Hannity, *The Nation* editor Katrina van den Heuvel, Rudy Giuliani, and Senator Barack Obama. How exactly did these prominent figures lack a public forum?

The most inexplicable decision came on the day five young girls were brutally murdered at an Amish school in Pennsylvania. That night's speaker was Brian Rohrbough, who had lost his son in the Columbine massacre, and who blamed the shootings on a moral vacuum caused by abortion and "expelling God from the school" and "replacing him with evolution." That was a provocative stance worthy of debate, but to put on Rohrbough, a self-promoting crusader, just hours after the girls had been shot to death seemed the height of insensitivity.

The broadcast did the same cute, end-of-show features as its rivals, but somehow at CBS they seemed lighter than air. Schools banning tag. Airborne pizza delivery to Alaska. Couric handled some of these segments herself. She spent time with choreographer Twyla Tharp in what served as one long commercial for a Broadway show based on the music of Bob Dylan, with Couric telling her: "I'd love to spend a day inside your brain." And when a study concluded that kids were being overloaded with too many activities, it was Couric who went out to Central Park to chat up other moms.

Formats could always be adjusted, but some at CBS began to get a sinking feeling: What if the viewers just didn't like Katie? What if the personality that had been so winning in the morning just didn't work at 6:30? What if the fatal flaw in the broadcast was that it made her the star attraction, rather than the news itself?

Couric occasionally chatted up the correspondents, as Schieffer had done so effectively, but she also took on the role of talk show host. One night she moderated a debate between James Carville, the high-decibel Democratic spinmeister, and Nicolle Wallace, who had been hired as a CBS consultant shortly after resigning as President Bush's communications director. They both spouted the usual talking points in sizing up the midterm elections.

One Friday afternoon Jim Murphy, the longtime *Evening News* producer for Rather and Schieffer who now ran *Good Morning America,* left his office early, had a couple of cocktails at home, and sat down to watch his old broadcast. He saw Couric conducting a panel discussion on Iraq with three experts: a retired general, a dean at Princeton, and a senior fellow with the Center for Strategic and International Studies. Couric asked such questions as "In the short term, what do you think must be done?" and "What is the solution in the long run?" It was deadly dull.

Murphy e-mailed a friend in the CBS control room. "I might be drunk, but you guys are crazy," he wrote.

He got a quick reply: "You wouldn't have wanted to be here today. That was all Katie. She made us do it."

CHAPTER 27

Reinventing the Wheel

Katie Couric was intrigued by Bill Clinton's angry moment, but Rome Hartman didn't think much of the story.

It was just before three o'clock when Couric walked into the Fishbowl, sat down, and dug into a plastic container of chopped chicken salad. She had been out at a meeting and had missed the daily editorial conference.

On the row of television monitors overhead, Clinton appeared every few minutes on the cable channels, wagging his finger and looking angry. It was one day after the former president's extraordinary appearance on *Fox News Sunday,* in which host Chris Wallace had gotten under Clinton's skin with a pointed question about why he hadn't done more to go after Osama bin Laden and al-Qaeda. Clinton, who had been promised that half the interview would be devoted to fund-raising for his Global Initiative, as part of it already had been, was seething. "So you did Fox's bidding on the show. You did your nice little conservative hit job on me," he said, even grousing that Wallace had "a little smirk" on his face. There were stories in the newspapers and plenty of buzz online. Nearly 1 million people had downloaded the interview on *YouTube.*

But Hartman felt that the story had come and gone. It had been all over the earlies, as he called the morning programs. Fox was recycling the confrontation in an endless video loop. Hartman was no fan of Chris Wallace— they had had a run-in when both were covering the Reagan White House—but more important, beyond its entertainment value, what did the interview really mean?

"It got a lot of press all weekend," Couric observed.

290

"Got a lot of press yesterday and was done to death this morning," Hartman said.

Couric took another forkful of salad and thought for a moment.

"Okay, crazy idea," she announced. "What about a 'Free Speech' reacting to it?"

"I feel it's old by tonight, unless it's a broader philosophical piece," Hartman said.

But what if Bill Clinton himself would come on the *Evening News* for an interview? "Should we call him?" Couric wondered.

Hartman was unenthusiastic.

"Really?" Couric said. "I think it's better than Brinkley for tonight." Historian Douglas Brinkley, a native of New Orleans and a newly hired CBS consultant, had already taped an essay on that night's reopening of the hurricane-battered Superdome for the first Saints football game on home turf in a year.

"That's the story everyone's talking about," Hartman said.

"Listen," Couric said, "if Clinton is willing to do it, don't you think it'd be better?" She kept pondering. "What about if Clinton would do a 'Free Speech' about it? I know that's pie in the sky."

The former president of the United States, taping a ninety-second commentary for a newscast that would be on the air in three and a half hours?

"It's no fun if he's not angry," said producer Katie Boyle, fearing that a taped statement would be too diplomatic.

Couric felt it was worth a try. She summoned her personal producer, Nicolla Hewitt. "Hey Nic," she said, "can you call Bill Clinton and see if he'd be interested in doing a 'Free Speech' about his testy interview with Chris Wallace and what made him so mad?"

It was in these daily, on-the-fly decisions that a newscast forged its identity, sending viewers signals about what was deemed vital and what was expendable. Couric functioned like a busy chief executive who was happy to delegate many day-to-day corporate functions to her staff. This meant that Rome Hartman, who was focused and efficient, functioned as a chief operating officer, to a much greater extent than John Reiss at *Nightly News* or Jon Banner at *World News*. Like any good number two, he was solicitous of his principal's views, and while Couric could slam on the brakes or change the route, he kept the train moving down the tracks.

The day had begun at 8 A.M., when Couric called Hartman from her Upper East Side apartment. She brought up a *New York Times* piece on female casualties in the Iraq war and said that they should think of a smart way of approaching the subject. Couric also talked about the paper's front-page scoop the day before, a leaked account of the administration's National Intelligence Estimate, which said that the U.S. occupation of Iraq had helped spawn a new generation of Islamic extremists and that the overall ter-rorist threat had grown since the 9/11 attacks.

Hartman felt that this was a very difficult subject for television to tackle. The *Times* was relying on unnamed sources, so it was not clear how they could advance the story. They weren't about to interview an anonymous per-son in silhouette.

In the office that morning, Hartman asked Bill Owens what he thought of the Clinton story.

"I covered him for six years," Owens said, "and I've never seen him that angry."

Wearing his signature white shirt with the sleeves rolled up, Hartman ran through the tentative lineup at the editorial meeting. They would lead with the Pentagon's announcement that four thousand troops in Iraq, scheduled to return home, would have their tours extended by a few more weeks. They had a taped report from Byron Pitts on an Army reserve captain being called back to Iraq, and the impact on his marriage. They had also put in a call to retired Major General John Batiste—a former Iraq commander who was calling for Don Rumsfeld's resignation at a hearing staged by House Democrats—about doing an interview with Couric. Bob Orr was tracking the easing of federal restrictions on carrying liquids and gels onto airplanes. And Jim Axelrod was poking around on the leaked intelligence report.

Beyond the first block, there was a Bill Whitaker report on falling hous-ing prices, pegged to some new statistics; Lee Cowan on a man with the world's first bionic knee; and a show-closer by Mark Phillips on how global warming was helping some British grape-growers make wine.

Lara Logan called from Baghdad. Her report on the militias prowling the slums of Sadr City was scheduled to run the next night, and she wanted to move it up because the AP was putting a similar story on the wire.

"Nobody's going to be able to match it on television," Hartman told his team. "Plus, we'd have to rip the whole show apart, because her piece is a minute longer than Cowan's is. Plus, we've already promo'd Cowan, and it's pretty cool."

Once Couric returned at lunchtime, they began worrying about the usual time crunch. If Batiste, the former general, agreed to an interview, Hartman said, they would have to hold Pitts's more personal piece on the reservist who had been ordered back to Iraq. Couric said that she was willing to bag the Batiste interview in favor of Pitts's taped report.

"That's really important," she said. "We've been talking about troop levels, but we haven't had much on the home front."

Couric returned to the flap over the National Intelligence Estimate, which Hartman had been lukewarm about in the morning.

"I don't know if it's too dated," she said. "How did it get released?"

"It was leaked," Hartman said. "Axelrod has spent the day chasing it."

Couric wanted the intelligence report in the show. She was slated to chat with David Martin, the veteran Pentagon correspondent, after his report on troop readiness.

"I'm wondering if I can talk to David and he can fold it into his spot," she said. "I think it got a little lost over the weekend. It's a question I asked Bush. It's a question I asked Rice." Couric's profile of the secretary of State had just aired on *60 Minutes.*

It was time to screen a feature story that Couric had begun reporting before she took over the anchor chair. The subject was a program in Alexandria, Virginia, not far from where she grew up, that helped disadvantaged kids by teaching them to build boats.

Beginning with strains of "I'm Your Captain," groups of young people were shown in woodworking shops. After the three-minute piece played on an oversize wall monitor, Hartman had a suggestion.

"I'm not sure I saw what they built," Hartman said. "I never saw it turn into a boat."

Couric turned to her producer. "Can we get some shots of the built boats?" she asked. "It would be nice to see them out on the water."

She reconsidered the soundtrack. "Maybe it's one too many musical interludes," Couric said. "I think 'Rock the Boat' was over the top. We should use instrumentals underneath that don't hit you over the head."

Katie Boyle took a call from one of the producers. They were playing catch-up up on a story about an American contractor in Iraq who had come under fire while in his truck and was abandoned by his boss. A CBS staffer who was pursuing the subject had heard that ABC's chief investigative reporter had already obtained some riveting video of the incident.

"I love the idea of sticking it to Brian Ross," Boyle told the producer. "But I don't think the story itself is worth displacing Lara Logan's piece from Sadr City."

Couric stepped into the newsroom to tape a pair of sixty-second Web commentaries for what was being billed as "Katie Couric's Notebook." One was about the Gap using the image of Audrey Hepburn "to sell a pair of skinny black pants which, trust me, on me isn't really that skinny." Couric's complaint was that Hepburn wasn't around to object to the commercial.

When she was finished, Couric told the staff: "I didn't say anything personal, but Audrey Hepburn died of colon cancer," the disease that Couric had been crusading against since it claimed her husband's life. "She's one of the most extraordinary people I've ever met. I adored her."

At 4:38 Hartman learned that General Batiste had called in from Capitol Hill and agreed to do the interview with Couric. After a brief huddle, they decided to take a pass rather than yank the Byron Pitts story.

Back in the Fishbowl, Couric watched as Hartman gave a second look to the feature on winemaking in an increasingly warm Britain. She found it flat. "This is where it could use an appropriate bit of classical music, to give it a little more of a happy feel, like Vivaldi's *Four Seasons,*" she said.

Next they looked at Douglas Brinkley's piece, which was illustrated with still photos of New Orleans after Katrina hit, one year earlier.

"Do we have any pictures of all the garbage?" Couric asked.

No one knew.

"We need a sense of the chaos and the filth that is captured in moving pictures. Have you checked with *48 Hours,* or *60?*" Suddenly a frantic hunt was under way for suitable garbage.

With an hour and a half until airtime, Couric walked into a corner of the newsroom and sat down next to Jerry Cipriano, the program's best writer, who supervised the anchor copy. This was the time of the afternoon when Brian Williams or Charlie Gibson would be at the keyboard, tapping away as they shaped and tightened the prose to make it punchier and fit their speaking style. But Couric dictated her thoughts, her fingers never coming near a computer. She had had less involvement with the scripts all day than her rivals, and now she delegated the final polishing, or at least preferred working with a collaborator. It was another snapshot of the busy CEO at work.

Couric looked at the introduction for the bionic man script. " *'This could be the smartest device yet'* . . . I don't know if you can say that . . . How many servicemen have lost their limbs?" She felt that the story of one Special Forces soldier, who had lost his leg in a helicopter crash in Somalia, had to be tied to a larger narrative.

A staffer suggested that five hundred soldiers had lost limbs in Iraq. No way, another said, it must be tens of thousands.

"Want me to try to call Walter Reed?" Couric asked. The staff promised to find out. Moments later someone found a *Time* citation: of the 20,000 wounded soldiers, 436 had lost limbs.

With fifty minutes to airtime, the pace was growing more frenetic. Couric headed to the set for live teases with several affiliate stations.

"Mary and Roz, back to you two."

"That's right, Wayne and Steve, more soldiers are staying in Iraq for longer tours. And is there actually a positive side to global warming? In Great Britain, they say yes."

Now it was time to pretape the "Snapshots" segment, featuring still photos from the day's reopening of the Superdome.

"Tonight's snapshots are of a city on the way back," Couric began. When it was over, she said: "Did that seem funny to you, Rome? Let me do that one more time."

One producer said that Couric had mispronounced *jambalaya*. She thought that it was right. "The consensus here is *jum*, not *jam*," Hartman said.

They retreated to the newsroom, where Couric and Cipriano began fiddling with the script about the reservists being kept in Iraq. She wanted to draw a sharper contrast with administration rhetoric. "Hey Rome, who said we're going to start troop reductions by the end of the year?" she asked. Hartman told her that General George Casey had made the announcement in 2005.

The plan was to raise the National Intelligence Estimate during the question-and-answer session with David Martin. Hartman suggested the wording: "I think you should say, 'David, our own classified study concluded that despite all of our troops and efforts, Iraq has gotten worse.' "

"Can you write it out?" Couric asked.

Minutes later she was back on the set to record the headlines for the top of the show. From his control room perch, the ever-vigilant Hartman noticed an omission: "Katie, the copy doesn't say 'I'm Katie Couric.' You probably should add that."

In the top row of the control room, one producer asked: "Where will we be whooshing?"

"We will not be whooshing. There is not one whoosh left in the show," his colleague replied. In CBS lingo, a whoosh was a brief sound effect used as a transition between items.

At 6:25, while wrestling with the fact that Bob Orr's earpiece wasn't working, Hartman told Couric that he was waiting to talk to David Martin at the Pentagon "so I can see exactly what he's going to say. You should plan on just doing what we said, with 'that can't be welcome news.' "

A moment later Hartman established contact with Martin, who provided what his ten-second answer to Couric would be. But the producer standing to Hartman's left said that the show was twenty-six seconds too long.

"Let's kill the Martin Q and A!" Hartman shouted. The only brief mention of the National Intelligence Estimate controversy that had drawn Couric's interest was gone.

The headlines rolled at 6:30, and Couric was into the first story about the reserve units being kept in Iraq. At that moment, Brian Williams was taking *Nightly News* in a different direction:

"It is a report from the very top of U.S. intelligence, and it is meant for the boss, the president and the very top of our government. The report, called the National Intelligence Estimate, or the NIE, has been leaked to the press. That is bad news for the Bush administration because of this report's conclusion, that the war in Iraq has created a new generation of Islamic radicals, and that the overall terrorist threat is now worse because this war has amounted to a huge recruiting tool for those who would do us harm."

Moments later, Charlie Gibson was teeing up another story on *World News*: "The issue of terrorism helped provoke an extraordinary outburst over the weekend from former President Bill Clinton, who was being interviewed by Chris Wallace on the Fox News Channel. When asked about efforts he made to get Osama bin Laden, the former president got angry. Was he really mad, or was he using anger to make a larger point?"

At almost the same moment, Brian Williams was tossing to Clinton's combative Fox interview as well, then turning to a journalist who had worked in the Clinton White House and for three other administrations.

It was then that Rome Hartman looked up and saw the *Nightly* segment on the row of monitors.

"Darn! NBC got David Gergen. What a get!" Hartman complained with mock jealousy. "This is a David Gergen–free zone."

Hartman returned his attention to their live broadcast. While Bob Orr's taped report on housing prices was playing, Couric said that she was unhappy with the line about the New Orleans segment that she was supposed to read before the break. Some anchors took these teases *very* seriously.

Hartman offered some new wording: "They're going to play a game in New Orleans tonight, but the city has already won."

Couric curled her lip disapprovingly.

Hartman tried again: "Why not what you said: 'Coming up next: Score one for New Orleans'?" That seemed to pass muster.

During the next commercial Couric asked Hartman whether the classical music had been added to the piece on British winemakers, as she had requested.

"Katie, they tried three different times. It's there, but it's so low it sounds like they were afraid to do it."

Couric sat on the edge of the anchor desk to introduce the piece, as the strains of *Hot! Hot! Hot!* came up under her. The tape rolled, Mark Phillips walked among the grape-growers, the strings came up on cue.

"And a little Vivaldi," Couric said, smiling sweetly, as if it were a personal triumph.

The next morning Couric saw Hartman in his usual seat in the Bowl.

"Did you see the Bush-Karzai thing?" he asked. Couric had missed the president's news conference with Afghan leader Hamid Karzai.

"They're declassifying the NIE."

"Is that the NIE from last weekend?" Couric asked.

"Parts of which were leaked last weekend," Hartman said.

Couric felt that they had missed an opportunity. Now they would have to catch up on the controversy over the intelligence estimate on Iraq.

She was also having second thoughts about the way they had blown off the Bill Clinton confrontation on Fox. She now wished they had pursued it. There was enough residual buzz surrounding the incident to warrant a story. What they should have done was taken the encounter, distilled it to its essence, and used that for a broader piece. They didn't need to yak about Clinton's motivation, that was pure speculation. But this whole debate about who did and who didn't do enough before 9/11, examining the actions of the Bush and Clinton administrations, that would have helped people understand what the flap was all about. There was no getting around it, Couric felt. They had probably made a mistake.

This was the frustration of doing an evening newscast, which Couric was suddenly feeling quite acutely. There just weren't enough minutes to do everything that she wanted to do. It wasn't like having two hours on the *Today* show, where you could pack in segment after segment. At night, the time was just so limited.

That night Couric began the broadcast this way: "President Bush has long insisted the war in Iraq is making us safer. So when a classified intelligence review was leaked and suggested the war had created more terrorism, his critics pounced." There was nothing in her opening that she couldn't have reported the night before. As the program described how Bush had made a portion of the secret estimate public—one that provided a more mixed verdict on his anti-terror efforts—they slipped in a sound bite of Bill Clinton, defending himself on Fox. It was a clear admission that the newscast had been late on both subjects.

In the following weeks the program included plenty of hard news, especially in the opening minutes. But Couric and Hartman passed up enough stories that political junkies began to feel that they were missing out. There was no mention of Republican congressman Bob Ney pleading guilty in a corruption probe that turned on his links to convicted lobbyist Jack Abramoff. No mention of the FBI conducting raids in an investigation of whether another Republican congressman, Curt Weldon, had improperly aided companies that hired his daughter as a lobbyist. No mention that Mark Warner, a highly regarded Democrat who had been governor of Virginia, had dropped out of the 2008 presidential race. No mention of a book by former White House aide David Kuo, charging that White House officials had privately dismissed evangelical Christian activists as "nuts" and "goofy." No mention of how Senate Democratic leader Harry Reid had turned a million-dollar profit on a questionable Las Vegas land deal and failed to fully disclose it, a story that Brian Williams covered twice.

Dropping any one of these stories on a busy day would have been understandable. Ignoring all of them, as Couric's rivals were covering them, added to the impression that the *Evening News* was drifting in a softer direction, especially since the program always made time for outside commentary and cute snapshots and interesting items from the Web. Without fully realizing it, Katie Couric was becoming a prisoner of the new format.

*   *   *

Every night Brian Williams lugged home stacks of printouts with all kinds of missives from viewers that most network anchors would have left for their staff or simply ignored.

It was the age of interactivity, and Williams wanted to show that he was listening. He loved to read e-mail on the air, to call in the heavy artillery on himself.

After an interview with Mahmoud Ahmadinejad in which Williams pressed Iran's confrontational president on his denial of the Holocaust and his pledge to wipe Israel off the map, his in-box was flooded with complaints about "giving our enemies an open platform to spew their propaganda," as one Atlanta viewer put it.

Williams quoted from the e-mail on *Nightly* and was tempted to defend himself—*"Well, madam, this is what we do"*—but he believed that would come off as holier-than-thou. Besides, he felt the critics were slightly frustrated that he did not respond.

Jeff Zucker loved the e-mail segments. He would run them every couple of days if possible. "Where are the e-mails?" Zucker would ask John Reiss.

Occasionally Williams would even chide his own program, as he did when introducing a report on gasoline dropping from well over $3 a gallon to about $2.60: "After some dire predictions on this broadcast and elsewhere that prices were rocketing to $4 a gallon, gas prices are coming down."

He had endured a summer of anxiety, bordering on obsession, about Katie Couric. Now he had roared back into first place, trouncing Katie in her fourth and fifth weeks on the job. He was beating her some nights by nearly 2 million viewers. Given the enormous publicity campaign that had accompanied her launch, this was no small achievement.

The chief executive of General Electric took notice. "Congratulations, so far, so good," Jeffrey Immelt told Williams in an e-mail. "I am proud of you. Keep it going."

Network executives were obsessed with the numbers, because that was what drove the advertising dollars. In just over a month Couric had dropped from 13.6 million viewers on opening night—an inflated figure, to be sure—to just over 7 million, a smaller number than Bob Schieffer had been drawing in his final week in the anchor chair. Williams, meanwhile, was pulling in 8.5 million viewers, and Gibson just under 8 million.

That didn't stop the CBS spin machine from trumpeting: "THE CBS EVENING NEWS WITH KATIE COURIC POSTS UNPRECEDENTED DOUBLE-DIGIT, ACROSS-THE-BOARD GAINS IN ITS FIRST MONTH IN YEAR-TO-YEAR COMPARISON." And that was true. The *Evening News* was up from its low base of a year earlier, especially in the money demo, while the others were slightly down. Of course, it would have been unrealistic to expect Couric to rocket to the top of the heap and stay there, given the difficulty of changing viewing habits. It had taken Peter Jennings and, later, Tom Brokaw years to climb past their rivals. But television writers cared only about the here and now, and their stories reflected the stark reality that Couric, who had been number one for a decade at *Today,* was in last place and sinking.

Williams was struck by the feedback that he was getting from his viewers. Some actually felt guilty for briefly abandoning him.

"My apologies to Brian Williams for skipping away to sneak a peek at Katie Couric's appearance as news anchor at CBS," one woman wrote. "Certainly wasn't worth my time."

"Tonight, for the first time in a long time, I did not watch your broadcast," a St. Louis man wrote. "Tonight, also for the first time in a long time, I felt I did not get the news of the day . . . I liked Katie much better on the *Today* show."

"On CBS, I saw very little news . . . Katie seemed ill at ease . . . I think her talent is misplaced and that she made a big mistake," another man said.

They had sinned, and now they were seeking absolution. As an NBC executive had put it to Williams, they had taken the long walk of shame to Katie's apartment and come back, smelling of cheap perfume and begging for forgiveness. Williams wrote back to every one of them. He felt as though they were members of his extended family.

But the quick surge back into first place did not put Williams at ease. In fact, he seemed incapable of relaxing. He carried a small notebook everywhere, pausing to write down story language during dinner or at other odd hours. He went home utterly exhausted every night. The only way he knew how to do the job was to go all-out. There were days when he needed to pick up toiletries at CVS or wanted to pop into Barnes & Noble to buy a book but spent the entire day at 30 Rock. He had a gnawing fear—an irrational fear, given the staff that supported him—that he would miss something.

Jane was concerned that her husband was working all the time. She wished that he could decompress, that he could take off two weeks in a row, that he wasn't constantly tethered to the job by the new 24/7 technology. But he just seemed hardwired for constant work. She feared that he would get to the end of his run and realize that he had made the outlandish leap from little boy who always wanted to be a network anchor to successful man who had gotten to do it and never took the time to enjoy it.

Sometimes, though, there was a rare chance to lighten up. Williams soon got an invitation that had been nothing more than a fantasy: How would he like to host *Saturday Night Live*?

Williams had become friendly with Lorne Michaels, the longtime executive producer of *SNL,* who had seen the anchor do his stand-up shtick at a number of charity dinners. Williams was a huge fan and loved taking his family to the show. He had attended rehearsals and gotten friendly with some of the cast members. So when Michaels broached the idea of Williams doing a star turn as guest host, a role that had been filled over the years by Steve Martin, Jerry Seinfeld, Jennifer Aniston, and Al Gore, it was enormously flattering. And, Williams felt, far too risky.

"I can't host," he told Michaels. "You'll have me dressed up in a ridiculous suit by the third skit."

But hosting the show was Williams's secret fantasy. For all his success as a news guy, he was aching to do comedy. During the late 1990s NBC entertainment chief Don Ohlmeyer had offered him, at least half-seriously, the late-night slot later occupied by Conan O'Brien. Williams watched David Letterman or Jay Leno every night, studied their moves, and was convinced he could handle that shift. He would be a latter-day Steve Allen or Jack Paar, with a little Johnny Carson thrown in. One day, if his job got too hard or the news division wanted a new face, he hoped to work that circuit.

But now, while he was still a news anchor? Williams told Michaels that he would make an appearance only if he could stay in character, as opposed to playing some buffoon. So the talk turned to *Weekend Update,* the spoof newscast that had been launched by Chevy Chase in 1975 and was about to get a new anchor team for the season premiere.

As it happened, Williams knew the comedians: Amy Poehler, who had been doing the fake news the previous season, and Seth Meyers, who would be taking over the coanchor role. Williams figured that the show would need a vehicle to introduce Meyers. They kicked around some ideas. Poehler came up with the concept: Brian shows up, expecting to anchor, and they have to break his heart.

Williams treated the entire venture as a state secret. He agreed to read his lines to Jane and their daughter, Allison, an aspiring actress, only under unrelenting pressure. If the thing was an unmitigated disaster at the Friday rehearsal and was dropped from the show, he didn't want anyone to know.

When he arrived after *Nightly,* Michaels was sitting there in a red sweater and khaki pants. Williams saw a finished script for the first time. As they ran through the skit, the crew members laughed, which Williams took to be a good sign.

The next day Williams flew to Boston for a meeting of the Congressional Medal of Honor Foundation, where he served as a director. By the time he got back to 30 Rock, he had missed the dress rehearsal by six minutes.

Michaels was concerned. "Brian, are you ready?" he asked. "We can hold the audience if you want to rehearse from the *Update* set."

"Lorne, the audience is already seated," Meyers said. That option was gone.

The final production meeting began in Michaels's office. This was a long, chaotic session where skits were chopped and added at the last minute. But Williams's walk-on was safe.

He was incredibly nervous, to the point of coping with flop sweat. This was not his field. His job was to speak into a camera with a guy named Barry behind it. Suddenly he would be on a stage with professional actors and a live audience that could hoot or howl. Jane had been worried that he would trip. The challenge was to make it look easy.

Williams got the cue and strode onto the set. "I'm so excited to be anchoring *Update* with you," he told Amy Poehler. "It's been a long wait."

"Oh gosh!" she said. "Did you get my messages?"

"You know what? I've been crazy busy. I've written a ton of material and—what did you need?"

"Oh, Brian, uh, we decided to go in another direction."

Williams looked as crestfallen as if he had just been told that his new job was to fetch Katie Couric's coffee.

Seth Meyers walked onto the stage. "I'm sorry it didn't work out," he said.

Williams, in a bit he had suggested, made fun of Meyers for lacking an anchor-style earpiece. And when Meyers congratulated him on being the number-one news anchor, Williams snapped: "Don't patronize me."

Poehler invited him to stick around for the rest of the show, but Williams began trudging off the stage. "Uh, Amy, I'm going to head home. I've got a wife and two kids and someone has to tell them that Daddy's not going to be on TV tonight."

Williams's shirt was soaked with sweat, but he felt that he had nailed it. He and Meyers embraced backstage, and he later joined the cast for a wrap party, downing cheeseburgers at 2 A.M.

What made the skit funny, Williams realized, was that most people thought he didn't have much of a life, and that was vaguely hurtful. He was Joe Sobersides on *Nightly News,* and that was the persona he had chosen. NBC was clearly trying to show the world that there was a lighter side to Brian, a funny man with an actual personality that he kept tightly under wraps. It was amazing how little people knew about him, and while one late-night comic turn was hardly going to change that, it was a start.

The following week Seth Meyers used his best anchor voice in reading a *Weekend Update* news item. "Last week," he said, "the *CBS Evening News with Katie Couric* finished in third place, earning her the nickname: Dan Rather."

CHAPTER 28

Scandal Time

Brian Ross was distracted when the tip came in.

A wiry man with the ice-cool demeanor of a detective, Ross was one of a vanishing breed, a classic investigative reporter valued more for his ability to coax information from sources than for his television presence. Ross ran a ten-person unit at ABC, sifting through their leads for potential *World News* stories.

It was late August, and Ross was busy with two major projects, looking at New Orleans a year after Hurricane Katrina and contributing to coverage of the fifth anniversary of 9/11. So when Ross heard about a questionable e-mail sent by a backbencher member of Congress, he was in no great hurry to jump on the story. It didn't seem all that pressing.

A source on Capitol Hill claimed to be in touch with a former member of the House page program, which was designed to allow teenagers recommended by their home-state lawmakers a taste of political life in Washington. The source, whom Ross trusted because he had worked with the man on other stories, had approached Rhonda Schwartz, one of Ross's reporters. Schwartz relayed the tantalizing message: Are you interested in a story about a congressman hitting on pages?

Sure, Ross said. Who wouldn't be?

The informant said that the boy, who was sixteen, was upset over an e-mail he had received from Mark Foley, a fifty-two-year-old Republican from south Florida who was widely believed on the Hill to be gay but refused to discuss his sexuality in public. And Foley wasn't just any congressman; in a bizarre, only-in-Washington twist, he was a crusader against pedophiles and headed the House caucus on exploited children. The boy was said to have complained about Foley to the office of Rodney Alexander, the Louisiana congressman who had sponsored him.

The source later provided a copy of the supposed e-mail from Foley to the Louisiana boy, asking what he wanted for his birthday: "how are you weathering the hurricane . . . are you safe . . . send me an email pic of you as well." And there was an e-mail reply to the Alexander staffer, showing the sixteen-year-old's reaction: "Sick sick sick sick sick sick sick sick sick sick sick sick sick . . ." The boy wrote that maybe he was just being paranoid, but "this freaked me out."

Ross could see that Foley's note was clearly inappropriate. His staff tried to reach the kid and the Alexander aides involved, but the effort went nowhere. Ross had bigger fish to fry at the moment, so he let it slide. After the September 11th remembrances passed, he decided to make another run at the story.

Still, Ross was extremely wary. He kept thinking about Dan Rather's National Guard story, and how Rather's producer, Mary Mapes, had blown up both their careers by accepting what were clearly suspect documents. What if the Foley e-mail was fake? What if this were some sort of political dirty trick? He had to be awfully careful about making a sensational charge against a member of Congress based on a single e-mail that, even if it were real, hardly proved that he was a pedophile.

Rather than spending days or weeks trying to authenticate the story, Ross came up with a simpler plan. "Let's just call up Foley and see what he has to say," he told Schwartz. Ross was unaware that an obscure blog called *StopSexPredators* had posted the e-mail days earlier.

Schwartz called Foley's chief of staff, Liz Nicholson, who said that the e-mail exchange was totally innocent and had been released by his opponents as part of an "ugly smear campaign."

Months earlier House Democratic staffers had given copies of the e-mails to the *St. Petersburg Times, The Miami Herald,* the Capitol Hill newspaper *Roll Call,* and *Harper's* magazine. All had contacted Foley's office, and all had decided that the exchange was too ambiguous to warrant a story.

Ross thought it over. What did they really have? A single e-mail didn't rise to the level of a *World News* story. But he wanted to make sure. He walked through two adjoining buildings to Charlie Gibson's office, asked Jon Banner to step inside, and showed them the message.

Gibson thought the e-mail was rather scummy. He flashed back to his days covering the House in the 1980s, when Gerry Studds, who had been a closeted gay, and Daniel Crane, who liked young girls, were censured for having sex with pages. Gibson remembered the drama and shame of that moment when they had to stand in the well of the House and be denounced by their colleagues.

"Is Foley gay?" Gibson asked. Yes, he was told.

Any member of Congress should know full well not to fraternize with these kids in any way, Gibson thought. But the House was such a clubby place that it was entirely possible other members had protected Foley. Still, this e-mail didn't really prove anything.

"Brian, this just isn't strong enough to go on the show," Gibson said.

Ross had one other option. He thought the Foley correspondence might be perfect for *The Blotter,* a blog that he had launched months earlier on ABC's Web site. The Internet, Ross felt, had changed the whole business. He had started spending more and more time in cyberspace, reading newspapers online, and he now viewed his blog as a tempting vehicle for big exclusives that might not hold until 6:30. The lingering problem was whether to give NBC and CBS a heads-up of several hours in which they might match the scoop before airtime. But Ross felt *The Blotter* was also a viable alternative for stories that were too minor or too questionable for national television.

The piece was posted online at 3:06 P.M. on September 28, 2006. "A 16-year-old male former congressional page concerned about the appropriateness of an e-mail exchange with a congressman alerted Capitol Hill staffers to the communication," it began. "Congressman Mark Foley's office says the e-mails were entirely appropriate and that their release is part of a smear campaign by his opponent."

Within hours the *Blotter* tip box was filling up with messages charging that Foley was lying, that he had engaged in far worse misconduct than an overly friendly e-mail. Another of Ross's associates, Maddy Sauer, made phone contact with two former pages, one a Republican, the other a Democrat. They sounded legitimate. By 10:30 the next morning they had forwarded dozens of instant messages that Foley had sent to other teenage boys from the program, filled with raunchy and graphic talk about sex.

Ross was revolted as he read the messages from the man whose screen name was nothing more mysterious than his initials and his birth year, Maf54:

"Did any girl give you a haand job this weekend"

"Where do you unload it . . . completely naked? . . . I always use lotion and the hand."

"Well I have aa totally stiff wood now"

"I am hard as a rock . . . so tell me when yours reaches rock"

"Get a ruler and measure it for me"

One of the former pages, using IM lingo for "be right back," had written, "brb . . . my mom is yelling," and then he said he had to finish his home-work—a stark reminder that these were, after all, teenagers.

Ross went to see Banner and filled him in. "This could be something," Ross said. "This might even be criminal. But we've got to authenticate it. And we've got to get someone who can tell us, does this violate the law?" Banner agreed that the top priority was making sure these messages were the real deal.

The question hung in the air: Had these boys actually saved all this real-time messaging back and forth with Foley? It was 10:30 on a Friday morning, and Ross figured that he would have to work over the weekend to have any chance of authenticating the messages by the following week.

Rhonda Schwartz, the ABC staffer who had gotten the original tip, called Jason Kello, Foley's spokesman. "You're not going to believe this," she said, and read him some of the thirty-six pages of IMs they had obtained. Kello said that he would get back to her. Kirk Fordham, a former chief of staff for Foley who was now the top aide to another Republican congressman, was having lunch at Foley's Capitol Hill home when Kello called him. Fordham asked the congressman whether the IMs were authentic.

"Probably," Foley said.

Fordham told him that he should resign. Foley walked to the offices of the National Republican Congressional Committee, where Speaker Dennis Hastert and others agreed that the Florida lawmaker had no choice but to quit. At 2:20, soon after the meeting, Fordham called Ross.

"He's going to resign," Fordham said. "I want to make a deal with you."

Ross was stunned. Just like that, Foley was quitting the House? And what did this guy mean by a deal?

"He's going to submit a letter to the speaker," Fordham said. "We don't want you to publish any of the e-mails, and we'll give you the exclusive on the resignation."

No way was Ross going to bite on that one.

"We're not going to make any deals about what we will or won't do," he said. "We're not going to tie our hands."

Everything was moving so fast that Ross could hardly believe it. He told Banner that they now had confirmation and began to crash a story for *World News,* but he had a problem. The IMs at the heart of the story were so raw, so explicit—how much could he really put on the air without being hugely offensive?

Fifteen minutes after he hung up with Fordham, Ross looked up at a television that was always tuned to CNN and saw a headline that Foley would not run for reelection. The story was coming out. But only ABC had the smoking-gun messages.

Less than four hours later, Ross was leading off *World News* with his exclusive. "Foley's resignation came just hours after ABC News questioned the congressman about a series of sexually explicit instant messages involving the congressional pages," he said.

Ross limited himself to reading, in a flat voice, a few of the IM exchanges between the teenager and Maf54:

"What you wearing?"

"T-shirt and shorts."

"Love to slip them off of you."

By now the *CBS Evening News* had jumped on the story as well. "As if the Republican Party needed any more bad news, a congressman was forced to resign today," Katie Couric said.

But Brian Williams made a huge misjudgment. Rather than run a story on the Foley mess, he folded it into the last part of a chat with Tim Russert that was mainly about the fallout from the new Bob Woodward book on the Bush administration. "And Tim, we've had a member of Congress resign late today, not just any member of Congress, but the co-chair of the Congressional Caucus on Missing and Exploited Children, a title I mention because it's germane to this case," Williams said.

Russert gave a two-sentence reply, saying people would view Foley's conduct as "very reprehensible," and that was the extent of the *Nightly News* coverage.

Williams was being too prim and proper for his own good. He had mulled it over and decided the story was so awful that he didn't want to go into the details during the dinner hour. At the same time, Williams undoubtedly would have felt differently had this been an NBC exclusive, and he recognized that it was a clean kill by Brian Ross.

Both NBC and CBS refused to credit ABC News, as virtually every other news organization was doing, and this amounted to more than mere pettiness. The two newscasts were deceiving their viewers by not explaining why a member of Congress was resigning, seemingly out of the blue. They did not have the e-mails or the instant messages, so not only were they blatantly ripping off Ross's story, they were airbrushing the dramatic circumstances—a resignation when faced with imminent exposure by a television network—that had produced Foley's hasty exit just hours earlier.

House Speaker Dennis Hastert was quickly caught in a tangle of conflicting accounts as his majority leader, John Boehner, and other Republican lawmakers and staffers insisted that they had warned him about Foley and the pages, and Hastert insisted he did not recall such warnings.

The finger-pointing was great fodder for *The Daily Show.* Jon Stewart played one clip after another of various Republican leaders saying it wasn't their fault but was the other guy's responsibility, an approach that captured the absurdity of the situation better than the sober summaries on the network newscasts. Stewart also played the footage of Ross reading the IMs on the air in his just-the-facts *Dragnet* style, mocking him as "the world's worst phone-sex operator."

By the following Monday, Williams had to set aside his reluctance and cover what was becoming a mushrooming scandal for the House Republican leadership. Hastert, Williams said, was "front and center" in the damage control effort. "Brian, Republicans are panicked," Russert declared.

CBS played up the story as well. But when ABC followed up, with new details from Ross, on the exclusive, Charlie Gibson did more than just read the introductions. In a chat with Ross, he said: "Brian, I read the e-mails this morning, and they are truly despicable."

"They are disgusting," Ross agreed.

Gibson wasn't through: "This is the party that talks about family values, and yet they put this guy at the head of the caucus that's worried about missing and exploited children. It seems very strange." Gibson had spent a decade covering the House, and he wasn't reticent about rendering a moral judgment rather than retreating to neutral anchor-speak.

Another former Hill correspondent, Bob Schieffer, matched the level of disdain, calling the congressional leadership's handling of the problem "disgraceful."

Brian Ross wasn't done breaking stories. Kirk Fordham, the former Foley aide, who promptly resigned from his House job, told Ross that he had warned Hastert's staff about Foley's misbehavior toward pages three years earlier.

A classic media frenzy had erupted. "Can Speaker Hastert survive?" Brian Williams was asking after kissing off the story days earlier.

George Stephanopoulos got a bit carried away. Relying too heavily on the daily buzz from the chattering classes, the onetime White House aide declared Hastert washed up.

"Charlie, I have not talked to a single person today, Republican or Democrat, who thinks Dennis Hastert will be speaker of the House next year," he said on *World News*. "That's not even a question anymore . . . Several top Republicans told me they don't think he can last the week," he said.

"The week?" Gibson asked, seemingly in disbelief.

The next day Stephanopoulos reversed himself as the winds of conventional wisdom shifted. Since Hastert had held a news conference and President Bush had called him, Stephanopoulos said, that "gives all other Republicans a reason to say Hastert can stay for now." He did not mention his previous prediction.

As the investigation continued, Ross was careful not to overplay his hand. Late in the week Ross nailed down another exclusive: three more former House pages describing sexual approaches from Foley. Ross posted the story on *The Blotter* at 5:20 P.M., and it was widely picked up by other news organizations. But *World News* did not carry a word that night.

Gibson had taken the broadcast to Philadelphia, where he had an interview with former president George H. W. Bush, so it was hard to squeeze in a late-breaking piece based on unnamed sources. No matter; Ross now saw the Net as a strong option.

David Westin had told Ross and Banner that they did not want to get too far ahead of themselves on this story. "We don't have to break every twist and turn in this," Westin said. "This is the point at which news divisions can get too big for their britches and make a mistake."

The Foley debacle was a godsend for the newscasts, and not just because it fed their love of scandal, sleaze, and an unraveling mystery. The real dividend was that it gave them a narrative for the congressional elections. The problem with the midterms was that they were a far-flung collection of state and local races involving candidates who were mostly unfamiliar to a national audience. The networks always tried to impose a national story line on these contests through polls, trends, and the prognostications of Beltway handicappers. But even in a year in which the Iraq war loomed so large, the House and Senate contests were still widely disparate in nature. The Foley melodrama opened the door for a wealth of reports about sexual misconduct, an ethical cesspool in Congress, anguish among gay Republicans, hypocrisy among GOP politicians who demonized homosexuals but tolerated gay staffers, and the daily drumbeat over whether this could cost Bush's party control of the House and perhaps even the Senate.

*   *   *

As October grew chillier, an urgent tone began creeping into the anchors' coverage of Iraq. No longer were they describing the war as a difficult battle whose outcome was in doubt, or depicting the military struggle as part of a larger effort to rebuild the battered country. Now it was all about the violence, and they were framing the situation as an unmitigated mess. The anchors were giving real weight to what had once seemed unmentionable, the possibility that the United States might have to pull out.

They were, to be sure, reflecting the rapid erosion of popular support for the war, and a level of killing and chaos that seemed to grow worse by the day. But given their huge platform, they were also shaping public sentiment, reinforcing the notion that three and a half years after the American invasion, the situation was all but lost.

"In plain English," Brian Williams said, "this has been a tough week to be hopeful about the prospects for victory in Iraq."

Charlie Gibson spoke of a "killing spree," a "horrific surge in religious violence, Iraqis killing Iraqis in unprecedented numbers." After correspondent Terry McCarthy reported that fifty to sixty dead people were turning up each day, Gibson could not remain silent. "Sobering to see people simply driving by a body in the streets," he said. "But such is life in Baghdad today."

They sounded almost apologetic at times, not because the stories were graphic but because of their repetitive nature. Listen up, they seemed to say, this is important, *pay attention*!

"Well," Katie Couric said, "you've heard it before but we have to say it again tonight, it's turning out to be an especially violent week in Iraq."

Couric, in particular, appeared to openly yearn for a pullout. "Pressure is building on President Bush to find a way out of Iraq, where the U.S. death toll is now approaching twenty-eight hundred," she said.

On another night Couric spoke of "opposition to the war in Iraq growing and no end in sight." And at times she came close to describing the situation as hopeless: "The day everyone is hoping for, the day American forces can finally come home from Iraq, seems more and more elusive."

The anchors looked for ways to dramatize the grim statistics. Williams, noting "the bloodshed that has become an all-too-common fact of life there for so many people," highlighted a report on how Baghdad coffin-makers could not keep up with demand. Gibson, reporting a United Nations finding on Iraqi casualties in July and August, tried to bring the impact home: "And just to put the sixty-six hundred Iraqi deaths over the past two months in perspective—if the U.S. lost an equivalent percentage of its population, that would represent seventy-five thousand American dead."

Even more ominous were the field reports from Iraq. Lara Logan told CBS viewers how death squads were invading hospitals and killing patients and the relatives who had come to visit them, even murdering mourners at morgues. Describing a gruesome wave of revenge killings from the town of Balad, Logan—never shy about offering her conclusions—said that "this slaughter highlights once again how powerless Iraq security forces are to stop the sectarian violence."

The common assumption was that the troops resented the negative media coverage as undermining their mission, and perhaps many did. But increasingly, some were voicing their doubts about the war, and television was a powerful medium for airing those doubts. Richard Engel interviewed a soldier named Rob Graves who said of the Iraqis: "If they want to kill each other, then why the hell are we here? Why is my buddy getting turned into Swiss cheese by an IED if it's meant for the Shiite that lives across street?"

The dedication required to cover the seemingly endless war was taking a toll on the correspondents. Not long after arriving in Iraq on the eve of the U.S. invasion, Engel had gotten divorced from his college sweetheart. Logan was separated from her American husband, who was living in the States. War reporting was not compatible with a normal family life.

The human depravity they chronicled, week after week, clearly made the situation seem beyond salvation and tended to blot out any fleeting signs of progress in Iraq. Of course, the broadcasts were just capturing the brutal reality of these attacks. But except for Bush's rhetoric about the conflict as a central front in the war on terror, no other story line was given much airtime. When the president abandoned a key catchphrase that critics had turned into a synonym for stubborn rigidity, Williams led his newscast with word that Bush would no longer use the phrase "stay the course" to describe his strategy in Iraq.

After eleven American servicemen were killed in two days, the senior military spokesman in Iraq admitted what was obvious to anyone with a television set, that the effort was falling short. The anchors pounced, as if to say, *See? We told you that the situation was far worse than the government is letting on.*

Like two tributaries feeding a rushing river, the surge in downbeat Iraq coverage gradually began to merge with the negative reporting on the Republican Party's chances in the midterm elections, until the two were virtually indistinguishable. Every setback in the war was cast as bad electoral news for Bush and his party. Iraq was now a nightly horror show, a proxy for the campaign itself.

CHAPTER 29

In the Trenches

Charlie Gibson, peering through his rimless reading glasses, looked transfixed as he watched the Pentagon briefing on a flat-screen wall monitor.

Donald Rumsfeld had been swinging away for half an hour, telling the assembled Pentagon reporters to "back off" in their coverage of the war, to stop trying to create "daylight" between the Bush administration and Iraq, to stop playing up the bad news and burying the good news, to stop making things up. "I find almost every day I see all kinds of mythology repeated in the press, day after day of things that never happened. Just unbelievable what I see," he declared.

The day's controversy centered on what President Bush had termed benchmarks, a series of goals and timetables that the Iraqis were said to have adopted in an effort to bring the deteriorating security situation under control. To make matters worse, Iraq's prime minister, Nouri al-Maliki, had promptly contradicted Bush by saying that his government was freely elected and had not agreed to any American demand for benchmarks.

NBC's Jim Miklaszewski, who was short and soft-spoken and had covered the Pentagon forever, rose to challenge Rumsfeld's dismissive attitude toward the war coverage.

"But given the record, Mr. Secretary, can you blame us for the tone, expressing some skepticism? Because every time a benchmark has been laid down in terms of security forces and the like, the Iraqis have been unable to meet them."

"That is just false," Rumsfeld snapped.

"You have no leverage—" Miklaszewski began.

"Just a minute. Just a minute! That is false!"

"That is not false," Miklaszewski said, standing his ground.

"Every time a security benchmark has been laid down the Iraqis have failed to meet it? Wrong! Just isn't true."

Miklaszewski modified his language, saying the Iraqis had shown no ability "to stand up and take control" and had failed to deliver most of the troops they had promised to secure Baghdad.

Rumsfeld would not let up: "Your assertion is flat wrong."

In the ABC newsroom, Gibson broke into a wry smile. "Very Rumsfeldian," he said.

The question for *World News* was simple: Was this news, or just another momentary clash that provided fodder for the cable channels? It was the sort of decision that each network, surrounded by the cacophony of cable news and the constant churning on the Net, faced every day.

The matter was complicated by the fact that the White House was challenging the translation of Maliki's earlier remarks and arguing that journalists had wrenched his answer out of context. The ABC producers were not terribly excited about the debate.

"It's dancing on the head of a pin," said Tom Nagorski, Jon Banner's deputy. "I'd rather have a piece from Iraq." In fact, correspondent Terry McCarthy had filed a report on Iraqi students who attended a school one block from where a bomb had recently exploded.

Gibson had lost friends in Vietnam, and now he had professional friends whose sons were dying in Iraq. His thoughts kept returning to one central question: When you commit kids to war, what are they fighting for? Just the other day, George Stephanopoulos had asked Bush whether we were essentially keeping our kids there to stop Sunnis from killing Shiites and vice versa. The president hadn't really answered the question. What was the mission in Iraq? How could a family say that the war was worth little Johnny's well-being?

Gibson was obsessed with this point. If you were president, and you decided to go to war, was there a calculus in your mind that the goal was worth so many American lives? After all, your generals would tell you that X number were likely to die. What was the acceptable trade-off? Gibson's own threshold would be one: Was the war worth one life?

For the moment, such momentous questions would have to wait. Gibson and his small circle of producers had to settle on a lead story. But first, it was time to head one flight up for the Webcast.

The online edition of *World News* was, as usual, more fun than the version that people saw on television. There was an interview with the crooner John Legend, a report on a video game built around Armageddon, and a story about the rock band KISS launching a line of perfume and deodorants—the kind of subjects that might attract younger viewers if they ever made it to air.

When Stephanopoulos appeared from Washington with a noticeable Band-Aid under his right eye, Gibson said: "George, a little bandage there, what did you do?"

"Charlie, it's embarrassing. I turned around and went right into a camera."

Gibson was looser as well, noting that a Republican gubernatorial candidate in Iowa had ducked a campaign appearance with Bush, claiming a commitment to a Rotarian lunch. "Come on!" he said. "That's a pretty thin veil to hide under."

When Gibson returned to the newsroom, the debate began in earnest. The producers wanted to lead with a wildfire that was raging in California.

"Why do I care if three firefighters were killed, as opposed to six people being killed in automobile accidents in Nebraska?" Gibson asked. "Which didn't happen, but would we lead with it?"

"It's the worst fire record for a season on record," Banner said.

"You think that rises above the threshold of ten and a half billion dollars in profits in three months?" ExxonMobil had just released the stunning figure, and Gibson wanted to lead the broadcast with the second highest quarterly corporate profit in American history, topped only by the same oil company in a previous quarter.

"To come on and say, 'Good evening, three people died in a fire today in California . . .'"

"We wouldn't say that," Nagorski said.

They drifted back to the debate over Maliki's swipe at the Bush administration over the timetables. Gibson said he was more interested in the prime minister saying that he could stop the violence in six months if the United States would give him the resources he needed. But Nagorski said they didn't have that interview on tape.

Gibson said he didn't want to "get in the weeds" on the dispute. But the report on Iraqi students didn't feel right either. "You just feel off the subject with McCarthy's piece on the school when Maliki is presenting his own Declaration of Independence," Gibson said.

The staff could not have been less enthusiastic about the diplomatic flap. "At the end of that spot," Banner said, "you're going to say Maliki and the White House are now on the same page—so?"

"When he rejects benchmarks and timetables, and then he turns around and says if you give me the resources I can do it in six months—that to me is news," Gibson said.

Banner dismissed the dispute as nothing but semantics. "The administration is playing a game of *it all depends on what the meaning of is, is,*" recalling Bill Clinton's famous hair-splitting testimony during the Monica Lewinsky investigation.

Nagorski began imitating Rumsfeld's style of asking and answering his own questions. "Is this worth doing two minutes of television tonight? No."

Gibson started channeling Rummy as well: "Am I being strong enough to get on the network news? Yes."

They screened a piece on Ford ending production of its once-popular Taurus. Gibson loved the story. "I just think it's the best single example of how totally fucked up the Ford Motor Company has become," he said. Maybe they could lead with ExxonMobil's profits and then run the Taurus story. "I just think if you can relate it to gas prices, that's a better lead than fires, though it's not as good a picture."

David Westin dropped by the second-floor newsroom to chat. Gibson asked him which story he would lead with.

"What do you say about ExxonMobil?" Westin asked. "What's the second line of the story? Okay, yeah, it's a lot of money, they're bad boys?"

Westin enjoyed being asked for his opinion. When Peter Jennings was the anchor, he never asked what the boss thought, deeming it a violation of church and state. Gibson laughed when Westin had mentioned this to him.

"We ask everybody. That doesn't mean we defer to you," Gibson said. It was his style to seek input from even the lowliest desk assistant. He loved to talk, to just about anyone, and was constantly running late as he got mired in conversation while aides kept checking their watches.

In a few short months, Gibson had taken command of the news division. Gone was the tentative approach when he first got the anchor job, seemingly surprised to find himself in charge without having to clear things with Diane Sawyer. He was writing more of the scripts and rewriting much of the rest. He was challenging the language in correspondents' pieces and suggesting which sound bites could be dropped. And he was putting more of his voice into the newscast.

When the program was airing a quirky feature on what would happen if you actually tried to dig a hole to China, Gibson said: "I really have no idea how to introduce the following story." After a report, lifted from *The*

Washington Post, on a teenager who had finished the University of Virginia in one year, Gibson said: "If he gets a Ph.D. before the end of the week, we'll let you know." For the fiftieth anniversary of the children's book *The Cat in the Hat,* he recited an item in Dr. Seuss rhyme. He began signing off as "Charlie," with a winsome smile and the words, "I hope you had a good day."

Westin had told him to lighten up and have some fun. Banner had encouraged him as well, but he knew that Gibson had very old-school notions about what an anchor should and should not do. Banner understood that Gibson was reluctant to step on the correspondents' toes.

Gibson, in fact, was starting to worry that he was interjecting too much. He knew the others wanted him to spout off more often, but he thought that it shouldn't become an everyday thing. The situation reminded him of his early days on *Good Morning America,* when the producers kept urging him to talk more about his family. One thing he had learned about television was that people projected a personality onto you, often based on your facial mannerisms or body language.

When he had been coanchoring with Joan Lunden, they were on camera together for maybe five minutes on each show. Yet viewers assumed they knew all about the nature of the relationship, and invariably they were right. When Lunden announced that she was getting divorced, Gibson thought the audience would be shocked, but people told him they saw it coming because she always talked about her children but not her husband. In some ways, you couldn't hide from the camera.

Gibson was now solidly ensconced in second place—the previous week, boosted by Diane Sawyer's reports from North Korea, he had finished just 200,000 viewers behind Brian Williams—and wondered what had happened to Katie Couric's program. Was the audience deserting *her* or the revamped newscast? Gibson was a big admirer of Katie and thought she was a terrific communicator, but the problem, he felt, was that she had tried to do too much, too fast. The *Evening News* now seemed schizophrenic—hard news one moment, three minutes of Katie chatting with Twyla Tharp the next, which was way too long. Couric should have done a very traditional newscast until she was established in the chair, and then started tweaking it.

That had been Gibson's approach. He had asked to start immediately once Westin decided to drop Elizabeth Vargas, figuring that he would work out the program's kinks by the fall. Gibson had very deliberately started out under the radar. That was where he liked to be.

Airtime was less than three hours away. Tom Nagorski, watching the

California wildfires on CNN's *The Situation Room,* said that the breadth of the blaze was greater than he had realized.

"So if Wolf Blitzer leads with it . . . ," Gibson teased him.

Just after five o'clock a wire-service bulletin reported that a fourth firefighter had been killed in the blaze. Gibson turned his attention to Jonathan Karl's piece about the tensions with Iraq. He didn't think that a sound bite from General Peter Pace, chairman of the Joint Chiefs, added much.

"I'd get rid of Pace and punch up Maliki," Gibson said.

Jon Banner remained unconvinced. "I'm not sure at the end of the piece why I care," he said.

Nagorski suggested that they tighten the language with some quick shorthand to summarize the back-and-forth about benchmarks.

"But that's what's dramatic," Gibson said. "Nobody's on the same page—nobody!" He smacked the script for emphasis.

Nagorski still wanted to spike the story. Gibson looked at the script again. Karl had begun by saying that the issues were complex.

"If you tell people it's complicated and confusing, they'll go away," Gibson said. He dictated a better lead: "Rumsfeld says the two sides are working together. But it certainly doesn't sound that way."

It was 5:09. Banner got up and put his jacket on. He was slipping out early to attend a school event for one of his kids.

"You're going to leave before we decide what the lead is? You're losing your vote," Gibson told him.

They had one more go-round without Banner. Gibson still didn't like the wildfires for kicking off the show.

"It's a weather story," he said. "It's a weather story that killed four people. I can't get past that."

The producers made their case, and Gibson yielded. In classic Quaker fashion, he had achieved a sense of the meeting. But Gibson stood his ground on the Iraq story that everyone else found to be a yawn.

At 6:30 all the networks led with the California fires. Gibson soon got to the story about Rumsfeld's eruption, and Brian Williams played it up as well. Williams asked Jim Miklaszewski about why things had gotten "a little hot" in the briefing room. "The Bush administration has become hypersensitive over any criticism of this new plan for progress in Iraq," Miklaszewski said.

Only Katie Couric didn't mention Donald Rumsfeld or the simmering dispute between the Bush administration and Iraq. She was totally focused on Michael J. Fox.

*   *   *

Sean McManus had a message for the troops.

It was fine for CBS staffers to argue among themselves in the office, he said. That was what journalists did. But these were family fights, and no one should talk about them to outsiders.

A woman in the London bureau had a question: Was McManus saying that there was a lack of loyalty at CBS?

No, McManus said. He just wanted to make sure that they kept their discussions in-house.

Rome Hartman often held these discussions with the staff on Fridays, with bureaus around the world joining by speakerphone, and this time the CBS News president was a featured participant. It was not the best of times for the *CBS Evening News*. With Katie Couric mired in third place, rumors were flying around the newsroom, some of them popping up on gossipy Web sites.

McManus assumed the role of a football coach whose team was behind at halftime. The important things to remember, he said, were "pride" and "loyalty." Ratings didn't matter; forget about ratings. All that counted was the demo, and they were doing better on that score than in the pre-Katie era.

It was the day after an extraordinary moment on the newscast. With a storm of controversy brewing around Michael J. Fox, the actor had arrived for an exclusive sit-down with Couric. But as the day wore on, the staff's curiosity turned to puzzlement and, finally, a sense of disbelief: *How* long was this interview going to run? Couric was going to turn over nine minutes of the broadcast to a celebrity spokesman for a crippling disease? All this other news was going to be tossed out? That, some staffers said, was crazy.

It was a move that at once showcased her hustle, her interviewing savvy, and her feel for pop culture, while also making some colleagues wonder about her judgment. Her personal ties to the subject merely added another layer of intrigue.

Couric was friendly with Fox, who had suffered for years from Parkinson's disease. She admired the former *Spin City* star and had contributed to his research foundation. And although few outside her circle of friends knew it, Couric's eighty-six-year-old father was suffering through the early stages of Parkinson's, which was causing tremors in one of his hands. Just as she had become a crusader against colon cancer after her husband's death, Couric had a strong personal interest in Parkinson's and in the broader debate about whether stem cell research could help those afflicted with such diseases. She knew that her experience had left her with greater sympathy for those with the disease, but also felt that she knew more about the science than most people.

Two days earlier Rush Limbaugh had ripped Fox for making political commercials for Democratic candidates who backed stem cell research. Moving his arms and body in the spastic, uncontrolled motions that afflict those with Parkinson's, Limbaugh accused the actor of either shamelessly exaggerating his symptoms or refusing to take his medicine, for maximum theatrical effect.

While Couric believed that Limbaugh's attack had been thoughtless, she did not want to be unfair to the radio host, who had insisted that he was not mocking Fox. Limbaugh, after all, had done a "Free Speech" segment for the broadcast a couple of weeks earlier and had taken considerable heat from some of his listeners for consorting with the likes of Katie Couric. So she called his office for comment, and the conservative commentator sent her an e-mail reply.

She also called her dad. Would it be all right, she asked, if she mentioned him in explaining her personal interest in the subject? John Couric told his daughter to go ahead, that he didn't care who knew he had the disease.

Couric's talk with Fox was sensitively handled, touching at times, and included a couple of bows to the other side of the argument, such as concerns that stem cell research might be a "slippery slope" and not properly regulated. It was also a friendly celebrity interview of the kind she had perfected over the years.

After screening the tape, she told Rome Hartman: "We cannot cut this short."

Hartman agreed that the interview was compelling without being exploitative. Hartman started cutting stories to give the Fox discussion and a related piece as much time as possible.

Was the flap of such overriding importance less than two weeks before the midterm elections? The decision to devote nearly half the broadcast to Michael J. Fox seemed to suggest that Couric still did not grasp the essential distinction between morning television and nightly news. But Couric didn't care if some of her colleagues were grousing about it. She considered the interview a watershed moment. The evening news, she felt, could use a little of the best of the *Today* show.

The next day's conference call made clear what the brass thought. Hartman said that he was delighted with the Fox interview, that this was where the broadcast was headed, and that every time they got a big story like this, they were going to make the most of it. McManus seconded the notion with great enthusiasm.

The great divide at CBS News was between the generals, who thought their war plan needed a few refinements at best, and some of the lieutenants and privates, who believed that the mission was deeply flawed. Hartman felt that this debate was healthy, that he and Katie were always looking for ways to improve the program. But he also felt there were some people in every organization who were constantly negative.

The program showed flashes of great promise but was maddeningly inconsistent. On the day when the *Sarasota Herald-Tribune* disclosed the name of the retired priest who Mark Foley said had abused him as a teenager, Couric was the only network anchor—in fact, the only network correspondent—to reach Anthony Mercieca in Malta for a taped phone conversation, during which he admitted to nude encounters with the young man. "Probably the weirdest interview I've ever done," she told viewers. Couric had followed this up with a strong discussion, mostly about Iraq, with John McCain.

But every time a broadcast worked up a head of steam, the flow would be interrupted by some silly item, pointless "Free Speech" segment, or trivial feature story, such as a company putting baseball logos on its funeral caskets—"for the diehard fan," as Couric put it. Or she would close with a morning show antic, such as handing Steve Hartman a pair of furry pink slippers after his report on a prison where inmates were required to wear pink.

At other times three minutes would be handed over to Couric's new political team—Mike McCurry, the former Clinton White House press secretary, and Nicolle Wallace, the former Bush White House communications director—to gently score points for their side. At moments like these, the *CBS Evening News* seemed like just another cable chat show.

The critics, quick to declare failure based on her last-place showing, were again piling on Couric. The trade magazine *Variety* declared: "The trajectory of her personality-driven leap to CBS has proven strangely predictable: enormous initial curiosity followed by a dawning realization there's not much 'there' there—a point starkly underscored by her 'How does one go about asking the secretary of State on a date?' interview with Condoleezza Rice on *60 Minutes*." That last point was unfair—the Rice segment had been a personality profile—but the article reflected a growing media consensus that Couric was a $15 million flop.

Couric was doing her best to ignore the naysayers. This constant charge that the newscast had gone "soft," she believed, was code for *she's a woman*. Brian Williams could do a piece on baby-boomer women and no one said that was soft. Besides, she thought, "hard" and "soft" were totally antiquated terms, trotted out by lazy reporters. They were acting like lemmings, and showing their ignorance of television news in the process. In fact, she believed, it was worse than that. It was incompetence. They clearly hadn't done their homework. She would never have been able to get away with that.

Foster kids being given addictive drugs: Was that soft? Soldiers struggling with emotional problems after returning from duty: Was that soft? The stories might be packaged as longer narratives, but that didn't render them lighter than air. Couric was open to critiques by reporters who dealt with facts and actually watched the program, but a recent swipe by Peter Bart, the editor of *Variety*, had really infuriated her. He suggested that Couric start "injecting some actual news back into your nightly equation and dropping some of your riveting 'lifestyle' stories."

At times she could be overly sensitive. When *The Washington Post*'s gossip column ran a series of bogus statements—including that her mother had told her hairdresser that she still watched Brian Williams—Couric was not mollified by the disclaimer that it was all a spoof.

Even when she walked out of the CBS building for lunch, paparazzi were staking her out on West 57th Street, snapping photos as soon as she emerged. Whatever her private frustrations, Couric felt that she shouldn't waste time responding to the chattering classes. The perpetrators, she believed, were driven by arrogance or insecurity. She wanted to win over the viewers, not the critics.

Toward that end, a growing share of the broadcast was being built around Couric. *She* would sit down with three military wives who described the difficulties of family life while their husbands were in Iraq. *She* would chat up four post-menopausal women about a new approach to hormone replacement therapy. These segments showed off her deft touch, her empathy, her ease at talking to ordinary people. But their heavy emphasis on women and family also made them seem like the kind of pieces that would appeal more to the heavily female morning audience after the first twenty minutes of news was out of the way.

When Couric led one newscast by reporting that cancer deaths had dropped for the second straight year, her favorite doctor, Jon LaPook, hastened to add that experts "do credit your efforts at increased colonoscopy, increased public awareness with the dramatic drop." And in the same show, during a piece about Muhammad Ali turning sixty-five, Couric noted that "I even went a few rounds with him myself"—cutting to a picture of her hugging the champ. Sometimes, it seemed, she *was* the news.

The more interviews and segments Couric handled, the less the correspondents were getting on the air, especially some of the female reporters who had thrived under Schieffer. Morale began to plummet. Who wanted to come to the office every day when you didn't feel like part of the product?

The result was a tense workplace in which unconfirmed gossip flourished. Would Rome Hartman keep his job? Was Bill Owens heading back to *60 Minutes*? Was one of Katie's bookers actually making half a million dollars a year? Had she gotten CBS to hire a freelance cameraman for her field reports who was getting five thousand bucks a shoot? Had Couric given Les Moonves a list of staffers she wanted canned? Some staffers noticed that McManus, who seemed such a perennial optimist, was looking rather subdued.

Couric was worried about the chatter because she knew that CBS management had told some of the correspondents to look for other jobs. Some of this had been in the works before she arrived, but Couric realized that she would be blamed. In fact, she felt that she took the hit for everything, whether it was her fault or not, and that seemed terribly unfair.

But the hard truth was that Couric was not happy with some of the correspondents. She felt that they needed a better and livelier ensemble for the broadcast. She wanted personalities who just popped off the screen. When Lara Logan reported from the field or David Martin delivered a scoop from the Pentagon, people paid attention. It was true that Couric had not asked for anyone to be fired. But it was obvious that if new reporters were brought in, others would have to be let go.

Hartman, too, believed that they did not have the best possible person in every slot, and plenty of outsiders wanted to come to CBS. It was little wonder that some of the existing staff was feeling insecure.

Couric believed that some of the pieces needed an injection of humanity, that she wasn't getting a sense of who the correspondents were. She wanted to see them walking and talking to people. When Cynthia Bowers did a piece on the minimum wage, she had opened with a shot of a Chicago pizza parlor before interviewing the manager about his teenage employees. Couric wanted a portrait of someone scraping by on $5.15 an hour, what his daily struggles were like, how a raise would change his life. She wanted to get inside the head of a General Motors worker who had to move to Wyoming because his job was eliminated, or see a long conversation with his nine-year-old daughter on how hard it was to relocate. It couldn't just be words on a script; there had to be room for emotion. She aspired, in short, to a feel-your-pain style of storytelling that was common on the morning and magazine shows but often deemed too cloying for nightly newscasts.

In her passion to improve the program, Couric was acquiring a reputation as a tough taskmaster, with some of the same whispering that had plagued her at *Today*. People would stop each other in the halls: Hey, did you hear that the technicians are upset because she wants to store her huge wardrobe in an equipment repair room? Did you hear that she wants the cables removed from the studio floor because women in heels are tripping over them? Some viewed Couric and her band of NBC expatriates almost as an occupying army.

But not all the grumbling was trivial. The two bookers who had come with Couric from NBC sometimes tried to line up interviews for her that the correspondents had been trying to snag for themselves. When Lara Logan was close to landing General John Abizaid, head of the U.S. Central Command, for *60 Minutes,* Couric's staff made a run at him before yielding to Logan.

Some foreign correspondents believed that Couric's requests for stories lacked sophistication. She would ask for pieces explaining the difference between Sunnis and Shiites, or what American soldiers thought of the latest Bush strategy, as if it were easy for the grunts to stand before a camera and criticize the commander in chief. And Couric was always pushing for more reports on the lives of the soldiers. When the reporters turned in such stories, she would ask: "Do you have anything more personal?"

As Couric's friends saw it, she was a hard-charging woman who was constantly throwing ideas at her staff, demanding responses, and prodding them to do more research. She was a micromanager, that was true enough, but had no choice because she felt that certain people weren't doing their jobs. Couric was not happy with the quality or the quantity of the work that she was getting from some of her colleagues. In this view, people were sniping because they were upset at having to work harder. Couric's camp dismissed them as chronic complainers or disgruntled Dan Rather holdovers.

But some CBS veterans saw Couric as a woman who was never satisfied with their efforts. The producers, too, had become highly critical of what some correspondents were turning in, prompting reporters to wonder if their superiors had drunk the Couric Kool-Aid. The honeymoon that had seemed

so hopeful when Couric's hiring was announced was giving way to a difficult marriage.

*   *   *

Tim Russert was constantly hearing from Dan Bartlett in the campaign's
final weeks.

The White House counselor was quick to contact Russert after he said on
Today that with the Republicans on the defensive over Iraq, Iran, and the
Abramoff and Foley scandals, "right now, a wave seems to be building."

He told Russert that the polling in individual races did not detect any kind
of wave. "This is a lot more fluid than the mainstream media is pronouncing," Bartlett said.

Russert, who had been trained in Buffalo precinct politics, never backed
away from a good fight. "I am not 'pronouncing' anything," he told Bartlett.
"I am reporting what Republican pollsters and campaign operatives are
telling me." Bartlett, for his part, felt that you could always find some
Republican somewhere to say just about anything.

Their next clash came over the war. After Richard Engel reported
from Baghdad that the Iraqi prime minister had accused Washington of
trying to "bully" him into setting timetables for military progress, Russert
said on *Nightly* that "the White House realizes they have to go back to
square one."

Bartlett told Russert that the wire-service accounts of Nouri al-Maliki's
comments were inaccurate. What Russert had said "seems way off," Bartlett
complained, and "it deserves a correction."

Russert checked with Engel, who said that he had just confirmed the
story with two more Maliki aides. "We are fine," Engel said.

Russert relayed this information to Bartlett, adding that both *The New
York Times* and *The Washington Post* were reporting a schism between the
two governments. Both Democrats and Republicans, Russert said, thought
that the situation in Iraq was a mess. Bartlett found that notion offensive.

When the conservative *Washington Times* reported that Maliki was publicly criticizing the Bush administration, Russert couldn't resist another shot
at Bartlett. "Do you consider them mainstream media?" he asked. Russert
pressed Bartlett to acknowledge that Engel's reports had been spot on and
that the White House criticisms were "off the mark."

Bartlett was struck by Russert's love of verbal combat. He would send
the man an e-mail and get a call thirty seconds later. Bartlett told Russert it

was hardly surprising that some people in high office, whether in Iraq or elsewhere, had their own agendas, and that Maliki was having to clarify his comments because he kept getting asked about positions that the Bush administration wasn't actually taking.

Russert said that they always talked to both sides, which was their job.

Bartlett said that none of this amounted to the situation in Iraq being "back to square one," as Russert had contended. But he seemed to be growing wearing of their daily duel.

"Okay, I give up," Bartlett said.

*   *   *

As Election Day approached, the nightly newscasts all but announced that the outcome was no longer in doubt. The anchors were convinced that a big Democratic wave was about to crest, and they decided to ride it.

"Some Republicans are privately admitting the Election Day forecast looks grim," Brian Williams said, putting aside his earlier doubts that the campaign might be tightening. Tim Russert quoted an unnamed GOP strategist as saying that the party expected to lose at least twenty-three seats in the House, well beyond the fifteen that would give the Democrats control.

"One senior Republican strategist told me their best case now is a loss of twenty seats," George Stephanopoulos said.

The polls were showing the Democrats in "a very good position to win back the House," Katie Couric said, and with the focus shifting to the Senate, "there's growing concern among Republicans that they could lose their majority in that chamber as well."

Whether the anchors were just reporting the news or, as conservative critics maintained, helping to shape it, they seemed caught up in the excitement. Williams worried at times that by constantly beating the Democratic House takeover drums, the networks might be creating the perception that such an outcome was inevitable. But he felt that they were reflecting what Democratic officials, both publicly and in off-the-record sessions, were telling them. Gibson believed that things could change in the closing days of a campaign and that Bush was right to be chiding his opponents for prematurely dancing in the end zone.

The day before the election, a new rash of polls prompted a sudden outbreak of caution. Brian Williams said that the latest numbers showed "a general tightening in most battleground races." Charlie Gibson said that things "always tighten at the end," and George Stephanopoulos said the Democrats' double-digit lead was "basically being cut in half and more."

Katie Couric talked about the battle for Congress "getting tighter by the minute," and Bob Schieffer warned that "Republicans nationwide are closing the gap."

They were in some ways like weathervanes, spinning with the prevailing polling winds. After months of all but predicting that the Democrats were headed for a major victory, the anchors were hedging their bets.

CHAPTER 30

Cliff-Hanger

Brian Williams was checking out the camera angles and had a suggestion.

"It's much better to have Tom closer," he said.

Tom Brokaw, who had anchored NBC's election coverage a dozen times, was sitting on Williams's right.

"As long as it doesn't feel like I'm shouting across the room," Williams said.

It was midafternoon on Election Day, and Williams was at the center of a massive, semicircular desk in a dazzling eighth-floor studio where the drama *Friday Night Lights* was taped. Above his head was an electronic zipper, with red letters saying **NBC News Decision 2006** moving slowly across the digital display. On either side were 107-inch Panasonic video screens showing rippling American flags and the Capitol. Behind him was a massive picture window reflecting a flag-bedecked Rockefeller Plaza, with its flowing waterfall and golden statue of the mythical Greek figure Prometheus. That was a fake—it was a projected moving picture of the actual scene outside the building, like the bogus backdrops on *The Daily Show*—but looked so real that it fooled the television critics.

As the cameras swiveled, testing various shots, Tim Russert, sitting on Williams's left, was trying out an electronic white board, a computerized version of the famous piece of cardboard on which he had scribbled "Florida, Florida, Florida" during the all-nighter of the 2000 presidential election. Russert was steeped in political intelligence, but he believed in keeping it simple for the viewers.

Betsy Fischer, his *Meet the Press* producer, was showing him how to use the contraption and how it would show up on the television screen.

"You can go through the states and X them out," Fischer said.

"Yeah, yeah," Russert said.

Brokaw was chatting about the Senate race in Montana, where Democrat Jon Tester was trying to unseat the Republican incumbent, Conrad Burns. "The Tester people think they're going to pull it out by this much," Brokaw said, holding his thumb and forefinger an inch apart.

This was not a rehearsal. Williams had refused to rehearse, because he didn't believe in sitting there and reciting a bunch of fictional vote totals. But he was pumped about the chance to anchor his first election after serving as Brokaw's apprentice for so long. He lived for big political nights like these. And he loved the idea of being flanked by these two heavyweights. Russert was like a walking computer. Even if Williams were a complete fraud when it came to politics, he felt, the magic word was, *Tim?*

Brokaw, who had first appeared on NBC during the 1966 elections, was particularly engaged in the campaign. The stakes, he felt, were huge. The country was at war, for Chrissake. It didn't get any bigger than that.

Steve Capus knew that Williams was facing a major challenge, the first time that the night would be *his.* They had covered their first election together at MSNBC in 1996, just months after the cable channel had launched, and had done several since then, but a broadcast network obviously provided a far bigger stage.

For half a century Election Night had been the big enchilada for the networks, a chance to trot out the A team and show off for the audience. But even with control of Congress at stake, NBC News, like the other news divisions, was slated to be on the air only for an hour at ten P.M., with another special at one A.M. for the West Coast, and occasional one-minute news cut-ins. This sort of truncated schedule would have been unthinkable in the days of Cronkite and Brinkley, but the economics of television had radically changed, with cable channels handling breaking news and the big networks rarely preempting their lucrative entertainment shows. Capus felt lucky to get the hour.

It was odd, in a way, for Williams to be the master of ceremonies and Brokaw reduced to a supporting role. But Williams felt comfortable because Tom didn't exude any weirdness about it. Williams didn't have to worry about watching his back. Whenever the producers had asked Brokaw what he wanted to contribute, he would say, it's Brian's show, whatever he wants.

This was the first national election in two decades not anchored by Brokaw, Rather, and Jennings, and Williams was acutely aware that the press was casting the event as a big-time showdown between him and his rookie rivals. He knew that the network that won during a big news event acquired a certain cachet that could spill over into the nightly news wars.

Williams had started the day in Connecticut, where he had voted and affixed a label from the polling place to his lapel. That, he felt, was the most important thing he would do all day. He had pored over the briefing books, and he was ready. Williams expected that the Democrats would take the House, and that the theme of the night would be voter anger, but in an election you never really knew how all the subplots might unfold.

The one thing that Williams did not want to do was to make a premature call. He vividly remembered anchoring at MSNBC on the night of the 2000 election and declaring, based on a producer's instructions in his ear, that Al Gore had won Florida. They were in a commercial later on when Williams was told that he would have to retract the call, and his face just dropped. He had been scarred by the experience, even though Brokaw, Rather, and Jennings had made the same blunder on the broadcast networks. And yet, like any anchor, he was dependent on his team, which would be crunching the numbers away from the cameras.

Williams had had no access to exit poll information all day. The National Election Pool, the network consortium that handled the surveys, had been embarrassed by the way the early numbers inevitably leaked to the *Drudge Report* and to various blogs, so the polling team had created what was dubbed the Quarantine Room. Two staff members from each network and the Associated Press were summoned to a windowless room in Manhattan—their laptops, cell phones, and BlackBerrys confiscated—and were barred from communicating with their offices until 5 P.M.

Finally, at 5:30, Capus, Williams, Russert, and the rest of the team huddled in a conference room with Sheldon Gawiser, the head of NBC's decision desk. The exit polls, he explained, seemed seriously skewed toward the Democrats, with some Democratic candidates projected to be so far ahead that it defied common sense. Williams thought that the surveys were trash, utterly useless. There was no House polling in any event, so they would have to make their projections the old-fashioned way, based on analyzing the raw vote totals and comparing them to previous elections. The Democrats needed a pickup of fifteen House seats and six in the Senate to take control of both chambers.

Phil Alongi, a twenty-eight-year NBC veteran, was producing the ten o'clock special. He had never handled an election before, had gotten no sleep, and his stomach was knotted. Williams had sent him an e-mail at 1 A.M., urging him on for the big night.

Alongi took his place in the darkened control room, filled with twenty-seven staffers, all of whom seemed to be talking at once. Twenty-one rows of monitors along the curved front wall were displaying every possible program and video feed. Williams had already done *Nightly News* and four updated versions for the other time zones.

"This will be a history-making midterm election," Williams declared as the special got under way. "We just do not know the extent of it quite yet."

He went to the Virginia race. Republican Senator George Allen was leading Democrat Jim Webb by 29,000 votes, with 85 percent of the precincts reporting. Too close to call. Missouri Senate race, too close to call. Montana Senate race, too close to call. Williams went to Russert, to Brokaw, to Campbell Brown. They were off and running.

The momentum screeched to a halt within minutes, however, when Williams interviewed John McCain and Barack Obama, two senators saying predictable things and shifting the focus from the vote-counting itself. After the interviews Russert decided that the computerized gizmo was too sluggish for his taste and that he would stick with scribbling on his plain old white board.

Capus, who wished that he was producing the event himself, reminded Williams to tell the audience that they were not actually sitting outside in Rockefeller Plaza, despite the picture behind him. Williams said that he had already made the disclaimer.

"I need something to do in the next segment, guys," Alongi told Williams and his team. He decided to order updates in the tightest Senate races—Virginia, Tennessee, Missouri, and Montana. "Then we would like to go back to Mr. Gregory, please. And then I'm going to give you time just for you guys to say goodbye."

At 10:53, during the last commercial break, Sheldon Gawiser, sitting in a third-floor control room, stopped poring over the voting data and made a projection. They had created a statistical model of each district and built in an overall margin of error of plus or minus five seats in trying to gauge which party would prevail. No monitors showing the other networks were allowed in the room, so Gawiser would not be influenced by what his competitors were doing, but there was no doubt in his mind. Gawiser cleared his decision with David McCormick, NBC's head of standards and practices, and then told Phil Alongi, who told Brian Williams in his ear.

One minute later, Williams announced: "We can now confirm our projection that Democrats will control the House of Representatives, 231 to 204."

"We have the first woman speaker in the history of the United States, Nancy Pelosi," Russert said.

NBC was the first network to make the call. Williams had been the one to tell the country that the Democrats would capture the House, just as he had been all but predicting on *Nightly News* for months.

Moments later the special was over, but there was still the question of whether the Democrats could take the Senate by winning all three remaining cliff-hangers. "If the Senate happens, do you want to do a special report?" Alongi asked.

Absolutely, Steve Capus said.

It was almost midnight, and Brian Williams was still on the set, spooning strawberry yogurt from a plastic cup. It had gotten so hot in the studio that he had been fanning himself with his script. John Reiss, the *Nightly* producer, walked over and gave him some news.

"That is such horseshit," Williams said with great exasperation. "We're misplacing our priorities. She's not going to make any news tomorrow."

It was one hour after NBC had projected that the Democrats would take the House, and Nancy Pelosi had sent word that she was willing to be interviewed the next day by the network anchors. Reiss had been told that the California congresswoman would accept no substitutes, meaning that she would not sit down with anyone below the anchor level. That meant the anchors, having worked half the night, would have to race down to Washington, sit down with Pelosi, and broadcast from the capital. Worse, the time that had been allotted for Williams was one in the afternoon, precisely when Bush had scheduled a postelection news conference. Williams was not happy.

While the anchor prepared for the 1 A.M. special, aides scrambled to see if they could charter a jet to Washington right after the program. The more immediate problem was finding a prominent Republican to appear on the West Coast edition. They were all running for cover. Republican Party officials had said that their chairman, Ken Mehlman, would be available for the 10 o'clock show, but then claimed he was on an hour-long conference call. Now, as the results turned from bad to worse for the GOP, party officials said that Mehlman wasn't available because he had left for the night.

Russert told Williams that Jim Webb was now ahead of George Allen by three thousand votes, with 99 percent of the Virginia precincts reporting. Jon Tester had won in Montana, and Claire McCaskill in Missouri, and the

Democrats were now one seat away. If Webb could hang on, they would pull off the improbable feat of winning the Senate as well.

After his daily battles with Dan Bartlett, Russert was feeling vindicated. The results, he felt, were bearing him out. Russert studied polls and called his sources every single day. He worked hard at the political game. He didn't make this shit up.

At 4 A.M., Brian Williams and his crew arrived at a darkened Newark airport. There would be no sleep this night.

* * *

Katie Couric was at a makeshift anchor desk, a spectacular view of the glittering Capitol dome behind her. She was about to tape a segment with Bob Schieffer, who was across town in the bureau, and Lara Logan in Baghdad.

"It's a threesome, Bob, your dream come true," Couric purred. She laughed at her sexual insinuation.

"Are you blushing?"

It was an hour before airtime on the day after the election, and Couric was exhausted but in high spirits, keeping up a constant patter with those around her. She was in a double-wide trailer mounted on the roof of the seven-story Capitol Hill headquarters of the Jones Day law firm, a cluttered tangle of computers, monitors, hanging lights, and cables snaking across the floor, which the network used for its gorgeous backdrop.

Once the tape was rolling, Couric asked her colleagues about the political bombshell that Bush had dropped hours earlier, that he was dumping Donald Rumsfeld at the Pentagon. What did this mean for the conduct of the Iraq war?

Schieffer said that he would be "very surprised if it didn't lead to some sort of withdrawal beginning sometime this year." Logan said the most common reaction among commanders and soldiers was "that this comes three years too late and that it won't change the reality on the ground for the troops here."

When they were done, Rome Hartman said that they would trim Schieffer's first answer. "What about the follow-up question?" Couric asked. "Can we shorten that answer too? Because he kind of repeated himself."

Couric was feeling good, almost giddy. Everything had seemed to fall into place when she anchored CBS's election coverage the night before. For a time, however, the program had seemed headed for failure.

On the Saturday before the election, Couric and her political team had done their second rehearsal for Election Night. They ran through pretend scripts and did mock interviews, with one CBS staffer playing John McCain and another Rahm Emanuel, the head of the House Democratic campaign committee. Couric chatted up their partisan duo, Mike McCurry and Nicolle Wallace, in the first few minutes of the program. Bob Schieffer was limited to two forty-five-second hits.

When it was over, Sean McManus was not happy. The program lacked a sense of urgency. He called his top executives into a conference room.

"This is not the show we're going to be doing on Election Night," he declared.

To a longtime sports producer who was already starting to prepare for the 2007 Super Bowl, it was not unlike covering football. "This is a postgame show," he said. "The first thing people want to know is the score." It was all about telling viewers what happened, why it happened, and what it meant for the country.

McManus told his team to throw out most of the scripts and the choreographed lineup. They had to be more flexible and follow the story wherever it went. They could not go to the correspondents stationed at key campaign headquarters unless there were results in those races. He also decided to junk the scheduled interviews with McCain and Emanuel. It would be better television to just keep reporting and analyzing the returns.

Schieffer questioned why McCurry and Wallace were seated at the anchor desk. He felt they didn't have much to say and that Wallace was just reciting talking points from the White House that she had so recently departed.

"Well, they're not going to be on much," McManus said.

"Then why are they sitting there?" Schieffer asked.

At the Monday rehearsal, McCurry and Wallace had been moved, their first appearance came later in the program, and Schieffer was given a larger role.

Couric was revved up for the big night. She had covered plenty of elections but always the next morning, never in real time. Couric thought of watching some tapes of past Election Nights, on CBS and the other networks, but decided against it. If their goal was to do something fresh and different, she didn't want to be influenced by the past.

What was daunting was that she had never worked with this collection of correspondents and producers on a big breaking story. She had to get a sense of everyone's rhythm to figure out how much they could rock and roll.

When the broadcast began on Tuesday night, Couric was on her game.

She immediately went to "our dean," as she called him, and Schieffer said: "Well, I tell you, Katie, this we knew was going to be a bad night for the Republicans, but it may be shaping up as their worst nightmare." Couric whipped things around—to Gloria Borger, to Sharyl Attkisson, to Lee Cowan, to Anthony Mason, to Jim Axelrod—at a pace that gave the broadcast a jolt of energy.

After ten minutes Couric glanced at the NBC monitor and saw Brian Williams interviewing John McCain. Where couldn't you find McCain these days? She was glad that they had decided to bag the politicians and stick with their own people.

While Couric was not as steeped in politics as Williams and Gibson, she tried to share interesting tidbits about the candidates. Lincoln Chafee and Sheldon Whitehouse, the Senate opponents in Rhode Island, were bluebloods whose fathers had roomed together at Yale. Jon Tester, the Montana Democrat, had lost three fingers in a meat-grinding accident. Jim Webb, the Virginia Democrat, had once described the admission of females to the Naval Academy as "a horny woman's dream." Couric wanted to get across that politics ranged from the sublime to the ridiculous.

Everything seemed to click. Schieffer thought that Katie had been under incredible pressure and had come through when the chips were down.

One thing that Couric did not get to do was announce the Democratic takeover of the House. After NBC made the call at 10:54, and ABC at 10:57, CBS's decision desk did not project a Democratic victory until 11:01, one minute after Couric had gone off the air.

Couric went home after the West Coast special but found herself up early, so she put on the *Today* show. There were Matt Lauer and Meredith Vieira, wearing red cooking smocks and making meatballs with celebrity chef Jamie Oliver. It was like a dream sequence, a flashback to the kind of fluff she had done so many times. The *Today* shtick never changed—it just ran like an endless loop.

Couric and her crew were driven to an airport in Morristown, New Jersey, to catch a chartered jet to Washington, but the flight was delayed by a driving rainstorm. At 1 P.M., when Bush was about to begin his news conference, Couric was in a car, racing from Dulles Airport toward the Washington bureau downtown, so Harry Smith, the *Early Show* cohost, had to anchor the beginning of their special report. Couric arrived during the news conference and handled the wrap-up, then left for her sit-down with Nancy Pelosi. Brian Williams showed up when she was finished.

While Williams was doing the interview, Steve Capus was on the phone with Jeff Zucker. There was so much to cover the day after the election, Capus said, that they wanted an hour for *Nightly News.* Zucker agreed, even though they had not yet checked with the affiliates to see how many would carry the extra half-hour.

Every network was jazzed over the elections. ABC was trumpeting the fact that Charlie Gibson had won the night, drawing 2 million viewers more than Williams had. Gibson had benefited from some fancy footwork. David Westin had been lobbying for days with Anne Sweeney, the network president, in Los Angeles and had gotten last-minute approval to start the special half an hour earlier than the others, at 9:30. The idea was to capitalize on the huge lead-in audience from *Dancing With the Stars.* When executives at the other networks heard about the maneuver, they instantly knew that ABC would prevail.

But Couric scored a moral victory. CBS's coverage finished just 300,000 viewers behind Williams and NBC, an impressive showing for a woman whose newscast was routinely a distant third. The CBS publicity office was crashing on a promo for that night's broadcast, with such blurbs as "Katie Couric proved herself"—*Washington Post.* "Did a particularly good job"— *USA Today.*

Rome Hartman had taken the 6 A.M. Amtrak express to Washington. He bumped into his old colleague Dan Rather on the platform, and they chatted about Rather's appearance the night before on *The Daily Show.* Rather had been there to play along with the gags, and Jon Stewart prodded him into reciting some of his vintage Rather-isms. Rather said that the segment had been fun. Had the National Guard story not blown up on him, he still might have been anchoring CBS's coverage.

Soon after Couric got to the double-wide trailer, Hartman told her it was time to record the headlines. "I'm Katie Couric in Washington," she said. "Tonight, casualties of war. Republicans are swept out of the House. The man running the war is ousted. But the president tells America's enemies, tells Iraqis, tells Americans in uniform—I don't know, I'm not hearing this right." Couric and Hartman, who was crammed into the far corner of the trailer, fiddled with the wording.

John Batiste, the retired general whom Couric had tried to book weeks earlier, arrived in the trailer for an interview. He asked whether he should look at the camera when he was introduced. "You should just look at me," Couric said. "I always think that looks cheesy: Hi!" She made an exaggerated face. "Like you're on *Hollywood Squares.*"

They were ready to go, but Couric was having hair issues. "Can I just check to see if I have flyaways?" she asked.

"I'm seeing a flyaway on that single shot, really sticking up and catching the light," Hartman said.

"Don't worry, we'll get it together," Couric told Batiste with a giggle.

The cameras rolled, and Couric asked Batiste a series of questions about Rumsfeld's firing.

"You don't think Donald Rumsfeld can be trusted?"

"What made him, in your opinion, such a weak secretary of Defense?"

"I don't mean to belabor this, General, but where did Donald Rumsfeld go wrong?"

The retired general was being diplomatic and deflecting the questions into broader discussions of Iraq strategy. But Couric didn't give up. She would feed him the language if she had to.

"Sounds to me that you're saying he was arrogant."

"Arrogant, dismissive," Batiste said. "Would have been a great peacetime secretary of Defense, perfect, but in wartime he was the wrong person."

With half an hour to go before the broadcast, Couric's hairdresser applied the curlers and blow-dryer. Once the styling was done, Couric practiced reading the lead-in to a story about the hanging-by-a-thread Virginia Senate race: "If Allen hangs on, it will be fifty-fifty, with Vice President Cheney breaking the tie."

Hartman tweaked it: "If Allen hangs on, the GOP hangs on."

Minutes later Jimmy Reyes, a wealthy Washington beer distributor who was regularly dating Couric, made his way into the back of the trailer. Couric shouted hello from the anchor desk.

The newscast began without a glitch. In the interview with Nancy Pelosi, the networks' first female solo anchor asked her about the significance of becoming the first female House speaker.

During the next break, Couric mocked the tease she was supposed to read for an upcoming series, "Aging in the Shadows."

"It's sort of like, why don't we do another series with a cheesy title?" Couric said with a grin.

In the final moments, Hartman suggested that she say something while signing off about how it had been an incredible day here in Washington.

"I'm too tired," Couric said. "I just don't want to flub and ruin a good show."

When she was finished, several crew members applauded. Couric slipped off her mike and joined Jimmy Reyes in the back of the trailer. She looked exhausted and exhilarated, as if she had just run a marathon.

The next afternoon George Allen, trailing by fewer than nine thousand votes, conceded defeat in Virginia, giving the Democrats control of the Senate by the slimmest of margins.

For much of the year, the evening newscasts had been strongly suggesting, even forecasting, that a big Democratic victory was taking shape, and now they had been proven right. Whether network news and the rest of the establishment media helped frame the debate in the Democrats' favor, or simply mirrored the growing anger in the country, was hard to say.

What was clear, though, was that the networks and the White House had been offering the country starkly different versions of reality for quite some time. In the days after Hurricane Katrina struck, Bush and his team had defended the federal government's response while Brian Williams, near the stench of the Superdome, bluntly declared that people were suffering and dying because the cavalry had never arrived. As the sectarian warfare intensified in Iraq, administration officials blamed television for playing into the terrorists' hands by playing up the violence, while the reporting of Lara Logan, Richard Engel, and others made clear that American soldiers were being overwhelmed by the deadly chaos. As congressional Republicans insisted that stories about corruption were isolated and overblown, Brian Ross revealed not just that Mark Foley was sexually soliciting former pages but that House GOP leaders had received ample warning about his predatory behavior and done little to stop it.

There was more than a whiff of advocacy as one story after another painted a dire picture in Iraq and an equally dire picture of the Republicans' political fortunes, but then, the administration and its allies seemed increasingly in denial on both fronts. For Bush to watch his party swept from power on the Hill and to fire Don Rumsfeld the next day confirmed that things were worse than he had acknowledged in war and in politics, and closer to the portrait carried by network news.

That night Brian Williams and Charlie Gibson led their newscasts with the Democrats cementing their control of both sides of Capitol Hill. But Katie Couric had a different lead story.

Ed Bradley, the *60 Minutes* veteran and one of the pioneering black journalists on television, died that day. Couric not only bumped the Democrats' Senate victory from the top of the show, she devoted half the newscast to mourning the passing of a colleague. On this day, for her, the personal had trumped the political.

CHAPTER 31

War Over Words

Brian Williams was more than ready to declare civil war.

But he didn't like the way the war plan was carried out.

For months Williams and the reporters and analysts on *Nightly* had been talking about whether Iraq was sliding toward civil war. Robert Wright, the NBC president, had become frustrated with all the on-air hedging. He decided to circulate an e-mail to the news division, asking whether the time had come to use the term that everyone had been dancing around.

For Steve Capus, the final straw came on Thanksgiving Day 2006, when more than two hundred Shiites in the slums of Sadr City were killed in a coordinated wave of car bombings, missiles, and mortar attacks. The phrase "sectarian violence" no longer seemed to capture the magnitude of the warfare. Capus asked that the question be put to a range of experts.

Jeff Zucker, who had been following the debate, sent a note to Alexandra Wallace, Capus's deputy: Whatever happened to that discussion about civil war? Are you guys going to do it?

Williams agreed that the network had to decide whether it was time to drop the qualifiers. The day after Thanksgiving he asked Wallace: "When will we call this thing what it is?"

Wallace was filling in for Capus, who was in Philadelphia, tending to his ailing mother in the last days of her fight against lung cancer. Williams suggested a list of experts for their consultations: Barry McCaffrey, the retired general and NBC analyst, who was already using the terminology, and another retired general and NBC consultant, Wayne Downing. Historians Doris Kearns Goodwin, David McCullough, and Richard Norton Smith. Richard Engel, who argued that the Arab media had regarded the conflict as a civil war for some time. There were calls back and forth over the weekend. John Reiss, the *Nightly* producer, was involved, and Jim Bell, *Today*'s executive producer, was pushing for the designation. The unanimous verdict was that "civil war" was an accurate description of the carnage in Iraq.

On Sunday Wallace sent Capus an e-mail outlining the consensus. Capus cautioned that they had to explain their decision to the viewers. They did not have editor's notes, as newspapers did, and couldn't start using the term out of the blue. Under the plan, Matt Lauer would be the first to weigh in, on *Today*.

Dan Bartlett's BlackBerry began to ping on Sunday night with requests for comment from NBC. He decided there was no percentage in picking a fight over terminology.

On Monday morning Lauer made the announcement in rather portentous fashion. "For months now, the White House has rejected claims that the situation in Iraq has deteriorated into civil war," he said, and NBC had "hesitated" to challenge that assertion. "But after careful consideration, NBC News has decided a change in terminology is warranted."

This stirred up quite a fuss—among White House correspondents, on talk radio, on the blogs—and MSNBC spent much of the day ginning up a debate over its use of the C-word.

It seemed a self-conscious attempt to replicate the moment in 1968 when Walter Cronkite returned from Vietnam and pronounced the war a stalemate. But that verdict from America's most trusted man, in an era when a television anchor could hold that designation, was based on first-hand reporting, while NBC's maneuver was simply a linguistic confirmation of what most Americans already believed to be the case. Of course the slaughter among revenge-minded Sunnis and Shiites amounted to some kind of civil war, despite the administration's refusal to use the term. On *The Daily Show,* Jon Stewart began mockingly referring to Iraq as a "Lauer-certified civil war," complete with a *Good Housekeeping*–style seal.

Brian Williams felt that the news division should not have treated the semantic shift as a major policy pronouncement. They often made changes to the network stylebook—and had long ago stopped using terms like "homosexual lifestyle" and "pro-life"—without any fanfare. By trumpeting the move, Williams believed, they had made themselves the center of attention and invited the criticism that followed.

After returning from a Pennsylvania memorial service for Jeannie Capus, Williams took a low-key approach that evening on *Nightly*. He said that it would be a "crucial week" for American involvement "in what has become a civil war in that country," and he had Andrea Mitchell point out that other news organizations had already been using the term.

In the Fishbowl at CBS, Rome Hartman brushed off the Lauer declaration as a gimmick. It was a political statement, he felt, not a news judgment.

At ABC, Charlie Gibson thought it was a lot of fuss over nothing. It was late in the game for that sort of thing. His network had been using the term occasionally for some time. The idea of NBC making an official declaration was silly.

But the rival news divisions found themselves reacting to NBC's move, even as they studiously avoided mentioning it, because the White House had been forced to react. A network news division still had the power to change the national conversation.

"You can call it anarchy, you can call it chaos, you can call it civil war," Gibson said. "Whatever you call it, the events of recent days demonstrate that the situation in Iraq is at a critical juncture."

"The Bush administration is still not calling it a civil war," Katie Couric said, "but national security adviser Stephen Hadley today gave the most ominous assessment yet of the violence in Iraq."

Couric and Hartman had reached a decision before the broadcast: They would fly to Jordan the next night to cover Bush's summit meeting with the Iraqi prime minister, Nouri al-Maliki. Couric thought it was important to show the network flag at such a major event. She was not sure whether she could arrange any big interviews, but figured the only way to find out was to fly to Amman and give it a shot.

Since Brian Williams and Charlie Gibson were also making the trip, Couric's first foreign foray for CBS was shaping up as an important test. Fortunately for Couric, she had struck up a friendship with Jordan's Queen Rania when she had visited Amman for *Today,* and the two had tea whenever the queen was in New York. Couric worked her Jordanian contacts in trying to line up an interview with Maliki. After landing at 5 P.M. local time, she spent the evening interviewing Iraqi refugees and the U.S. ambassador to Iraq before doing the broadcast in the middle of the night. Couric got to bed at 4 A.M.

At 9:30 a producer woke her with word that she might have a chance at getting Maliki if they headed to Amman's military air base, where the prime minister, who had finished his breakfast meeting with Bush, was doing a scheduled half-hour sit-down with Gibson. It was a fairly audacious move, trying to horn in on a rival's exclusive with a head of state.

When they walked into a reception room at the small VIP terminal,

Maliki, seated on a sofa, had just wrapped up his session with Gibson. He did not recognize Couric and did not seem willing to sit for another American television interview. But the Iraqi foreign minister, Hoshyar Zebari, interceded on her behalf, persuading Maliki to give Couric a few minutes. She saw that the ABC producers looked crestfallen.

Gibson, though, could not have been more gracious to his longtime morning rival. "My people are really upset," he said. "I told them, 'Don't worry, good for Katie.' "

Couric had fifteen minutes to ask the prime minister whether he was worried that American support for his government was slipping. Gibson's interview was far more newsworthy; Maliki had told him he could bring the violence under control by June 2007 if Bush would give him greater authority over the security forces. But Couric, at least, had gotten in the game.

That afternoon Couric drove to the Dead Sea Marriott to interview Condoleezza Rice. The secretary of state was running late, so Couric was part of a small group, including Brian Williams, who made small talk as they waited. Couric considered it a coup that she was the only anchor to have gotten both Maliki and Rice.

With Iraq appearing to descend into chaos, meeting the country's top leaders was an education for Couric. She had always felt uncomfortable with the war, and sometimes that showed in the way she framed the story. She kept booking interviews with prominent figures who had turned against the conflict—Democratic lawmakers such as Jack Murtha and Carl Levin; John Batiste, the retired general; Ken Adelman, a former Rumsfeld confidant who had turned on him; and Tom Friedman of *The New York Times.*

When Bush had been marshaling support for the invasion, Couric felt, the country seemed to be swept up in a patriotic furor and a palpable sense of fear. There was a rush to war, no question about it. She could never quite figure out how Iraq became Public Enemy Number 1, or how the United States wound up making many of the same mistakes as in Vietnam. She was happy, like most people, when the war initially seemed to be going well. Nobody wanted to see all these young kids getting killed. But the frenzied march to war had been bolstered by a reluctance to question the administration after 9/11, and Couric believed that the climate was poisonous.

She had firsthand experience with what she considered the chilling effect on the media. Two months before the 2004 election, Couric had asked Condoleezza Rice on *Today* whether she agreed with Dick Cheney's declaration that the country would be at greater risk for terrorist attacks if John

Kerry won the White House. Rice sidestepped the question, saying that any president had to fight aggressively against terrorism.

Couric interrupted and asked the question again. Would a Kerry victory put America at greater risk? Rice ducked again, saying that the issue should not be personalized.

Soon afterward Couric got an e-mail from Bob Wright. The NBC president was forwarding a message from an Atlanta woman who complained that Couric had been too confrontational with Rice. Wright had thanked the woman for writing.

What was the message here? Couric felt that Wright must be telling her to back off. She decided to write him a note. She said that she tried to be persistent and elicit good answers in all her interviews, regardless of the political views of her guests. If Wright had a problem with that, she would like to discuss it with him personally.

Wright wrote back that such protest letters usually came in batches, but that he had passed along this one because it seemed different.

Couric was troubled. There was, she felt, a subtle, insidious pressure to toe the party line, and you bucked that at your peril. She wanted to believe that her NBC colleagues were partners in the search for truth, but that was clearly not the case. She knew that the corporate management viewed her as an out-and-out liberal. When she ran into Jack Welch, the General Electric chairman, he would sometimes say that they had never seen eye to eye politically. The whole attitude was pretty disturbing. If you weren't rah rah rah for the Bush administration and the war, you were considered unpatriotic, even treasonous.

Couric believed that many viewers were now suffering from Iraq fatigue. She tried not to lead with the conflict every night, unless there were significant developments. And when the day's Iraq events were too big to ignore, Couric made clear—in starker terms than the other anchors—her disgust with the whole enterprise. One night she began, "With each death, with every passing day, so many of us ask, 'Is there any way out of this nightmare?' "

The visit to Jordan seemed to symbolize a transformation that had been slowly gathering force at the broadcast. No one would admit it, at least not in public. But step by incremental step, CBS was abandoning the very changes that Katie Couric had brought to the *Evening News*.

The network never announced that it was all but pulling the plug on "Free Speech," the sound-off segment that had become shorthand for a lack of

commitment to news. Suddenly, two weeks went by without a single install-
ment. Finally Rome Hartman tried to salvage the concept by saying that the
segments would run once a week or so and would focus more on average
folks. Hartman knew that most of his correspondents detested the segment, because they felt that pure opinion had no place on the broadcast and
was sucking up the oxygen that they needed to get on the air.

"Snapshots," the periodic roundup of interesting images, faded to black.
So did the summary of offbeat items that were hot on the Web. Couric felt
that these brief segments had gotten a little gimmicky and were too often
using second-rate material. Hartman even stopped opening the show with
Couric taking a step forward to a brief burst of music, instead having her
read the opening headlines at the anchor desk.

What was left was something closer to a traditional newscast. Couric was
spending more time chatting with her reporters and with newsmakers and
experts. Hartman began having correspondents file thirty- and forty-second
reports and running three of them back to back. As the experiments and
cutesy stuff withered, except for the occasional interview with a Michael J.
Fox, the nutritional content of the program grew. There was more news in
the *CBS Evening News.*

Sean McManus felt that they had run too many features in the first few
weeks and was encouraging the harder direction. He would often e-mail
Couric, or call Hartman, with suggestions about clearer, more definitive
writing—using "today," "tonight," "new medical study," anything to create
a sense of urgency. He asked them to tease stories from the following night
after seeing research that the average viewer watched only once a week.

The Couric team still had a tendency to blow off major stories. When
Rupert Murdoch's News Corporation announced that it was publishing a
book by O.J. Simpson called *If I Did It*—a sickening but hypothetical discussion of the two murders that much of the country believed he committed—and would air a Fox television special, Brian Williams jumped on the
appalling spectacle that night. Charlie Gibson did it the next night. But
Couric, who had interviewed Simpson twice on the *Today* show, argued that
the project was so sleazy that anything they did would amount to an
infomercial for Fox. Hartman agreed that they should not become part of the
hype machine.

Other Fishbowl producers argued that everyone was talking about the
controversy and that they could do a piece that made their disapproval
clear. Couric, however, found the whole thing so distasteful that she

announced to viewers, "We didn't think that was worth your time or ours." Instead, she introduced a "Free Speech" essay by a woman who worked for a domestic violence hotline. But this quickly proved to be a head-in-the-sand approach. When a wave of public revulsion forced Murdoch to cancel the Simpson book and prime-time special, the *Evening News* covered the decision along with the rest of the media.

On some nights Couric would hit it out of the park—reporting from Fort Stewart, Georgia, for instance, and leading with a world exclusive from David Martin about a U.S. missile strike against al-Qaeda terrorists in Somalia. But most of the broadcasts were decidedly ordinary.

Couric kept pushing for more medical segments and reported a number of them herself, on back pain, on obesity, on hormone therapy. She fervently believed that a newscast couldn't be only about what happened today, that it had to plug into issues that mattered in people's lives.

Whatever editorial choices she made, the negative reviews mounted. McManus was surprised by the degree of vitriol aimed at Couric in the press. Some of the columnists couldn't wait for her to fail. They seemed to feel that her *Today* show experience was insufficient and that she didn't deserve to be an evening news anchor.

As they tinkered with the format, Couric and her colleagues got no credit from the press for trying new approaches and discarding what didn't work. Couric grew frustrated as they groped for the right formula. How did you come up with something new and innovative without alienating your most loyal viewers?

Rome Hartman reluctantly reached the conclusion that they had moved too quickly, that the nightly news audience was uneasy with too much change at one time. He also came to believe that many viewers were uncomfortable getting their news from a woman, at least at night. But that could change if they found a way to lure new viewers who lacked that particular hang-up. For all their difficulties, the answer was not to go back to the same show that the boys were doing. The arrow was pointing south on the old, traditional newscast, and there had to be a better way.

In an effort to reverse the tide, Hartman sent McManus and other executives a memo outlining a major bureaucratic reorganization at the broadcast.

"We want to have a powerful team focused full-time on asking these questions: What should we be launching *right now* that will make tomorrow's broadcast better than our competition?" he asked. "What's that great story we ought to be doing for Friday that's going to end the week with a bang? What ground-breaking series can we launch today that will be smart, original, and attention-getting next month?"

The following day Couric had the half-dozen Fishbowl executives over to her Upper East Side apartment for coffee and pastries. She wanted a chance to talk, away from the phones. Couric told them that they could all do better. They kept coming up with story ideas that sounded great but were never executed. What they needed was better research, people who were willing to roll up their sleeves, work the phones, and sniff out the latest trends. They should dig into these story pitches and figure out which ones were good enough to put on the air.

Even the correspondents and producers who were dissatisfied with the broadcast's direction had to admit that CBS News had long been a dysfunctional family. Some people who had been there since the glory days of the Tiffany Network would bitch no matter who the anchor was.

Brian Williams got the word that things were not happy at his old network. At one event, a former NBC producer who had joined CBS confided to Williams that she was miserable as part of the Couric team. A former CBS News staffer e-mailed Williams with the latest rumor that Rome Hartman was on his way out. "Everything has to be done on what is called Katie time," this person wrote, describing how Couric would complain about the way she was being lit or shot.

But others at CBS felt that the network, after being saddled for a decade with the smallest news team, was finally beginning to make headway. The flip side to running fewer stories by the correspondents each night, in this view, was that they were being given more time to report and refine in-depth pieces.

Jim Axelrod felt that some nights were better than others. They were not yet firing on all eight cylinders. It was no surprise, he believed, that at the outset some people had said, *Wait a minute, we need a little more news here.*

Byron Pitts was more optimistic, but he was frustrated that they had gone out and hired a superstar quarterback and still weren't gaining any yardage. CBS had done a tremendous amount of planning for Couric's arrival, but clearly, Pitts believed, the accumulated problems at the network were not going to be fixed overnight. He was reminded of what Mike Tyson used to say: *Everyone has a plan until they get hit in the mouth.*

They suffered another blow in the first week of 2007. The ratings showed not only that Brian Williams was beating Couric by nearly 2.5 million viewers but that Charlie Gibson was ahead by 2 million. In some weeks she had fallen behind the audience that Bob Schieffer had been drawing a year earlier. The broadcast was now losing ground, especially among the senior citizens who formed the core of the nightly audience.

"We've got to do what we can to get some of these older viewers back," Sean McManus told another top executive. He began asking colleagues whether returning to the harder-edged broadcast of the Schieffer days would boost the ratings.

McManus wanted to make sure that Couric didn't get down about the negative press and kept repeating, like a mantra, that it had taken Tom Brokaw thirteen years to take *Nightly News* to the top. "As difficult as it is to do," he told Couric, "forget what they're writing. The only control we have over the situation is what we put on the air."

Les Moonves, who had courted the new anchor so ardently, was getting a bit discouraged. He did not like being stuck in third place and had stopped reading most of the press coverage. Moonves felt that there was a prejudice against female anchors, jealousy of Couric's salary, a feeling that her morning talents were antithetical to what was needed at night, and a perception—unfair, in his view—that Couric was biased to the left. But Moonves had seen in CBS's own research a problem that was not so easy to dismiss. Some viewers were not comfortable getting their news from a woman. And more women than men fell into this category. Moonves was surprised to learn that it was a significant percentage. But he gave Couric positive feedback during their occasional lunches and meetings.

Moonves expected that her ratings would gradually improve over the next year, but at least they were making modest gains among younger viewers. Relying too heavily on the over-sixty crowd meant marching toward obsolescence. For the moment Moonves was confident that his big investment would ultimately pay off.

Couric had expected an uphill struggle and, when she initially stormed into first place, she felt that CBS executives had been too quick to see her as a magic bullet. She had lost track of the number of people who had come up to her and said, I loved you on *Today* but I can never watch you at night. Many of her younger fans were still working at 6:30 or were busy with their kids. They no longer had time for her or the evening news ritual itself.

But the inescapable reality was that many others had checked out her first few shows and never returned. What if the problem was her tone, her often bubbly approach, which had worked so well on a rollicking morning show?

What if that was fatally undercutting her image as a serious presenter of the news? What if viewers just didn't find her convincing as an evening news anchor?

Some CBS staffers, even those who were critical of Couric, felt sorry for her. Others found her personally charming, liked the way she had made an effort to learn everyone's name, but blamed her for the show's direction, which they saw as Katie sucking up too much of the airtime and squeezing out important news. The numbers backed them up: In the last four months of 2006 Couric reported 103 stories on her own, one more than Brian Williams had done during the entire year.

The bosses were in a bubble, these staffers felt. Some saw Sean McManus as a sports guy who did not seem inclined to listen to the news professionals at CBS. This would end badly, and since Katie was untouchable, they figured, Rome Hartman would be the fall guy.

As the tension mounted, Couric began asking for more advice and offering to take correspondents to lunch. She seemed rattled, her confidence shaken.

Her workload was taking a personal toll as well. Whenever her cell phone rang, she would quickly check to see if it was her children's nanny. Carrie and Ellie watched the broadcast most nights, and sometimes they would discuss the war and other issues over dinner. But the schedule was proving difficult. Couric had been unable to attend parents' night at their school, because it ran from 5:30 to 7:30, when she was crashing the newscast. She was trying to decide whether to go to Cotillion, the ball at Ellie's school. If she went, she had to dance with Ellie, who might be mortified, but if she didn't show up, she would be wracked by guilt. Nothing was more important than her girls, and despite her fame and wealth, she wanted them to have a normal life. Now that she was carrying the burdens of an entire news division, juggling her job and single parenthood was harder than ever.

*   *   *

Elizabeth Vargas was pleasantly surprised when she returned to the newsroom.

It was just over a month after she had given birth to her second son, Samuel, on the one-year anniversary of Peter Jennings's death and the shooting of her husband. She brought the baby to the *World News* offices, along with his nurse. The staff had gotten her a big bouquet of flowers, and she saw a poetic aspect to the moment: They were getting to see, in the flesh, what had rocked her world. After all, if she had not gotten pregnant, she might still be in the anchor chair.

Vargas had just returned to work full time, and her first piece for *20/20* had been pegged to her own heartache in leaving *World News*. Now Vargas was filling in for Charlie Gibson for the first time since she had been dumped from the newscast the previous May. Gibson had sent her a nice note, saying it had been good for the program for her to be back in the chair. It felt surprisingly comfortable to Vargas, and easier than when she had had to stick around until 10 for the West Coast update.

But it was a long day nonetheless, and Vargas now had to admit to herself what she had forcefully denied six months earlier. Perhaps David Westin had been right. She could not imagine being the *World News* anchor while also dealing with Zachary and Samuel. She had forgotten how exhausting it was to cope with a new baby. Vargas still hoped to get another shot at the anchor chair one day, but for now, the woman who had fought like hell to keep her high-pressure job felt fortunate to have relinquished it.

*   *   *

Steve Capus was horrified when he began attending General Electric budgeting sessions in the spring of 2006, soon after taking over the news division. Here he had been thinking of NBC News as a great success story, number one in the morning, in the evening, and on Sunday, but it quickly became clear that declining revenues would force them to make fundamental changes in the way they organized things. It was nothing short of depressing. Capus began to speak of NBC as a "legacy business," an old-media relic compared to the digital delivery of news to Web sites and mobile phones.

The first of the GE budget meetings, known as S-1, had convened on the fifty-second floor of the network's skyscraper with Bob Wright; Jeff Zucker; Randy Falco, the chief operating officer of the NBC Universal Television Group; and other executives. Capus made a proposal to save money by merging the operations of NBC News and MSNBC, which would involve closing the cable channel's campus in Secaucus, New Jersey, where Brian Williams had anchored his cable show, and transferring everything to 30 Rock. The plan was under consideration for a while, then taken off the table, then resurrected in time for the S-2 budget meeting. Finally, in October, Capus had pitched the idea to Jeffrey Immelt, the GE chairman, and it was ultimately approved.

There was more pain to come. Jeff Zucker imposed a 5 percent budget cut on every division of the network. Layoffs were clearly inevitable, and Capus was determined to rein in the salaries of the correspondents, some of whom made $300,000, or $600,000, even as much as $800,000.

Williams was not especially worried. Capus was his pal, his control room buddy. They usually talked on Sundays about mundane family matters and, in the fall and winter, about football. They had been in the trenches together, dating back to their days in Philadelphia, before Steve was elevated to the executive suite.

"If this ever hurts, I expect you to stand up and yell," Capus told him.

Jeff Immelt made sure to meet with his anchor. They lived near each other in Connecticut, and Williams had bought his Manhattan apartment in the same East 50s building where Immelt lived. He was the big boss, but he had also become a friend.

"This is more about the third- and fourth-string weather people at our owned stations," Immelt said. "If you think the news is starting to be affected by any of this—if you start to *feel* these cost savings in what you do for a living—you tell me."

In the end Williams dodged a financial bullet. *Nightly* lost only one producer.

*   *   *

In the weeks after the election Dan Bartlett felt that he was fighting a losing battle. For all his hectoring—he would send reporters e-mail complaints at 6:30 in the morning, shortly after arriving at his West Wing office—the media narrative was set. Bush was in a bubble. He didn't listen. They had their heads in the sand.

The coverage of the war was endlessly frustrating for Bartlett. On any given day the networks could, and did, air footage of some suicide attack to show how bad things were in Iraq. Bartlett would hear from one network or another about a correspondent who had risked his or her life to go out and report a good-news story, about a school that was thriving, or a program that was working. Then it would get held for weeks and never show up on the air. But the footage of an attack that some Iraqi stringer had brought back was guaranteed to run.

What the newscasts were doing, Bartlett believed, was oversimplifying things, casting the president as being in denial about the carnage in Iraq and trying to sell the country a bill of goods. That was the story line: *"On a day when fourteen car bombs went off, the president unbelievably tried to say we are winning . . ."*

Of course things were tough in Iraq, they all recognized that. Far from being insulated, Bush lived with it every minute of every day. What the networks failed to recognize, in Bartlett's view, was that it was one thing for reporters and pundits to opine about how badly the war was going, and far different for the commander in chief to do so. Bush had to keep in mind that he was speaking to multiple audiences: Our troops. The Iraqi insurgents. The American people. Our coalition partners. He had to worry about morale, had to calibrate his language carefully.

Sure, they had made mistakes. The president had sometimes blurted out things that gave the media more fodder. Cheney had assured Tim Russert before the war that we would be "greeted as liberators." But Bush was not going to throw up his hands and say this was all for naught, was not going to express doubts about the ultimate outcome.

Bartlett was struck by the litany that Russert recited on *Meet the Press* when he was interviewing Steve Hadley, the national security adviser.

"Could the president step forward and say, 'I acknowledge we were wrong about WMD, we were wrong about troop levels, we were wrong about the length of the war, we were wrong about the cost of the war, we were wrong about the financing of the war, we were wrong about the level of sectarian violence, we were wrong about being greeted as liberators. We made some fundamental misjudgments, and they were wrong, but now we're all in this together'? Could he do that?"

That was the prevailing media mindset, that the war had been a terrible mistake and the chances of success were practically nil. And Russert seemed to have convinced everyone at NBC of that view.

As Bartlett saw it, Bob Schieffer had turned against the war even earlier, while he was anchor, and was even more opinionated than Russert on the air. Bartlett had monitored what Schieffer was saying in radio appearances and in his *Face the Nation* commentaries. He wondered whether the wounding of Kimberly Dozier and the death of her two crew members had taken a psychological toll on CBS and its view of the war. ABC, he felt, was the closest to being even-handed, which Bartlett saw as reflecting Charlie Gibson's straightforward style and Jon Banner's approach as well.

The tensions were bubbling over in the White House pressroom, where Tony Snow was taking on David Gregory in unusually personal terms.

Snow's genial, talk show style, honed at Fox News, belied his tendency to bluntly challenge the motivation of reporters asking tough questions. And day after day, Gregory was the most aggressive of the correspondents in pressing the president's spokesman about new information that administration officials themselves harbored severe doubts about the debacle in Iraq.

When *The New York Times* obtained a preelection memo in which Don Rumsfeld admitted that the war effort was "not working well enough or fast enough" and outlined such options as redeploying some U.S. troops, Gregory asked Snow: "So why wasn't the president leveling with the American people? Why wasn't he saying publicly what top members of this administration who were running the war were saying privately?"

They went at it again when the bipartisan Iraq Study Group proposed a possible redeployment of troops, who would shift to a role of training the Iraqi forces.

Gregory summarized the panel's findings: "The cochairs say the following: 'Stay the course' is no longer viable. The current approach is not working. The situation is grave and deteriorating. Chairman Hamilton says he is not sure whether the situation can be turned around. Can this report be seen as anything other than a rejection of this president's handling of the war?"

Snow bristled at Gregory's approach. "You need to understand that trying to frame it in a partisan way is actually at odds with what the group itself says it wanted to do," he said.

Gregory sensed what was happening. He believed that the White House had a strategy of trying to make *him* the issue, as a way of deflecting aggressive questions and casting the daily briefings as a freakish sideshow. That would set off a predictable reaction in the right-wing media and shift the focus from the administration's conduct to the behavior of the press corps. He had been through this with Scott McClellan, and Snow was so much smoother at playing this particular game. Gregory had decided that the best way to deal with this strategy was to call attention to what the press secretary was doing.

"I just want to be clear," he told Snow. "Are you suggesting that I'm trying to frame this in a partisan way?"

"Yes," Snow said.

"You are? Why? Based on the fact that—"

"Because what—"

"Wait a minute. Wait a second. Based on quoting the report and the chairmen, and I'm asking you a straight question which you're not answering straight. You're actually—you're trying to answer it by nitpicking it."

Gregory believed that Snow was playing to what was left of the Republican base by trying to pillory him as the embodiment of an unfair liberal media. Gregory was no shrinking violet, and perhaps he interrupted and annoyed Snow, but he did not believe he was playing to the cameras. This was serious stuff. They were in the middle of a fucking war, more than 2,900 American kids were dead, and it was his job to press the White House for answers about a faltering strategy.

Snow, for his part, had just come out of a meeting with James Baker and the other commissioners, who were very upbeat about how they all needed to work together to solve the crisis. Now Gregory was trying to use the report to beat them over the head and accuse them of being a bunch of idiots. Of course the Iraq strategy wasn't working. Everyone knew it wasn't working. But Gregory's use of the phrase "stay the course" had set him off, since Bush had dropped that terminology a couple of months earlier. Snow felt badly that he had started up their feud again. If he had it to do over again, he would probably have answered the question differently.

What happened next was exactly what Gregory predicted. Video of the exchange was posted on *YouTube,* and the anchors at Fox News repeatedly took aim at Gregory.

"NBC News has taken a dramatic turn to the left in pursuit of liberal viewers," Bill O'Reilly declared on the highest-rated cable news show. "Mr. Gregory is a partisan. He has come to the conclusion that Iraq is a loser. While Gregory may be correct, using loaded questions to bolster his point of view is not what straight news reporting is about."

But Fox seemed to have little interest in straight reporting when it came to Gregory. The morning show *Fox & Friends* flashed the headline "Grouchy Gregory," and cohost Brian Kilmeade said: "It's all about David Gregory. It's never about the issue with that guy. . . . He wants to be famous." Never mind that Gregory had asked about the substance of the Baker report. Kilmeade also said, without offering a shred of evidence, that Gregory had wanted Al Gore and John Kerry to win the White House. The program then posted its question: "Should NBC Ditch David?"

Brian Williams had been with his wife, coming out of Martin Short's Broadway play *Fame Becomes Me,* when he got word on his BlackBerry about O'Reilly's attack on David Gregory. Williams thought Tony Snow's conduct had been outrageous. Gregory had only been quoting from the report, and that had somehow been twisted into a "partisan" attack?

Williams later called Gregory to offer moral support. He said it had been hard sitting at home and watching various cable types hurling unfair accusations at Gregory.

The problem, in Williams's view, was that Gregory stood out in the

White House press corps, and not just because of his six-foot-five frame. He was the only reporter constantly banging on senior administration officials. In this era when pushy journalists could be painted as ideologically driven, Gregory needed some reinforcements. That, Williams felt, might help people to understand that the system actually worked better when journalists were pressing the country's leaders.

As the controversy continued to simmer, Tony Snow came to believe that he had gone too far in essentially accusing David Gregory of being a spokesman for the Democrats. That, he felt, had been too harsh. He walked over to the NBC booth in the White House pressroom and told Gregory that he regretted what he had said, and felt he should make amends in public. At the next briefing, when Gregory rose to ask a question, Snow said: "I've thought a lot about that, and I was wrong. So I want to apologize and tell you I'm sorry for it."

It was a rare admission by a White House that remained on a war footing with the networks.

*   *   *

Sometimes the Iraq war was too graphic for network television.

When Lara Logan filed a report on the gruesome violence that had gripped Baghdad's notorious Haifa Street, Rome Hartman refused to put it on the *Evening News.* There was footage of dead Iraqi soldiers, who appeared to have been shot multiple times, some at close range. Logan had also obtained video of the bodies of Sunni residents who appeared to have been tortured, and locals were telling her this was done by the Iraqi army. All this was too raw for a television audience, Hartman felt, and he had editorial concerns about the thrust of the piece as well. Since a young aid worker had been killed in Iraq, there was no room for Logan's two-minute report anyway, so Hartman had it posted on CBS's Web site.

Logan and Hartman often had shouting matches over her scripts from Iraq, but she felt that he was one of her biggest supporters. In this case, though, Logan understood what she was up against. The entire American media establishment, she believed, was too squeamish about covering Iraq. People fucking died in wars, and it wasn't pretty. Logan was passionate about this point because she spent so much time with the soldiers.

In frustration, Logan sent an e-mail to some friends and relatives, complaining that her story was "largely being ignored."

"Our crew had to be pulled out because we got a call saying they were about to be killed, and on their way out, a civilian man was shot dead in front of them as they ran.

"I would be very grateful if any of you have a chance to watch this story and pass the link on to as many people you know as possible. It should be seen. And people should know about this.

"If anyone has time to send a comment to CBS—about the story—not about my request, then that would help highlight that people are interested and this is not too gruesome to air, but rather too important to ignore."

The e-mail wound up on a site called *MediaChannel.org* and spread across the Net like a virus. The Haifa Street report was posted on *YouTube*. Some bloggers said that Logan was trying to pressure her network into airing the piece. She felt stupid for having sent the e-mail but also believed that someone had violated her trust. She wasn't trying to bludgeon CBS into running the story. She just wanted the video to get plenty of hits, which would amount to some kind of vindication.

What was really troubling was that some bloggers were accusing Logan of having obtained the torture pictures from a terrorist group affiliated with al-Qaeda. Logan certainly would have mentioned if it had come from some organized group, but in this case the video had come from a person who had risked his life to provide it. She complained to a CBS colleague about the wild charges thrown around by bloggers. "Why am I accountable to these fucking idiots whose lives aren't at risk?" Logan asked.

Covering Iraq was a constant journalistic battle. She had gotten a weekend piece on the air about the wounding and killing of young Iraqi children, and an editor had asked her to tone it down for re-airing the following morning, and not show the blood on the steps of a school where two mortars had ripped through the classrooms, killing five students. Lara Logan was determined to capture the ugly reality of this horrifying civil war. Sometimes she had to fend off requests from New York for feature stories. If she wanted to do softer pieces, she would have gone to the *Today* show, which had dangled the prospect of a huge salary.

One day Logan was asked to put together a story on female soldiers who were distracting themselves by keeping cyber-pets online.

"I would rather stick needles in my eyes than spend one second of my time on that story," she e-mailed back.

CHAPTER 32

A Softer Touch

Tim Russert was out of breath when he called Brian Williams.

Russert was on crutches, hobbling toward a waiting car at LaGuardia Airport after having broken his right ankle while playing with his dog Buster. He had just gotten a call on his cell phone from a senator, who was not-so-subtly suggesting that he might make an ideal guest for *Meet the Press,* when Russert asked him what else was going on.

"We're worried to death about Tim Johnson," the senator said.

"What do you mean?" Russert asked.

"He had a stroke. They brought him out of his office and he wasn't speaking."

"Is this out yet?"

"No."

Oh my God, Russert thought. Johnson, the Democratic senator from South Dakota, had been rushed to the hospital. Russert happened to know that the state's governor, Mike Rounds, was a Republican. If Johnson were to die, the Democrats would almost certainly lose the razor-thin Senate majority that they had captured just weeks earlier. The governor would name Johnson's replacement, most likely from his own party, which would put the Senate at fifty-fifty, with Dick Cheney breaking the tie in the GOP's favor.

Russert alerted the Washington bureau and then dialed Williams's number.

"Man, you will not believe this," Russert said. He quickly explained the situation. "You obviously have a new lead."

It was just over two and a half hours before airtime. The balance of power in the Capitol now hung on the failing health of one obscure lawmaker. It was, Williams realized, a slam-dunk of a story.

Moments later correspondent Chip Reid was on MSNBC, delivering the scoop as a BREAKING NEWS logo filled the bottom of the screen.

Williams called Tom Brokaw and gave him the news. Then he called a senator to find out what he could about Johnson's condition. Brokaw, the man with the South Dakota roots, called a second senator, and Russert called a third.

Brokaw came down to the third-floor newsroom and joined Williams in John Reiss's office. They were buzzing about the story, piecing together the latest tidbits, and there was an intoxicating feeling in the air. Brokaw left to check on an e-mail he was expecting from Tom Daschle, the former South Dakota senator. It felt to Williams like a scene from the great newspaper movie *The Front Page*.

Charlie Gibson was in a meeting when a staffer held up a sign outside his office window: "We Need To Meet."

After learning what had happened to Tim Johnson, Gibson agreed that the story belonged near the top of the newscast. He called a source on Capitol Hill, who told him that the senator's condition was really bad. George Stephanopoulos got hold of someone very close to Johnson's office, who said the senator appeared to have suffered a massive stroke.

But Gibson was worried. What if Johnson were still conscious and watching in his hospital room? To what extent should they raise the issue of his ability to serve? They had so little information—he didn't want to go too far and write the guy off. For the moment, he felt that they should stick with their original lead story, on the growing spate of airline mergers.

With five minutes to air, Gibson got miked on the *World News* set. Jon Banner was on his way to a White House Christmas party for the press when the other senior producers reached him on his cell. This potentially could change control of the Senate, Gibson said. The airline piece was not that strong. They decided to flip the stories and lead with Johnson.

At CBS, Katie Couric was not convinced that Tim Johnson's medical emergency was a story at all. She asked her staff what impact his illness could have on control of the Senate and somehow got the impression that it wouldn't really change things. Couric was also concerned that a dramatic story might make it appear that Johnson had one foot in the grave. Rome Hartman, too, was squeamish about the situation. With Johnson fighting for his life, were they going to go into a cold political piece about what this meant for the Senate committee chairmanships? They concluded that it just seemed like bad form. Couric felt that she could handle it with a simple "tell," a brief read from the anchor desk.

Hartman left town for the White House party. The Washington bureau, meanwhile, was pushing the story hard. If Johnson could not continue in office, it would produce a political earthquake. Bob Schieffer said that he thought it was a pretty big deal. Gloria Borger was working the phones but was concerned about appearing ghoulish.

"The big deal here is that he's still alive," one producer e-mailed Schieffer.

"Especially for him," Schieffer wrote back.

Half an hour before airtime, the Fishbowl finally decided that the Johnson saga at least warranted a discussion with Borger.

At 6:30, the newscasts hit the air.

"A member of the U.S. Senate has suffered a stroke," Brian Williams said, and "while our thoughts and prayers are with the senator and his family, of course, in Washington, with control of the U.S. Senate decided by a single vote for the Democrats, this could affect the balance of power."

"There is late news breaking in Washington tonight that could have enormous political implications," Charlie Gibson said. "There is word today that Senator Tim Johnson, a Democrat from South Dakota, has suffered a stroke."

CBS went in a different direction. "I'm Katie Couric. And it's beginning to look a lot more like Christmas in the checkout lines at the shopping malls. Tonight, all of a sudden, it's looking like the holiday shopping season won't be so bad for retailers and the economy after all. The government reported today that sales actually shot up one percent in November."

Couric then turned to big bonuses on Wall Street before reporting that Johnson "may have had a stroke" and briefly chatting with Borger about his condition. A few sentences later they were done.

Much of the staff at CBS was amazed. It was one thing to decide, for reasons of delicacy, not to lead with a senator who had just been rushed to the hospital with severe symptoms. But to play it down for an utterly routine story about Christmas shopping seemed to make little sense.

Couric later concluded that they had made the wrong call. It was, without question, a bigger story than they had realized.

Johnson, who underwent extensive surgery for bleeding in the brain, soon began to recover, but CBS's reputation for solid news judgment did not. Rome Hartman realized that they had made a mistake. A very human mistake, in his view, but a mistake nonetheless.

*   *   *

If one moment seemed to capture Couric's more emotional approach to the news, it was her interview with Karen James.

Couric flew to Dallas four days after the body of James's husband was recovered on Oregon's Mount Hood, during a search for three climbers that cable news had turned into a round-the-clock melodrama.

CBS labeled the sit-down "Exclusive," although James, who married the man after he had four children, had been interviewed on television a number of times. She choked back tears as Couric led her through Kelly James's final days.

"I can't imagine what that week was like for you," Couric said.

"Is there any part of you that's angry that he did this?" Couric said.

"Sounds as if your faith was strengthened by this whole ordeal, but it must have been tested, too," Couric said.

It was at once a moving, sensitive interview and an orchestrated, over-the-top encounter with a grieving widow. It also took up nine minutes of the *CBS Evening News.*

Many staffers could not believe what they were seeing. What the hell was this? Some found it tawdry and invasive, while others said the interview was difficult to watch. Even less clear was why this sit-down with one woman, discussing the loss of a husband with a dangerous hobby, was being trumpeted as a major scoop. What, one staffer asked, have we become?

Couric's view could not have been more different. People had really been obsessed with the mountain climbers' saga. The interview with Karen James had been meaningful and memorable. A good evening newscast did not have to be formulaic. She gave herself an *attagirl* for pulling it off.

But the interview seemed to crystallize much of the unhappiness with Couric, judging by the flood of negative comments on her CBS blog.

"Katie," one person wrote, "I am sorry but you should be ashamed of yourself. I loved you on the *Today* show, but this one lost my faith in your talents."

Said another: "Katie, STOP! You are not doing the *Today* show. Les, STOP KATIE and Save CBS News."

And: "I'm sorry the guy died and I'm sorry for his widow. No one tunes in the *CBS Evening News* to watch this kind of interview."

And: "The *CBS Evening News* has become the *People* magazine version of television news—all soft and fuzzy human interest reports, and not much real news."

And: "Katie, you should be ashamed. To prey on a woman who just lost her husband with a sleazy 'How do you feel interview' is disgraceful. You of all people who lost a husband should know better. I'll stick to Brian Williams and I will let all of my friends and family know how sleazy you have become."

Couric's dilemma had become increasingly clear. If she stuck to a standard newscast, she had no way of distinguishing herself from her rivals. If she highlighted her interviewing skills and sought out stories that packed a greater emotional punch, she was accused of conduct unbecoming an evening news anchor. Couric wanted to break the mold, but it turned out that many viewers liked the old mold.

She was in the same box when it came to the press. Couric was revealing about herself in ways that few television stars allowed themselves to be, which was precisely what made her fascinating to read about. But even her friends felt that she complained a bit too much about her plight and risked being seen as the kind of wealthy woman who held her fiftieth birthday party at Tiffany's—where she was serenaded by Tony Bennett—but griped about her press coverage. Couric also lacked a filtering mechanism to stop herself from saying things that detracted from her dignity as an anchor, at least as that role had long been defined. Everyone at CBS, it seemed, was buzzing about Couric's exceedingly candid interview with *Esquire.*

She said she hated the word *panties.* She said that sometimes she barely remembered to put on deodorant. She said she had had a perfect life until she turned forty, when Jay died. She said she was open to love but that it was difficult at forty-nine with two kids and a very public life. She said there were a lot of "circling vultures" out there ready to eat her alive. She said she played the piano and cried when she was depressed.

Couric also complained that *Esquire*'s editors had said in a cheeky column called "Obscure Women We Love" that they no longer felt they knew the anchor. Her response: "You don't know me any more? Bite me."

For days, CBS reporters and producers, at the slightest provocation, walked around inviting a biting from each other. One jokingly wondered whether the official motto of CBS News had gone from "Good night and good luck," to "That's the way it is," to "Bite me."

*　　　*　　　*

For a man who blogged every day, sharing his musings with anyone who cared to click his way, Brian Williams was remarkably skeptical of the digital world.

Our culture of self-absorption, he believed, was out of control.

When *Time* magazine invited Williams to a nominating luncheon for its 2006 Person of the Year issue, he came prepared. Williams took these sorts of outings seriously. He had written for *Newsweek,* he had written for *The New York Times,* and while it was an ego kick and a way of extending the brand, Williams, more than the other anchors, saw himself as helping to lead a national conversation.

At the luncheon, where he sat in a red director's chair, the names of past winners on a screen behind him, Williams said he could nominate George W. Bush but wanted to go for the "long ball." His suggested winner: You.

"Because it's all about you," he said. "Our celebration of self and marketing toward self, I believe, is tearing us apart and could kill us." And Williams didn't hide his stake in the argument: "We are choosing cat-juggling videos over well-thought-out, well-researched, well-reported evening newscasts."

Arianna Huffington, the liberal blogger who was in an adjoining director's chair, dismissed Williams's argument as obsolete. "I'm not sure what universe Brian inhabits," she said in her Greek-accented English.

Rick Stengel, *Time*'s managing editor, had already been considering the idea, and You got the nod, with Williams writing a dissent from the magazine's isn't-this-cool tone.

What worried him most was the fragmentation of society. It was now possible, he knew, to go through the day and watch only networks that agreed with your point of view, Internet shows that filtered out anything you found dull or objectionable, and to listen to your personal iPod playlist without risking exposure to unfamiliar music. How could that be a healthy thing for America? Wasn't there plenty of important information that people in a democracy needed to know, whether they instinctively sought it out or not?

The paradox was that Williams eagerly partook of the fruits of the digital culture. Once Allison went to college, he had installed an Apple laptop with a video camera on his kitchen island, which, when it worked, even enabled his daughter to see the family dog. He prided himself on his stream-of-consciousness blogging, right on deadline. On the *Early Nightly* he would write about seeing a deer outside the Washington bureau, buying a six-dollar fudge cake in Columbus, watching customers in a Manhattan department store take photos of a visiting rock star. He loved reading e-mail, even negative missives, from his viewers. But now that anyone could create content, where did that leave the platform he had hungered for all his life?

Maybe he was just an old Irish romantic, but Williams believed that television news mattered, even if young people were leaving the flock. On some nights he still reached nearly 11 million viewers. His person of the year was indeed all the you's out there, but he still wanted them to need him.

*   *   *

They were gathered around a long conference table in the Roosevelt Room, listening to Stephen Hadley, the president's national security adviser, describe the administration's latest strategy for Iraq.

Brian Williams and Charlie Gibson were there, along with Tim Russert, Bob Schieffer, George Stephanopoulos, Jim Lehrer, and several cable news anchors. As Katie Couric surveyed the scene from one end of the table, she couldn't help but notice that she was the only woman in the room, except for a couple of female support staffers. She would later note the disparity on her blog.

They had been summoned for a background briefing, hours before President Bush was to make a prime-time announcement that he was sending 21,500 more troops to Baghdad. Anything gleaned from the discussion was supposed to be attributed to senior officials. The president's top aides had leaked news of the so-called "surge" well in advance, but it was a measure of how seriously they took the network newscasts that they felt the need to sell the anchors who would report and analyze the latest initiative. The anchors had spent the past year pounding home the message that the war effort was a shambles, but with a majority of Americans now favoring a gradual withdrawal, the president's political position was weaker than ever. In a very real sense, he needed the likes of Williams, Gibson, and Couric to understand, and to convey to millions of viewers, what he was trying to do.

A few minutes after 10 o'clock, Bush walked into the room, which was adorned with a portrait of Teddy Roosevelt, and took over the briefing. The president was wound up and spoke uninterrupted for the first fifteen minutes. George Stephanopoulos tried to ask a question, but Bush cut him off.

"I didn't come in here to do an interview, I came in here to talk," he said.

In blunter language than he employed in public, Bush said that his patience with Nouri al-Maliki's performance as prime minister was running out. "The question he needs to be asking is, 'Am I about to lose George Bush?' He is in danger of losing his number-one benefactor."

The anchors were struck by the not-so-subtle threat.

"What is Plan B?" Couric asked.

"You ought to ask Maliki what his Plan B is," Bush shot back.

The scene was striking. The president could not flout diplomatic convention by assailing the man he had defended for so long, so he was counting on the anchors to deliver his message. It was, in short, a leak at the highest possible level. Bush placed a few of his comments off the record, but the rest was fair game.

Fox's Chris Wallace asked about Moqtada al-Sadr, the Shiite leader who had inherited his father's anti-American militia and was a crucial supporter of Maliki. "Look, this guy walked in on his father's coattails. It's sort of a small club, but you'd understand, Chris," Bush said, shooting a bemused look at Mike Wallace's son.

"I know my neck is on the line here," Bush declared. "I know I'm going against public opinion."

The discussion lasted for more than an hour before Bush started saying his goodbyes. As Brian Williams shook the president's hand, he slipped in a final question: Had Bush seen the cell phone video of Saddam Hussein's bungled hanging?

The president said he had, and that in terms of the war's mistakes, the way it was handled ranked just below the prisoner abuse at Abu Ghraib.

Before Bush left the room, Williams hustled over to a group of White House officials. "Okay," he said. "So we can say we were with him, we can say we asked him questions, and we can indicate what he said and how he answered—just no direct quotes, right?"

Right, he was told.

On the North Lawn, as CNN's Wolf Blitzer and Fox's Brit Hume headed for the exit gate, Williams walked to the MSNBC camera position for a live shot. Bush's background comments were embargoed until 12 o'clock, and as the noon hour arrived, Williams repeated much of what they had been told. On *Nightly* that evening Williams turned to Russert, who dished about the meeting.

"It was quite striking, Brian, how the president confided with advisers, and they are open about it, that he has told the Iraqis that 'My neck is on the line, and that if you lose Bush, if you lose the primary benefactor of this war in Iraq, you are in grave straits.' " They went into more detail on MSNBC after Bush's address.

His rivals were more circumspect about their ultimate source. On *World News,* Gibson said that Bush would say in his speech that his patience with the Iraqi government was not infinite, and that "high administration officials have made it clear today he has said as much in no uncertain terms to Iraq's Prime Minister Maliki."

On the *Evening News,* Couric said: "Bob, we were both briefed by senior administration officials today, and they admitted the president is really sticking his neck out here."

"He knows he is going against public opinion," Schieffer said.

The other anchors were steamed at Williams. What was up with that? Couric wondered. She was new to this game, but that wasn't her understanding of the ground rules at all. Schieffer was surprised to learn that Williams had attributed the response about Saddam's hanging directly to Bush. He hated the restrictions of these background briefings but felt that he had played by the rules and been scooped. Charlie Gibson believed Brian had clearly violated the agreement, which was that information could be attributed only to officials familiar with the president's thinking.

Williams checked the next day with a top White House official, who said that the press office was not wild about his question on the Saddam execution video. But it was a smart question, the official said, and Williams had not violated the deal with the White House. Williams felt that he had smoked his rivals simply by being more aggressive.

The presidential courtship had little effect. The next night CBS and ABC aired instant polls showing that less than a third of the country was supporting the military escalation. The year 2007 was beginning as the previous one had ended, with the network newscasts portraying a president whose support for his war of choice had all but collapsed.

CHAPTER 33

The Premature Campaign

As the 2008 presidential race began to take shape, the networks needed a superstar, a ratings winner, an exciting personality whose meteoric rise they could chart while awaiting a possible flameout.

And so they helped create one.

"He's getting rock star treatment all across the country," Tim Russert said on *Nightly News.*

Russert was talking about Barack Obama, and he was no passive observer. Two weeks before voters went to the polls in the 2006 midterm elections, Russert had coaxed the freshman Democratic senator into all but declaring his candidacy on *Meet the Press.*

"It's fair to say you're thinking about running for president in 2008?" Russert asked.

"It's fair, yes," Obama said.

"And so when you said to me in January, 'I will not,' that statement is no longer operative." Obama allowed that he was mulling the matter.

Therefore, said Russert, "it sounds as if the door has opened a bit."

"A bit."

That bit was all that the networks needed. It mattered little that Obama had been an Illinois state senator two years earlier, or that most people knew little about his record, or that no African-American had ever had a serious shot at the nation's highest office. That, in fact, was part of his appeal. What could be a better television story than a Democratic primary showdown between Hillary Clinton, aiming to become the first woman in the Oval Office, and Barack Obama, who would be the first black president?

All the evening newscasts aired stories on Obama the next night. Every serious White House contender had to compete in what insiders had dubbed the Russert Primary, and Obama had scored well, even before declaring his candidacy. He had appeared days earlier with Oprah Winfrey, who had urged him to run for president, but had shrewdly saved his trial balloon for NBC's Washington bureau chief.

"He's changed his mind and now says he is considering running for the Democratic presidential nomination," Katie Couric said on the *Evening News*, without explaining that Obama had done so on her old network.

Charlie Gibson had watched Obama campaigning on C-SPAN and had not seen such a visceral reaction to a candidate since Jack Kennedy in 1960. But what was Obama really about? What did he really think? Was it really an advantage to run for president as an unfinished canvas?

Gibson was restrained on *World News,* which credited NBC by running a bite from Russert's interview. "He is very new to the national political stage, having spent less than two years in the U.S. Senate," Gibson said.

In the final weeks of 2006 Obama made a quick trip to New Hampshire, trailed by 160 journalists, and the evening newscasts all carried reports on his visit to the first primary state. "One New Hampshire legislator said he hasn't seen anything like what happened there this weekend since John F. Kennedy," Brian Williams observed.

It was, Gloria Borger said on CBS, "a triumph." She did point out that Obama had "no national security credentials," while ABC's Jake Tapper noted that the senator was "untested, with so much unknown." But such details did not detract from the main narrative.

On NBC, correspondent Chip Reid highlighted how little media attention the other Democratic candidates were drawing with a clip from *The Daily Show.* The newscasts could no longer resist Jon Stewart.

"In Iowa," Stewart was seen saying, "the first official announcement of a 2008 presidential candidacy from Iowa Governor Tom—what's his name?" An animated talking duck waddled onto the screen to honk the answer: "Vilsack!"

That was more coverage than Vilsack had gotten on the *Evening News,* where Couric did not mention the declaration by the governor of the state with the first presidential caucuses. Gibson gave Vilsack's announcement two sentences, and Williams one, and Vilsack would drop out before long, starved for media attention and money. Obama, meanwhile, got a second story on *World News* and *Nightly News* when he did a pregame gag on ESPN's *Monday Night Football,* pretending that he was ready to make a big announcement about going "all the way" when he was really just rooting for his hometown Chicago Bears.

There were no such free publicity stunts for John Edwards when the former senator announced his candidacy. Edwards may have been the Democrats' vice presidential nominee in 2004, but CBS kissed him off in five sentences and ABC in four, plus a brief clip. Only NBC carried a full report by Chip Reid, who was on the scene in New Orleans, where Edwards was using the damage from Katrina as a backdrop for his launch.

Network television simply did not have the inclination or the attention span to deal with nearly twenty candidates for a presidential nomination. A two-person race was so much easier to package, and cheaper to cover. So the newscasts were attempting to perform a classic winnowing function by providing airtime to their preferred contenders and depriving the others of oxygen. What was unusual was that these broadcasts were narrowing the field absurdly early, a full year before the primaries would begin.

The media had long been touting Hillary Clinton not just as the party's front-runner but as the most fascinating candidate, given her political history, her husband's infamous affair, and the unprecedented spectacle of a former president's wife trying to win his old job. But the networks were openly skeptical of the New York senator's chances. "Obama is not Hillary Clinton, whom some Democrats worry is just too much of a lightning rod to win the election," Gloria Borger said on the *Evening News.*

On the weekend in early 2007 when Clinton declared her candidacy, her team let the network anchors know that she was willing to pay each of them a house call on Monday. But there was a catch: The interviews would have to be done live to tape, with no possibility of slicing and dicing.

When Charlie Gibson heard about the ground rules, he balked. The problem was that in a three-and-a-half-minute interview like this, the first question had to be some version of *why do you want to be president,* and if Clinton went on and on, he would barely have a chance to ask about anything else. And what if Rudy Giuliani or Bill Richardson or any other candidate asked for the same treatment? It would set a terrible precedent.

"You've got to go back to them," Gibson told Jon Banner. "We just don't do that. We don't do that for the president of the United States."

Gibson stewed about it through Sunday. He thought of calling Brian and Katie at home and saying, "You guys do what you want, but I'm going to say no, and we should all say no." But he decided it would be wrong to engage in that kind of collusion.

On Monday, Gibson told David Westin that he was turning down the interview.

"I'm going to back you up," Westin said. "But please understand, you're putting *Good Morning America* at a competitive disadvantage." The morning show, he explained, was being frozen out by the Clinton family because ABC's entertainment division had recently aired a movie, *The Path to 9/11,* that contained fictional scenes of top Bill Clinton aides undermining efforts against Osama bin Laden. Gibson told Westin that he would think about it.

Finally, Gibson said that he would interview Hillary if they could do it live, so that neither side would have a built-in advantage. The Clinton team agreed but said that it would have to be done by satellite because she had to be back in Washington for Senate business.

That afternoon Hillary Clinton went to 30 Rock and sat down with Brian Williams. His first question was whether she had moved up her announcement to follow Obama's within days. Not at all, Clinton said, they had planned it this way all along. He had trouble believing her answer. And when a Clinton aide later told him that of course they had speeded up their timetable, Williams concluded that she had not been straight with him.

Clinton also went to West 57th Street to chat with Katie Couric. They had known each other for years, and posed for pictures. When Couric first got the anchor job, Hillary had quietly passed on some words of advice. Couric obviously identified with another woman looking to break the ultimate glass ceiling. But she was determined to ask the candidate some challenging questions. Clinton was highly intelligent, she felt, and understood the role of journalists.

Couric let fly: Wouldn't another Clinton administration feel like *Groundhog Day*? Hadn't the health care plan she pushed as first lady been a disaster? Didn't even her supporters have doubts about her electability? The senator calmly responded with canned answers.

Gibson conducted the most probing interview by far, fueled in part by an air of annoyance about the format restrictions that Hillary had imposed. But it was more than that. He just had a disarming directness that came with age and experience.

"You are a strong, credible, female candidate for president of the United States and I mean no disrespect in this, but would you be in this position were it not for your husband?"

Clinton seemed taken aback.

Would she take a pledge not to raise taxes? Could the country finance the war without raising taxes? Had her vote to authorize the Iraq war been a mistake? Clinton regained her footing but still seemed on the defensive.

Gibson asked whether Barack Obama was qualified to be president.

Clinton said that he was "a terrific guy" and she looked forward to a good contest.

"Well, but that's something of a dodge," Gibson said. "In your mind is he qualified to be president?"

Clinton ducked again.

Gibson may have had just under four minutes, but he got the most out of the allotted time.

The next day the anchors were back at the White House, this time for the State of the Union luncheon with Bush. Gibson, Couric, Chris Wallace, and George Stephanopoulos took the lead in needling Brian Williams for having attributed Bush's answer on the Saddam hanging directly to the president. Williams turned very serious, insisting that White House officials had given their approval—which none of the other anchors had heard. Several found him to be rather defensive.

When the luncheon began, Dan Bartlett offered an extra note of caution. "Now, once and for all, this is on background," he said. "You can reflect the president's thinking, but you can't say you saw him."

Chris Wallace interjected a lighter note. "Mr. President, be careful, or Katie's going to blog about the fact that she's the only woman at this briefing," the Fox anchor said.

"I'm with her on that," the president replied.

Bush made clear that he understood the unpopularity of his Iraq escalation and why politicians of both parties were running for cover. "Nobody wants to be seen dancing with old POTUS right now," he said.

Then the president made a major mistake. He blurted out a bit of classified information having to do with Middle East strategy. As his aides turned ashen-faced, Bush stopped and glared at each of the anchors, one by one.

"Now, I'm telling you, that is off the record," Bush said. "If that ever left this room, it would be heavily damaging." The anchors silently acquiesced.

The luncheon lasted two hours, and there was considerable chatter about the 2008 race. Bob Schieffer asked whether the president saw John McCain as the Republican front-runner. Bush said he did, and that he believed Hillary Clinton would win the Democratic nomination, and that she would be a tough opponent. For dessert, the president served a chocolate concoction in the shape of a television set with rabbit ears.

As they left the White House, Katie Couric told Schieffer how much fun she was having, and how Bush was much more likable in person than he appeared on television. Couric and Schieffer had presided over several special events recently, as they would for that night's presidential address, and she increasingly seemed to lean on his deep knowledge of Washington's ways. Sean McManus had told Schieffer that they made a good coanchor team.

As a car ferried them up Independence Avenue for a briefing with the new Democratic congressional leaders, Nancy Pelosi and Harry Reid, Schieffer looked out the window and saw a familiar figure in a trench coat. It was Dan Rather, who was in town to cover the State of the Union for his digital network, HDNet. The car did not stop. Schieffer figured that the last people Rather wanted to see were his two successors in the anchor chair.

In the hothouse environment of presidential politics, the networks helped determine whether a gaffe by one of the candidates blossomed into a thorny controversy or wilted from view.

Brian Williams had MSNBC on in the background as he sat down to write the script about Joe Biden declaring his candidacy for the White House. The long-winded Delaware senator, whose mouth sometimes outran his brain, had upstaged himself with an interview in *The New York Observer,* calling Obama the first mainstream black candidate for president who was "clean" and "articulate." The words, however unintentionally, reeked of racial condescension.

On the screen, the voluble *Hardball* host, Chris Matthews, was unperturbed: "Hey, I measure people by their heart. I don't think Biden was saying anything more than somebody of his generation would say."

Williams had heard other guests chattering on like that. They were giving Biden a pass. This was the liberal media in action, he thought, cutting slack for one of their own. Williams knew Biden slightly. He saw him occasionally at meetings of the Council on Foreign Relations, the ultra-establishment group to which the anchor belonged, and the senator had once called him at home to discuss some legislation. But this was the reason Williams avoided even casual friendships with public officials. Sometimes you just had to kick them in the balls.

It might have been a verbal misstep, and Biden had already apologized, but Williams decided to lead *Nightly* with the story. The man was running for president, Williams said, but "it's how he described his fellow senator and fellow presidential candidate Barack Obama that tonight has Joe Biden in trouble. It's a story about race and politics and the power of words."

Charlie Gibson had the opposite reaction. The onetime Capitol Hill correspondent thought that the criticism of Biden was unfair. It had been an unfortunate choice of words, nothing more. In the pantheon of insults about political rivals, this wasn't much. In fact, Gibson was lukewarm about mentioning it on the air at all, but his producers insisted. Gibson gave the Biden story a tepid lead-in: "Tonight he might be wishing for a do-over, after being accused of making a racially insensitive remark."

Katie Couric ran a piece as well—"Sources close to Biden say they've warned him repeatedly about his big mouth," Gloria Borger said—and the networks had certified the media buzz that Biden's blunder was more important than why he was running for president. His candidacy seemed badly wounded.

Gradually the networks began to suggest that, just maybe, Barack Obama did not walk on water. It would be a long campaign, Brian Williams felt, and Obama might make a rookie mistake that could blow up on him. *Nightly News* was the first to pick up on newspaper stories saying that some African-Americans did not find the biracial, Harvard-educated candidate "black enough" for their liking. *World News* jumped on the senator's first gaffe after he said that the lives of those killed in Iraq had been "wasted." But the overall focus was on the issue that had dominated the coverage for the past year, how Obama wanted a quick pullout from Iraq while Hillary Clinton was refusing to apologize for her 2002 vote authorizing the war, even as she stepped up her rhetoric against Bush's handling of the conflict.

Each major candidate got one introductory piece on the network news, and if there was a deeply embedded skepticism toward that politician, it became all too obvious. When Mitt Romney—the former governor of Massachusetts, the savior of the 2002 Salt Lake City Olympics, and widely viewed as one of the top three Republican contenders—announced that he was running, the newscasts depicted him as facing one overwhelming obstacle.

"Can a Mormon be elected president of the United States?" Katie Couric asked.

Brian Williams combined the Mormon issue with the candidate's lurch to the right on social issues. Romney, he said, was "facing questions about abortion, gay rights, and religion." And NBC's Campbell Brown spelled it out: "His biggest hurdle, though, may be Romney's religion. He's Mormon. And a recent poll found about half of Americans had at least some reserva-tions about a Mormon candidate." Would such polls be passively cited, with-out comment, if they showed widespread resistance to a Jewish candidate?

It was fairly remarkable: Anchors and correspondents could prattle on about the excitement being generated by the first potential female president or black president—both of whom were Democrats—but when it came to a Republican who happened to be a Mormon, the story was framed as if he were a strange creature attempting a near-impossible feat.

The anchors were more sympathetic when John McCain stumbled in announcing his candidacy or, in the standard ritual of drawing more television attention, his intention to announce. In keeping with the *Daily Show* era, the Arizona senator confirmed the obvious on the *Late Show with David Letterman,* the better to reach a younger audience and show off his sardonic sense of humor.

Most journalists were personally fond of McCain because he was a wise-cracking maverick constantly bucking his own party, as well as a constantly available television guest, and were inclined to give him the benefit of the doubt. But when he told Letterman that "we've wasted a lot of our most precious treasure, which is American lives over there," they took notice.

On the *Evening News,* which had not reported Obama's misstep, Bob Schieffer attributed the criticism to others, telling Katie Couric: "The blogs and the Democrats attacked him. Today he had to apologize and say what he meant to say was a lot of lives were being sacrificed."

Charlie Gibson did not mention the gaffe, even though *World News* had reported Obama's apology for using the same word. And on *Nightly,* Brian Williams, who had not covered Obama's "wasted" comment, tried to soften the blow: "As a former Navy aviator and a longtime prisoner of war in Vietnam, nobody questions John McCain's military credentials. But it's something he said when he announced his presidential campaign last night that has some people today questioning his choice of words." McCain's mistake was attracting more attention than Obama's, perhaps because he was a staunch supporter of Bush's escalation in Iraq.

The subsequent coverage of McCain conveyed a sense of disappointment in a man who was no longer a rebel challenging his own party but a candidate of the Republican establishment. Journalists had clearly preferred the funnier, more liberal-sounding McCain of the 2000 campaign. And with the early polls showing Rudy Giuliani pulling ahead of McCain, they quickly concluded that his fortunes were fading. This was especially noticeable on the *Evening News,* where Couric declared that McCain's candidacy "has stalled in recent weeks."

"You're not a rookie. Do you feel like you should be a little farther ahead at this point?" CBS correspondent Sharyn Alfonsi asked McCain on his first bus trip, in Iowa, in March 2007, ten months before the first caucuses and primaries. For good measure, she quoted unnamed "insiders" as saying that "the magic of 2000 may be gone" and declared, in her stand-up, that "some wonder" whether the seventy-year-old lawmaker might be "too old" to be president.

Giuliani managed to fly beneath the networks' radar during this period, and the reason was simple: Many of their journalists lived in New York, had watched his two terms as mayor up close, and did not believe that he could be elected president. The only real coverage that Giuliani got on the newscasts was when he filed his preliminary papers to pave the way for a White House bid, and the skepticism was palpable.

Couric's take was typical: "Giuliani supports abortion rights, gay rights, and gun control. And given the conservative Republican base that comes out during the primary process, does he have a chance?"

Giuliani's popularity, Ron Allen reported on NBC, "is built on celebrity and an image as a strong leader, especially after September eleventh." How did he know? "Many analysts say." What's more, Giuliani had had "two divorces, three marriages with unflattering details splashed across New York's tabloids."

Here the New Yorkers were showing their parochialism. While they credited Giuliani as the crime-busting mayor who rallied the city after 9/11, they were smugly certain that his GOP support would collapse once folks out in the heartland learned of his social liberalism and what many of the journalists viewed as his bullying and confrontational style. That was certainly a possibility, but how did the newscasts take it upon themselves to decide that in advance?

World News, which had devoted all of three sentences to Giuliani's filing, decided weeks later to do a story on the former mayor—after *The New York Times* quoted his twenty-one-year-old son, Andrew, as saying that he had been estranged from his father and had problems with Giuliani's new wife, Judith Nathan. While describing Giuliani as having a Teflon coating stemming from the terrorist attacks, correspondent Jake Tapper recalled the pre-9/11 Rudy: "With racial tensions and an in-your-face style and a messy personal life, he had become a polarizing figure."

The next time Giuliani made *World News,* he was described as being "on the defensive" after giving an interview, with his wife, to Barbara Walters. She asked him on *20/20* whether Judith was responsible for the breakup of his previous marriage, which he denied, and whether as first lady Judith could sit in on Cabinet meetings, which he said would be fine. The same evening, Brian Williams followed up a *New York Times* report that Giuliani had failed in grand jury testimony to recall an investigator's warning that his nominee for police commissioner, Bernard Kerik, had connections to a company suspected of mob ties, a connection that later led to Kerik's guilty plea for accepting favors from the firm. When it came to examining the candidates, the newspapers were still setting the broadcast agenda.

The emergence of the former mayor was ideal from a television perspective. The newscasts liked the idea of a Giuliani-McCain showdown as much as they prized a Hillary-Obama face-off, for that would minimize the messy process of covering all those other candidates. During this period, when NBC conducted a presidential preference poll, Tim Russert told viewers that the network had added a second question in which voters of each party were asked to choose between the top two finishers. This enabled Russert to report that Clinton had an 8-point lead over Obama and that Giuliani was 21 points ahead of McCain, with the other contenders, from John Edwards to Mitt Romney, simply airbrushed out of the picture.

But the field was not even set. When Fred Thompson, who was better known for his role as a prosecutor on *Law & Order* than for his eight years as a Tennessee senator, formed a committee to explore running, two of the newscasts saw that his entry had the potential to shake up the Republican race. Charlie Gibson ran a story on Thompson's probable candidacy, and Brian Williams discussed the impact with Tim Russert. Katie Couric, who lacked the political addiction of her rivals, gave the move only a few sentences. Whether that was a miscalculation remained to be seen.

The media's slavish adherence to conventional wisdom was soon exposed. John McCain, whom the networks had depicted as the Republican front-runner, struggled for months, his backing of the Iraq war and a divisive immigration reform measure making it difficult for him to raise money as he steadily sank in the polls. In the summer of 2007, when McCain laid off nearly half his staff and then ousted his campaign manager and chief strategist, the newscasts portrayed him as a dead man walking. The McCain effort was "in crisis," David Gregory said on NBC. The campaign "smelled like a loser," George Stephanopoulos said on ABC. No mention was made of the media's earlier assessments that he was the man to beat. That was then, and this was now.

The most wide-open presidential race in half a century would go through many more twists and turns before actual voters went to the polls in 2008. Web sites, blogs, and online video would become vital tools in the campaigns. But even in the *YouTube* era, no medium would be more important than the network newscasts, especially to the candidates who were trying to draw enough media attention to compete with the anointed front-runners.

CHAPTER 34

Taking the Fall

Sean McManus's secretary told him that Katie was on the line.

"I thought things on Sunday worked out really, really well," he said.

They had just gotten back from the Super Bowl in Miami, where, while coping with a torrential rainstorm that knocked out two of his cameras, McManus had watched Couric pal around with his football analysts. He had been struck by how she got rock star treatment wherever she went, how all the sports guys had loved her.

"Well, we can knock that off our things-to-do list," McManus said. "All right, kiddo, good job."

They had used the game's huge audience to promote a new *Evening News* segment that Couric hoped would banish memories of "Free Speech" and other failed experiments: a look at people who were solving problems in ways that might be utilized across the country. One working title was "What's Right with America." McManus decided that they would go with "American Solutions." But he later told Couric and Rome Hartman in an e-mail that he had made a mistake and would defer to their choice: "The American Spirit."

Couric reported the first three pieces herself. She touted a program in Kalamazoo, Michigan, that guaranteed a free college education to all public school students who maintained a C average, and she was seen exchanging closed-fist high-fives with several students. It was not clear how the rest of the country might benefit, since the Kalamazoo effort was being financed by anonymous donors. And the effort bore a striking resemblance to the occasional *Nightly News* segment "What Works." But the stories blended substantive reporting with Couric's personal touch, a marked improvement over the frilly material of her first weeks.

Couric now recognized that the changes they had initially made to the broadcast, with snapshots and Web videos and people on soapboxes, were too gimmicky. Beyond that, she had come to admit, they had changed too many things at once. The evening news audience was fairly set in its ways, Couric realized, and didn't want too many new wrinkles too quickly. Having a new anchor in the chair was change enough, especially the first woman to hold the job. The nightly news format was so steeped in tradition, she now believed, that even small changes could feel exaggerated.

The dilemma was, in essence, just what the skeptics had predicted when Couric agreed to leave *Today.* The constricted evening news format did not allow Couric to display the winning personality that had made her so popular in the morning. When she tried, she offended part of the audience because precious news was being squeezed out. When she retreated, she was left with a largely conventional newscast that barely reflected her sparkle.

CBS was getting rid of more correspondents—Lee Cowan jumped to NBC, Jim Acosta to CNN, Trish Regan to CNBC, and Sharyn Alfonsi was let go, along with several producers—but gradually enough that there were no media reports of a purge. Gloria Borger, who had been hired under Schieffer, quit to look for another television job. Bill Owens, Hartman's deputy, returned to *60 Minutes.* McManus, meanwhile, was hiring new reporters in an effort to give the broadcast a fresher look.

The press, Couric felt, had finally moved on from kicking her around, now that her third-place status was no longer news. These things moved in cycles, and reporters seemed more interested in such distractions as Rosie O'Donnell feuding with Donald Trump.

She had come to regard herself as a human Rorschach test, someone in whom people saw what they wanted. Maybe she was too famous for the job. Couric had always tried to manage her fame. When she had first moved to New York, Kathie Lee Gifford was on all the magazine covers, a ubiquity that Couric wanted to avoid. At *Today* she had limited herself to one women's magazine cover a year. She didn't want to be Greta Garboesque, but she also wanted to avoid overexposure.

It was the nature of morning television, Couric believed, that accounted for her special kind of celebrity. *Today* had created a sense of family that made viewers interested in her life. They knew that she had lost her husband, they knew when she was dating.

The realization, confirmed by CBS researchers, that some viewers did not want to get their news from a woman was disappointing, no question about it. Once the initial novelty wore off, you still had something to prove. But Couric believed that she could win over some of the doubters. The more you showed that you were as capable as your male counterparts, the more comfortable people would become. A big contract could put you on the anchor set, she thought, but over time, the right to sit in that chair had to be earned.

*   *   *

Charlie Gibson was having breakfast in Chicago, where he was to be inducted into the Illinois Broadcasters Hall of Fame, when his cell phone rang.

"I'm probably the fifth person to call you, but isn't this great?" Paul Slavin, ABC's senior vice president, was on the line from New York.

Gibson said he didn't know what was supposed to be great.

"You won the ratings last week," Slavin said.

"Overall?" Gibson knew that the networks liked to trumpet different kinds of demographic numbers.

Yes, Slavin said. It was February 13, 2007, and for the first full week since Gibson had taken over eight months earlier, *World News* was number one. He had beaten Brian Williams by 200,000 viewers, and Katie Couric by 1.7 million.

Gibson tried to pay as little attention to ratings as possible. Otherwise, he thought, if you knew that you did well by running several medical stories, you would feel pressured to run more medical stories the next week. In the Internet age, he believed, an anchor had to guide viewers toward what was important, not just the enjoyable fluff that people would click on if left to their own devices. Besides, ratings were fleeting. They went up and down. What was lasting, he felt, was building up trust with people over time.

The previous week Gibson and his producers had been sitting in the newsroom when word came in midafternoon that Anna Nicole Smith had died. They quickly began debating what to do about the former stripper and *Playboy* playmate who had married an eighty-nine-year-old billionaire and, after his death, spent her life fighting for his money. Obviously they could goose the ratings if they played up the story.

"What's important about this?" Gibson asked. "What did she ever do to warrant an obituary on an evening newscast?" The answer, everyone agreed, was not much. They ordered up a piece on the public fascination with Smith and put it toward the end of the show.

When Gibson saw a tape of *Nightly News,* he thought that Williams was going to lead with Anna Nicole. Williams had come out of the headlines with a picture of the buxom blonde over his shoulder, but it was just a tease, a way of telling viewers to stay tuned.

Williams understood the legitimate interest in a minor celebrity's death but was amazed at how the cable channels had turned it into an afternoon soap opera. When Williams got to the story that night, he didn't hide his feelings: "This may say a lot about our current culture of celebrity and media these days when all the major cable news networks switched over to nonstop live coverage this afternoon when word arrived that Anna Nicole Smith had died."

Couric, who jumped on Smith's sudden death as well, found the whole Anna Nicole saga seductive. It was hard to take your eyes off the spectacle. This, she felt, was when discipline and self-control were needed the most. Covering Anna Nicole was the cheap, easy thing to do, and they had to make sure not to go overboard, the way the morning shows were doing.

In the endless debate over story selection, Gibson had slowly gravitated toward leading *World News* with pieces that had kitchen-table appeal, that offered relief from the steady diet of war and politics. An insurance industry list of the safest cars. The theft of credit card information from a major department store chain. An outbreak of *E. coli* poisoning in produce. A recall of laptop batteries that were catching fire. New government rules that would reduce the mileage claims that automakers could make. And that old local-news standby, rising gas prices. Even major Washington stories sometimes took a backseat to such news-you-can-use fare. Gibson wondered what viewers did during commercials. Did they run to the bathroom, make sure the peas were boiling? He wanted to stop people from flipping around.

When the racehorse Barbaro was put to sleep after breaking a leg, Brian Williams had been struck when a female producer in his editorial meeting cried upon hearing the news. But while Williams used Barbaro's fate as the show's kicker, Gibson led with the story. Every person that Gibson saw that day had had a strong reaction to the horse's death, and that was good enough for him.

The approach seemed to be paying off. Gibson won the February sweeps, the first time *World News* had prevailed in such a key ratings period since Peter Jennings did so in 1996, before losing his lead to Tom Brokaw. Gibson now looked to be the tortoise in the race. For much of his tenure he had seemed to be the forgotten anchor.

"Remember Charles Gibson?" asked *MarketWatch.com,* as if commenting on a long-lost relative. Gibson reveled in his low-key approach and did little to promote himself, as if that would amount to some sort of crass commercialism. But he had been quietly building an audience.

What had happened was not all that complicated. At sixty-three Gibson was more in tune with the older audience that watched network news. Many of them had gravitated to Bob Schieffer when he replaced Dan Rather, and then switched to Gibson when the much younger Couric took over. And Gibson's easygoing style made them feel at home. In the first two months of 2007 he had gained 460,000 viewers from a year earlier, when Elizabeth Vargas was in the chair, while Williams, whose broadcast had a slightly harder edge and featured more Washington news, had lost 310,000 viewers. Couric had lost 410,000 viewers from the Schieffer newscast a year earlier.

The irony, of course, was that ABC had passed over Gibson the first time, and he almost fumbled away the job the second time when he balked at coanchoring with Vargas. But with his decades of seasoning and the goodwill he had accumulated at *GMA,* Gibson was always the strongest player off the bench, even if his network had trouble recognizing that.

                    *   *   *

The tension had been building for months.

Brian Williams never thought that John Reiss was a good match as his executive producer. Reiss, who had been a compromise choice, was smart and dedicated, but they often didn't seem on the same wavelength. Williams was interested in stories that affected families and the great mass of suburbia, and he felt that Reiss, as a single guy who lived in Manhattan, did not have an innate feel for those subjects. He liked the man personally—they had taken the subway to the Bronx for Yankees games—but thought that Reiss did not crack the whip on some underperforming producers. And he was always disappointed when he e-mailed Reiss at one A.M. and didn't get a response.

One nagging thing came to symbolize what Williams viewed as the former *Dateline* producer's lack of daily-deadline experience. When Reiss was in the control room and spoke to the anchor in his IFB, as the earpieces are known, he would always say, "Brian?" or "It's John." That forced Williams to ask him what he wanted, wasting precious seconds. Aggressive producers were always peppering their anchors with instructions.

"Go ahead, just bust in, I'm expecting to hear from you," Williams would tell him, but Reiss never did.

There were other times when Williams showed his annoyance. When the death toll from tornados in Florida rose while he was on the air, they had to update the story for the Midwest feed at seven P.M. Reiss said from the control room that one of the writers would bang out a new top.

"Don't you get that's exactly what I *don't* want to hear?" Williams snapped. "Give me the salient facts and tell me how long it has to be." Williams despised cold copy, always fearing that he would stumble over it. In the minute he had before moving to a standing position to open the new broadcast, Williams updated the script.

Another time, Williams heard Reiss telling David Gregory that the program was packed and he would have to trim his package on Joe Biden's gratuitous remarks about Barack Obama.

"Damn it, I don't want to nickel-and-dime our lead piece," Williams declared. "This needs more time, not less." Reiss quickly went along.

But such minor incidents were rare. Williams was a demanding boss, but he did not like confrontations; he almost never raised his voice. Reiss was a quiet personality. The anchor made no direct complaints. The way you found out that Brian was unhappy with your work was that you would hear about it from others on the staff.

In the final weeks of 2006, Reiss sensed that after a year and a half in a relentlessly demanding job, perhaps it was time to end things on a graceful note. Anchors worked under tremendous pressure and were entitled to pick their team. Reiss went to Steve Capus and said that it was time to talk about an exit strategy. By doing that when *Nightly* was number one, he could go out on top.

Capus could see the problem festering. Brian liked to rock and roll, to jump on last-minute developments, while John was methodical, deliberate, set in his ways. Reiss had been Capus's deputy when he was the *Nightly* producer and had done an excellent job. But as another NBC executive had told him, "Steve, he was a great colonel. He is not a great general."

Reiss had been worried about the ratings in the first weeks of 2007. When the overnight numbers were about to come in each afternoon at 4:30, he would feel tense. ABC's lead-in audience from local programming kept growing, and Reiss knew that his old boss, Charlie Gibson, was good enough to take advantage of it. When Elizabeth Vargas was fronting the program, Brian kept managing to overcome the ABC lead-in, and people thought that Reiss was a genius. Now it was getting tougher.

The plan was for Reiss to find a new assignment at NBC. But in March 2007, word leaked to the online magazine *Radar,* which reported, wrongly, that Reiss was being replaced at Jeff Zucker's insistence. He went to see Capus.

"What the fuck do we do now?" Reiss asked. "You can't completely deny this, because I do want out."

The next day *The New York Times* played up the ouster in a front-page story, saying that Reiss's downfall was being "widely interpreted" as "fall-out" from *Nightly* losing the ratings lead. Williams, Reiss, and everyone else in the office felt terrible about the implication that this was a panicky move tied to Gibson taking over first place, rather than a reassignment that the producer had requested two months earlier.

Capus went haywire over the *Times* story. To portray the month of February as a major setback for *Nightly* was, in his view, a huge overreaction. Capus had argued to Bill Carter, the savvy television reporter at the *Times,* that ABC always got a bump during sweeps. Oprah Winfrey booked terrific guests, the local ABC newscasts did stories on killer iced tea, and *World News* got a stronger lead-in audience. Gibson's lead-in advantage over Williams, Capus explained, had jumped from 225,000 viewers in January to 709,000 in February. That more than accounted for ABC's margin of victory.

Carter told Capus he had made those very points in the story but that they were excised when his editors cut seven paragraphs for space. "In my view, what you end up with is a bit unbalanced and totally pro-Charlie," Carter said.

Williams was furious about the leak. It was driving him crazy to think that there was a mole in their midst. Someone he looked at every day was spilling their secrets. Williams wanted to administer polygraph tests, pull staffers' phone records, and search their e-mail, at least until he calmed down. Of course, had Capus moved more quickly when Reiss asked to leave the job, the whole mess would have been avoided.

Despite the humiliation, John Reiss, ever gracious, sent Williams a hand-written card: "I didn't want to let this moment pass without noting what an honor it has been to work with you . . . You, sir, are an immensely talented broadcaster."

The ABC surge was not a complete shock. Williams had heard Gibson's footsteps as he watched his once-impregnable lead shrink. He had increasingly come to like Charlie, so there was nothing personal in their competition. Gibson had been extremely nice to his father-in-law when the two families ran into each other at a Yale-Princeton football game while

Williams was visiting his daughter in New Haven. They had spent time together while waiting for the New York shuttle at Washington's National Airport, grousing about the number of promos they had to do for local affiliates. Charlie was a class act. Williams viewed their relationship as similar to that of Ronald Reagan and Tip O'Neill: slug it out by day, share a drink at night.

Williams could hardly complain about his backing at the company, beginning with Jeff Zucker. When Zucker was named chief executive of NBC Universal Television, succeeding Bob Wright—and finally putting him on par with Les Moonves at CBS—Williams sent him a congratulatory note. Zucker was the first person from the news division to run the network, and that was comforting.

But Williams also realized that he was being hurt by Zucker's budget cuts, even though *Nightly* had largely been spared. The vision of a more digital network, which Jeff was calling NBC 2.0, was accompanied by a sharp budget ax at the local NBC stations, where anchors and top correspondents were being laid off. That, Williams felt, had hurt his lead-in audience during the February sweeps. The network's promotional budget had also been slashed. Now they were paying the price.

Williams took enormous pride in being number one, more than he wanted to admit. But he had no idea what he would do differently if his slide to second place turned out to be permanent. Put on nude mud wrestling? Williams wasn't about to muddy up the newscast. He was already working as hard as he possibly could, reporting, writing, and blogging. He had allowed himself to be talked into cooperating with a cover story for *Men's Vogue,* even though he knew no one who read the magazine, and had posed with Jane in the book-lined den of their Connecticut home. Although he studiously avoided the word "I" in the newscast, he had done a piece on his relationship with his eighty-nine-year-old father, Gordon, who was struggling in an assisted-living facility not far from where they had lived in New Jersey. Williams had been deluged by the reaction, people literally stopping him on the street and sending him photos of their parents. It was only the second time in his career that Williams had put himself in a story, but that seemed to be what people wanted. In the end, you couldn't control the ratings. All that Williams could do was put himself out there every night and hope that the viewers stuck around.

*   *   *

Bob Woodruff was sitting next to him on the set, and the irony was not lost on Charlie Gibson.

For Woodruff to be able to appear on television, to lucidly discuss what had happened to him in Iraq, amounted to an incredible comeback. Even the man's doctors had been surprised. A year earlier, he had been missing a sizable chunk of his skull. Six months earlier, he was struggling to remember common words. Now he had completed a prime-time special about his ordeal and was ready to be interviewed by the anchor of *World News.*

Had Woodruff not encountered that roadside bomb, Gibson knew, Bob would be in the anchor chair, and he would still be at *Good Morning America.* Gibson had lost count of the number of people at ABC who had told him that he shouldn't feel guilty about the situation. And the truth was, he didn't. You would never want to get a job this way, after a double tragedy, Jennings's death and Woodruff's brush with death, but that was what had happened. Gibson felt very warmly toward Woodruff, who had filled in on *GMA* from time to time, and toward his wife Lee, who had been an occasional guest on the morning show.

There was so much that Gibson wanted to ask, but one question loomed above all. When the U.S. embassy in Kenya was bombed by terrorists in 1998, Gibson, who was filling in for Jennings, went on the air with a special report. The first picture he saw was of his college roommate, out on the street, his face dripping with blood. When he later spoke to the foreign service officer, the man had terrible survivor's guilt, wondering why he had been spared when several others had been killed. And so, as the cameras rolled, Gibson asked his predecessor whether he felt that he had been allowed to live for a reason.

"Well, I still don't understand it, to tell you the truth," Woodruff said. "I don't know how these rocks went through my neck and came up through the artery on the other side and stopped one millimeter from it, and I still lived. To this day I just don't know why this has become such a miracle for me."

As the interview ended, Gibson said, "It is, as I say, very good to have you back." He looked to be on the verge of choking up.

*   *   *

From the moment Katie Couric took over the anchor chair, Sean McManus wasn't hesitant about asking people for advice.

Four weeks after her debut, McManus was chatting with his friend Rick

Kaplan, the brilliant, intense television executive who had bounced around the business and left a trail of admirers and detractors. Kaplan thought there were problems with the program.

"Every show starts rocky," Kaplan said. "You want me to just give you my thoughts?"

"Boy, would I love that," McManus said.

Kaplan had a special affection for CBS. He had started his career at the CBS station in Chicago, where he grew up, and worked on the old Cronkite broadcast in the 1970s. But he had become legendary—for both his brains and his bombast—at ABC. He had been Ted Koppel's producer at *Nightline,* run *Primetime Live* for Diane Sawyer and Sam Donaldson, and produced *World News Tonight* for Peter Jennings. Kaplan was a volatile man who thought nothing of dressing down a subordinate and apologizing afterward. But he was a dynamo who made things happen.

Kaplan later became president of CNN, where he had a tumultuous tenure, especially after the network had to retract a documentary charging that American forces had used nerve gas during the Vietnam War. He also stirred controversy by sleeping in the Lincoln Bedroom while his longtime friend, Bill Clinton, was in office, insisting that this had no effect on his journalistic judgment. Kaplan was fired after three years, returned to ABC as an executive, was hired as president of MSNBC, and let go two years after that. Now he was lecturing at universities and happy to offer McManus some advice.

Kaplan had expected Couric to tank in the ratings initially, because she was making the switch from another network and because viewers were accustomed to Dad, not Mom, talking to them at 6:30. He sent over a memo about the newscast. McManus later asked him whether he thought Rome Hartman could make the proposed changes. Kaplan said he was sure that Hartman could.

"Why don't you call Rome?"

"I don't know Rome, he doesn't know me," Kaplan said. "Why would he want to sit down with some asshole he doesn't know?"

When the Chicago Bears reached the Super Bowl, Kaplan hit his friend up for tickets, and McManus got him seats thirty-five rows from the field.

In late February McManus invited Kaplan to lunch at an obscure Italian restaurant where they would not be spotted. At six foot seven, Kaplan was a big man with a big personality, towering over the slightly built McManus.

"Look, I need to do something with the *Evening News,*" McManus said. "It's not working out."

Kaplan said he didn't have any interest in coming on board as some kind of consultant. The press would immediately speculate that Hartman was dead and he was taking over. And, Kaplan said, there were practical problems as well.

"If Rome tells Katie to do one thing and I tell her to do something else, what do you think Katie's going to do? Who will she listen to?"

McManus conceded the point. As they talked, he could not help being struck by Kaplan's sheer confidence. This was a man who knew what he wanted in a television show. Still, he had concerns about Kaplan's temper.

"I don't mind people insisting on excellence," McManus said. "I don't mind people being impatient—"

"You can stop right there," Kaplan said. "You're not going to have a problem with me. I demand a lot, but you're not going to have any behavioral issues with me."

By the time the coffee came, McManus had basically reached a decision. But Kaplan wasn't leaving things to chance. He looked McManus in the eye.

"You have the best anchor," Kaplan said. "If you have the best show, you're going to win in the ratings. If you give me the opportunity, I'm going to get it done."

McManus knew full well that Kaplan had been ousted from his last two management jobs, but he wasn't considering him to run CBS News. He needed someone to rejuvenate a single broadcast and showcase Katie's abilities. Kaplan reminded him of Don Ohlmeyer, one of the best sports producers he had ever seen.

McManus had claimed in one interview after another that he was willing to be patient, but the truth was, he was running short on patience. He needed to see some ratings growth. The show was drifting, and it was time to stop experimenting. They had asked Hartman to do something different, and he had, but they had discovered to their chagrin that different didn't work at 6:30. Rome had taken the telecast as far as he could, and now it was time for someone who could push things to the next level.

What McManus needed most of all was someone who could handle Katie. She had so many ideas, and someone had to channel those ideas and turn them into programming so that she could concentrate on being the anchor. Sometimes it seemed that Couric was trying to produce the broadcast on top of her other duties. McManus was beginning to worry that she lacked focus. She needed more direction.

Kaplan, he thought, could also advise her on the most fundamental aspects of her job. Her inflection, her pacing, her overall presence could be much stronger. Katie had never been a news anchor before, and Rick had worked with the best.

Whatever strides the *Evening News* had made, the biggest problem was that it was inconsistent. McManus would watch one night and the show would be terrific, but he had no confidence that they could sustain the pace for five straight nights. The writing, the story selection needed to improve. McManus needed someone with a vision of a fully realized program.

The following week he called Kaplan. "I need to make a change," McManus said. "Do you want to do it?" He was offering the executive producer's job.

Kaplan said that he would.

"I've got to take it to Katie," McManus said. "I can't imagine she's not going to be happy, but I need to run it past her. And I need you to meet Moonves."

It was a stunning moment. Sean McManus had decided to change executive producers without telling his anchor and managing editor. She would be informed only after the fact and given a chance to object. McManus felt that she had enough to worry about without being saddled with a difficult personnel move, and that she would have to trust his judgment. Yet there was something else at work: Couric may have been the richest celebrity in the news business, but McManus was reminding her who was in charge.

It was time to call his own boss. "I know this is really tough to do, because I love Rome," Les Moonves said. He asked McManus to make sure that Hartman stayed with CBS.

On the morning of March 7, 2007, Kaplan sat down with Moonves, and both expressed surprise that they had never met. Moonves was impressed with his take-charge demeanor. McManus wanted to make a change, and Moonves's approach was to hire the right coach and let him manage the team. But Moonves wanted Kaplan to understand one thing about the relationship between the chief executive's office and the news division.

"I know it's church and state," Moonves said, "but I hope you don't mind if I call you if I have an opinion." Kaplan said he had no problem with that.

By the afternoon the deal was done. In two phone calls that lasted twenty minutes, Kaplan reached an agreement with McManus without involving his agent. Now it was time to let the anchor in on the secret.

Katie Couric had heard rumors that Hartman was getting the ax, and now there were murmurs in the newsroom that Rick Kaplan would be his replacement. Just after 2 o'clock, McManus summoned her to his office. He got right to the point.

"I think we need to make a move," McManus said. "I think it's best for the broadcast. I have someone good, but you need to spend some time with him."

Couric felt conflicted. She felt sad for Rome. They had become very good friends. But it was invigorating to think about working with someone who had Kaplan's wealth of experience.

Couric instinctively understood why she had been kept out of the loop. Sean had realized that she was in an awkward position. The network didn't want it to look as though she had wielded the hatchet. He was giving her plausible deniability.

The truth was that Couric had found herself increasingly at odds with Hartman. After five Amish schoolgirls were killed in Pennsylvania, she had wanted to go to the scene, but he decided against it. Couric had made a big push to visit Afghanistan, where a Taliban resurgence was fueling violence, but the network decided to send Lara Logan instead. Just as Hartman seemed to be asserting himself, which was of course his job, Couric's relationship with McManus was also growing a bit strained. His regular critiques of the broadcast—which were part of *his* job—began to grate on her, and Couric did not feel that his notes and calls were balanced by enough positive feedback.

As the meeting was ending, McManus offered her veto power. "You can stop this whole thing," he said. "If you feel strongly about it, it won't happen. I personally feel it's the right thing to do." But Couric was new to the evening news arena. She wasn't sure who would make the best producer. Besides, she felt, the train had pretty much left the station.

McManus called Kaplan back soon afterward.

"Katie's really loyal to Rome," McManus said. "But she understands what needs to be done and she's excited to work with you."

Moments later, Couric was calling.

"We need to talk," she told Kaplan. "How about nine tonight at my house?"

After the newscast, McManus summoned Rome Hartman to his first-floor office.

"This is going to come as a big surprise to you," McManus said. "I'm sorry to have to lay it on you right now. But I think we need to make a change."

The words hit Hartman like a ton of bricks. He had no inkling, none, that this was coming. He was being fired.

Just like that, six months after launching Couric in the anchor chair, after all the endless hours, the predawn flights from his home in Washington, he was being shown the door. He had helped recruit Katie, had planned the program with her, had accompanied her on the listening tour, had crafted the feature segments she wanted, had hosted the video chats when she was busy. This was one brutal business. In the space of one week, two of the three evening news producers had gotten canned.

Hartman's mind was racing as McManus said that it had been a difficult decision, one that he regretted making, and that he hoped to find him another slot at CBS. The producer made no effort to hide his disappointment, but tried to be gracious.

"I completely respect that," Hartman said. "It's your call." Sean could be a tough customer, but he was decisive.

Hartman felt like a baseball manager being fired in the middle of the season. He had known that, with the *Evening News* mired in third place, his job might eventually be in jeopardy. But he believed that he would be given more than six months to fix the problems.

Rome Hartman had never produced a daily news show before coming over from *60 Minutes,* and sometimes it showed. His dedication was extraordinary, but his news judgment was sometimes spotty. The previous week NBC and ABC had led with Vice President Cheney making a surprise visit to Pakistan and threatening a cutoff in U.S. aid unless the country's leaders got tougher in hunting down al-Qaeda terrorists. The *Evening News* did not carry a word.

Hartman felt he had probably failed to put on a consistent broadcast, but there was a reason for that. Plenty of people—Couric, McManus, and others—had strong opinions about what the show should look like. They were pushing him to retrench, to dial back, to make the show more traditional. It could make your head hurt at times. He had complained now and then that too many cooks were ruining the soup, but to no avail. They were taking away what made Katie distinctive, casting her as an ordinary anchor who happened to wear a skirt. But it was out of his hands now.

McManus checked back with Kaplan one more time, to report that Hartman had taken the news like a gentleman. McManus told Kaplan and Couric to let him know how their meeting went, but not to call after 10:30, when he would be going to bed.

To Rick Kaplan, a news program succeeded or failed based entirely on the anchor. Katie had the right stuff, but she had not been presented in the best light. She was the only evening news anchor who had changed networks as well as day parts. Brian Williams had sat in for Tom Brokaw for years, and Charlie Gibson had been subbing for Peter Jennings forever. But when *Evening News* viewers tuned in, instead of seeing a middle-aged white guy, they saw a woman who had never been part of CBS, and that had been jarring.

In the incestuous world of network television, Kaplan knew most of the players. Just two weeks earlier he had had lunch with Gibson, his old friend from their *GMA* days.

"You're absolutely going to beat Brian Williams, no question about it," Kaplan told him.

"No, it will take a long time," Gibson said.

"No, it won't. You've got the best evening news I've ever seen, and your persona is just terrific."

Now he would be going up against Charlie on Katie's behalf. Kaplan had come to know Couric socially over the years. As he headed to her Upper East Side apartment that night, after picking up two boxes of cookies, he realized that this was the second time they would be having a conversation about the possibility of working together.

In the spring of 2005, when Kaplan was running MSNBC, Jeff Zucker had made a surprise request. "Listen," Zucker asked, "would you do the *Today* show for me if I asked?"

Kaplan said that he probably would. The situation at the morning show was no secret: Couric was unhappy, the ratings were slipping, and Tom Touchet's job as executive producer was hanging by a thread.

"Why don't you meet with Matt and Katie?" Zucker said. "They're expecting your call."

Things went well in the sit-down with Lauer. Then Kaplan went to Couric's apartment.

He told her what he didn't like about *Today,* and some of the ideas, it turned out, were hers. Couric asked why he didn't like them and seemed interested in his answers. That said to Kaplan that she was capable of taking advice.

"If I come over and do the show, we're going to soar together," he said.

But there had been a complicating factor. "I've got to tell you, I don't know if I'm going to be around," Couric said. Dan Rather had surrendered the CBS anchor chair three months earlier, and Couric was already contemplating leaving *Today*. In the end Zucker decided to leave Kaplan at the cable network.

Now it was time to try again. But when Kaplan arrived at Couric's apartment, his star was occupied in the kitchen. A woman was slowly fingering the strands of Couric's hair, searching for nits. The painstaking examination, well known to most parents, had been prompted by an outbreak of lice at one of her daughters' schools.

Once the treatment was over, Kaplan sat down in Couric's living room and began sipping a cup of coffee. But their discussion was further delayed when one of Couric's dogs pooped on the floor and she had to clean it up.

Finally a free-flowing conversation got under way. Kaplan was his usual blunt self.

"You know, Katie, I'm a real anchor's producer," he said. "When you're doing special events, election stuff, I'm going to be in your ear."

Couric wanted to make sure that Kaplan knew what he was getting into. "I can be a handful," she warned.

"You know what? I've worked with handfuls that you can't even compete with, and I'd work with them again tomorrow. You're right in there with them, Katie. It's not about disagreements. It's not about having a mind of your own. It's about knowing how to make up."

"I couldn't agree more," Couric said.

They talked about the direction of the newscast. Kaplan wanted to harden it up. Couric thought that he was buying into the conventional wisdom about the program being too feature-oriented, a diagnosis that bugged the shit out of her. But he had an endless stream of ideas.

Couric chuckled to herself about his chest-thumping style. There was a fine line between self-confidence and all-out hubris. But she liked the fact that Kaplan was a kick-butt-and-take-names kind of guy. She felt that he would protect her, would come up with ways to make her shine. It was nice to hear that Rick thought she was so talented. After the last six months her confidence was not exactly at an all-time high.

It was after eleven when Kaplan left the apartment. He felt like he was walking on air. Had Couric expressed any trepidation about him coming on board, he would have called McManus and backed out, but now he was raring to go. This would be one heck of a challenge, trying to overtake Brian and Charlie and make Katie number one.

Couric had one piece of unfinished business. She called the man who had just been fired.

"Rome, I'm so sorry," she said. "I've loved working with you and I care about you so much as a person. This was a very last-minute thing when I found out about it."

Hartman sounded downbeat and disappointed. Couric felt as though she had let him down. "I'm sorry I couldn't make things better for you," she said.

Sean McManus had already dozed off, but he stirred around midnight and dragged himself to his computer. As dazed as he was, he couldn't wait until the next morning to find out what had happened.

McManus saw that he had e-mails from Couric and Kaplan. Both said that the meeting had gone very well. He went back to bed, certain that he had made the right decision.

CHAPTER 35

Journey to Iraq

The Black Hawk helicopter was staying low, no more than a hundred yards off the ground, to avoid any antiaircraft fire as Brian Williams surveyed the Iraqi landscape below.

From above, F-16 attack jets formed a protective canopy. Apache helicopter gunships rode shotgun. Inside, door gunners wielding M-4 rifles peered out, looking for signs of trouble. Williams, wearing ear mufflers, sunglasses, and body armor, chatted with a three-star general, Ray Odierno, about how the war was going. Odierno said that the new American strategy of placing smaller military outposts in dangerous Iraqi towns was putting a damper on the violence.

After landing, Williams heard the same refrain from a lieutenant colonel in Ramadi, which had long been plagued by urban warfare. But just as the Army officer was boasting how much safer the area had become, a command sergeant major thought he saw something and that Williams and the colonel were sniper targets. He broke up the interview and hustled them inside the command center.

Williams had wrestled for months with the question of whether to return to Iraq for the first time since the 2003 invasion. He was acutely conscious of the risks involved, and yet felt guilty about staying away. Iraq was the story of our time, it led the newscast night after night, and Williams felt a responsibility to touch it and feel it and not just observe from a safe distance.

There had been long conversations with Jane in the den of their Connecticut home. It had been devastating for Jane to watch what her friend Lee Woodruff had gone through, and to think that this could so easily have happened to her family. For one year after Bob's injury, Jane Williams could not imagine her husband returning to Iraq. It felt too risky, too scary. Yes, the story was crucial to the national dialogue, but was any job, any assignment worth the destruction of a human life?

Now that a return to Baghdad was a real possibility, Jane reacted, on one level, like the television producer she had once been. She could not live paralyzed by fear. "I think you need to go to Iraq sooner rather than later," she said.

But Jane also leveled with her husband about her emotional reaction. This is insane, she said. Look at what happened to Bob Woodruff.

"I reserve the right to be sad that you're walking out the door," Jane said.

The anchor's toughest sales job was with his two teenagers. "I'm going to be heavily guarded, I'm not going to do anything stupid, and I will be back," he assured them.

In early 2007, Jeff Zucker came to Williams's third-floor office and sat on his couch.

"Are you sure about this?" Zucker asked.

"This is a decision I've reached," Williams said. "I really want to go."

"Just tell me that you're going with the safest security package," Zucker said.

Williams knew that Woodruff's prime-time ABC documentary on his ordeal was coming up, and he asked Jane to find out from Lee Woodruff when it would air. He did not want to be perceived as trying to steal his friend's thunder. When Williams learned the date, he pushed his trip back by a few days.

With no publicity, Williams and his wife threw a party for the Woodruffs at their New York apartment to celebrate the couple's new book. Williams felt that Bob and Lee needed friends who were not trying to profit from their sudden fame. During the same period Williams ran into Kimberly Dozier, the CBS correspondent, who was in good spirits despite considerable pain in her leg from the Iraq bombing that had killed her two crew members. The danger in Iraq was no abstract concept for Williams.

The trip was in some respects a selfish move, Williams felt, since it was mainly about his need to feel connected to the story. He made clear to his team that this mission was totally voluntary. Subrata De, the producer who accompanied him to New Orleans and just about everywhere else, was among the first to sign up.

The danger was apparent on the approach to the Baghdad airport, when the plane had to conduct a corkscrew landing to avoid possible enemy fire. That in itself, Williams felt, was telling about the state of the war. Four years into the conflict, and the airport was still not secure.

But Williams was a fatalist when it came to spending time in war zones. He would take precautions—he was not a cowboy—but he did not feel nervous. Either bad things were going to happen or they were not.

If Bush's surge was making progress, Williams wanted to report that. He noticed a difference in the level of security. But by the time he began the broadcast at 2:30 A.M. Baghdad time, the story had taken a depressing turn.

"Despite the upbeat tone of some U.S. commanders that we just might be turning a corner in parts of this fight," Williams began, "tonight there is awful violence to report." Ten American soldiers had been killed in three separate roadside bombings. And at least ten coordinated attacks had been launched against Shiite pilgrims, killing more than one hundred of them.

This, Williams thought, captured the dichotomy of Iraq. He could report on the valiant efforts of American soldiers to pacify Iraq, one block at a time, but the image that *Nightly* viewers would remember was of the big car bombing, the big civilian massacre. That would overshadow everything else.

The mass murder of the pilgrims was nothing if not sobering. Williams had planned to visit a Shiite open-air market the next day and attempt to interview ordinary Iraqis. But Richard Engel, who had logged more time in Iraq than any other network reporter, objected.

"You're not doing that," Engel told him. "I'm not sure I would on a day like today." Besides, he said, Williams would be the only one wearing a blue vest, the designated color for journalists, making him even more of a target. Williams canceled the visit.

He enjoyed spending time with Engel, whose work Williams admired enormously. By virtue of his longevity and his Arabic language skills, Engel was now considered such an expert on the conflict that he received an invitation from a most unlikely source. Bush asked Engel to join him in the Oval Office for a private, hour-long chat. It was all the more surprising in light of the administration's four-year record of criticizing media coverage of Iraq as too negative. Here was the president, away from the cameras, losing political support, turning to a journalist for his perspective on the war effort. White House officials saw the encounter as a chance for the man calling the shots to make his case to a high-profile correspondent. Engel scribbled one of his signature maps for Bush, an elaborate diagram with the Green Zone at the center, and Bush was so struck by the conversation that he discussed it with his senior staffers.

While Williams was utterly absorbed with the Iraq visit, he also had to deal with domestic news. In the middle of the trip, a jury in Washington convicted Lewis "Scooter" Libby of perjury and obstruction of justice in the Valerie Plame leak investigation—a case that turned on the testimony of Tim Russert. The jurors believed Russert when he said that he and Libby had never discussed the covert CIA operative during a phone call in 2003, in which the vice president's chief of staff was complaining about criticism by Chris Matthews on MSNBC. Undergoing cross-examination had been an unpleasant experience for Russert, who kept commenting on the political impact of the trial even as he became a participant, and Williams made sure to interview his colleague on the day of his testimony and again on the day of the verdict. He felt that other news organizations were calling Russert for comment and that NBC's Washington bureau chief had to be front and center on his own network.

But the Libby trial, important as it was back home, proved a minor distraction for Williams. He was totally immersed in Iraq, working crazy hours, taping trash bags to the windows to try to get some sleep in the early morning after being up half the night. Williams hung out with the infantry at Camp Victory, living the life of a soldier. He spent two days staring at the armored Humvees and noting how they had evolved since his last visit. He was fascinated by a tour of one of Saddam's luxury palaces, with its gold-plated fixtures, that now provided a home for American soldiers.

Williams was extraordinarily grateful to the troops. He felt that he had placed his life in their hands and that they had his back. It was an intoxicating feeling, being protected by the United States military.

But the picture he got of the war that he had been talking about for four years was as muddled as ever. Williams told friends that if they wanted to find good news in Iraq, he could show them plenty of examples. And if they wanted proof that Iraq was a lost cause, he could provide considerable evidence of that as well. Still, when he looked at the big picture, he wondered how the war effort was ever going to succeed.

When Williams called home, he learned that some critics were questioning whether he had gone to Iraq as a ratings stunt, because Charlie Gibson had just moved into first place for a couple of weeks. He was stunned by the news. It was just bloody offensive. Here he was, risking his neck to report on the war, and these cheap-shot artists thought it was all about Nielsen numbers? Besides, they obviously knew nothing about the extensive preparations required for a Baghdad trip. NBC had started making these plans weeks ago, when *Nightly* was still ahead of Charlie, so the whole notion was absurd.

Williams and his seven colleagues spent every night in sleeping bags in a cinderblock building. For three straight nights his dinner consisted of envelopes of tuna on crackers, picked up at the local PX. Several times, as Williams worked in the back of a hollowed-out truck, his fingers got so cold that he had to stop typing. This was no ploy to attract an audience. You had to want this.

Four days after his arrival, Williams and his crew were sitting in the dark, cavernous lounge at the Baghdad airport when they heard five straight explosions. Subrata De ran to the windows and saw smoke rising just beyond the taxiway. It was incredible. The insurgents could still land mortars at an airport under American military control. Seven minutes later Williams heard a boarding announcement. He and his team hustled onto the Fokker jet and were happy to clear Iraqi airspace.

He had made a good-faith effort to report on the pluses and minuses of the war effort, but the truth was that most of the audience had made up its mind. Polls were showing that three-quarters of the public believed that things were going badly in Iraq and that six in ten thought that the invasion had been a mistake.

Williams needed to decompress after the intensity of Iraq, and he got to spend a rare week at the beach with his family. When they returned home to Connecticut, he went to the laundry room to do a bleach load. He yelled at Jane for having turned off the water before they left. For all the globe-trotting, an anchor's life was rarely as glamorous as it seemed from the outside.

Dan Bartlett was pleased that Williams had gone to Iraq. He had been encouraging network executives, correspondents, and bureau chiefs, including Tim Russert, to make the trek, offering access to top commanders, in the belief that such trips would provide the public with a clearer picture of the war. Bartlett remained frustrated by the media narrative that had Bush insisting, in the face of overwhelming evidence, that progress was being made in Iraq, when in Bartlett's view the president was constantly warning that the military faced increased casualties as part of the troop surge. He had made the argument with the press as forcefully as he could, but he was making little headway, and he was tired.

*   *   *

Katie Couric's face filled the flat-screen monitor on the wall, and Rick Kaplan was in the Fishbowl, his sizable frame filling Rome Hartman's old chair.

It was the fourth anniversary of the U.S. invasion of Iraq. That morning, Couric, Charlie Gibson, and Brian Williams had all anchored special reports when Bush addressed the nation, asking for "courage" and "resolve" in supporting the war until victory could be achieved. Couric had convinced the administration to grant her an exclusive interview with Zalmay Khalilzad, the U.S. ambassador to Baghdad. Kaplan, wearing a sleeveless gray sweater over his blue shirt, was making notes on a yellow legal pad as Couric began the satellite interview.

"What, specifically, are the signs of progress?" she asked. Khalilzad said that killings by death squads had declined.

"Roadside bombs are up. Attacks on helicopters have increased, Chemical weapons are being used with increasing frequency," Couric said. "Would you concede the level of violence has gotten worse?" Khalilzad would not.

Couric pressed on: "Why should this latest assessment by the Bush administration be deemed credible?" "Can the Sunni and Shiite populations really come together in your view?" "Not to sound pessimistic, but what is Plan B if this surge does not work?"

"Good question, Katie," Kaplan said under his breath.

The ambassador gave no ground: "Plan B is to make sure Plan A works."

Couric said that good military planners always had a Plan B.

"Way to go, Katie," Kaplan said. But he was frustrated with the guest. "It's like a tennis game where all he's doing is trying to block the shot."

Couric made one more try, asking whether Bush's military surge could last into 2008.

"We can make this interview useful if he gives a responsive answer to this," Kaplan said. But Khalilzad swatted away the question.

"He was programmed to give her only what he was programmed to give her," Kaplan told Katie Boyle, the producer watching from his left. He strode onto the anchor set as soon as the interview ended.

"He didn't do it, did he?" Couric said.

Kaplan decided on the spot to kill the interview. It would piss off the White House, but that wasn't his problem. He could imagine the audience groaning, *The fucking guy didn't say anything.* He wasn't going to waste three precious minutes of his newscast on diplomatic double-talk.

Kaplan had made his presence felt even before he officially took over. At a staff meeting, he reviewed a story on sleepless women that had closed the show earlier that week.

"The character was fine," he said. "The story was fine. The writing was fine. The editing was fine. But we don't do 'fine' on the *CBS Evening News.*" He was sending a message that routine pieces would no longer cut it.

Kaplan soon quickened the pace and hardened up the newscast. He decreed that each program would have only one feature story. Couric's one-on-one interviews—one of her strengths—were greatly reduced, and chats with the correspondents were all but eliminated.

Some changes were more subtle. Couric switched her greeting to "Hello everyone" from the more informal "Hi." She began opening the newscast from behind the desk. And she seemed to dress more conservatively.

Kaplan's edginess was balanced by his gregarious nature. He thought nothing of planting a loud kiss on Couric's cheek in front of others.

Couric enjoyed their bantering relationship. "You can tell me when you don't like my makeup, or don't like my jacket," she said on his second day at the office. "But dude, deep-six that aftershave."

"I have no sense of smell," Kaplan protested. He was infamous for his Polo cologne.

"Well, I do," said Couric, who later brought him some Sea Breeze.

Kaplan touched one other important base. He called Bob Schieffer, who was weighing whether to retire. Kaplan, who had known Schieffer when he worked at CBS three decades earlier, insisted that the former anchor remained an important part of the program.

In his first week on the job Kaplan made clear that he believed in a big-story approach to the news. When Alberto Gonzales, the attorney general, suddenly seemed to be in hot water, Kaplan announced to his staff: "We're going to own the attorney general story."

In fact, the network newscasts had been appallingly slow to grab even a piece of the story, let alone take ownership. The controversy over how the Justice Department had fired eight U.S. attorneys for what appeared to be political reasons had been building for two months, since *The Wall Street Journal* broke the news in the middle of January. The *Los Angeles Times, New York Times,* and *Washington Post* had quickly followed up, and the newspapers had carried dozens of articles as the administration's cover story—that the prosecutors had been dumped because of their performance—slowly unraveled.

The story was complicated for broadcasts that had to report most news in under two minutes. After all, presidents had a perfect right to dismiss the U.S. attorneys they had appointed. The problem was that Gonzales had testified before Congress that he was not involved in the firings, that the White House had played no role, and that partisan considerations were not a factor. But the newspapers found that the U.S. attorney in New Mexico had been canned after two Republican members of Congress had called to pressure him about a vote-fraud investigation that targeted Democrats, and that the U.S. attorney in Arkansas had been pushed aside to install a former White House deputy to Karl Rove. The papers also reported that Gonzales planned to replace the prosecutors, without Senate confirmation, under an obscure provision that had quietly been added to the Patriot Act.

But the newscasts seemed oblivious. They carried not a single word until early March, and then only on a pair of weekend shows. That changed on March 13, when *The Washington Post* published e-mails showing that the White House had suggested ousting all ninety-three U.S. attorneys after Bush's reelection, and Gonzales's chief of staff resigned over his role in the fiasco.

"How many people have any clue what the prosecutors do?" Kaplan asked his staff. He ordered up two pieces, one on the e-mails and a second story explaining the job of U.S. attorneys. The *Evening News, World News,* and *Nightly News* all began with the scandal that they had so steadfastly ignored. But only Couric led with the story for four straight nights. She interviewed David Yglesias, the prosecutor in New Mexico who had been fired, a far newsier encounter than her sit-down with the mountain climber's widow.

A cascade of developments followed: Bush said that "mistakes were made" and acknowledged having discussed Republican complaints about some of the prosecutors with Gonzales. Rove had also been involved in some of the discussions. Newly uncovered e-mails described efforts to protect the "loyal Bushies" from dismissal.

But the other newscasts were not quite as fixated on the story. Gibson led one evening with bad winter weather. Campbell Brown, filling in for Williams, began one broadcast with a government warning about side effects from sleeping pills.

In earlier months Couric would have mixed things up as well. There would have been complaints that the Gonzales story was too inside-Washington, the developments too incremental. But Kaplan was convinced that Gonzales was going to resign, and he was now driving the journalistic train.

As Democrats, and several Republicans, called for Gonzales to step down, Charlie Gibson and his team heard from numerous sources that the attorney general was about to quit. But Gibson refused to speculate on the broadcast. There was only one source who mattered, he felt, and that was Bush.

At CBS, however, the drumbeat about Gonzales was growing louder. "Are his days numbered?" Katie Couric asked. "Pressure is building for the removal of Attorney General Gonzales in the uproar over the firing of eight U.S. attorneys"—an uproar that the networks had been unable to hear until that week.

Jim Axelrod climbed out on a limb from the White House lawn. "Sources also say it is now inevitable that Gonzales will be fired," he reported.

But Bush quickly embraced Gonzales, temporarily quieting any talk of resignation, and Gibson sounded as though he was chiding the rival newscast for repeating Beltway chatter. "Washington has been filled with people in the last couple of days who thought they knew and said they knew what was going to happen to the attorney general, but he serves at the pleasure of the president," Gibson said on *World News*.

When Gonzales struggled to answer questions at a Senate hearing, the *Evening News* stole a technique from *The Daily Show,* using quick-cut editing to show the attorney general saying "I don't recall" again and again—and, for good measure, played a clip of Jon Stewart proclaiming: "There you have it: Alberto Gonzales doesn't know what happened." The Stewart style was now embedded in once-sober network newscasts.

As the coverage intensified, Sean McManus knew that the daily focus on Washington politics might bore some viewers, and that they might have done a better number that first week if they had led with winter storms. But over time, he felt, they would forge a reputation as a place that covered serious news. That, in the early months, was an image that the Couric broadcast, with all its experimenting, most definitely did not have.

The networks soon swarmed over a presidential candidate they had barely found time to mention in their attempt to narrow the field to two contenders on each side. When John and Elizabeth Edwards announced that her breast cancer had spread to her bones and was now considered incurable, the media were faced with a compelling human drama. The former North Carolina senator's decision to continue campaigning sparked an intense debate about illness, ambition, and the age-old conflict between public pressures and family responsibilities. That was a dilemma all too familiar to the anchors: Charlie Gibson had lost his parents and his sister to cancer; Brian Williams had lost his sister; and Katie Couric, of course, had lost her husband as well as her sister.

The candidate whose announcement had warranted only a few sentences on CBS and ABC was now the subject of one story after another at the top of the evening newscasts, his marriage suddenly scrutinized as closely as Hillary Clinton's. That afternoon Couric called Jeff Fager, the *60 Minutes* producer, and asked whether they should pursue an interview with the couple.

"Before I call them, I wanted to check with you," she said.

As it happened, CBS's political director had already pitched the idea of a Couric sit-down to the Edwards campaign, but Fager had all but decided against it. The candidate and his wife at their news conference, had just finished sharing their feelings with the world in considerable detail.

"They said everything there is to say," Fager said. "I don't want to do it just for emotion."

Couric still felt that it was a compelling story.

"Are you sure?" she asked. She thought of arguing, but decided against it. She wasn't Mike Wallace, who had had his share of epic battles with the bosses at *60 Minutes.* Jeff was the executive producer, and the decision was his.

Fager soon noticed that everyone in the office was buzzing about the Edwards saga. He checked in with Sean McManus.

"Give it another thought, Jeff," McManus said.

The next morning, a Friday, Fager changed his mind and put in an official request. He had heard that John Edwards and his wife were going to talk to Brian Williams, probably for *Dateline,* if *60 Minutes* passed it up.

Williams had, in fact, tried to land the interview. He had gone to North Carolina the previous fall to interview Elizabeth Edwards, and they had really bonded. She was promoting a book on her battle against cancer, and he had recently lost his sister, Mary Jane, to the disease. Williams felt that Elizabeth had been incredibly nice to him, and now he reached out to her.

But Elizabeth Edwards told Williams that she could not give him an exclusive again. She and her husband had to be fair to other networks or they would pay a price. Williams said that he understood.

As Couric was about to board a plane with her daughters for a long weekend in Sun Valley, Idaho, she called CBS. She was told that the Edwardses might wait several weeks before granting any television interviews.

When Couric landed in Idaho, she had a voice-mail message from Fager. The interview was on. All she had to do was get to Las Vegas the next day.

Couric had interviewed the couple before and was particularly impressed by Elizabeth, who seemed a strong and unpretentious woman. They had talked after her breast cancer diagnosis in the aftermath of the 2004 election. Couric felt that continuing the presidential campaign was the couple's decision and no one else's. She knew from her own experience that maintaining a sense of normalcy was critical when coping with a life-threatening disease.

On the Saturday morning flight to Las Vegas, Couric read a *New York Times* piece in which a number of voters questioned how the Edwardses, whose youngest children were six and eight, could possibly continue on the campaign trail. She realized that she had to include questions that reflected this critical point of view, even though she didn't agree with it. She would be a conduit for the negative reaction so that the couple would have a chance to address it. After all, they weren't sitting down with her just to have a do-over of their press conference. Even people sympathetic to Edwards, she thought, wondered how a president would cope with a seriously ill wife.

Couric spoke with Fager about the sequence of the questions: How did Elizabeth get the diagnosis? What did they tell their kids? How did they reach the decision to stick with the campaign? Fager listened from New York on a phone line as the interview began.

Couric could not have appeared more empathetic, her tone and facial expressions reflecting her concern. It was strange, though, that she did not simply acknowledge what everyone watching knew, that she had faced the same wrenching decision when Jay was dying and that she had opted to keep working at *Today*. But Couric felt that it would have been inappropriate to mention that. In her mind, it was a balancing act: talking to a couple who had just gotten devastating health news while asking important questions of a presidential candidate. She wasn't there as a support group. She was a journalist, and she had to be dispassionate about it.

When the time came, Couric pressed the couple, always attributing the views to others:

"Some say what you're doing is courageous. Others say it's callous. Some say, 'Isn't it wonderful they care for something greater than themselves.' And others say it's a case of insatiable ambition."

To Elizabeth, Couric said: "Here you're staring at possible death, and you're thinking 'I don't want to deprive the country of having my husband lead it.' "

And: "Some people watching this would say, 'I would put my family first always, and my job second.' And you're doing the exact opposite."

It was Couric doing what she had always done in the mornings, with enough time to feel her subjects' pain.

The interview was widely picked up, including on *NBC Nightly News,* which did not show Couric in the clip. It was, by any measure, a major success. But it didn't take long for the backlash to build. And in the digital age, critics had an instantaneous way of expressing their displeasure. Couric's detractors, many of them women, saw her as badgering the couple and denigrating Elizabeth Edwards as she valiantly battled a deadly illness, though Couric had done nothing of the sort. And they vented on CBS's Web site.

"I will not watch Katie Couric again. The way she handled this interview was an absolute disgrace . . . Shame on all of you," wrote PAMELA10231.

"Ditch Katie! Her judgment and cut-throat ways will do nothing to help CBS ratings," said CarolRobbin1.

"CBS should ask her to resign immediately. I will not watch CBS as long as she gets money to do such hateful/mean interviews," declared Patcrawford3.

"This was the most cruel interview I have ever seen any journalist do. Katie attacking Elizabeth Edwards . . . CBS should do the right thing and rid themselves of the disastrous Katie Couric." This writer's screen name suggested a partisan point of view: Bushsucks11.

Fager was flabbergasted by the onslaught. He thought that Couric had done a terrific job, that if anything she had been too cautious in attributing every skeptical observation to others. Hateful? Cruel? Couric had asked tough questions, but her tone was clearly sympathetic. Fager doubted that the reaction would have been the same had Steve Kroft or some other *60 Minutes* correspondent asked the very same questions. Maybe the talk at CBS was right, that gender was a factor, that some people were rooting for her to fail.

Fager called Couric to buck her up. The Edwards campaign put out a statement defending her. Elizabeth Edwards called to say that she didn't understand the criticism.

"We thought it was great," she told Couric. "You asked the questions that we wanted to answer."

Couric was proud of what she had done and felt that people were projecting their own feelings onto the interview. She was getting it from the left and the right. People were so passionate about politics and about cancer, she believed, that the whole controversy, and her role in it, had touched some kind of exposed nerve. She had just rubbed some people the wrong way with this interview. Maybe it was more than that. People were accustomed to seeing her as a very sympathetic person, and here she was having to ask some uncomfortable questions. That, she suspected, was what was causing the disconnect.

It was a moment that captured the swirling debate around Katie Couric. Had she gushed over her subjects, she would have been mocked as too soft. By simply doing her job, she was derided in some quarters as too heartless. Many people, it was now clear, did not accept her, refused to accept her, as an evening news anchor. She had made mistakes, to be sure, but there was a visceral quality to the criticism, a hurdle that some would not allow her to overcome. Perhaps that would change over time, but for now, Katie Couric was trapped in a contest that, for all her natural talent, she could not seem to win. What should have been a moment of triumph had, in the end, been tarnished.

*   *   *

It was a difficult phone call for Brian Williams.

He had always enjoyed bantering with Don Imus when he called in to the morning man's radio program, which was simulcast on MSNBC, but now Imus's career was hanging by a thread. A professional curmudgeon who sprinkled his show with locker-room insults while also conducting smart interviews with leading politicians and journalists, Imus had gone way too far by dismissing the Rutgers women's basketball team as a bunch of "nappy-headed hos." The comment, Williams felt, was downright hateful. Imus had repeatedly apologized, but the criticism was growing deafening. NBC and CBS, which syndicated the radio show to sixty stations across the country, had both suspended Imus for two weeks.

The situation was awkward for Williams, who was viewed as part of the Imus "gang"—along with Tim Russert, David Gregory, Bob Schieffer, Dan Rather, Tom Brokaw, and more recently Charlie Gibson—whose members were now being chided for lending their prestige to the controversial radio host. They had plenty of company in the political world: John McCain, Joe Lieberman, and John Kerry were frequent callers, and Senator Chris Dodd had declared his presidential candidacy on the show. NBC had clearly benefited from the exposure, so Williams had kept calling the program and had also contributed to the various Imus charities. Imus was usually nice to him but sometimes would carve him up, as Williams would later hear from his wife.

The truth was, Imus remained an enigma. Williams didn't really know him. They had met twice and spoken on the phone three or four times, but Imus seemed to be the wizard behind the curtain. Some of the crude talk on the show had always made him wince, and it was hard for him to defend Imus from these charges of racism and sexism, Williams felt, because they had no off-air relationship.

When Williams called Imus at home, he told him about his visit to the Rutgers campus in New Jersey that afternoon to interview the team's coach and players, most of whom were African-American. The meeting had had a profound emotional impact on Williams. Maybe it was because he had a daughter in college, but he was moved by these remarkable young students who had been deeply hurt by the insulting remarks. He devoted the first eleven minutes of *Nightly News* to the story, feeling an extra responsibility because the Imus show aired on MSNBC. Now Williams had some words of advice for Imus, who had been trying to arrange a meeting with the team to apologize in person.

"They are so extraordinary they may make your job easier," Williams said. "A lot of them have already found the route to forgiveness and redemption. Many of them grew up in religious households."

Imus had stopped watching television and reading the papers. He told Williams that the students might be surprised to hear that more than 10 percent of the children with cancer who visited his New Mexico ranch under the charitable program Imus had created were minorities, or that he personally knew three hip-hop stars. Williams was disappointed that Imus was offering the same defenses that he had been making on the air, but found him to be contrite. Williams told Imus that he should visit Iraq, that such a trip would be a valuable experience for him and help him change the subject. But it was not a good phone call. The man seemed close to despondent.

At the office, Williams made it his mission to gather reaction in the newsroom. Ron Allen, an African-American correspondent for *Nightly* whose father and sister had attended Rutgers, felt strongly that Imus should be dropped because of a history of racially insensitive remarks. One woman burst into tears while watching the Rutgers women on television. Williams reported all the negative feedback to Steve Capus, who heard similar complaints at an emotional meeting with two dozen black staffers that stretched on for two hours.

Capus had also gotten advice from Tom Brokaw, who had forged a friendship with Imus over the years and felt that he was not getting adequate credit for his charitable endeavors. Brokaw called Imus and then approached Capus.

"You go to him and say, 'Don, take yourself off the air for two or three weeks, a month, and say you've got a lot to learn,' " Brokaw told him. He said Imus could then donate the money he would have earned to a Rutgers scholarship fund. But Brokaw recognized that perhaps too many days had elapsed since he made the suggestion, and he later heard that Imus had rejected it. The suspension imposed by MSNBC and CBS soon made the matter moot.

Now, after taking the staff's temperature, Capus concluded that Imus had simply gone so far over the line that the relationship could not continue. Capus made the case to Jeff Zucker, who checked with the GE chairman, Jeffrey Immelt, who signed off on the decision. Zucker had been in touch with his old rival, Les Moonves, who had to decide whether CBS could keep the show. In a brief call, Zucker told Moonves that MSNBC was dumping *Imus in the Morning*.

That night Williams was at a cocktail reception for NBC's affiliate stations. It fell to him to make the announcement to the assembled executives.

Now Moonves faced a difficult decision. The Imus radio show was far more valuable to CBS, bringing in $25 million a year in revenue, than it had been to NBC. But Moonves was coming under the same kind of intensifying pressure from employees at his network. Twenty-four hours after Zucker dropped the cable simulcast, Moonves called Imus at home to say that he was killing the show.

The whole thing had been painful for Williams to watch. It had been a good program in many ways. But Imus had always done things his own way, Williams felt, and in the end he paid the price.

CHAPTER 36

A New Champion

The essays lasted all of one minute, but they were a way for Katie Couric to extend her brand. Each day she taped a brief "Katie's Notebook" commentary, and it ran on CBS television stations, radio stations, and her blog.

They were bland and inoffensive, for the most part, tackling such subjects as childhood obesity, grade inflation, bacteria on everyday objects, and the need for more female columnists. One of her few political posts was to praise Al Gore's Capitol Hill testimony on climate change and to urge Congress to "act boldly on global warming."

Network insiders knew that Couric didn't write most of these commentaries, not even the folksy ones. They were scripted by members of her staff. Couric's main involvement was to suggest the topics at planning meetings.

CBS had asked Bob Schieffer to do a daily radio commentary when he succeeded Dan Rather. But Schieffer had refused, saying he didn't have enough time to write them and didn't want to be stretched too thin, as he believed Rather had been. When CBS executives said that staff members could easily bang out the pieces, Schieffer said that he wouldn't feel comfortable reading someone else's work product.

Couric's decision to employ ghostwriters blew up on her in early April 2007. She began with a seemingly personal remembrance: "Hi everyone. I still remember when I got my first library card, browsing through the stacks for my favorite books."

But Couric was borrowing more than just books. *The Wall Street Journal* soon contacted CBS to complain that the commentary had been ripped off, almost verbatim, from a column by one of its writers, Jeffrey Zaslow.

"For kids today," Couric said, "the library is more removed from their lives. It's a last-ditch place to go if they need to find something out."

Zaslow had written in March: "The library is more removed from their lives. It's a last-ditch place to go if they need to find something out."

Couric said: "Sure, children still like libraries, but books aren't the draw."

Zaslow had written: "Sure, there are still library-loving children, but books aren't necessarily the draw."

Couric even cited the same statistic as Zaslow—a 60 percent rise in sales of hardcover juvenile books—as "an encouraging sign that kids value reading," just as Zaslow had called it "an encouraging sign that kids still value books."

CBS blamed the blatant plagiarism on a twenty-eight-year-old producer who was promptly fired. The network had to admit that most of "Katie's Notebooks" weren't written by Katie. She was widely mocked, with media columnist Jon Friedman calling her CBS career a "train wreck." It was an embarrassing episode for the anchor that caused many of her colleagues to cringe, and it could have been avoided had Couric insisted on doing her own writing.

She had hit another of those rough patches, when not much seemed to go right. *The Philadelphia Inquirer* reported, based on unnamed CBS sources, that there was a growing feeling among the rank and file that Couric was "an expensive, unfixable mistake" and that eventually she might have to leave the anchor chair.

The CBS press office hit back hard, calling the article "beyond ridiculous—unfounded, gratuitous, utterly malicious and, most importantly, untrue."

The reality was that Les Moonves and Sean McManus still had confidence in Couric, even if some of her colleagues did not. This was an extraordinarily difficult period for Couric. Even as the broadcast, under Rick Kaplan's direction, continued to make incremental improvements, the ratings kept sinking, reaching a twenty-year low in the spring of 2007 and then dipping further, to fewer than 6 million viewers.

While Couric would not say so publicly, she was giving some thought to abandoning the *CBS Evening News,* perhaps after the 2008 elections, and trying something else, maybe becoming a full-time *60 Minutes* correspondent. It wasn't that management, which had made a $75 million investment in her, was wavering, but that she was losing confidence in herself. There were days when she wondered whether she should have left the *Today* show in the first place, so constricting was the nightly straitjacket into which she now had to fit, her personality all but squeezed out in the process.

Even Couric's friends acknowledged that she had made mistakes, that perhaps she should have been more vigorous in reaching out to the staff, but no matter what she did, she was getting pounded by the press. How long did she want to live under that kind of pressure?

As the mess at CBS drew wave after wave of publicity, Sean McManus was hashing over the situation with Les Moonves.

"In retrospect," McManus said, "if we did the exact same show we're doing now from September fifth, and got the same ratings, we'd all have been fired. Everyone would say, 'You didn't do shit. You're doing the same thing as Schieffer.'"

Moonves agreed. "I'm not ashamed of anything we did," he said. "We had a format much more conducive to her talents, and it didn't work, but I'm glad we tried it."

Couric's competitors were beginning to feel sorry for her. Brian Williams thought it was absolutely seditious for some of her colleagues to be dumping on her from behind a veil of anonymity. "How do you think Katie must feel today?" his wife asked him in an e-mail.

Charlie Gibson pulled Couric aside the next time he saw her. "Nobody's cutting you any slack, and I feel badly about that," he said.

Gibson thought that Couric looked shell-shocked and was starting to second-guess herself. While watching her interview John and Elizabeth Edwards, he had thought that she was perfect for the task, that nobody grasped the difficulty of coping with cancer better than she did. How moving it would have been had Katie said that she understood all too well the conversations the couple had been having. When she made no reference to losing her husband, she was criticized for appearing insensitive. But if she had done so, Gibson thought, she would have caught hell for making the interview about herself. She couldn't win.

Gibson wanted Couric to succeed—not too much, of course, but he wanted her to make it. Otherwise, he felt, the concept of a solo female anchor would be judged a failure, and unfairly so.

The television world began buzzing with speculation as to who was behind the *Philadelphia Inquirer* story. Roger Friedman, the Fox News online columnist, wrote that Bob Schieffer was being "frequently mentioned" as one of the culprits.

But Schieffer had not cooperated with the article and had told friends that he wanted Couric to thrive. He had criticized the softer direction of the broadcast in the early months, and sometimes he'd joined in the newsroom banter about this or that story, but he kept telling colleagues that it was in everyone's interest that Couric do well, since their fate was hitched to hers. Schieffer found it typical of the blogosphere that someone could accuse him of something but never bother to call him for comment.

He decided to consult Sean McManus.

"You don't think I did this?" Schieffer asked.

McManus said that he did not. "Listen, I'm not accusing you of anything," he said.

Schieffer wasn't sure what to do next. "Should I call Katie?"

McManus didn't think so.

"Are you sure?" Schieffer asked. "Look, I can do this with a clear conscience."

But McManus felt it wasn't necessary.

Schieffer had just signed a new multimillion-dollar contract that would carry him through the 2008 elections. Far from hungering for more airtime, Schieffer had made clear that he wanted to reduce his workload, that he would be away at times to make speeches or work with the journalism school named for him at Texas Christian University. He had a standard clause inserted in the contract that if his assignment changed, CBS would have to renegotiate. But Schieffer saw no possibility that Couric would be stepping down anytime soon, and even if by some strange turn of events she did, he had no interest in filling in again. He was seventy years old, he had already served his time in the chair, and he was through with anchoring.

A big chill soon set in. Schieffer heard through the grapevine that Couric and Rick Kaplan were grousing about him. Two months went by, and he received not a single request to appear on the *Evening News*. He was, it was clear, being blackballed. A relationship that had begun with Schieffer offering Couric friendly advice over lunch, and had blossomed into an easy on-air rapport on Election Night and during major political stories, had now gone sadly sour. Schieffer felt that he could get along with anyone—he had remained friends with Dan Rather for 30 years—but decided, under the circumstances, to lay low. This was getting to be like fucking high school. It was typical of the malaise that had enveloped CBS News that the current anchor and the former anchor were now in opposite camps.

Kaplan had concluded that Schieffer was not a team player, and when he stopped inviting him on the broadcast, Couric had made no objection.

McManus decided to intercede. He told Schieffer that he would be playing an important role at Couric's side during the 2008 campaign, and that he had made this clear to his anchor as well. Whatever hard feelings lingered from the past had to be put aside.

"We need you on the team," McManus said.

Schieffer eventually decided to call Couric, to tell her that the rift wasn't helping either one of them and it was time to patch things up and move on. She did not return the call.

The larger problem, Kaplan believed, was that the *Inquirer* story was debilitating because it changed the conversation. It had spawned an urban myth, that Couric was on her way out. Even Kaplan's son-in-law had asked him, "Is Katie going to be fired?" The debate was no longer about the quality of the *Evening News* or how Couric was performing as anchor. It was about her job security.

At the regular Friday staff meeting, Mo Cashin, the twenty-five-year veteran who served as the program's broadcast manager, spoke up about the negative publicity. "How long are we going to take this?" she asked. "When are we going to start fighting back?"

Kaplan was surprised by her stance, since Couric did not think that Cashin particularly liked her. The chatter that followed turned the session into a pep rally. This, Kaplan believed, was a defining moment. The show had become Katie's. Even those who were not big Couric fans seemed to sense that they were a team, he felt, and the team was under siege from the outside. Kaplan was struck by Couric's determination, by how she persevered through all the criticism as if it didn't exist.

That, however, was the brave face that Couric presented at the office. Friends knew that she felt wounded. As if things weren't going badly enough, the *National Enquirer* came out with a "Boozing Katie Collapses!" cover. The story was hyperventilating in depicting her supposed battle against depression, but it was quite specific in describing her new boyfriend, Brooks Perlin—"a 33-year-old financial analyst who's a former triathlete"—and their vacations together, including their trip to the 2007 Super Bowl. Even worse, a "source close to her" recounted how Katie had bragged about his sexual stamina.

Couric's friends believed that the source in question was a lower-level assistant who had worked with her and had recently left CBS. Couric was stunned by the breach of trust after she had confided in the woman. That had been devastating to her. And it exposed her to a new round of ridicule.

"Poor Katie! Her new boytoy's so young," said a *Boston Herald* headline.

Friends were glad to hear that Perlin was making her happy. But even those most sympathetic to Couric questioned her judgment in discussing her sex life with a colleague who then blabbed it to others. As a fifty-year-old who had been widowed for nearly a decade, Couric was free to date anyone she pleased, younger or not, but she had to realize that, given her level of celebrity, the relationship would eventually become public. The bad publicity over the plagiarism incident had been deserved, but the *National Enquirer* humiliation was over the top. No matter what strides she made journalistically, Katie Couric seemed destined to remain tabloid fodder.

Everyone seemed to be piling on, and soon the man who had held the job for a quarter-century could not resist a hard shot. Dan Rather, in an interview on MSNBC, accused Couric's evening newscast of attempting "to dumb it down, tart it up in hopes of attracting a younger audience."

Tart it up? Rather had used the phrase before, but this time it sounded squarely aimed at his female successor. The truth was that Rather did not watch the broadcast much, and clearly did not realize the extent to which Rick Kaplan had returned it to a more traditional format. Just as clearly, Rather was still bitter at his old network for refusing to renew his *60 Minutes* contract. Though he had made his share of compromises with commercialism during his *Evening News* tenure, Rather fancied himself a lonely champion of hard news, and by unloading on Katie, he got to burnish that reputation while denigrating hers.

Couric, who had gotten in touch with Rather after getting the job but never followed up, was irritated. Several female staffers were furious. Rick Kaplan felt that the attack was beneath Rather, especially given the damage that the former anchor had inflicted on CBS News with the Memogate scandal, and sent him a sharp note expressing his disappointment.

Les Moonves was being driven to a public forum when he saw an article about Rather's remarks in the paper. No way that should have been said. Moonves knew he had no way to duck it—the moderator, Ken Auletta of *The New Yorker,* would surely bring up the matter—but he didn't want to escalate the battle to a higher level. At the same time, Moonves thought, it was important for CBS management to respond. They couldn't just leave such a disparaging comment about their star anchor hanging out there. You wouldn't use "tarting it up" against a male anchor, no matter how much of a lightweight he might be. The constant criticism of Couric, her looks, who her boyfriend was, had become a way of life for them, but this one was different.

When the question came, Moonves shrugged and said that the remark sounded pretty "sexist" to him. He wasn't looking to blow up Rather, just to firmly defend Katie. But his effort to use a light touch was lost on the print press. He was surprised by all the "Moonves Blasts Rather" headlines.

Rather wasn't done, not when his new antagonist was the man who had criticized him after the investigative report on the National Guard fiasco and who had approved the decision to cut him loose a year earlier. Within hours Rather took on his old boss, telling Fox News that "Les Moonves knows about entertainment, but he doesn't know about news," and resurrecting Moonves's old crack about blowing up the news division.

It was almost a cry for attention from the former CBS newsman who had risen so high from the days of covering hurricanes in Texas and was now relegated to the near-obscurity of a digital cable channel. Just as Couric was struggling to regain her footing, her predecessor had publicly deemed her unworthy.

Moonves decided to let it pass rather than drag out the fight for another round. He was struck by the irony of Rather appearing on Fox, which had vilified him for years as the personification of a liberal network anchor, especially after the National Guard debacle. Moonves knew that Rather still harbored resentment toward him and CBS over his messy departure, but he didn't share those feelings. He still felt a certain degree of affection for Rather and all that he had done for CBS News.

As the exchanges reverberated through the media echo chamber, Couric came to believe that there was a silver lining. Her network colleagues were aggressively defending her, decrying the focus on her gender. They were telling the world that despite her abysmal ratings, the network still backed its embattled anchor. Couric was so accustomed to coming under attack, so inured to constant criticism, that she now took comfort in the rallying of her remaining allies.

Couric picked up the phone and called Moonves. "Thanks for standing up for me," she said.

*　　*　　*

Brian Williams had just landed in New York after two awful days at the Virginia Tech campus when he got a BlackBerry message from his new producer, Alexandra Wallace.

The deranged student who had murdered thirty-two people at the college, in the worst gun massacre in American history, had sent NBC a package. It had been discovered in the mailroom at 30 Rock. Steve Capus wanted Williams in his executive suite the moment he got back.

There had never been any question, after the horrifying shootings on April 16, 2007, that the three anchors would go to Blacksburg, Virginia. The magnitude of the tragedy required their presence, and they needed to assume a comforting role after a trauma that had hit the country particularly hard, given the youth of most of the victims and the sheer senselessness of the attacks.

Williams, Couric, and Gibson conducted sensitive interviews with friends and relatives of those who had been killed. They were each granted a few minutes with George and Laura Bush during the president's visit there. Gibson gently asked him about gun control, just as he had raised the matter with President Clinton after Columbine. Williams invoked the gun issue by noting that he had a daughter in college and that the Bushes' two daughters were recent graduates. Couric was the most pointed, asking Bush: "Is it too easy, in your view, for unstable people to purchase guns in this country?"

Williams understood all too well the horror for parents, having just sent Allison off to college. He had called her and they talked about what happened.

When Williams got to Capus's office, he found the boss hunched over his computer. The DVD sent by Seung-Hui Cho, the South Korean student who had gone on the rampage before killing himself, was already in the machine. Capus would click on a little box, and a new photo—Cho glaring at the camera, Cho with his arms outstretched, each hand clutching a gun—would pop up on the screen. It was revolting to think that this psychopath had methodically mailed the package during a two-hour break in his shooting spree. Each time Capus clicked, a fresh vision of hell would appear.

Capus handed Williams the killer's scrawled manifesto. It bordered on incoherent, each profanity-filled sentence seemingly unconnected to the next. Worst of all was the videotaped diatribe in which Cho railed against rich people. Poring over this collection of hate was one of the creepiest experiences of Williams's life.

He called Pete Williams, the network's justice correspondent, and asked him to hop on the next shuttle to New York and handle the story. Pete said he wanted to remain in Washington to finish his piece on the day's Supreme Court ruling restricting partial-birth abortion.

"People will be talking about the abortion decision long after this manifesto has faded," he said.

"I know, but I need your eye and your hand and your judgment on this."

There was no question in Brian Williams's mind, and none in Steve Capus's, that they had to air some of this material once they got the green light from the Virginia State Police officials who were reviewing the originals. Williams knew that the images would be painful for many viewers. It had been painful to watch pictures of American soldiers setting fire to peasants' huts in Vietnam. It had been painful to look at the photos of Abu Ghraib, painful to watch the coffins coming back from Iraq. But this was news. This was journalism. This was what they did. The only question was how best to pare back this garbage.

"Take all the time you need at the top of the broadcast to explain what's about to happen," Capus said. This was the portrait of a killer, Capus felt, and they had to run it.

Jeff Zucker joined the meeting at 4:30. He approved of Capus's plan to broadcast two minutes and twenty seconds of the twenty-five-minute video and a handful of the forty-five photos. Williams began writing the "good evening" script, and when *Nightly* began, he sounded a note of caution.

"We are sensitive to how all of this will be seen by those affected, and we know we are, in effect, airing the words of a murderer here tonight," he said.

Six and a half minutes after *Nightly* began, Charlie Gibson was showing the Cho video on *World News*. When Gibson heard about the tape, he cursed the news gods for NBC's good fortune. But as airtime approached, he realized what an awful position NBC was in, having to wrestle with whether the video had news value or whether broadcasting it would be sheer exploitation. He was grateful for having been spared that burden.

Two and a half minutes after ABC picked up the story, Katie Couric was airing the footage on the *CBS Evening News*. Both broadcasts had simply lifted the video and replayed it as the anchors explained that it had been sent to NBC.

When Williams got home to Connecticut that night, he and Jane were surfing the cable channels. The haunting Cho footage was everywhere. It had become video wallpaper. Williams couldn't watch anymore and clicked off the set.

The backlash erupted immediately. On the radio airwaves, conservative and liberal hosts alike hammered NBC for its decision. Rival network executives took their potshots. And the majority of comments posted on Williams's blog seethed with anger.

"You should be ashamed," a Tennessee viewer said. "While the families of those that died are trying to deal with this horrible act of violence you provide the killer with exactly what he wanted, worldwide viewing of his hatred."

"I have watched NBC News for 28 years," a Michigan woman wrote, "but tonight when you reported on the material you received from that demented killer, you gave him a platform to legitimize his rantings, and the exposure that make legends . . . I have turned off my TV and I will get my news from another source from now on."

"Oh, my God," an Indiana man said, "your newscast has made me so enraged I cannot even see straight."

Williams understood the emotional response, but he was absolutely convinced that they had done the right thing and had acted with restraint. Still, they were taking a beating on the PR front. When an invitation arrived from Oprah Winfrey, Williams thought about it that night and decided against it. But the next morning he changed his mind. She was going to do an hour with families of the victims, and his network wouldn't be represented? Journalists were e-mailing with words of thanks for making the difficult call. Every other network, every newspaper in the country, had made the same decision by picking up the video and the photos.

Williams talked it over with Capus. Oprah had a huge and influential audience. They should both go to Chicago and tape the show. They were two guys with daughters who were college freshmen. This wasn't a decision made by some corporate monolith. They had to be the face of NBC News. Capus reluctantly agreed.

The taping went well. Williams was on the set, while Capus fielded questions from the audience, and Winfrey gave them a respectful hearing.

When Williams got back to Manhattan at four o'clock, he had to crash on the upcoming newscast, and there was no chance to catch his breath. He was scheduled to fly to South Carolina the following night to moderate the first televised debate involving all the Democratic presidential candidates, which would be carried on MSNBC.

When he got to the campus of South Carolina State University, Williams did not want to be buttonholed by people pushing questions or agendas. He took refuge in the office of the school's assistant vice president for academic affairs and stayed there all day, refining the questions that he and his staff had developed. He emerged to anchor *Nightly*, then slipped into the debate hall to moderate the ninety-minute session.

Williams was at his sharpest when he asked a series of what he called "elephant in the room" questions, designed to raise uncomfortable topics that put the candidates on the spot. He told Hillary Clinton that a majority of the public had an unfavorable view of her and asked why the Republicans were so zealously looking forward to running against her. He asked Barack Obama about his ties to a Chicago donor under indictment and whether the senator was practicing old-style politics. He asked Joe Biden whether he had the discipline to control his mouth or would remain what one newspaper called a "gaffe machine." He asked John Edwards why he had gotten a $400 haircut and paid for it out of campaign funds.

When it was over, Williams shook hands with the eight candidates. He had already turned down invitations to appear on three MSNBC programs. He did not want to critique the contenders' answers or analyze his own performance. Instead, he slipped out a back door and headed for the airport.

Such was the life of a network anchor. Williams had ricocheted from a trip to Iraq to the Imus uproar to the Virginia Tech tragedy to the Oprah appearance to a starring role in the first major face-off of the 2008 presidential campaign, all the while reporting, editing, blogging, and anchoring an evening newscast, and squeezing in his son's high school baseball game. If the breakneck pace sometimes meant that he had little time to think, if snap decisions had to be made largely on instinct, that came with the territory.

Sometimes, though, his prim approach to the news clouded his judgment. One day Williams left his competitors in the dust, topping the broadcast with a breakthrough in which researchers had created stem cells in mice without the use of embryos; his science correspondent delivered the late-breaking news at the afternoon meeting. The next day he boasted about refusing to cover an uproar over Paris Hilton being released from a Los Angeles jail after serving just three days of a sentence for driving with a suspended license, a spectacle that was consuming the cable networks hour after hour.

Although Hilton was far more renowned for her bad-girl antics than for any discernible talent, Gibson and Couric carried reports on the raging debate over a double standard of justice. The following day, when the wealthy heiress was ordered back to jail, Williams capitulated, making the Paris melodrama the second story on *Nightly News.* His lonely stand against celebrity news had lasted all of twenty-four hours.

After an eruption involving Paris Hilton or Anna Nicole Smith or other famous-for-being-famous starlets, the networks generally drifted back toward serious news, the kind that matters to people's lives but unfolds at a maddeningly slow pace. The long-running debate over illegal immigration was a classic example.

If there was a day when the evening newscasts seemed to declare the Bush presidency over, at least on the domestic front, it was when Republican lawmakers killed his immigration reform bill, the last major initiative of Bush's second term.

"It's a big loss for President Bush," Williams announced, and the analysis that followed made clear that the journalists were rendering a judgment on more than just a single piece of legislation.

The Senate vote against debating the measure was "a stinging political defeat," said NBC's David Gregory; reflected a "serious loss of clout by the unpopular president," said ABC's Jake Tapper; produced "a strong sense that Washington is just broken," said NBC's Tim Russert; and, in the words of CBS analyst Douglas Brinkley, had left the country with "a dead duck president." The networks, in a sense, were moving on from the Bush era, except for the war that would be his defining legacy, and increasingly focusing on the campaign to replace him.

There was a similar sense of turning the page on Iraq. At a news conference, David Gregory asked the president: "Why shouldn't people conclude that you are either stubborn, in denial, but certainly not realistic about the strategy?" Days later, when the House voted to withdraw most American troops by April 2008—even as the Senate remained stalemated—the anchors' narrative was set. They were tightly focused on the search for an exit strategy. They did not dwell on the consequences of withdrawal; rather, they reflected a growing political consensus that no more American blood should be spilled.

Brian Williams thrived on such politically charged stories, but the hard slog of journalism had a way of bumping up against the realities of the marketplace. As *Nightly*'s ratings had started to decline in the early months of 2007, a gossip reporter for the *New York Post* called Tom Brokaw to ask about a bogus rumor that some insiders wanted him to reclaim to his old job. "God, no! Brian's doing a great job," Brokaw said. The idea was absurd, not least because Brokaw, at sixty-seven, was happy to have abandoned the daily grind. Williams laughed at the item, called Brokaw, and thanked him for being classy about it. But after more than two years on top, the anonymous carping had started. Somehow, in network news, everything got reduced to the numbers.

Williams had responded once again by hitting the road. There were trips to London—for an exclusive sitdown with Tony Blair—and to New Orleans, where the anchor assessed the slow progress on his thirteenth visit to the once-drowned city, and then to Boston and Chicago and Los Angeles. Outside Brian was back. Williams came alive on the road, was far more animated and provocative, shedding the reserved persona of the studio. He seemed to sense that, as the second-place contender, he needed an extra kick.

Privately, Williams's frustration was mounting. He hated losing—*hated* it!—even though he loved Charlie Gibson. And there were nights when the *World News* gang kicked their butts. But although *Nightly* had lost half a million viewers from the previous year—even more than Couric had shed, as CBS executives kept reminding reporters—Williams was convinced that none of it, not a tenth of a percentage point, was his fault.

Sure, he was distracted at times. His dad had broken his other hip, and Williams was commuting each day from Connecticut to the hospital in New Jersey and then to Manhattan. But what was killing the newscast, he thought, were the budget cuts at the network's ten O-and-Os, or owned-and-operated stations. At every station he visited, he could still smell the gunpowder from people being shot.

When Williams was at NBC's Dallas station, staffers there were livid over layoffs that had cost five top on-air people their jobs—and applauded when word came that day that the NBC executive in charge of the local stations had been transferred to a General Electric job. At NBC's Washington station, a top anchor, a nationally known sportscaster, and an entertainment reporter who was a fixture in the capital had all been axed. In New York, the 5 p.m. newscast that led into *Nightly* had been cut to one anchor. All these cutbacks, Williams believed, were slicing into his lead-in audience in the major markets in a way that coincided with his ratings slide, as if someone had flipped a switch. Local executives at these stations kept asking him to fix his newscast, but *Nightly,* in his view, was not the problem.

Williams took his case to Jeff Zucker. "These cuts are killing me," he said. He also appealed to Jeff Immelt at GE.

"You're the most important single asset to the company," Immelt assured him. It was nice to know that he was even more vital than lightbulbs, Williams thought, but that didn't make the problem go away. Immelt and Zucker both said they would look into the matter, but Williams was not optimistic.

Williams thought *Nightly* was as good as ever, but this was really starting to sting. The horse-race coverage was maddening, especially since most television writers never bothered weighing the merits of the newscasts. It was always numbers, just numbers.

And for Williams, the numbers were personal. The ratings slide was being hung like an albatross around his neck. Every news story on the subject began, "Williams has lost X hundred thousand viewers . . ." Did people actually believe that he had been on top for two years and suddenly became an awful, unwatchable presence?

There were other factors at work, of course. Perhaps the audience just hadn't warmed up to Williams, or thought he did too many Washington stories, or found Gibson easier to watch. But those were intangibles that could never quite be measured.

Maybe, Williams thought, he was tilting at windmills. Maybe he just needed a villain to blame. But in trying to climb back to the mountaintop, he felt, the biggest obstacle was beyond his control.

* * *

Charlie Gibson had no desire to tell the world about prostitution in the nation's capital.

His ace investigator, Brian Ross, had the goods from the woman known as the D.C. Madam. Deborah Jeane Palfrey, who had been indicted on charges of running a high-end escort service, had given Ross four years' worth of phone records that enabled him to identify about a thousand of her male clients. Palfrey believed that the publicity would aid her defense, and Washington was brimming with speculation about who might be on the list. Brian Williams did the story, Katie Couric did the story, and Ross was touting the investigation on his blog. But Gibson wanted no part of it.

On a Wednesday at the end of April 2007, Ross called Randall Tobias, the deputy secretary of State, who supervised a worldwide effort to curb prostitution and promote abstinence. The married official admitted that he patronized the escort service but said he had not engaged in sex, had merely had "gals come over to the condo to give me a massage." The next day, late in the afternoon, Tobias abruptly quit. Other news organizations jumped on the story, but *World News* reported nothing. There was a simple explanation: Ross was at his son's high school debate and knew nothing about the resignation. He posted the story on ABC's Web site at nine o'clock that night.

The following Monday Ross sat down with Gibson and Jon Banner to make his case. The Bush administration had a strong moralistic streak, he said, and federal prosecutors spent large sums of money to go after services such as Palfrey's, even setting up classes on the dangers of prostitution for johns who had been arrested. "That's nice treatment for the men," Ross said, "but women don't get the same special handling."

Ross sensed that Gibson and Banner seemed squeamish about the subject. To Gibson, the idea of airing a bunch of names of the male clients, of getting embroiled in this woman's legal battle, just didn't feel right. If both the men and women were acting voluntarily, Gibson thought, wasn't this a victimless crime?

In the end, Ross concluded that Palfrey's other clients, however important, were not prominent enough to be outed on national television, and when he did the story that week for *20/20,* he named no one who had not already been identified. But *World News* never even mentioned the Tobias resignation that its own reporter had caused. A year earlier, when Gibson was still searching for Quaker-style consensus, he might have yielded and done the story. If he wasn't absolutely certain that he was right, he didn't want to impose his own views. But now, Gibson was far more willing to go with his gut. He trusted his instincts. There was no longer any doubt that the program was his.

On the air, Gibson had never looked more relaxed. He ad-libbed lines, slipped in jokes, and most of all, conducted smart conversations with his correspondents. Night after night he would chat up George Stephanopoulos and Martha Raddatz, whom he privately called "Toots," about the day's developments. He was doing Bob Schieffer's old show, and everything seemed to be clicking.

When Gibson beat Brian Williams the first couple of weeks, David Westin was so pleased that he sent a congratulatory box of chocolates down to the newsroom. At a morning planning meeting, Gibson chided the boss.

"When we won in the old days, Roone would send champagne."

Westin played along: "If you win the sweeps, you can have champagne." When Gibson registered his first sweeps victory at the end of February, a case of fine bubbly appeared in his office.

By the summer of 2007, as Gibson recorded three months of first-place finishes—sometimes beating Williams by as much as 1 million viewers—the media crowned him the new winner of the anchor wars. It was, on a personal level, a remarkable achievement. The man had once been booted off the morning show. He had been passed over for the evening news the first time. Fate had given him the job he never expected to have. What an irony, given the publicity cocoon surrounding Couric, that Gibson celebrated his first anniversary in the job as America's top-rated anchor.

He shied away from anything that smacked of self-promotion, frustrating his publicists by refusing to talk to the likes of *People* and *GQ.* He was the anti-Katie, the most self-effacing of the anchors, who had tiptoed onto the stage without fanfare. He did not blog, or even read blogs, and the daily Webcast, was his only bow to the new technology. He spent no time plotting how to attract younger viewers, as he was satisfied with the graying crowd. He was an old-school reporter in an age of razzle-dazzle.

Gibson was genuinely puzzled by the obsession with ratings, by the way that so many people talked and wrote about the numbers. He had never set an overriding goal of getting to number one, and he refused to look at the detailed Nielsen figures, for fear of distorting his journalistic decisions. He just did what came naturally.

Why *was* there such an unrelenting focus on ratings? Why was an anchor who reached 7 million viewers each night, an enormous audience by news standards, derided as a flop because a rival had 8 million people tuning in? The answer was that they sat atop a media edifice built on keeping score. Journalists wrote about television the way they covered sports and politics: by the numbers. There had to be winners and losers. There had to be an attempt to quantify who was the best and who was an also-ran. The *American Idol* mentality permeated the process. Just as the most talented singer didn't always win the most votes, the most inspiring politician didn't always win the election, and the most athletic baseball team didn't always reach the World Series, the newscast with the most stellar journalism didn't necessarily finish on top. A newscast was the ultimate reality show. Victory required some intangible combination of personality, savvy, ambition, graceful writing, solid reporting, good producing, a strong lead-in audience, and a few lucky breaks.

Gibson was the lead horse now, but Brian Williams was still running strongly, and Katie Couric, with a new jockey cracking the whip, was several lengths back. Still, fans could be fickle, and it was not hard to envision the lead changing again.

*   *   *

Shortly before Memorial Day 2007, CBS aired a prime-time tribute to Walter Cronkite on his ninetieth birthday. Charlie Gibson talked about being riveted as a boy by Cronkite's coverage of the 1952 political conventions. Katie Couric, who had sought his advice over dinner before taking the job, recalled Cronkite announcing with great sadness that JFK was dead—how he had handled it as a human being first and an anchor second, which was how she saw herself as well. Brian Williams, who had insisted on visiting the old set when he joined CBS, said that on the day of Cronkite's last newscast in 1981, he could not shake the feeling that something more than one man was leaving the chair. And he was right. Cronkite had presided in an era when journalists were implicitly trusted, when he could close by saying "That's the way it is," and for much of America, that's the way it was. No anchor would ever wield that authority again, not in a world of instantaneous information and constant criticism, and Gibson, Couric, and Williams, in paying their respects to the old lion, knew that better than anyone.

After more than two decades of Dan Rather, Tom Brokaw, and Peter Jennings lending an aura of permanence to the network newscasts, the competition now has a wide-open feel. The new anchors are feeling their way in a different political environment, one in which the precipitous decline of the Bush presidency, the growing unpopularity of the Iraq war, and the Democratic takeover of Congress has left the country more polarized than at any time since Vietnam. But they are also having to adapt to a world of blogging and Web video and endless cable chatter, as they seek to retool the nightly programs that they inherited.

For Gibson, the looming question is whether he wants to continue after his contract expires in early 2009. He had planned to retire from *GMA* by now and canceled trips to Canada and New Zealand that he and his wife were to take with friends. Every six weeks or so he sits down with Arlene and asks if she minds that he is working while she is retired, and as long as the answer is no, he feels comfortable. He is convinced that when the time comes to hang it up and spend more time with the grandchildren, he will sense it. The worst thing would be to stay too long. Charlie Gibson, unlike so many in the television business, does not need to be a network anchor.

Katie Couric is still grappling with the consequences of her midcareer move, the bold gamble that she now hopes to salvage. There is a frenetic quality about Couric, a restless energy that prompted her to abandon her throne as the queen of morning television and seek to conquer a new kingdom. Couric is not shy about sharing her emotions, which makes her approachable, or taking chances, which makes her a risk-taker, but she was savvy enough to seek a midcourse correction after her news makeover proved too extreme for the viewers. Her first-woman status and celebrity coverage magnify each misstep as she struggles to prove that she has the seasoned judgment and seriousness of purpose required of an evening news anchor. Katie Couric is a star whose blinding light sometimes obscures her many talents.

Brian Williams is still enjoying the culmination of a dream, a chance to fulfill the childhood fantasy that once seemed remote for a college dropout. He revels in being an anchor, in communicating, in writing a daily blog, in being the man in front of the camera. Williams enjoys the vindication of life at the top after years of being dismissed as a good-looking lightweight and enduring the relative obscurity of cable exile. His round-the-clock drive reflects both a love affair with news and a lingering insecurity that success, like his first-place standing, could one day prove fleeting. Yet his natural caution, and the on-air suppression of his natural humor, sometimes seems to be holding him back. Brian Williams is a traditionalist in an era of transformation, lightly retouching the contours of the network newscast while clinging to its past glory.

For ABC, CBS, and NBC, how these new faces fare will be, above all, a matter of commercial success. But for the news business and the country, the stakes are higher than a matter of ratings share and demo numbers. Williams, Gibson, and Couric have the considerable burden of keeping their franchises afloat as an important method of information delivery when their usefulness is no longer entirely clear. They must overcome the odds or be remembered as fleeting figures who managed the inevitable decline of the evening news. The ghosts of television history are watching.

Rome Hartman left CBS News in the summer of 2007, joining the BBC to produce an hourlong nightly newscast in Washington for the American market.

John Reiss remained at NBC but did not immediately come to terms with management on a new assignment.

Dan Bartlett resigned as President Bush's counselor, several months after the birth of his third son, following a long period of frustration with the coverage of the Iraq war as Bush's military surge fell short in stemming the tide of violence.

Kimberly Dozier returned to CBS, regaining the ability to walk after more than twenty-five operations, and did a prime-time special on the Iraq bombing that wounded her and killed her two crew members.

Ben Karlin gave up his dual jobs as executive producer of *The Daily Show* and *The Colbert Report* to pursue a book and other projects while still consulting for Jon Stewart.

EPILOGUE

As he was packing up his office at NBC for the last time, John Chancellor took a moment to reflect on his anchoring days and the future of nightly newscasts.

"Maybe they will end up in a kind of extinction, like *Collier's* and *Look* and the *Saturday Evening Post,*" he said.

That was in the spring of 1993, at about the midpoint of the long tenures of Tom Brokaw, Dan Rather, and Peter Jennings, and barely a day has gone by since without someone suggesting that the creaky old jalopies known as evening newscasts should be dismantled, packed up, and shipped to history's junkyard. But somehow they just keep lurching along.

When I began work on this book at the end of 2005, I wanted to get inside the culture of the network newscasts and learn how they planned to cope with the erosion of their audience and with the rise of insta-news in our new, lightning-quick digital culture. But that quest became, as any human endeavor does, a story about people—talented, driven, smart people, sometimes cocky, and yet concerned and confused, trying to regain their footing in a world far different from the one in which they grew up. No one is more acutely sensitive to the whims of public preference than those who live and die by a nightly box office.

The questions about how nightly newscasts can compete in a wired age have grown louder as the ratings have declined. The CBS, NBC, and ABC programs were still drawing 35 million viewers in 1996, and 30 million in 2002, and by 2007 viewership had dropped to 25 million. It was still the biggest arena out there, but the crowds were thinning. As the baton was passed to Brian Williams, Katie Couric, and Charlie Gibson, the obituary writers were once again sharpening their quills.

First, the good news. This trio of anchors is as good as any in the past. Whether the measure is experience, journalistic savvy, or on-camera skills, they all understand the ingredients of a solid newscast. Couric, with her morning show background, obviously spent far less time as a reporter, but she is a skilled interviewer with a great capacity for empathy. All three are crisp and comfortable on the air.

They are surrounded by groups of smart producers and hardworking correspondents, some of whom routinely risk their lives in war zones. The reporters understand the art of storytelling, the use of pictures, and the demand for sharp writing better than many of their predecessors, and those in charge are supremely mindful of the need to connect with the audience. They *have* to be, given that at any second the viewer can flick away to a hundred other stations or simply click off the set and turn to the computer screen or the iPod.

For all the griping about evening newscasts, they provide a reasonably intelligent, if somewhat shallow, fill on the day's news, coupled with interesting features, trend stories, and human interest fare. They are polished, concise, and sometimes evocative.

Now, the bad news.

It's not enough. It's not even close to being enough.

The newscasts have an aging audience because they systematically cater to that audience, squeezing out, or simply ignoring, all kinds of cool developments that might appeal to younger people. That is a ticking demographic time bomb.

The newscasts break little news because their reporting ranks are strikingly thin, given the millions of viewers they serve, a consequence of their takeover by huge conglomerates that view the programs as a financial burden. A medium-sized local newspaper has more reporters than any of the network newscasts.

The broadcasts are largely predictable because they follow an agenda set by a handful of national newspapers, yielding a kind of groupthink in which all three programs do the same stories, and beyond that the same kinds of stories, night after night.

The newscasts are of little interest to a sizable segment of the population because they are so wedded to the traditional 6:30 time slot—or 5:30 in some markets—that they have come and gone before many people get home from work.

And it's a shame. With their massive megaphone, they could have a much bigger impact on the country, break new ground, and drive the media agenda. Instead, they increasingly resemble Detroit's Big Three automakers, churning out a product that fewer customers want, even as they equip the latest models with shinier chrome and better tail fins.

The focus on viewers ranging from middle-aged to elderly—many of them women—is so intense that it badly skews the journalistic selection process. Barely a week goes by without a report on breast cancer or the demands on working mothers. The seemingly endless flow of health and medical stories on these programs makes the newscasts look and feel like a clinic at *General Hospital*: autism, ADHD drugs, children's vaccines, Ambien, low-fat diets for women, sperm banks, back pain, ear infections, menopause, chemotherapy, sunscreen, healthy cooking, children and hazardous chemicals, vitamin supplements, childhood obesity, hormone therapy, breast-feeding, postpartum depression, sleep deprivation, custom-made bladders, migraines, prostate cancer, and Alzheimer's.

And just in case any older viewers were feeling left out, the newscasts have also featured segments on new retirement communities, custody battles, parents tracking kids through cell phones, and separate series on baby boomers on both *Nightly News* and *World News*. One edition of *Nightly* carried a piece on women being more likely than men to get lung cancer, which was followed by Brian Williams reporting that "researchers feel they have a better handle now on what it is women really do want most of all"—more time away from the job with their families. Not exactly a news flash.

Taken individually, these stories can be important and informative. Collectively, they hang a giant "Young People Not Wanted" sign on the newscasts. Even when the programs cover a subject that might appeal to, say, college students, they do it from an older person's perspective, such as the hidden dangers lurking at MySpace or Facebook, rather than the attractions of online social networking, or the addiction, rather than the excitement, of video games.

It's not that network staffers are hopelessly unhip—ABC routinely puts items about rock stars and high-tech gadgets in its Webcast, but by the time *World News* rolls around, they have dropped off the radar screen. One day Brian Williams walked into a *Nightly* editorial meeting buzzing about the hottest thing online: video of a Comcast repairman fast asleep on a customer's couch, having succumbed while on hold with his own company. The footage, which had spread across the Net, would have made a hilarious item for the newscast, but it was never even considered.

In a broader sense, the slavish devotion with which ABC, NBC, and CBS follow the lead of the major papers—especially *The New York Times*—betrays more than a lack of imagination. It is an abdication of news judgment, a form of pack journalism that also reflects how the staffs of these programs are constantly a step behind. They are packagers and popularizers, not groundbreakers.

When the three Duke University lacrosse players were accused—wrongly, as it turned out—of raping a woman hired to strip for them at a late-night party, Martin Savidge, the NBC correspondent in Atlanta, asked his bosses if they were interested in the story. He was told to keep an eye on the situation, which he took to mean, don't go anywhere and don't spend any money. Days later, when *The New York Times* ran a front-page story on the Duke case, NBC immediately dispatched Savidge to North Carolina to report that night on what had previously been deemed less than newsworthy.

Such an approach suggests a kind of intellectual dishonesty on the part of the newscasts, which pretend that they are unearthing all manner of fascinating information and ideas on the viewers' behalf when they are merely playing a modified form of rip 'n read. Yes, they do their own reporting in these pieces, often humanize the stories by finding people who are affected, and carry the news to a wider audience. But they should be able to think for themselves about what is important and have better antennae for spotting emerging trends. Otherwise, they are just another copycat medium in a world in which millions of commentators, radio hosts, and bloggers are regurgitating and rating the reporting of a few large newspapers.

The reason, in part, is that they are making do with less. In 2005 ABC had forty-seven correspondents; NBC, forty-five, and CBS, forty-one. The contraction of foreign coverage is beyond debate. The number of overseas network bureaus has been cut roughly in half since the 1980s: NBC has ten, CBS six, and ABC five. Even the average time allotted for news has shrunk, from 21 minutes in 1988 to 18.7 minutes in 2005. There are more commercials, more teases, more promos, and less actual news content.

That content, while serious much of the time, sometimes slides into pandering. The soap opera journalism that increasingly infects cable news and the morning shows has slowly spread to the evening newscasts as well. There is no plausible reason for these broadcasts to be leading with a fabricating drifter who claimed to have killed JonBenet Ramsey, or a week-old search for missing mountain climbers who obviously must be dead, other than as a surrender to sensationalism that might produce an uptick in the ratings.

The era of polarization has also taken its toll on the networks. While 38 percent of Democrats regularly watch the nightly newscasts, according to one survey, only 24 percent of Republicans are loyal viewers. This gap between the partisans nearly tripled from 2004 to 2006, no doubt because of inflamed passions surrounding the Bush presidency and the Iraq war. Many network staffers are essentially in denial about the extent to which conservatives believe that they tilt to the left, which is more true on social issues than on politics, although the properly skeptical coverage of the war seemed at times to drift into advocacy. Even if the problem is largely one of perception, the prospect of news programs that increasingly appeal to Democratic Party voters, while a rising percentage of Republicans gravitate to such outlets as Fox News, is nothing short of troubling.

Katie Couric made perhaps the boldest attempt to break with tradition by introducing more outside voices, eye-catching images, juicy Web items, and long interviews on emotionally charged subjects. These were lively additions to a staid format, but they wound up shortchanging viewers on important news, and within weeks Couric was forced to retreat. The lengthy sit-downs with celebrities and grieving widows felt jarring, and the lighter fare made Couric seem less serious. The overriding message was that an evening anchor could not cut back on the meat and potatoes of daily events in favor of tastier, but less filling, ingredients from the journalistic salad bar. In the morning Couric could do both; the evening platter proved too small.

The puzzle that no one has been able to solve is how to fit all the jagged pieces—breaking news, politics, foreign affairs, finance, health care, culture, and longer narratives that provide a colorful slice of America—into those measly nineteen minutes of airtime. The truth is that the half-hour newscast is as outmoded as the fifteen-minute version was when CBS became the first network to junk it in 1963. On the handful of occasions when *World News* and *Nightly News* squeezed in a few more minutes by lining up a single sponsor willing to settle for fewer commercials, the improvement was striking.

An hour-long program would have a far better chance of combining news, features, and original reporting in a way that would live up to the networks' potential and reclaim part of their franchise. But no one talks seriously about the prospect. A network newscast that ran from 7 to 8—a time, incidentally, when more people are home from work—would mean cutting into the affiliates' lucrative profits from such fare as *Wheel of Fortune, Entertainment Tonight,* and *Seinfeld* reruns. And a 10 P.M. newscast would have to compete against prime-time dramas.

Instead, everyone in television is comfortable with an arrangement that is just barely good enough. Just good enough that the networks can enjoy the prestige of putting on nightly newscasts. Just good enough that they plant their flag in the soil of major national and international events, only to move on moments later in an effort to shoehorn other headlines into the allotted time. Just good enough so live interviews that break from the scripted choreography last no more than a few minutes. Just good enough that the audience for these sixty-year-old programs does not decline too precipitously. But not good enough to reverse that decline, or to get anyone terribly excited, or to put on newscasts that are as compelling as the best entertainment shows.

The networks have taken a few tentative steps in the right direction by expanding their presence on the Internet. In making available more video, blogs, and footage of the programs themselves, by hooking up with the likes of *YouTube* and iTunes, they are reaching a generation that is unaccustomed to getting information by sitting passively on the living room couch. More important, they are starting to circumvent the 6:30-or-nothing dilemma. From reality shows to rock music, the entertainment world is inching toward a model of providing content when the user wants it, in as large or as small a dose as he or she wants it. If a teenager can download a single song to an iPod instead of being forced to go to the mall and buy the entire CD, why would the networks insist on making you watch their once-a-day news offering at a fixed time, in the sequence of stories they have determined?

But just moving the programs into cyberspace is as rudimentary as the early days of television, when it resembled radio with pictures. Why not make available speeches, news conferences, supporting documents, and background chats by correspondents related to a story for which only one minute and forty-five seconds is available on the air? Why not show the full interviews that were sliced and diced into broadcast snippets? Why can a couple of guys in a California garage launch a site called *YouTube* and get people downloading 100 million videos a day, leaving the news sites run by Viacom, Disney, and General Electric in the dust? Why not have the anchor online, talking about the difficulty of covering the story, or show the newsroom debate over whether it was a story at all? The possibilities are almost endless once you pull back the curtain, move away from the half-hour mindset, and turn the broadcasts into a cornucopia of online information and images.

The network blogs have also been rather tepid. Charlie Gibson does not indulge. Katie Couric has a writer help with her posts, and they are generally as short, polished, and bland as Hallmark cards. Brian Williams is the most ambitious blogger, often commenting on buzzworthy subjects and providing links to various articles. But when it comes to *Nightly,* Williams generally limits himself to billboarding the night's upcoming stories rather than discussing how he handled a controversial piece or what mistakes his team might have made. The underlying problem is that blogs, by their nature, are supposed to be provocative, while anchors are in the business of trying to avoid offending even a sliver of their mass audience. It is an awkward fit at best. The NBC and CBS videologs have also become routine and unremarkable. CBS has broken some ground by taping editorial meetings, but only once or twice a year. The overall sense is of a big toe barely being dipped into the online waters.

Most of what the anchors and correspondents do is based on carefully crafted scripts, but there is no script for an uncertain future with an eroding audience. They are being forced to rethink the essence of their approach, just as other digital choices—for news, video, opinion, argument, gossip—are multiplying by the minute.

Embedded in the early months of Katie Couric's run as anchor is a lesson about the limitations of the evening news. Whatever the flaws in her execution, she tried a different approach, one aimed at expanding the breadth of the audience, mainly by attracting younger viewers who might prefer a more informal and slightly hipper version of the old format. By abandoning that approach, Couric and her network essentially decided to fight for a larger share of the existing audience whose average age hovers around sixty. Whether a different retooling of the newscast, or a different anchor, might have been more successful is open to debate. What is beyond debate is the demographic reality that catering mainly to aging customers amounts to slow suicide for the networks.

A Gallup poll in the spring of 2007 found Couric maintaining the highest negative ratings—33 percent, compared to 16 percent for Gibson and 18 percent for Williams—but the partisan verdict was equally troubling. Sixty-five percent of Democrats, but only 36 percent of Republicans, approved of Couric. The split was narrower, but no less real, for her rivals: 71 percent of Democrats approved of Gibson, compared to 56 percent of Republicans. And 75 percent of Democrats, but only 47 percent of Republicans, approved of Williams. The figures were no doubt influenced by the reporting on the

Iraq war, but also reflected a lack of confidence on the right in network newscasts in general and in Couric in particular.

Were the evening newscasts to fade into history, something important and irreplaceable would be lost. They are still the biggest tent in the media village, still explaining the world—a few chunks of it, anyway—to those too busy to be surfing the Net or watching cable all day. They have the power to cut through the static and give a story a national profile. And because their divisions are essentially constructed to support them, they set the pace for the other network news shows.

In the end, news is not just words, sound bites, and pictures. It is people guiding us through the dizzying swirl of events. The importance of Brian Williams, Katie Couric, and Charlie Gibson is that they come on the screen when terrorists attack, when the country goes to war, when a space shuttle blows up, when the votes are counted on Election Night. They will never have the audience share of the Cronkite era, but they are national explainers, inquisitors, and hand-holders. And even in an info-saturated society, that matters.

But if they want to hang on to their day jobs, and the networks want to protect their storied franchise, they have to cast off the barnacles of tradition and bring more edge, urgency, and originality to their programs. Williams made a start with his New Orleans crusade and showcasing of e-mail feedback, Schieffer through his homespun chats with his colleagues, Gibson with his everyman persona and affinity for consumer issues, Couric with her humor, informality, and more emotional interviews, but they still face an uphill battle. The anchors are certified celebrities as well as talented communicators, but in an era when fame has been so devalued, that is no longer enough. They must reinvent the ancient ritual of the evening newscast or face the cruelest fate of all: irrelevance.

ACKNOWLEDGMENTS

My thanks to Dominick Anfuso and Martha Levin of Free Press, who instantly grasped the potential of this project and buoyed me with their enthusiasm and advice. I am indebted to Rafe Sagalyn, my agent, for his unerring instincts about journalism and publishing. And I appreciate the generosity of the more than 125 people associated with the networks who patiently and graciously provided their insights about the television business.

Most of all, I am thankful for the love and support of Sheri Annis, my wife, and Judy, Bonnie, and Abby, my daughters, who kept me grounded during the bookwriting process.

NOTES

CHAPTER 1

5   "the audience for TV network news . . .": Alvin P. Sanoff, *U.S. News & World Report,* June 9, 1980.

CHAPTER 2

7   "He looks so good . . .": Tony Schwartz, *New York Times,* July 14, 1981.
7   "younger, richer, prettier": Tom Shales, *Washington Post,* July 22, 1981.
7   "I'm not looking to be the Farrah Fawcett . . .": Tony Schwartz, *New York Times,* July 14, 1981.
9   "a built-in anti-Washington bias . . .": Tom Shales, *Washington Post,* July 27, 1983.
11 "Tom Brokaw was sharpening . . .": Bill Carter, *New York Times,* October 12, 1995.

CHAPTER 3

13 "I think you'd be fabulous . . .": Roone Arledge, *Roone: A Memoir* (New York: Harper-Collins, 2003).
14 "Roone Arledge, know this now . . .": Ibid.
14 "Some people have told me . . .": Tom Shales, *Washington Post,* March 12, 1980.

CHAPTER 4

23 viewed anchors as high-priced slaves: Robert Goldberg and Gerald Jay Goldberg, *Anchors: Brokaw, Jennings, Rather and the Evening News* (New York: Carol Publishing, 1990).
24 "You *have* to take it . . .": Arledge, *Roone: A Memoir.*

24 He mispronounced the name of Bowie Kuhn . . .: Sally Bedell Smith, *New York Times,* August 10, 1983.

24 Jennings was humiliated . . .: Goldberg and Goldberg, *Anchors.*

25 "gossip at the highest level . . .": Ibid.

CHAPTER 5

37 "Perhaps for Tom . . .": Jim Rutenberg, *New York Times,* July 26, 2004.

CHAPTER 6

42 "Look, we made a terrible mistake . . .": Gail Shister, *Philadelphia Inquirer,* November 12, 2004.

43 Schieffer "could be tapped": Peter Johnson, *USA Today,* December 13, 2004.

52 "I want to bomb . . .": Lynn Hirshberg, *New York Times Magazine,* September 4, 2005.

CHAPTER 7

56 the network was breaking off the talks: John Carmody, *Washington Post,* February 12, 1996.

56 "could very well turn out": Johnnie L. Roberts, *Newsweek,* June 24, 1996.

57 "We're both kind of bummed . . .": Peter Johnson, *USA Today,* July 11, 1996.

57 "two-camera shoots whenever": Scott Williams, *Daily News,* June 10, 1997.

58 "Hamptons buzz . . .": George Rush and Joanna Molloy, *Daily News,* August 1, 1997.

59 "Seems the budding romance . . .": Bill Zwecker, *Chicago Sun-Times,* October 8, 1997.

59 "**MICHAEL DOUGLAS** isn't giving . . .": George Rush and Joanna Molloy, *Daily News,* March 2, 1998.

59 "The New York press is churning . . .": Bill Zwecker, *Chicago Sun-Times,* September 23, 1998.

59 They fell in love . . .: Lois Smith Brady, *New York Times,* July 28, 2002.

61 "Don't screw it up": Lee Woodruff and Bob Woodruff, *In an Instant* (New York: Random House, 2007).

66 "It is going to be hard . . .": Ibid.

68 "Vargas is hot . . .": Tina Brown, *Washington Post,* December 8, 2005.

68 Vargas's "histrionic" facial expressions: Robert P. Laurence, *San Diego Union-Tribune,* January 9, 2006.

68 "pretty boy android": Maureen Dowd, *New York Times,* December 10, 2005.

68 Banner called to discuss . . .: Jacques Steinberg, *New York Times,* January 9, 2006.

CHAPTER 8

73 "go-to network anchor": Paul Bedard, *U.S. News & World Report,* February 15, 2005.

CHAPTER 13

119 "one of the more laughable claims . . .": John Consoli, *Mediaweek,* May 21, 2003.

120 Her image of Jeff . . .: Bill Carter, *New York Times,* December 9, 1991.

120 "I'm not trying to be a bully": Bill Carter, *New York Times,* October 25, 1999.
125 "My sources now say that Diane Sawyer . . .": Roger Friedman, *FoxNews.com,* March 9, 2006.

CHAPTER 15

139 "C'mon, DAN": Roxanne Roberts, *Washington Post,* May 21, 1991.
142 "She has a comfortable . . .": Walter Goodman, *New York Times,* April 22, 1991.
144 Katie was the girl next door . . . Elisabeth Bumiller, *New York Times,* February 9, 1997.
148 "Lately her image has grown . . .": Alessandra Stanley, *New York Times,* April 25, 2005.
149 "disgruntled ex-employees": Meryl Gordon, *New York,* June 6, 2005.

CHAPTER 16

164 "The woman who dressed . . .": David Bauder, Associated Press, April 5, 2006.
164 "Star power is the reason . . .": Tim Goodman, *San Francisco Chronicle,* April 6, 2006.
164 "I've seen Katie Couric swoon . . .": Florangela Devila, *Seattle Times,* April 6, 2006.
165 "She doesn't fit the image . . .": Peter Johnson, *USA Today,* April 6, 2006.

CHAPTER 19

206 "reinforcing many women's fears . . .": Bridget Hall-Grumet, *St. Petersburg Times,* June 29, 2006.
206 "Elizabeth Vargas did not deserve . . .": Tom Jicha, *Fort Lauderdale Sun-Sentinel,* May 29, 2006.
206 "a message to all women . . .": Jesse Noyes, *Boston Herald,* June 24, 2006.

CHAPTER 20

209 "That's because of Katrina . . .": Joe Hagan, *New York,* June 12, 2006.
211 "because of our strong belief . . .": Stephen Isaacs, *Washington Post,* May 5, 1975.
213 "I love this": Bob Priddy, *Communicator,* April 2006.
215 "the dogged, authoritarian air . . .": Jacqueline Trescott, *Washington Post,* May 12, 1987.
215 "Washington reporter who has demonstrated . . .": Howard Rosenberg, *Los Angeles Times,* February 21, 1987.
217 "ABC executives are scouting . . .": Peter Johnson, *USA Today,* December 17, 1996.

CHAPTER 21

230 Morley Safer had been mad at Rather . . .: *New York Post,* June 5, 2006.

CHAPTER 23

253　"dressed in a black suit": Vanessa O'Connell, *Wall Street Journal,* August 5, 2006.
253　"The problem of Katie Couric's hair color": Olivia Barker, *USA Today,* August 9, 2006.
253　"My kids are thriving . . .": Jacqueline Mitchard, *Parade,* August 13, 2006.
257　no "on-air charisma": Allison Benedikt, *Chicago Tribune,* June 26, 2006.

CHAPTER 25

272　"cuddly news": Barry Garon, *Hollywood Reporter,* September 6, 2006.
272　"Her presence actually gave . . .": Jonathan Storm, *Philadelphia Inquirer,* September 6, 2006.
272　"If this is the new direction . . .": Glenn Garvin, *Miami Herald,* September 6, 2006.
272　"Maybe *The CBS Evening No-News* . . .": Tom Shales, *Washington Post,* September 6, 2006.
272　"Her face was Botoxed . . .": Andrea Peyser, *New York Post,* September 6, 2006.

CHAPTER 29

321　"The trajectory of her . . .": Brian Lowry, *Variety,* October 15, 2006.

CHAPTER 32

360　"You don't know me . . .": Tom Junod, *Esquire,* January 2007.

CHAPTER 34

378　"Remember Charles Gibson?" Jon Friedman, *MarketWatch.com,* September 27, 2006.
381　"widely interpreted": Bill Carter and Jacques Steinberg, *New York Times,* March 1, 2007.

CHAPTER 36

409　"train wreck": Jon Friedman, *MarketWatch.com,* April 18, 2007.
409　"an expensive, unfixable mistake": Gail Shister, *Philadelphia Inquirer,* April 22, 2007.
412　"a 33-year-old financial analyst . . .": *National Enquirer,* April 23, 2007.
419　"God, no!" *New York Post,* May 8, 2007.

EPILOGUE

430　ABC had forty-seven correspondents . . .: Andrew Tyndall, *Tyndall Report,* 2006.
431　While 38 percent of Democrats . . .: Pew Research Center for the People and the Press, July 30, 2006.

INDEX

ABOUT THE AUTHOR

Howard Kurtz is the media reporter for *The Washington Post* and also writes a weekly column for the newspaper and a daily blog for its Web site. He is the host of CNN's *Reliable Sources,* the longest-running media criticism show on television. His previous books include *New York Times* bestsellers *Spin Cycle: Inside the Clinton Propaganda Machine* (1998) and *The Fortune Tellers: Inside Wall Street's Game of Money, Media, and Manipulation* (2000). His book *Hot Air: All Talk All The Time* (1996) was named by *Business Week* as one of the ten best business books of the year, and *Media Circus: The Trouble with America's Newspapers* (1993) was chosen as the best recent book about the news media by *American Journalism Review.* Kurtz joined *The Washington Post* in 1981, and his work has appeared in *Vanity Fair, Newsweek, New York,* and other national magazines. He lives with his family in Chevy Chase, Maryland.